# 1 MONTH OF FREE READING

at

www.ForgottenBooks.com

---

By purchasing this book you are eligible for one month membership to ForgottenBooks.com, giving you unlimited access to our entire collection of over 1,000,000 titles via our web site and mobile apps.

To claim your free month visit:

www.forgottenbooks.com/free760111

\* Offer is valid for 45 days from date of purchase. Terms and conditions apply.

ISBN 978-0-484-41597-2
PIBN 10760111

This book is a reproduction of an important historical work. Forgotten Books uses state-of-the-art technology to digitally reconstruct the work, preserving the original format whilst repairing imperfections present in the aged copy. In rare cases, an imperfection in the original, such as a blemish or missing page, may be replicated in our edition. We do, however, repair the vast majority of imperfections successfully; any imperfections that remain are intentionally left to preserve the state of such historical works.

Forgotten Books is a registered trademark of FB &c Ltd.
Copyright © 2018 FB &c Ltd.
FB &c Ltd, Dalton House, 60 Windsor Avenue, London, SW19 2RR.
Company number 08720141. Registered in England and Wales.

For support please visit www.forgottenbooks.com

# Three *Physico-Theological* DISCOURSES,

CONCERNING

I. The Primitive CHAOS, and Creation of the World.
II. The General DELUGE, its Causes and Effects.
III. The Dissolution of the WORLD, and Future Conflagration.

Wherein are largely discussed,

The Production and Use of Mountains; the Original of Fountains, of Formed Stones, and Sea-Fishes Bones and Shells found in the Earth; the Effects of particular Floods, and Inundations of the Sea; the Eruptions of *Vulcano*'s; the Nature and Causes of Earthquakes.

Also an Historical Account of those Two late remarkable Ones in *Jamaica* and *England*.

With PRACTICAL INFERENCES.

By *JOHN RAY*, late Fellow of the *Royal Society*.

The Third Edition, Illustrated with Copper-Plates, and much more Enlarged than the former Editions, from the Author's own MSS.

London: Printed for WILLIAM INNYS, at the Prince's Arms in S. Paul's Church-yard, 1713.

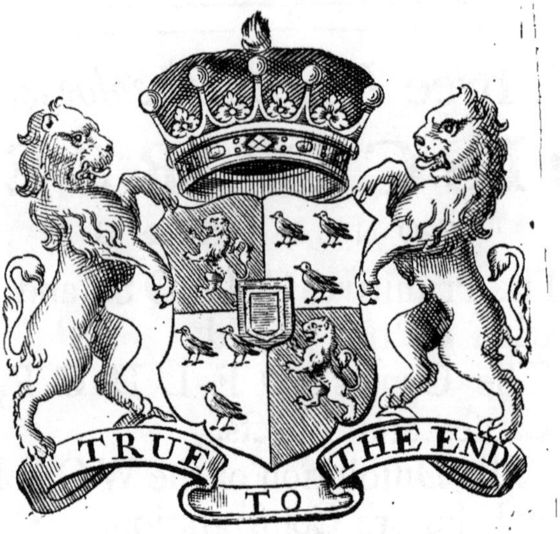
TRUE
TO
THE END

TO THE

Most Reverend FATHER in GOD,

# JOHN,

Lord Arch-Bishop of *Canterbury*, Primate of all *England*, and *Metropolitan*.

My Lord,

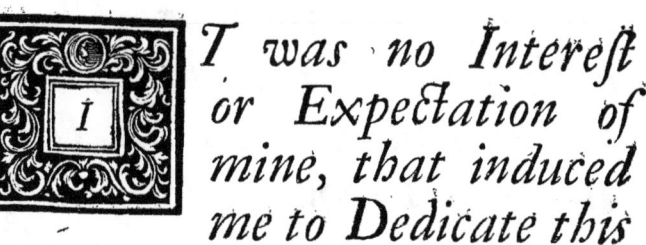

*I* was no *Interest* or *Expectation* of mine, that induced me to Dedicate this Discourse to Your Grace. I am not so well conceited of

## DEDICATION.

*my own Performances, as to think it merits to be inscribed to so Great a Name, much less that I should Oblige Your Lordship, or indeed a far meaner Person, by such Inscription. My principal Motive was, that it would give me Opportunity of Congratulating with the Sober Part of this Nation, Your Advancement to the Archiepiscopal Dignity; and of acknowledging His Majesty's Wisdom in making Choice of so fit a Person to fill that Chair, endued with all Qualifications requisite for so high a Calling; so able and skilful a Pilot to govern the Church,*

## DEDICATION.

*Church, and so prudent and faithful a Counsellor to serve Himself. But I will not enlarge in just Praises, lest I should incurr the unjust Censure or Suspicion of Flattery. Give me leave only to add, what I may without Injury of Truth, and I think without Violation of Modesty, that Your* Grace's *Election hath the concurrent Approbation and Applause of all good Men that know You, or have had a true Character of You; which may serve to strengthen Your Hands in the Management and Administration of so difficult a Province, tho' You need no such Support,*

A 3 *as*

## DEDICATION.

*as being sufficiently involved and armed by Your Vertues, and protected by the Almighty Power and Providence. Those that are Good and Wise are pleased and satisfied when Great Men are preferred to Great Places; and think it Pity that Persons of large and publick Spirits should be confined to narrow Spheres of Action, and want Field to exercise and employ those rich Talents and Abilities wherewith they are endowed, in doing all the Good they are thereby qualified and inclined to do.*

M y

# DEDICATION.

My Lord,

*I am sensible that the* Present *I make You, is neither for Bulk nor Worth suitable to Your* Person *and* Greatness; *Yet I hope You will favourably accept it, being the best I have to offer: And my Boldness may pretend some Excuse from ancient Acquaintance, and from my Forwardness to embrace this Opportunity of professing my Name among those that Honour You, and of publishing myself,*

My Lord,
Your Grace's most devoted Servant,
and humble Orator,

**JOHN RAY.**

# THE PREFACE,

*Shewing what Alterations were made in the* Second Edition.

Having altered the Method of this Treatise, and made considerable Additions to it, it may justly be expected that I should give some Account thereof to the Reader. In the Preface to the former Edition, I acquainted him, that I had taken notice of five Matters of Ancient Tradition. 1. That the World was formed out of a *Chaos*, by the Divine Wisdom and Power. 2. That there was an universal Flood of Waters, in which all Mankind perished, excepting some few, which were saved in an Ark or Ship. 3. That the World shall one day be destroyed by Fire. 4. That there is a Heaven and a Hell, an *Elyſium* and a *Tartarus*, the one to reward good Men, and the other to puniſh wicked; and both eternal. 5. That bloody Sacrifices were to be offered for the Expiation of Sin. And that of four of them I had occaſion to treat in this Book; of two, that is to ſay, of the Diſſolution of the World by Fire, and the Eternal State that was to ſucceed (in reference to Man) either in Heaven or Hell, more directly: Of the other two, *viz.* The Primitive *Chaos* and Creation, and the General Deluge, occaſionally and by way of digreſſion, at the Requeſt of ſome Friends. But now this Treatiſe coming to a ſecond Impreſſion, I thought it more convenient to make theſe ſeveral Diſcourſes upon theſe Particulars, ſubſtantial Parts of my Work, and to diſpoſe them according to the Priority and Poſteriority of their Subjects, in Order of Time, beginning with the Primitive *Chaos*.

Concerning theſe Traditions, it may be enquired what the Original of them was; Whether they were of Divine Revelation, or Humane Invention? In anſwer whereto,

As to the Second, That there was once a General Deluge, whereby this whole ſublunary World was drown'd, and all Animals, both Man and Beaſt, deſtroyed, excepting only ſuch as were preſerved in an

Ark;

*The Preface.*

Ark; it being Matter of Fact, and seen and felt by *Noah*, and his Sons, there can be no Doubt of the Original of that.

THE First, concerning the *Chaos* and Creation of the World, if it were not ancienter than the Scripture, it is likely it had its Original from the first Chapter of *Genesis*, and the *Chaos* from the second Verse; *And the Earth was without Form, and Void, and Darkness was upon the Face of the Deep.* But if it were more ancient, it must still, in all likelihood, be Divinely revealed, because Man being created last, and brought into a World already filled and furnished: And GOD being an Omnipotent, and also a Free Agent, who could as well have created the World in a Moment, or all together, as successively, it was impossible for Man by Reason to determine, which way He made choice of.

THE Third, concerning the future Dissolution and Destruction of the World by a General *Conflagration*, there being nothing in Nature that can demonstrate the Necessity of it: And a second Inundation and Submersion by Water, being in the Course of Nature a hundred times more probable, as I have shewn in the ensuing Discourses. And, therefore, we see GOD Almighty, to secure Man against the Apprehension and Dread of a second Deluge, made a Covenant

nant with him, to give him a visible Sign in Confirmation of it, never to destroy the World so again. And the Ancients, who relate this Tradition, delivering it as an Oracle or Decree of Fate, *Ovid Metamorph.* 1. *Esse quoque in fatis reminiscitur affore tempus, &c.* was likewise probable of Divine Revelation.

The Fourth, That there shall be a future State, wherein Men shall be punished or rewarded accordingly, as they have done ill or well in this Life, and that State Eternal: Tho' the First Part may be demonstrated from the Justice and Goodness of God, because there being an unequal Distribution of Good and Evil in this Life, there must be a Time to set things streight in another World; yet it being so difficult to Humane Reason, to reconcile the Eternity of Punishments with the Justice and Goodness of God, this Second Part of the Tradition had need be well back'd by Divine Authority, to make it credible and current among Men.

As for the Last, tho' I meddle not with it in this Treatise, yet I will take Leave to say so much concerning it, That, I think, those who held Sacrificing to have been a positive Command of God, and to have had its Original from Divine Institution, have the better Reason on their side. For that

that it is no eternal and indispensable Law of Nature, is clear, in that our Saviour abolished it. And many of the ancient Fathers look upon Sacrificing as so unreasonable a Service, that therefore they thought GOD commanded it not to the Primitive Patriarchs; and though He did command it to the *Jews*, yet He did it only in condescension to their Weakness, because they had been used to such Services, and also the Nations round about them, to restrain them from Idolatry, and Sacrificing to strange Gods. *Origen. Homil.* 17. *in Numer. Deus sicut per alium Prophetam dicit, non manducat carnes taurorum, nec sanguinem hircorum potat. Et etiam, ut alibi scriptum est, Quia non mandavi tibi de Sacrificiis vel victimis in die qua deduxi te de terra Ægypti. Sed Moyses hæc ad duritiem cordis eorum, pro consuetudine pessima qua imbuti fuerant in Ægypto, mandavit eis, ut qui abstinere se non possent ab immolando, Deo saltem & non Dæmoniis immolarent.* Other Quotations to this purpose may be seen in Dr. *Outram De Sacrificiis*. Indeed, it seems absurd to think or believe, that GOD should take any Pleasure in the Slaughter of innocent Beasts, or in the Fume and *Nidor* of burnt Flesh or Fat. Nor doth the Reason these Fathers alledge, of the Institution of Sacrifices, or Enjoining them to the *Jews*, satisfy, whatever Truth there

there may be in it: For it is clear, that the main End and Design of GOD in instituting of them, was for Types and Adumbrations of the great Sacrifice of CHRIST to be offered upon the Cross for the Expiation of Sin: And, consequently, it is probable, that those also that were offered by the Ancient Patriarchs before the Law, had their Original from some Divine Command or Revelation, and the like Reason of their Institution, in reference to CHRIST.

BUT to leave that, I have in this *Edition* removed one Subject of Apology, and added another; so that there still remain as many things to be excused or pleaded for. They are,

FIRST, *Writing so much;* for which some perchance may censure me. I am not ignorant, that Men as they are mutable, so they love Change, and affect Variety of Authors as well as Books. Satiety even of the best things is apt to creep upon us. He that writes much, let him write never so well, shall experience, that his last Books, though nothing inferiour to his first, will not find equal Acceptance. But for mine own part, tho' in general I may be thought to have written too much, yet is it but little that I have written relating to Divinity. It were a good Rule to be observed both by Writer and Reader, *Not how much, but how well.*

*well.* He that cannot write well, had better spare his Pains, and not write at all. Neither is he to be thought to write well, who though he hath some good things thin set and disperfed, yet encumbers and accloys the Reader with a deal of useless and impertinent Stuff. On the contrary, he that writes well, cannot write too much. For, as *Pliny* the Younger saith well, *Ut aliæ bonæ res, ita bonus Liber eò melior est quisque, quò major: As other good Things, so a good Book; the bigger it is, the better is it:* Which holds as well of the Number as Magnitude of Books.

SECONDLY, *Being too hasty in huddling up, and tumbling out of Books;* wherein, I confess, I cannot wholly acquit myself of Blame. I know well, that the longer a Book lies by me, the perfecter it becomes. Something occurrs every Day in Reading or Thinking, either to add, or to correct and alter for the better. But should I deferr the *Edition* till the Work were absolutely perfect, I might wait all my Life-time, and leave it to be published by my Executors. Now my Age minding me of the Approach of Death; and posthumous Pieces generally proving inferiour to those put out by the Authors in their Life-time, I need no other Excuse for my Haste in publishing what I write. Yet I shall farther add, in Extenuation of the Fault, if it be one, that however hasty and precipitate I am in writing, my Books are but small, so that if they be worthless, the Purchase is not great, nor the Expence of Time, wasted in the Perusal of them, very considerable. Yet, is not the Worth of a Book always answerable to its Bulk. But on the contrary, Μέγα βιβλίον is usually esteemed ἴσον τῷ μεγάλῳ κακῷ; for, ὀκ ἐν τῷ μεγάλῳ τὸ εὖ, ἀλλ' ἐν τῷ εὖ τὸ μέγα.

THIRDLY, The last thing for which I had need to apologize, is the Rendring the former *Edition* of this Treatise worthless, by making large Additions to this latter: In Excuse whereof I have no more to say, than I have already written in an *Advertisement* to the *Reader*, premised to my Discourse concerning the *Wisdom* of GOD; to which, therefore, I referr those who desire Satisfaction in this Particular.

TO

# TO THE READER.

*LEST the Additions made to this* Third Edition *of these Discourses should lie under any Suspicion of being spurious, by reason they have lain above seven Years unpublished after their justly celebrated Author's Death; I think it necessary to assure the Reader, that they were written in* Mr. Ray's *own Hand, and (as I find by his Papers) towards the latter End of the Year* 1703, *or Beginning of* 1704: *And in April,* 1704, *they were transmitted to his Booksellers, who had been very importunate for them, and hasty for a* Third Edition; *the former Impression being sold off, and the Book*

much

*much called for, as they say in their Letters.* But amongst other Hindrances, that which chiefly retarded the intended Impression of the Book, was an ill State of Health befalling the principal Bookseller, which necessitated him to retire often into the Country from his Business, which was succeeded by his Death, and some time after by the Death of the other Partner also. By which means the Affairs of the Booksellers, who had the Right of the Copy, being in some Confusion, this Third Edition could not be attended unto till of late, when the Right of this and other of Mr. Ray's Copies came into another's Hands.

As for the Reasons inducing our excellent Author to make Additions to this, and other of his justly admired Pieces, he had (besides the Solicitations of the Booksellers) the earnest Requests of some of his most judicious and best Friends. And considering that his Additions tended to the greater Perfection of his Books, there is no great Reason for the Purchasers of the former Editions to complain of Injury, especially

where

*where the Purchase was but small. But for a farther Answer, I shall referr the Reader (as our Author in his Preface doth) to the Advertisement in his* Wisdom of God. *And that I might do what lies in me to obviate Complaints, and be serviceable, as far as I could, to the Purchaser's Profit, I have noted the Additions made to this* Third Impression, *that they that bought the former Edition may transcribe them, if they think it worth their while.*

WILLIAM DERHAM.

# THE ADDITIONS
## IN THIS
## *Third Impression.*

PAG. 10. *From* In this manner, *to* illustrate it.

Pag. 12. *From* When I say, *to* Mountain that way, p. 13.

Pag. 41. As for the Wells, *to* improbable.

Pag. 58. But notwithstanding, *to* insist upon it, p. 59.

Pag. 59. I think I have, *to* I am less inclinable.

Pag. 62. The first in, *to* in the 5th Chap.

Pag. 65. Consonant to the preceding Words of *Abydenus*.

Pag. 67. *Pliny* saith of the City of *Joppa*, that it was built before the Flood.

Pag. 70. To this may be replied, *to* the lightest, p. 71.

Pag. 73. Natural; and that no ordinary, *to* Heavens were opened.

Pag. 74. *After* no inconsiderable thing, *seven Lines of the former Edition are left out.*

Ibid.

*Ibid. From* Cloud, who knows? *the following Part of the Paragraph is left out, and in its room is set,* That the Ocean, *to* Scriptures, *p.* 75.

*Pag.* 79. *Madidus Notus alis.* Ovid. Metam.

*Pag.* 84. But to put, *to p.* 101, 102.

*Pag.* 89. Dr. *Hook*'s, *to* believe there are not.

*Pag.* 114. That Rains, *to the Bottom of the Page.*

*Pag.* 115. The Fruitfulness, *to* of *Nile.* Q. *Whether this Paragraph be not misplaced?*

*Pag.* 116. But because (as I said before) *to* touch the Ground. *After which, three Paragraphs in* p. 117, 118, 119, 120. *of the former Edition, are left out.*

*Pag.* 118. *I shall leave the Reader to compare the Alteration made, from* This Hypothesis, *to* highest Mountains, *with p.* 122. *of the former Edition,* If any object.

*Ibid.* (as credibly Authors, *to* those of *Mexico*) *p.* 119.

*Pag.* 120. But because, *to* former Account.

*Pag.* 126. Dr. *Woodward*, *to* Deluge.

*Pag.* 129. Another the like Bed, *to* so far Mr. *Brewer, p.* 132.

*Pag.* 138. This Argument is, *to* living Shark, *p.* 139.

*Pag.* 140. as Signor *Agostino, to* from them both.

*Pag.* 143. Two farther Arguments, *to* out of *Agostino Scilla, p.* 145.

*Pag.* 146. and 13 days, *to the Bottom of the Page.*

*Pag.* 149. This to me, I confess, is at present unaccountable.

*Pag.* 155. Upon farther Consideration, *to* Species under it.

*Pag.* 156. To this may be answered, *to* Islands of *Scotland, p.* 157.

*Pag.* 165. Dr. *Woodward*, *to* Bed or *Stratum, p.* 167.

## Additions, &c.

*Pag.* 172. This Conjecture, *to* thence might.

*Pag.* 174. According to my Hope, *to* with their Fellows, p. 204.

*Pag.* 208. To which may be added, *to* Working of the Sea, p. 209.

*Pag.* 211. Notwithstanding these, *to* selves beholding it, p. 212.

*Pag.* 215. Moreover, *to* thereabout.

*Pag.* 218. Notwithstanding all these, *to the End of the Page* 226.

*Pag.* 228. Here I might take, *to* I have digressed, p. 241.

*Pag.* 276. For, 1. It could, *to* a Flame.

*Pag.* 291. In this Conjecture, *to* discoursed at large, p 294.

*Pag.* 443. Now that it is unjust, *to* enforce Obedience to his Laws, p. 446.

§ *And in the same Place, in the former Edition, p.* 395. *from* How can it be just, *to the End of the Paragraph, is left out.*

*Pag.* 450. *Instead of* punishing an Offender, *it is* having an Offender punished by the Magistrate, or by GOD.

*Ibid.* He hath not permitted, *to* I will repay.

*Ibid. After* Veracity? *compare the Alterations, viz. what is left out in the former, and added in this Edition, from* Veracity, *to* digressed, p. 452.

*Pag.* 452. I shall add farther, *to* groundlesly imagine, p 453. *Compare also the Variation from the former Edition.*

*Pag.* 453. After go on in Sin, *see what is left out of what is in the former Edition, p.* 402, 403.

# THE
# CONTENTS.

### Discourse I.
### Of the Primitive CHAOS, and Creation of the WORLD.

CHAP. I. *Testimonies of the Ancient Heathen Writers, Hesiod, Ovid, Aristophanes, Lucan, Euripides, concerning the Chaos, and what they meant by it,* pag. 2, 3, 4.

Chap. II. *That the Creation of the World out of a Chaos, is not repugnant to the Holy Scripture, if soberly understood,* p. 5, 6, 7, 8.

Chap. III. *Of the separating the Land and Water, and raising up the Mountains,* p. 8, &c *By what Means the Waters were gathered together into one Place, and the dry Land made to appear,* p. 9. *That subterraneous Fires and Flatus's, might be of Power sufficient to produce such an Effect, proved from the Force and Effects of Gunpowder, and the Raising up of new Mountains,* p. 10, 11, 12, 13. *The Shaking of the whole known World by an Earthquake,* p. 13, 14. *That the Mountains, Islands, and whole Continents were probably at first raised up by subterraneous Fires,*

# The Contents.

*Fires, proved by the Authority of* Lydiate *and* Strabo, p. 15, 16, 17. *Of subterraneous Caverns passing under the Bottom of the Sea,* p. 19, 20, 21, &c. *A Communication between* Ætna, Stromboli, *&c.* p. 22, &c. *A Discourse concerning the Equality of the Sea and Land, both as to the Extent of each, and the Height of one, to the Depth of the Other, taken from the Shores,* p. 25, 26, 27, 31, 32, 33. *That the Motion of the Waters levels the Bottom of the Sea,* p. 28, 29, 30. *A Discourse concerning the Use of the Mountains,* p. 34, 35, 36, 37, &c. *The Way of digging Wells in the* Lower Austria, *&c.* p. 39, 40, 41. *The Sum of what hath been said of the Division and Disposition of the Water and Earth,* p. 43, 44.

Chap. IV. *Of the Creation of Animals: Some Questions concerning them resolved,* p. 45. *That God Almighty did at first create either the Seeds of all Animate Bodies, and dispersed them all the Earth over: Or else, the first Sett of Animals themselves, in their full State and Perfection, giving each Species a Power by Generation to propagate their Like,* p. 45, 46. *Whether God at first created a great Number of each Species, or only two, a Male and a Female,* p. 46, 47. *Whether all individual Animals which already have been, and hereafter shall be, were at first actually created by God, or only the first Setts of each Species, the rest proceeding from them by way of Generation, and being anew produced,* p. 48, 49, *&c. Objections against the First Part answered.* 1. *That it seems impossible, that the Ovaries of the first Animals should actually include the innumerable Myriads of those that may proceed from them in so many Generations as have been, and shall be to the End of the World. This shewn not to be so incredible from the Multitude of Parts, into which Matter may be, and is divided, in many Experiments,* p. 50, 51, 52, 53, 54. 2. *If all the Members of Animals already formed, do pre-exist in the Egg, how can the Imagination of the Mother change the Shape, and that so notoriously sometimes, as to produce a Calf's Head, or Dog's Face, or the like monstrous Members? Several Answers to this Objection offered,* p. 55, 56, 57, &c.

# The Contents.

### Discourse II.

Of the General DELUGE, in the Days of Noah; its Causes and Effects. Pag. 61.

CHAP. I. *Testimonies of Ancient Heathen Writers, and some ancient Coins or Medals, verifying the Scripture-History of the Deluge,* p. 62, 63, 64, 65. *That the ancient Poets and Mythologists, by* Deucalion *understood* Noah, *and by* Deucalion's *Flood the General Deluge, proved,* p. 65, 66, 67, 68.

Chap. II. *Of the Causes of the General Deluge,* p. 69. 1. *A miraculous Transmutation of Air into Water rejected,* p. 69, 70, 71, 72. *That* Noah's *Flood was not Topical,* p. 72, 73. 2, *and* 3. *The Emotion of the Center of the Earth, or a violent Depression of the Surface of the Ocean, the most probable partial Causes of the Deluge: But the immediate Causes assigned by the Scripture, are the* Breaking up of the Fountains of the Great Deep, *and the* Opening of the Windows of Heaven, p. 73. *That those Causes are sufficient to produce a Deluge, granting a Change of the Center of the Earth, to prevent the Waters running off,* p. 73, 74, 75. *That all the Vapours suspended in the Air, might contribute much towards a Flood,* ibid. *Concerning the Expence of the Sea by Vapour,* p. 76, 77, 78, &c. *Of the Water's keeping its Level. An Objection concerning an Under-current at the* Propontis, *the Streights of* Gibraltar, *and the* Baltick Sound, *proposed and replied to,* p. 81, 82, 83, 84. *Concerning the Breaking up of the Fountains of the Great Deep, and how the Waters might be made to ascend,* p. 84, 85. *The inferiour Circulation, and perpetual Motion of the Water disapproved,* p 86, &c *That the Continents and Islands are so equally dispersed all the World over, as to counterbalance one another, so that the Centers of Motion, Gravity, and Magnitude, concurr in one,* p. 86, 87, 88.

*An*

*lar Account of the late remarkable and far-extended Earthquake which happened here with us in England, and in other Parts of Europe, upon Sept. 8. 1692. p. 272, &c. to 281. Of Vulcanos,* p. 282.

*Of extraordinary Floods caused by long-continuing Showers, or violent Storms and Shots of Rain,* p. 283 to 287.

*Of boisterous and violent Winds and Hurricanes, what Interest they have in the Changes wrought in the Earth,* p. 287, 288, 289.

*That the Earth doth not proceed so fast towards a general Inundation and Submersion by Water, as the Force and Agency of all these Causes seem to require,* p. 291. *The Earthquakes in* Sicily *and* Naples, p. 291, 292, 293, 294.

### DISCOURSE III.

## Of the Future Dissolution of the World, and the General Conflagration.

THE *Introduction, being a Discourse concerning Prophecy,* p. 296, &c.

Chap. I. *The Division of the Words* [2 Pet. iii. 1.] *and the Doctrine contained in them, with the Heads of the following Discourse, viz.* I. *Testimonies concerning the Dissolution.* 1. *Of the Holy Scriptures.* 2. *Of ancient Christian Writers.* 3. *Of Heathen Philosophers and Sages.* II. *Seven Questions concerning the Dissolution of the World, proposed,* p. 300, &c.

Chap. II. *The Testimonies of Scripture concerning the Dissolution of the World. And Dr.* Hammond's *Expositions, referring the most of them to the Destruction of the City and Temple of* Jerusalem, *and the Period of the* Jewish *State and Polity considered, and pleaded for,* p. 303 to 320.

Chap.

Chap. III. *Testimonies of the Ancient Fathers and Doctors of the Church, concerning the Dissolution of the World,* p. 320 to 335.

Chap. IV. *The Testimonies of some Heathen Philosophers, and other Writers, concerning the Dissolution; the Epicureans,* p. 326. *the Stoicks,* p. 327, &c. *who held certain Periods of Inundations and Conflagrations.* p. 328, &c. *That this Opinion of a Future Conflagration was of far greater Antiquity than that Sect, proved,* p. 333, &c.

Chap. V. *The first Question concerning the World's Dissolution; Whether there be any thing in Nature that may probably cause or argue a Future Dissolution? Four probable Means propounded and discussed,* p. 338.

Sect. 1. *The first is the Probability of the Waters naturally returning to overflow and cover the Earth,* ibid.

*The old Argument from the World's Dissolution, taken from its daily Consenescency and Decay, rejected,* p. 339.

*The Necessity of such a Prevailing of the Waters daily upon the dry Land, till at last it proceed to a total Submersion of it, in the Course of Nature, as things now stand, unless some Stop be put, proved, from the continual streightning of the Sea, and lowering the Mountains and high Grounds by Rains, Floods and Rivers washing away, and carrying down the Earth, and from the Seas encroaching upon the Shores,* p. 344 to 356.

*The Reason why there are no Rains nor Springs in Egypt,* p. 349.

*A large Quotation out of* Josephus Blancanus, *demonstrating some of the former Matters,* p. 356 to 365.

*Of the Sinking of ancient Buildings,* p. 368.

Sect. 2. *The second probable Means or Cause of the World's Destruction in a Natural way, viz. the Extinction of the Sun,* p. 373.

Sect. 3. *The third possible Cause of the World's Destruction, the Eruption of the Central Fire,* p. 375. *That the Being of such a Fire is no way repugnant either to Scripture or Reason,* p. 377. *Mines run generally East and West,* p. 378, &c.

Sect.

## The Contents.

Sect. 4. *The fourth possible Cause of the World's Dissolution, the Earth's Dryness and Inflammability in the Torrid Zone, and the concurrent Eruptions of* Vulcano's, p. 381, &c.

*That the Inclination of the Ecliptick to the Æquator doth not diminish,* p. 381. *That tho' there were such a Drying and Parching of the Earth in the Torrid Zone, it would not probably inferr a Conflagration,* p. 382, 383. *That there hath not yet been, nor in the ordinary Course of Nature can be, any such Drying or Parching of the Earth in the Torrid Zone,* p. 384. *The Possibility of the Desiccation of the Sea by Natural Means, denied,* p. 385, &c. *The Fixedness and Intransmutability of Principles secures the Universe from Dissolution, Destruction of any present Species, or Production of any new,* p. 387.

Chap. VI. *Containing an Answer to the second Question, Whether shall this Dissolution be effected by Natural or Extraordinary Means? and what they shall be?* p. 388.

Chap. VII. *The third Question answered, Whether shall the Dissolution be gradual and successive, or momentanous and sudden?* p. 391.

Chap. VIII. *The fourth Question resolved, Whether shall there be any Signs or Fore-runners of the Dissolution of the World?* p. 393.

Chap. IX. *The fifth Question debated, At what Period of Time shall the World be dissolved? and particularly, Whether at the End of Six thousand Years?* p. 397.

Chap. X. *How far shall this Dissolution or Conflagration extend? Whether to the Ætherial Heavens, and all the Host of them, Sun, Moon, and Stars, or to the Aerial only?* p. 403.

Chap. XI. *The seventh and last Question, Whether shall the whole World be consumed and destroyed, or annihilated, or only refined and purified,* p. 406.

*The Restitution and Continuance of the World, proved by the Testimonies of Scripture and Antiquity, and also by Reason,* p. 411, &c.

*The Arguments for the Abolition and Annihilation, answer'd,* p. 412, &c.

Chap. XII. *The Inference the Apostle makes from the precedent Doctrine: Of future Rewards and Punishments. The Eternity of future Punishments proved from the Authority of Scripture and Antiquity. How the Eternity of Punishments can consist with the Justice and Gooodness of God,* from p. 416. to the End of the Book.

*The great Usefulness of Shame,* p. 429. *The Blotting out of Sins,* p. 430, &c.

*A* CATALOGUE *of the* Author's Works,
*fold by* WILLIAM INNYS.

Hiſtoria Plantarum, Species hactenus editas aliaſque inſuper multas noviter inventas & deſcriptas complectens. Tomi duo. *Fol.* 1686.

Ejuſd. Tomus tertius, qui eſt Supplementum duorum præcedentium, cum acceſſionibus *Camelli* & *Tournefortii*, 1704.

Catalogus Plantarum circa Cantabrigiam naſcentium. *Octavo, Cantab.* 1660. cum Appendice.

Catalogus Plantarum Angliæ, *&c.* 8vo. 1670. & 1677.

Faſciculus Stirp. Britann. poſt editum Catal. præd. 1688.

Catalogus Stirpium in ext. region. obſervat. 1673.

Methodus Plantarum nova cum Tabulis, 1682; 1703.

Synopſis Methodica Stirp. Britann. in qua tum Notæ Generum Characteriſticæ traduntur, tum Species ſingulæ breviter deſcribitur, &c. 1690.

Ead. Synop. multis Stirpibus & Obſervationibus curioſis paſſim inſertis, cum Muſcorum Methodo & Hiſtoria pleniore, &c. 1696.

Epiſtola ad D. *Rivinum* de Methodo Plantarum in qua Elementa Botanica D. *Tournefort* tanguntur, 1696.

Diſſertatio de variis Plantarum Methodis, 1696.

Stirp. Europ. extra Britannias naſcentium Sylloge, 1694.

Synopſis Methodica Avium & Piſcium, 8vo. 1713.

Synopſ. Methodica Animalium Quadrupedum & Serpentini Generis, 1693.

Franciſci Willughbeii Hiſtoria Piſcium cum Fig. Recognovit, digeſſit, ſupplevit *Jo. Raius, Oxon.* Fol. 1686.

Ejuſd. Ornithologia cum Fig edente eod. 1676.

*The ſame much enlarged, in* Engliſh. 1678.

*Obſervations Topographical, Moral, and Phyſiological, made in a Journey thro' ſeveral Parts of* Europe, 8vo. 1673.

*Collection of unuſual or local* Engliſh *Words, with an Account of preparing* Engliſh *Metals,* &c. 1674, *and* 1691.

*Collection of* Engliſh *and other Proverbs*. Camb. 1678.

Methodus Inſectorum: ſeu Inſecta in Methodum aliqualem Digeſta. 1705.

Hiſtoria Inſectorum. *Lond.* 1710. 4to. Opus Poſthumum.

*A Perſuaſive to a Holy Life*, 1700.

*The Wiſdom of God manifeſted in the Works of the Creation*. In Two Parts. *To which are added, Anſwers to ſome Objections*. 8vo. Sixth Edition. 1713

*Three* Phyſico-Theological *Diſcourſes*, &c. *With Practical Inferences*. 1713.

Dictionariolum Trilingue, ſec. Locos Commun. 1672, 689, 1696.

# DISCOURSE I.

## *Of the Primitive* Chaos *and Creation of the World.*

IN the First Edition of this Treatise, this Discourse concerning the *Primitive Chaos* and *Creation* of the World, and that other concerning the *Destruction* thereof by the Waters of the *General Deluge*, in the Days of *Noah*, were brought in by way of Digression; because I designed not at first to treat of them, but only of the *Conflagration* or *Dissolution* of the *World* by *Fire*; but was afterwards, when I had made a considerable Progress in the *Dissolution*, at the Instance of some Friends, because of their Relation to my Subject, prevailed upon to say something of them. But now that I am at Liberty so to do, I shall not handle them any more by the by, but make

B  them

them substantial Parts of my Book, and dispose them, as is most natural, according to their Priority and Posteriority in Order of Time, beginning with the *Chaos* and *Creation*.

## Chap. I.

*Testimonies of the Ancient Heathen Writers concerning the* Chaos, *and what they meant by it.*

IT was an ancient Tradition among the Heathen, that the World was created out of a *Chaos.*

First of all the ancient *Greek* Poet *Hesiod*, who may contend for Antiquity with *Homer* himself, makes mention of it in his *Theogonia*, not far from the Beginning, in these Words:

Ἤτοι μὲν πρώτιϛα Χάος γένετ᾽·

*First of all there was a Chaos.* And a few Verses after, speaking of the immediate Production or Offspring of the Chaos, he saith,

Ἐκ Χάεος δ᾽ Ἔρεβός τε, μέλαινά τε Νὺξ ἐγένοντο.

*From* Chaos *proceeded* Hell, *and* Night, [*or* Darkness] which seems to have its Foundation or Occasion from the second Verse of
the

## and Creation.

the firſt Chapter of *Geneſis*; *And the Earth was without Form, and void; and Darkneſs was upon the Face of the Deep.* Of this Teſtimony of *Heſiod*, *Lactantius* takes notice, and cenſures it, in the firſt Book of his *Inſtitutions*, cap. 5. *Heſiodus non à Deo conditore ſumens exordium, ſed à Chao, quod eſt rudis inordinatáque materiæ confuſæ congeries.* Heſiod not taking his Beginning from GOD the Creator of all Things, but from the Chaos, which is a rude and inordinate Heap of confuſed Matter. And ſo *Ovid* deſcribes it in the Beginning of his *Metamorphoſis*;

*Quem dixere* Chaos, *rudis indigeſtáque moles,*
*Nec quicquam niſi pondus iners congeſtáque*
 *eódem*
*Non bene junctarum diſcordia ſemina rerum.*

That is;
One Face had Nature, which they Chaos nam'd,
An undigeſted Lump, a barren Load,
Where jarring Seeds of things ill-join'd abode.

Others of the Ancients have alſo made mention of the *Chaos*, as *Ariſtophanes* in *Avibus*,

Χάος ἦν καὶ Νὺξ, Ἐρεβός τε μέλαν πρῶτον, &c.

And *Lucian* in the Beginning of his firſt Book,

*Antiquum repetent iterum Chaos omnia, &c.*

Of the Formation of all the Parts of the World out of this *Chaos*, *Ovid*, in the place fore-

fore-quoted, gives us a full and particular Description; and *Euripides* before him a brief one,

'Ο δ' Οὐρανὸς καὶ γαῖά τ' ἦν μορφὴ μία,
Ἐπεὶ δ' ἐχωρίσθησαν ἀλλήλων, &c.

*The Heaven and Earth were at first of one Form; but after they were separated, the Earth brought forth Trees, Birds, Beasts, Fishes, and Mankind.*

The like Account also the ancient Philosopher *Anaxagoras* gives of the Creation of the World, beginning his Philosophy thus; Πάντα χρήματα ἦν ὁμῦ· εἶτα Νῦς ἐλθὼν αὐτὰ διεκόσμησε· that is, *All things* (at first) *were together*, or mingled and confused, *then Mind supervening disposed them in a beautiful Order.*

That which I chiefly dislike in this Opinion of theirs, is, that they make no mention of the Creation of this *Chaos*, but seem to look upon it as self-existent and improduced.

CHAP.

## Chap. II.

*That the Creation of the World out of a* Chaos, *is not repugnant to the Holy Scripture.*

THIS Opinion of a *Chaos*, if soberly understood, not as self-existent and improduced, but in the first place created by God, and preceding other Beings, which were made out of it, is not, so far as I can discern, any way repugnant to the Holy Scripture, but on the contrary rather consonant and agreeable thereto. For *Moses*, in the History and Description of the Creation, in the first Chapter of *Genesis*, saith, not that God created all things in an instant in their full State and Perfection, but that He proceeded gradually and in Order, from more imperfect to more perfect Beings, first beginning with the Earth, that is, the Terraqueous Globe, which was made *tohu vabohu*, without Form, and void, the Waters covering the Face of the Land, which were afterwards separated from the Land, and gathered together into one place. Then He created out of the Land and Water, first Plants, and then Animals, Fishes, Birds, Beasts, in Order, and last of all formed the Body of Man of the Dust of the Earth.

## Of the Chaos

AND whereas there is no particular mention made of the Creation of Metals, Minerals, and other Fossils, they must be comprehended in the Word *Earth*, as the Water itself also is in the second Verse of this first Chapter.

IT seems, therefore, to me consonant to the Scripture, That God Almighty did at first create the Earth or Terraqueous Globe, containing in itself the Principles of all simple inanimate Bodies, or the minute and naturally indivisible Particles of which they were compounded, of various but a determinate Number of Figures, and perchance of different Magnitudes; and these variously and confusedly commixed, as though they had been carelesly shaken and shuffled together; yet not so, but that there was Order observed by the most Wise Creator in the Disposition of them. And not only so, but that the same Omnipotent Deity did create also the Seeds or Seminal Principles of all Animate Bodies, both Vegetative and Sensitive; and dispers'd them, at least the Vegetative, all over the superficial Part of the Earth and Water. And the Notion of such an Earth as this is, the Primitive Patriarchs of the World delivered to their Posterity, who, by Degrees annexing something of Fabulous to it, imposed upon it the Name of *Chaos*.

THE next Work of the Divine Power and Wisdom, was the Separation of the Water from

from the dry Land, and Raising up of the Mountains, of which I shall treat more particularly in the next Chapter.

To which follows the Giving to both Elements a Power of hatching, as I may so say, or quickening and bringing to Perfection the Seeds they contained; first the more imperfect, as Herbs and Trees; then the more perfect, Fish, Fowl, Four-footed Beasts, and creeping Things or Insects. Which may be the Meaning of those Commands of GOD, which were operative and effectual, communicating to the Earth and Water a Power to produce what He commanded them, *Gen.* i. 11. *Let the Earth bring forth Grass,* &c. and *v.* 20. *Let the Waters bring forth abundantly the moving Creature that hath Life, and Fowl that may fly above the Earth,* &c. And *v.* 24. *Let the Earth bring forth the living Creature after his Kind, Cattle and creeping thing, and Beast of the Earth after his Kind.*

So the Earth was at first cloathed with all Sorts of Herbs and Trees; and both Earth and Water furnished with Inhabitants. And this the Ancients understood by their διακόσμησις.

But whether out of præ-existing Seeds, as I suppose, or not, certain it is, that GOD at that time did give an extraordinary and miraculous Power to the Land and Water, of producing Vegetables and Animals; and after there were as many of every kind brought forth,

forth, as there were Seeds created at firſt; or as many as it ſeemed good to the Divine Creator to produce without Seed; there remained no farther Ability in thoſe Elements to bring forth any more; but all the ſucceeding owe their Original to Seed; GOD having given to every *Species* a Power to generate or propagate its Like.

## CHAP. III.
### Of the Separating the Land and Water, and Raiſing up the Mountains.

SUPPOSING that GOD Almighty did at firſt create the Terreſtrial Globe, partly of ſolid and more ponderous, partly of fluid and lighter Parts; the ſolid and ponderous muſt needs naturally ſubſide, the fluid and lighter get above. Now, that there were ſuch different Parts created, is clear, and therefore it is reaſonable to think, that the Waters at firſt ſhould ſtand above and cover the Earth: And that they did ſo, ſeems evident to me from the Teſtimony of the Scripture. For, in the Hiſtory of the Creation, in the firſt Chapter of *Geneſis*, ver. 2. it is ſaid, That *the Spirit of* GOD *moved upon the Face of the Waters,* intimating that the Waters were uppermoſt. And GOD *ſaid*, ver. 9. *let the Waters under the Heaven be gathered together*

*together into one place, and let the dry Land appear.* Whence, I think, it is manifest to any unprejudiced Reader, That before that time the Land was covered with Water: Especially, if we add the Testimony of the Holy Psalmist, *Psalm* civ. ver. 6, and 9. which is as it were a Comment upon this Place of *Genesis*, where, speaking of the Earth at the Creation, he saith, *Thou coveredst it with the Deep as with a Garment; the Waters stood above the Mountains* .... and, ver. 9. *That they turn not again to cover the Earth.* And that this Gathering together of Waters was not into any subterraneous Abyss, seems likewise clear from the Text: For it is said, That GOD called this Collection of Waters *Seas*, as if it had been on purpose to prevent such a Mistake.

WHETHER this Separation of the Land and Water, and Gathering the Waters together into one Place, were done by the immediate Application and Agency of God's Almighty Power, or by the Intervention and Instrumentality of Second Causes, I cannot determine. It might possibly be effected by the same Causes that Earthquakes are, *viz.* subterraneous Fires and *Flatus's*. We see what incredible Effects the Accension of Gunpowder hath: It rends Rocks, and blows up the most ponderous and solid Walls, Towers, and Edifices, so that its Force is almost irresistible. Why then might not such a proportionable

tionable Quantity of such Materials set on fire together, raise up the Mountains themselves, how great and ponderous soever they be, yea the whole Superficies of the dry Land (for it must all be elevated) above the Waters? And truly to me the Psalmist seems to intimate this Cause, *Psalm* civ. 7. For, after he had said, *The Waters stood above the Mountains;* he adds, *At Thy Rebuke they fled, at the Voice of Thy Thunder they hasted away.* Now, we know that an Earthquake is but a subterraneous Thunder, and then immediately follows, *The Mountains ascend, the Valleys descend,* &c. In this Manner of raising up the dry Land at first, and casting off the Waters, I was well pleased to find the Right Reverend Father in GOD, *Simon*, Lord Bishop of *Ely*, to agree with me in his excellent Commentary upon *Genesis*, cap. i. ver. 9. ' This, saith he, we may conceive to have ' been done by such Particles of Fire as were ' left in the Bowels of the Earth, whereby such ' Nitrosulphureous Vapours were kindled, as ' made an Earthquake, which both lifted up ' the Earth, and made Receptacles for the Wa' ters to run into; as the Psalmist (otherwise ' I should not venture to mention this) seems ' in the forementioned Place to illustrate it. If there might be a high Hill raised up near the City *Trœzen*, out of a plain Field, by the Force of a subterraneous Fire or *Flatus*, as *Ovid* tells us:

*Est*

*Est prope Pitthæam tumulus Træzena sine ullis*  Ov. Me-
*Arduus arboribus, quondam planissima campi*  tamorph.
*Area, nunc tumulus; nam (res horrenda relatu)*  lib. 15.
*Vis fera ventorum, cæcis inclusa cavernis,*
*Expirare aliqua cupiens, luctatáque frustra*
*Liberiore frui cœlo, cum carcere rima*
*Nulla fuit toto, nec pervia flatibus esset,*
*Extentam tumefecit humum, ceu spiritus oris*
*Tendere vesicam solet, aut derepta bicornis*
*Terga capri; tumor ille loci permansit, & alti*
*Collis habet speciem, longóque induruit ævo:*

*A Hill by* Pitthæan Trœzen *mounts, uncrown'd*
*With Sylvan Shades, which once was level*
  *Ground,*
*For furious Winds (a Story to admire)*
*Pent in blind Caverns, struggling to expire;*
*And vainly seeking to enjoy th' Extent*
*Of freer Air, the Prison wanting Vent,*
*Puffs up the hollow Earth extended so,*
*As when with swelling Breath we Bladders*
  *blow:*
*The Tumour of the Place remained still,*
*In time grown solid, like a lofty Hill:*

A parallel Instance hereto we have of later Date, of a Hill not far from *Puzzuolo* [*Puteoli*] beside the Gulf of *Baiæ*, which I myself have view'd and been upon. It is by the Natives call'd *Monte di cenere*, and was raised by an Earthquake, *Sept.* 29. 1538. of about one hundred Foot perpendicular Altitude,
                    though

though some make it much higher: According to *Stephanus Pighius*, it is a Mile Ascent to the Top, and four Miles round at the Foot: We indeed judged it not near so great. The People say it bears nothing; nothing of any Use or Profit, I suppose, they mean: Else I am sure, there grows *Heath, Myrtle, Mastick-Tree*, and other Shrubs upon it. It is a spungy kind of Earth, and makes a great Sound under a Man's Feet that stamps upon it. The same Earthquake threw up so much Earth, Stones and Ashes, as quite filled up the *Jacus Lucrinus*, so that there is nothing left of it now, but a fenny Meadow. When I say, that this Mountain was raised by an Earthquake, I do not mean, that the meer Succussion, or Shaking of the Earth, raised up the Mountain; but that the same Cause which shook the Earth, that is, subterraneous Fire, cast up the Materials which raised the Mountain, and of which it doth consist, that is, Stones, Cinders, Earth, and Ashes. Indeed, under the Word *Earthquake*, in this Work, I comprehend the Concomitants and Consequents of an Earthquake, and the efficient Cause of it; which is a subterraneous Fire, as I have expressed myself, *pag.* 10. *line* 8. of the First *Edition*.

NEITHER, by the Elevation of Mountains, do I mean, that they were all heaved up, as it were by a *Flatus*, but only such, where the enclosed Fire was not of Force sufficient

to

to make its way out, or found not *Spiracula* to vent itſelf. Otherwhere, where it was ſtrong enough to rend the ſuperincumbent Maſs of Earth, or found ſome Rifts or *Spiracula* to break out by, there it iſſued out with great Force, and threw up abundance of Stones, Aſhes, and Earth, and ſo raiſed up a Mountain that way.

If ſuch Hills, I ſay, as theſe, may be, and have been elevated by ſubterraneous Wild-fire, *Flatus*, or Earthquakes, *ſi parvis liceat componere magna*, if we may compare great things with ſmall, why might not the greateſt and higheſt Mountains in the World be raiſed up in like manner by a ſubterraneous *Flatus* or Wild-fire, of Quantity and Force ſufficient to work ſuch an Effect; that is, that bears as great a Proportion to the ſuperincumbent Weight and Bulk to be elevated, as thoſe under theſe ſmaller Hills did to theirs?

But we cannot doubt this may be done, when we are well aſſured that the like hath been done. For the greateſt and higheſt Ridge of Mountains in the World, the *Andes* of *Peru*, have been, for ſome hundreds of Leagues in Length, violently ſhaken, and many Alterations made therein by an Earthquake that happened in the Year 1646. mentioned by *Kircher* in his *Arca Noæ*, from the Letters of the Jeſuites. And *Pliny* tells us, of his own knowledge, that the Alps and Appennine have often been ſhaken with Earthquakes:

quakes: *Exploratum est mihi Alpes Appenninúmque sæpius tremuisse*, lib. 2. cap. 80. Nay, more than all this, we read, that in the time of the Emperor *Valentinian* the First, there was an Earthquake that shook all the known World. Whilst this Innovator [that is, *Procopius*] was yet alive, (saith *Amm. Marcellinus*, lib. 26. cap. 14.) *Horrendi tremores per omnem orbis ambitum grassati sunt subitò, quales nec fabulæ, nec veridicæ nobis antiquitates exponunt. Paulò enim post lucis exortum, densitate prævia fulgurum acriùs vibratorum tremefacta concutitur omnis terreni stabilitas ponderis, maréque dispulsum retrò fluctibus evolutis abscessit, ut retecta voragine profundorum species natantium multiformes limo cernerentur hærentes, valliúmque vastitates & montium, ut opinari dabatur, suspicerent radios solis quos primigenia rerum sub immensis gurgitibus amandavit,* &c. That is, *Horrid Earthquakes suddenly raged all the World over; the like whereto, neither Fables nor true Antiquities ever acquaint us with, or make mention of. For soon after Break of Day, redoubled, smart, and violent Flashes of Lightning preceding, the stable and ponderous Mass of the whole Earth was shaken, and made to tremble; and the Sea, with revolved Waves, was driven backwards, and forced so far to recede, that the Bottom of the great Deeps and Gulfs being discovered, multiform Species of Fishes, forsaken by the Water, were seen*

seen lying on the Mud; and those vast Valleys and Mountains, which the primigenial Nature had sunk deep, and concealed under immense Waters, (as we had reason to think) saw the Sun-beams. Wherefore, many Ships resting upon the dry Ground, the Mariners wandring carelesly up and down through the small Reliques of the Waters, that they might gather up Fishes, and other things, with their Hands; the Sea-Waves being, as it were, grieved with their Repulse, rise up again, and making their way backward through the fervid Shallows, violently dashing against the Islands and extended Shores of the Continents, threw down, and levelled innumerable Edifices in Cities, and where else they were found. Where, see more of the Effects of it. Of this Earthquake we find mention also in *Zosimus* and *Orosius*.

If this Story be true, as certainly it is, we have no reason to doubt of the Possibility of the dry Land being thus raised at first by subterraneous Fire. And with us agrees the learned *Thomas Lydyat*, in his *Philosophical Disquisition concerning the Origine of Fountains*, &c. being of Opinion not only that it might be so, but that it was so. I shall give you his own Words, *Ubi aliud quoque summæ admirationis plenum Terramotús atque Ignis subterranei effectum notandum venit, montium sci. generatio.* And then having mentioned the raising up Islands in the

Sea

Sea by subterraneous Fires, he proceeds thus, *Quomodo etiam omnes montes qui uspiam sunt, unà cum ipsis terris Continentibus (quæ nihil aliud sunt quàm sparsi in Oceano majores montes sive insulæ) in mundi primordiis, (quando nimirum Ignis de quo loquimur, in terræ visceribus à potentissimo mundi Conditore accensus est) extitisse maximè fit verisimile; mari in cava loca recedente, & terrestribus Animalibus (ejusdem Divini numinis sapientissimo consilio) habitandi locum relinquente.* That is, *After which Manner also all the Mountains in the World, together with the Continents themselves, (which are nothing else but great Mountains or Islands scattered in the Ocean) in the beginning of the World, when the Fire of which we speak was first kindled in the Bowels of the Earth by the Almighty Creator, were (as it is most highly probable) originally raised up; the Sea receding into the Cavities and depressed Places, and by the most wise Counsel of the Supreme Deity, leaving Room for Terrestrial Animals to inhabit.* Than which nothing can be said more consonant to what we have written: And I was highly pleased and satisfied to find such Philosophy in so learned and judicious a Writer.

AND in Confirmation of this Doctrine, *Strabo* himself, though he had not, nor could have any Knowledge at all of the prodigious Effects of Gunpowder, yet makes no Difficulty to affirm the Possibility of raising up as well the Continents and Mountains, as the Islands, by Earthquakes and subterraneous Fires; toward the latter end of the first Book of his Geography, discoursing thus: Καὶ γὰρ σεισμοὶ, καὶ ἀναφυσήματα, καὶ ἀποιδήσεις τῆς ὑφάλυ γῆς μετεωρίζυσι καὶ τὴν θάλασσαν. Οὐ γὰρ μύδρι μὲν ἀνενεχθῆναι δύνανται, καὶ μικραὶ νῆσοι, μεγάλαι δ' ὒ· ὐδὲ νῆσοι μὲν, ἤπειροι δ' ὒ. And a little after, Καὶ τὴν Σικελίαν ὐδέν τι μᾶλλον ἀπορρῶγα τῆς Ἰταλίας εἰκάζοι τὶς, ἂν, ἢ ἀναβληθεῖσαν ὑπὸ τῦ Αἰτναίυ πυρὸς ἐκ βύθυ συμμεῖναι. That is, *For Earthquakes and Eruptions of* Flatus [*Blasts*] *or sudden Tumors of the Submarine Earth, or Bottom of the Sea, may swell and elevate the Sea; so that not only small Lumps or Masses of Matter, but even Islands may be raised up in the midst of it. Neither if small Islands can be raised, may not great ones too; neither may Islands be heaved up, and not Continents as well. And* Sicily *may as well be thought to have been thrown up out of the Deep by the Force of the* Ætnæan *Fire, and sticking together to have continued above Water, as to have been a Piece broken off from* Italy. And the like may be said of the Islands of *Lipara* and *Pithecusa*.

Of the Possibility of doing it we need not doubt, when we have sufficient Proof of the thing done in lesser Islands thus heaved up in the midst of the Sea, by submarine Fires. *Strabo*, lib. 1. Ἀνὰ μέσον γὰρ Θήρας καὶ Θηρασίας ἐκπεσῦσαι φλόγες ἐκ τῦ πελάγυς ἐφ' ἡμέρας

ρας τέσσαρας, ὡςε πᾶσαν ζεῖν καὶ Φλέγεσθαι τὴν θάλασσαν, ἀνεφύσησαν κατ᾽ ὀλίγον ἐξαιρομένην ὡς ἂν ὀργανικῶς καὶ συντεθειμένην ἐκ μύδρων νῆσον, δώδεκα ςαδίων τὴν περίμετρον. *That is, Between* Thera *and* Therafia *Flames issuing out of the Sea for four Days, (so that the whole Sea boiled and burned) blew up by little and little, as if it had been raised by Machines, and composed of great Lumps or Masses, an Island of Twelve Furlongs Circumference.*

And *Pliny* tells us, that the Island *Hiera*, near *Italy*, in the Time of the Social War, together with the Sea itself, did burn for several Days. His Words are, *In medio Mari Hiera insula juxta* Italiam *cum ipso Mari arsit per aliquot dies.*

And *Strabo*, lib. 1. reports, That about *Methone*, in the Bay of *Hermione*, there was Earth raised, and as it were blown up to the Height of seven Furlongs by a fiery Breath or Exhalation, which by Day-time was unaccessible by reason of Heat and sulphureous Stench, but smelling sweet by Night, and shining so as to be seen afar off, likewise casting such a Heat, as to cause the Sea to boil for five Furlongs, and to render it troubled for the Space of twenty; raising up therein a Baich or Bank of Stones as big as Towers.

These Instances I alledge, principally because they seem to demonstrate a Possibility of the Accension of Fire in the Earth when it was wholly covered with Water, and had no Entercourse or Communion with the superiour or external Air; which is the main and most material Objection against the Elevation of the dry Land at the beginning by subterraneous Fires.

You will say, If the Mountains be thus heaved, or else cast up, by subterraneous Fires, the Earth must needs be hollow all underneath them, and there must be vast Dens and Caverns dispers'd throughout them.

I ANSWER, 'Tis true indeed, so there are; as may undeniably be proved by Instances. For the new Mountain we mentioned at *Puteoli*, that was thus raised, being of a Mile steep Ascent, and four Miles round at the Foot, a proportionable Cavity must be left in the Earth underneath: And the Mountain *Ætna*, at the last Eructation alone, having disgorged out of its Bowels so great a Flood of melted Materials, as if spread at the Depth and Breadth of three Foot, might reach four times round the whole Circuit of the *Terraqueous Globe*, there must likewise an answerable Vault be left within. You will demand, How then comes it to pass, that they stand so firm, and do not founder and fall in, after so many Ages? I answer, that they may stand, appears by the foresaid new-raised Mountain. For notwithstanding the Cavity under it, it hath stood firm and staunch, without the least Sinking or Subsidency, for above an hundred and fifty Years; neither is there

there any great Sinking or Falling in at *Ætna* itself; at least in no degree answerable to its ejected Matter. This Assertion is confirmed by the unanimous Vote and Testimony of all Writers, Ancient and Modern, who have handled this Subject. But *Alphonsus Borellus* supposes them not to have duly considered the Matter, and calculated the Quantity of the ejected Materials, and the Bulk of the Mountain, and compared them together; but to have been carried away by the Prejudices and Persuasions of the People, who looking upon the Top of the Mountain at a Distance, think it but a small thing in Comparison of the ejected Sand and Ashes that cover'd whole Countries; and those vast Rivers of liquid Stones, and other Ingredients, that ran down so many Miles, whereas he, by a moderate Computation, found out that the Total of what the Mountain disgorged at the last Eruption, amounted not (as I remember) to the fourteen thousandth Part of the Solidity of the whole Mountain. The reason is the Strength and Firmness of their Vaulture and Pillars, sufficient to support the superincumbent Weight. And yet in some Places there are Sinkings and Fallings in, which have afterwards become Valleys, or Pools of Water. But as for the Cavities that are lower than the *Superficies* of the Ocean, the Water, where it could insinuate and make its Way, hath filled them up to that Height. I say, where it could

could make its Way, for that there are many empty Cavities even under the Sea itself, appears by the shaking and heating too of the very Water of the Sea in some Places in Earthquakes, and raising up the Borders or Skirts of it, so as to drive the Water a great way back, and the raising up new Islands in the middle of the Sea; as *Delos* and *Rhodes*, and *Anaphe*, and *Nea*, and *Alone*, and *Hiera*, and *Thera*, mentioned by *Pliny*, Hist. lib. 2. c. 87. and *Thia* in his own time; and *Therasia* in the *Ægean* in *Seneca*'s time, which was heaved up in the Sight of many Mariners then present and looking on.

I am not ignorant, that the learned Man I lately quoted, I mean *Alph. Borellus*, in his Book *De Incendiis Ætnæ*, is of Opinion, that the middle Part, or, as he calls it, the Kernel of that Mountain, is firm and solid, without any great Caverns or Vacuities, and that all those Vaults and Cavities in which the Fire rages, are near the Superficial or Cortical Part: And derides those who fancy that *Ætna*, the *Æolian* Islands, *Lipara*, *Strongyle*, &c. and *Vesuvius*, do communicate by subterraneous Channels and Passages running under the Bottom of the Sea. But saving the Respect due to him for his Learning and Ingenuity, there is good Authority on their Side; and our Ratiocinations against the Possibility of such a thing must give place to the clear Proof of Matter of Fact. *Julius Ethnicus*,

## Of the Chaos

an ancient Writer, quoted by *Ludovicus Vives*, in his Annotations upon S. *Augustin, De Civitate Dei*, gives us this Relation; *Marco Æmilio, Lucio Aurelio Consulibus, Ætna mons terræmotu Ignes super verticem latè diffudit, & ad Insulam Liparam mare efferbuit, & quibusdam adustis navibus vapore plerosque navaleis exanimavit: Piscium vim magnam exanimem dispersit, quos Liparenses avidiùs epulis adpetenteis contaminatione ventris consumpti sunt, ita ut novâ pestilentiâ vastarentur insulæ.* That is, Marcus Æmilius, *and* Lucius Aurelius, *being Consuls, Mount* Ætna *being shaken by an Earthquake, cast forth and scattered Fire from its Top far and wide. At which time, the Sea, at the Island of* Lipara, *was boiling hot, and some Ships being burnt, most of the Seamen were stifled with the Vapour: Besides, it dispersed abroad a power of dead Fish, which the* Liparensians *greedily gathering up and eating, were consumed with a contagious Disease in their Bellies; so that the Islands were wasted with a new sort of Pestilence.* And Father *Kircher* the Jesuite, in the Preface to his *Mundus Subterraneus*, giving a Relation of an Earthquake which shook a great Part of *Calabria*, and made notable Devastations there, which himself saw, and was, in *Anno* 1638. clearly demonstrates, that *Ætna, Stromboli*, and the Mountains of *Calabria*, do communicate by Vaults and Caverns passing under the Bottom of the Sea.

I shall

I shall insert but one Passage out of him, referring the Reader to the fore-quoted Preface for the rest. *Hisce calamitatibus* (saith he) *dum jactamur, ego curiosiùs intuitus* Strongylum, 60 *ferè milliarium intercapedine dissitum, illum insolito modo furere notavi, &c.* i. e. *While we were tost with these Calamities, I beholding curiously the Island* Stromboli, *about* 60 *Miles distant, observed it to rage after an unusual manner, for it appeared all filled with Fire in such Plenty, that it seemed to cast forth Mountains of Flame; a Spectacle horrid to behold, and formidable to the most undaunted Spirit. In the mean time, there was a certain Sound perceived as it were of Thunder, but by reason of the great Distance from whence it came, somewhat obscure, which by degrees proceeding forward in the subterraneous Conduits, grew greater and greater, till it came to the Place just underneath us,* [they were at *Lopez* by the Sea] *where it shook the Earth with such a Roaring, or Murmur and Fury, that being not able to stand any longer upon our Legs, we were forced, to support ourselves, to catch hold upon any Shrub or Twig that was near us, lest our Limbs should be put out of Joint by too much Shaking and Concussion.* At which time happened a thing worthy of immortal and eternal Memory, viz. the *Subversion* of the famous Town of *S.* Eufemia; which he goes about to relate. As for *Vesuvius*, if that be not hollow down to the very Roots and Foundations of it, how comes it to pafs, that at the Times of its Deflagrations it fhould vomit out fuch Floods of boiling Waters? as, if we had not read of them in Hiftories, and been told fo by our Guide when we afcended that Mountain, we muft needs have perceived ourfelves, by the mighty Gulls and Channels in the Sides thereof, it being of itfelf near the Top fo fpungy and dry, that it is more likely to imbibe than to caft off much Rain in the Winter-time. And again, what caufes the Sea to recede at thofe Times, and that to fo great a Diftance, that the Galleys have been laid dry in the very Haven of *Naples?*

HOWBEIT, I cannot pofitively affert the Mountains thus to have been raifed. But yet, whether without Means, or by whatfoever Means it were, a Receptacle for the Waters was prepared, and the dry Land and Mountains elevated, fo as to caft off the Waters, on the third Day, and which is wonderful, the Cavities made to receive the Waters, and the whole *terra firma,* or dry Land, with its Mountains, were fo proportioned one to the other, as that the one was as much depreffed below the Shores, as the other was elevated above them. And, as if the one had been taken out of the other, the Sea, with all its Creeks, and Bays, and Inlets, and other Appendants, was made, and is very near equal to the whole dry Land,

with

with its Promontories and Mountains, if not in *Superficies*, yet in Bulk or Dimenfions, though fome think in both. Which Equality is ftill conftantly maintained, notwithftanding all Inundations of Land, and Atterations of Sea; becaufe one of thefe doth always nearly balance the other, according to the vulgar Proverb we have before-mention'd, *What the Sea lofes in one Place, it gains in another.* If any fhall demand, How the Sea comes to be gradually depreffed, and deepeft about the Middle Part; whereas the Bottom of it was in all likelihood equal while the Waters covered the whole Earth? I anfwer, the fame Caufe that raifed up the Earth, whether a fubterraneous Fire or *Flatus*, raifed up alfo the Skirts of the Sea, the Afcent gradually decreafing to the Middle Part, where, by reafon of the Solidity of the Earth, or Gravity of the incumbent Water, the Bottom was not elevated at all. For the enclofed Fire in thofe Parts where its firft Accenfion or greateft Strength was, raifed up the Earth firft, and caft off the Waters, and thence fpreading by degrees, ftill elevated the Land, and drove the Waters farther and farther; till at length the Weight of them was too great to be raifed, and then the Fire brake forth at the Tops of the Mountains, where it found leaft Refiftance, and difpers'd itfelf in the open Air. The Waters alfo, where they found the Bottom fandy, or yielding,

ing, made their way into all those Cavities the Fire had made and left, filling them up as high as the Level of the Ocean. Neither let any Man imagine, that the Earth under the Water was too soft and muddy to be in this manner raised by subterraneous Fire; for I have shewn before, that the Bottom of the Sea is so saddened and hardened by the Weight of the incumbent Water, that the High-ways, beaten continually by Horses and Carriages, are not more firm and solid. But omitting this (which is only a Conjecture) I shall discourse a little more concerning the Equality of Sea and Land.

It hath been observed by some, that where there are high Cliffs or Downs along the Shore, there the Sea adjoining is deep; and where there are low and level Grounds, it is shallow; the Depth of the Sea answering to the Elevation of the Earth above it: And as the Earth from the Shores is gradually higher and higher, to the Middle and Parts most remote from the Sea, as is evident by the Descents of the Rivers, they requiring a constant Declivity to carry them down; so the Sea likewise is proportionably deeper and deeper from the Shores to the Middle. So that the Rising of the Earth from the Shores to the Mid-Land, is answerable to the Descent or Declivity of the Bottom of the Sea from the same Shores to the Mid-Sea. This Rising of the Earth from the Shores gradually to the

Mid-

Mid-land, is so considerable, that it is very likely the Altitude of the Earth in those Mid-land Parts above the *Superficies* of the Sea, is greater than that of the Mountains above the Level of the adjacent Lands. To the Height of the Hills, above the common *Superficies* of the Earth, do answer, in *Brerewood*'s Opinion, the extraordinary Depths or Whirl-pools that are found in the Sea, descending beneath the ordinary Bottom of the Sea, as the Hills ascend above the ordinary Face of the Land. But this is but a Conjecture of his; and to me it seems not very probable, because it is not likely there should be, in the Sea, extraordinary Depths of that vast Length and Extension, as those huge Ridges of Mountains that run almost quite through the Continents: And because I have observed the Waters of Rivers that flow gently, but especially of the Sea, to level the Bottoms of their Channels and Receptacles, as may be seen in those Parts of the Sea whose Bottoms are uncovered at Low-water; and in dry Lands that have been deserted by the Sea, as the Fens in the Isle of *Ely*, and the *Craux* in *Provence* in *France*, &c. which appear to be a perfect Level, as far as one can ken. Though possibly the Motion of the Sea may not descend down so low as those Depths, and so may not level the Bottoms of them.

BUT

But againſt what I have ſaid concerning the Leveling of the Bottom of the Sea, it may be objected, That Mariners and Divers find no ſuch thing, but the quite contrary, *viz.* That the Bottom of the Sea is as unequal as the Land, ſometimes ten or twelve Fathoms on one Side of the Ship, and one hundred on the other, as Mr. *Boyle* tells us in his *Relations about the Bottom of the Sea,* conſonant whereto are the Accounts of Divers. *And I have* (ſaith my worthy Friend Dr. *Tanc. Robinſon,* in one of his Letters to me) *read in Voyages, of vaſt Rocks of Salt obſerv'd in ſome Places under the Sea.*

To which I anſwer, That I ſhould indeed have excepted ſuch Places as are rocky, which bear a very little Proportion to the Latitude and Extent of the Sea, and are for the moſt part not far off the Land. I myſelf have ſeen ſo much of the Bottom of the Sea, round about the Coaſts of *England,* and a good Part of the Low-Countreys, of *Italy* and *Sicily,* that, I think, I may boldly pronounce in general, That where the Bottom of the Sea is not rocky, but Earth, Owze, or Sand, (and that is incomparably the greateſt Part of it) it is by the Motion of the Waters, ſo far as the Reciprocration of the Sea extends to the Bottom, brought to a Level; and if it ſhould be now unequal, would in time be level'd again. By Level, I do not mean ſo as to have no Declivity, (for the Reciprocration preſerves that,

that, the Flood hindring, in good meafure, the conſtant Carrying down of the Bottom) but only to have an equal, uniform, and eaſie Deſcent from the Shores to the Deeps. Now, all thoſe Reports of Divers and Navigators referr, for the moſt part, to rocky Places. For Mariners ſeldom found but in ſuch Places, and in Shallows; and Urinators have no reaſon to dive where the Bottom is level and ſandy. And that the Motion of the Waters deſcends to a good Depth, I prove from thoſe Plants that grow deepeſt in the Sea, becauſe they all generally grow flat in manner of a Fan, and not with Branches on all ſides, like Trees; which is ſo contrived by the Providence of Nature, becauſe the Edges of them do, in that Poſture, with moſt eaſe, cut the Water flowing to and fro: And ſhould the flat Side be objected to the Stream, it would be turned Edgewiſe by the Force of it; becauſe, in that Site it doth leaſt reſiſt the Motion of the Water: Whereas, did the Branches of thoſe Plants grow round, as in Trees, they would be thrown down backward and forward every Tide. Nay, not only the herbaceous and woody ſubmarine Plants, but even the *Lithophyta* themſelves affect this manner of Growing, if they be any thing Ramoſe, and riſe to a conſiderable Height, as I have obſerved in various Kinds of *Corals* and *Pori*. Hence I ſuſpect thoſe Relations of Trees growing at the Bottom of the Sea,

and

and bringing forth Fruit there. As for the *Maldiva Nut*, till better Information, I adhere to *Garcias* his Opinion, That the Trees that bare those Nuts were, of old time, together with the Land on which they grew, overwhelmed by the Inundations of the Sea, and there hardned in the Earth, and afterwards cast up by the Working of the Sea again. Which thing is very probable; for to this day, some of those *Maldiva* Islands are now and then drowned, and swallowed up by the Sea. Farther, I do believe, that in the great Depths of the Sea there grow no Plants at all, the Bottom being too remote from the external Air; which, though it may pierce the Water so low, yet I doubt, whether in Quantity sufficient for the Vegetation of Plants. Nay, we are told, that in those deep and bottomless Seas, there are no Fish neither: Yet, not because there are no Plants or Insects to feed them; for that they can live upon Water alone, *Rondeletius* his Experiment about keeping them in a Glass, doth undeniably prove; but because their Spawn would be lost in those Seas, the Bottom being too cold for it to quicken there. This Answer and Discourse, though it be inserted into another Treatise, yet properly belongs to this place, to which I have, therefore, restored it; begging the Reader's Excuse for this Repetition. I now proceed.

THAT

## and Creation.

THAT it is confonant to the beſt Obſervations of the Height of the Earth and its Mountains above the *Superficies* of the Sea; and of the Depth of the Sea; that the one is anſwerable to the other. *Varenius*, in his *Geogr.* witneſſeth, p. 152. *Cæterùm ex obſervata hactenus in pleriſque locis profunditate Oceani, manifeſtum eſt, eam fere æqualem Altitudini ſive Elevationi montium & locorum Mediterraneorum ſupra littora, nimirum quantum hæc elevantur & extant ſupra littorum horizontem, tantum alvei maris infra eum deprimuntur; ſive quantum aſſurgit terra à littoribus versùs mediterranea loca, tantundem paulatim magis magiſque deprimitur uſque ad medii Oceani loca, ubi plerumque maxima eſt profunditas.* That is, *From the Depth of the Ocean, as far as hath been hitherto obſerved in moſt Places, it is manifeſt, that that* [Profundity] *is near equal to the Altitude or Elevation of the Mediterraneous Places above the Shores; that is to ſay, as much as theſe are elevated, and ſtand up above the Horizon of the Shores, ſo much are the Channels of the Seas depreſſed below it: Or, as much as the Earth riſeth from the Shores towards the Mediterraneous Places; ſo much it is by little and little, more and more, depreſſed to the middle Parts of the Ocean, where the greateſt Depth for the moſt part is.*

AND *Brerewood*, in his Enquiries, pertinently to our Purpoſe, ſuppoſeth the Depth of the Sea to be a great deal more than the Height of the Hills above the common Surface of the Earth. ---*For that in making Estimation of the Depth of the Sea, we are not to reckon and consider only the Height of the Hills above the common Superficies of the Earth, but the Advantage or Height of all the dry Land above the Superficies of the Sea; Because the whole Mass of the Earth, that now appeareth above the Waters, being taken, as it were, out of the Place which the Waters now possess, must be equal to the Place out of which it was taken; and consequently it seemeth, that the Height or Elevation of the one should answer to the Depth or Descending of the other.* And, therefore, as I said, in estimating the Deepness of the Sea, we are not to consider only the Erection of the Hills above the ordinary Land, but the Advantage of all the dry Land above the Sea. Which latter, I mean the Height of the ordinary Main Land, is in my Opinion more in large Continents above the Sea, than that of the Hills is above the Land. For, that the plain and common Face of the dry Land, is not level or equally distant from the Center, but hath great Declivity and Descent towards the Sea, and Acclivity or Rising toward the Mid-Land Part, although it appear not so to the common View of the Eye, is to Reason notwithstanding manifest. Because, as it is found in that Part of the Earth which the Sea covereth, that it

descendeth

descendeth lower and lower toward the midst of the Sea; (for the Sea which touching the upper Face of it is known to be level by Nature, and evenly distant from the Center, is withall observed to wax deeper and deeper the farther one saileth from the Shore towards the Main) even so, in that Part which is uncovered, the Coursings and Streamings of Rivers on all Sides, from the Mid-Land Parts towards the Sea, (whose Property we know is to slide from the higher to the lower) evidently declare so much. * This Author, with *Damascen*, supposes, that the Unevenness and Irregularity, which is now seen in the *Superficies* of the Earth, was caused either by taking some Parts out of the upper Face of the Earth in sundry Places to make it more Hollow, and laying them in other Places to make it more Convex: Or else (which in effect is equivalent to that) by raising up some, and depressing others, to make Room and Receipt for the Sea; that Mutation being wrought by the Power of that Word, *Let the Waters be gathered into one Place, that the dry Land may appear.* This Proportioning of the Cavities appointed to receive the Seas, to the Protuberancy of the dry Land above the common *Superficies* of the Ocean, is to me a sufficient Argument, to prove, that the Gathering together of the Waters into one Place, was a Work of Counsel and Design; and if not effected by the immediate

* *De fide Orthod. l. 2. c. 10.*

mediate Finger of GOD, yet at least govern'd and directed by Him. So the Scripture affirms the Place to receive the Sea, to have been prepared by GOD, *Psal.* civ. 8. Now in things of this Nature, to the giving an Account whereof whatever *Hypothesis* we can possibly invent, can be but meerly conjectural; those are to be most approved that come nearest to the Letter of Scripture, and those that clash with it to be rejected, how trim or consistent soever with themselves they may seem to be: This being as much, as when GOD tells us how He did make the World, for us to tell Him how He should have made it.

But here it may be objected, That the present Earth looks like a Heap of Rubbish and Ruins; And that there are no greater Examples of Confusion in Nature, than Mountains singly or jointly considered; and that there appear not the least Footsteps of any Art or Counsel, either in the Figure and Shape, or Order and Disposition of Mountains and Rocks. Wherefore it is not likely they came so out of GOD's Hands; who by the Ancient Philosophers is said ἀιεὶ γεωμετρεῖν, and to make all things in Number, Weight, and Measure.

To which I answer, That the present Face of the Earth, with all its Mountains and Hills, its Promontories and Rocks, as rude and deformed as they appear, seems to me a very

## *and Creation.*

ry beautiful and pleafant Object, and with all that Variety of Hills, and Valleys, and Inequalities, far more grateful to behold, than a perfectly level Country, without any Rifing or Protuberancy, to terminate the Sight: As any one, that hath on the one hand feen the Ifle of *Ely,* or any the like Country exactly level, and extending on all Sides farther than one can ken, or that hath been far out at Sea, where nothing is to be feen but Sky and Water: And on the other, from the Downs of *Suffex* enjoyed that fpacious and ravifhing Profpect of the Country on one hand, and the Sea on the other, comparing both Objects, muft necetfarily confefs.

2. They are ufeful to Mankind in affording them convenient Places for Habitation, and Situations of Houfes and Villages; ferving as Skreens to keep off the cold and nipping Blafts of the Northern and Eafterly Winds, and reflecting the benign and cherifhing Sun-Beams, and fo rendring their Habitations both more comfortable and chearly in Winter; and promoting the Growth of Herbs and Fruit-Trees, and the Maturation of their Fruits in Summer. Befides, cafting off the Waters, they lay the Gardens, Yards and Avenues to the Houfes dry and clean, and fo as well more falutary as more elegant. Whereas Houfes built in Plains, unlefs fhaded with Trees, ftand bleak and expofed to Wind and

D 2  Weather;

Weather; and all Winter are apt to be grievoufly annoyed with Mire and Dirt.

3. A Land fo diftinguifhed into Mountains, Valleys and Plains, is alfo moſt convenient for the Entertainment of the various Sorts of Animals, which God hath created, fome whereof delight in cold, fome in hot, fome moift and watery, fome in dry and upland Places, and fome of them could neither find nor gather their proper Food in different Regions. Some Beafts and Birds we find live upon the higheft Tops of the *Alps*, and that all the Winter too, while they are conftantly covered with Snow, as the *Ibex* and *Rupicapra*, or *Chamois* among Quadrupeds, and *Lagopus* among Birds.

4. The Mountains are moft proper for the putting forth of Plants; yielding the greateft Variety, and the moft luxuriant Sorts of Vegetables, for the Maintenance of the Animals proper to thofe Places, and for medicinal Ufes, partly alfo for the Exercife and Delight of fuch ingenious Perfons as are addicted to fearch out and collect thofe Rarities, to contemplate and confider their Forms and Natures, and to admire and celebrate the Wifdom of their Creator.

5. All manner of Metals, Minerals and Foffils, if they could be generated in a level Earth, of which there is fome Queftion, yet fhould they be dug or mined for, the Delfs muft neceffarily be fo flown with Water,

(which

(which to derive and rid away, no *Adits* or *Soughs* could be made, and I much doubt whether Gins would suffice) that it would be extremely difficult and chargeable, if possible to work them at all.

6. NEITHER are the very Tops of the highest Mountains barren of Grass for the feeding and fattening of Beasts. For on the Ridges of the high Mountains of *Jura* and *Saleve* near *Geneva*, and those of *Rhætia*, or the *Grisons* Country, which are the highest of all the *Alps*, excepting the *Vallesian* and *Sabaudian*, there are Multitudes of Kine fed in Summer-time, as I myself can witness, having in my Simpling Voyages on those of *Jura* and *Saleve* observed Herds of Cattle there, and many Dairy-Houses built, where I have been more than once refreshed by their Milk, and Milk-Meats. Nay, there are but very few, and those of the highest Summits of the *Alps*, that keep Snow all Summer: And I was told by the Inhabitants, that one time or other, in seven or eight Years Space, for the most part there came a Summer that melted all the Snow that lay on them too.

7. ANOTHER great Use and Necessity of the Mountains and Hills, is for the Generation and Maintenance of Rivers and Fountains, which (in our *Hypothesis*, that all proceed from Rain-water) could not be without them, or but rarely. So we should have only

Torrents, which would fail in Summer-time, or any dry Seafon, and nothing to truft to, but ftagnating Water referved in Pools and Cifterns. Which how great an Inconvenience it would be, I need not take Pains to fhew. I fay, that Fountains and Rivers would be but rare, were there no Mountains: For, upon ferious Confideration, I find that I was too hafty in * concluding, becaufe I had obferved no Fountains fpringing up in Plains, therefore there were, or could be, abfolutely none; and do now grant, that there is Reafon to believe the Relations made of fuch. For the whole dry Land being but one continued Mountain, and afcending all along from the Sea to the Mid-Land, as is undeniably proved by the Defcent of Rivers even in plain Countries; the Water finking into the Earth, may run under Ground, and according as the Vein leads it, break out in the Side of this Mountain, tho' the Place, as to outward Appearance, be a Plain.

* *Obfervat.Phyfical, &c.*

I shall now add, That tho' it be poffible that without Mountains there may be Springs, if there fhould be Rains, (which it is fomething queftionable were there no Mountains, whether there could be or no, at leaft in hot Countries) yet it is probable, that moft of thofe Springs we find in Plains, or depreffed Places diftant from Mountains, may come along in fubterraneous Channels

from

from the next Mountains, and there break out. Monsieur *Blundel* related to the *Parisian* Academy, what Device the Inhabitants of the Lower *Austria*, which is encompassed with the Mountains of *Stiria*, are wont to use to fill their Wells with Water: They dig in the Earth to the Depth of twenty or five and twenty Foot, till they come to an *Argilla* [clammy Earth] then they bore a Hole in the midst of a Stone about five or six Inches broad, and through it bore the *Argilla* so deep, till the Water breaks forcibly out; which Water, it's probable, comes from the neighbouring Mountains in subterraneous Channels. And *Cassinus* observed, That in many Places of the Territory of *Modena* and *Bologna* in *Italy*, they make themselves Wells of springing Water by the like Artifice. They dig in the Earth till they come to the Water (which stagnates in common Wells) which they draw quite out. Then within this new digged Well they make two cylindrical Walls, concentrical one to another; the Space or Interstice between them they fill and ram close with well-wrought *Argilla*, or Clay, to keep out the ambient Water; which done, they sink the Well deeper into the Ground, and continue the inner Wall so low, till the Earth underneath seems to swell by the Force of the Water rising up: And lastly, they bore this Earth or Soil with a long Wimble; whereupon the Water breaks forth

forth through the Hole with a great Force, so that it doth not only fill the Well, but overflows and waters the neighbouring Fields with a constant Stream: By this means the same Signor *Cassini* made a Fountain at the Castle of *Urbin*, that cast up the Water five Foot high above the Level of the Ground. It is very probable that these Waters descend by subterraneous Passages from the *Appennine* Mountains, which are about ten Miles distant. If such things may be done by Art, why may they not also by Nature? Nay, that the like are done, we find by Experience, in the *Lacus Lugeus*, or *Zirchnitzer-Sea* in *Carniola*, which after it is empty of Water running out at Holes or Pits in the Bottom, (which it doth yearly in the Summer-time, in the Months of *May*, *June*, and *July*) in the Autumn, when it rains moderately, the Water spouts out of some of the forementioned Pits two or three Fathoms perpendicularly; but when it rains very hard and long together, especially with Thunder, then the Water breaks forth with great Force, not only from the foresaid Pits, but likewise at a thousand other Caves and Holes, spirting several Fathoms high, from some perpendicularly, from others obliquely, so that there is not a pleasanter Sight than this, and in a short time fills the Lake. A full Description, and an Account of all the *Phænomena* of this admirable Lake, see in *Philosoph.Transact.* Numb.

Numb. 191. p. 411, &c. So we see, Water may be brought down from the Mountains, and raised up naturally in strait Channels, with that Force, and to that Height, as to exceed all the artificial Jets in the World, if not in the Altitude of the Spout, yet in the Bigness of the Stream abundantly.

As for the Wells about *Modena*, because wheresoever you dig about that City for some Miles, at the Depth of 63 Foot you meet with Water under such a Bed of *Argilla*, which spouts up, and rises as high, and higher than the adjacent Country; I guess there is a subterraneous Lake, whose Waters are compressed between, perhaps, the Sea or fresh Water on one hand, which forces them upward, and the Bed of *Argilla* on the other, which keeps them down; which Bed, when it is bored through, they rush upwards, *quâ data porta*, with great Force, and fill the new digged Well. This I propose as Conjecture not altogether improbable.

This End and Use of Mountains, I find assigned by Mr. *Halley*, in his Discourse concerning the Original of Springs and Rivers, in these Words: *This, if we may allow final Causes,* (and why may we not? what needs this Hesitancy and Dubitation in a thing that is clear?) *seems to be the Design of the Hills, that their Ridges being placed through the midst of the Continents, might serve, as it were Alembicks,*

lembicks, to diſtill freſh Water for the Uſe of Man and Beaſt, and their Heights to give a Deſcent to thoſe Streams to run gently, like ſo many Veins of the Macrocoſm, to be the more beneficial to the Creation.

But ſome may ſay, Granting there be ſome Uſe and Benefit of moderate Hills and Riſings; what neceſſity is there of ſuch extended Ridges of vaſt and tow'ring Mountains, hiding their Heads among the Clouds, and ſeeming for Altitude to contend with the Skies? I anſwer, There is very great Uſe of them, for repelling the Vapours exhaled by the Sun-beams in the hot Regions, and hindring their Evagations Northward, as we have already ſhewn, and ſhall not repeat. I might add hereto,

8. Thoſe long Series and Chains of Mountains are of great Uſe for Boundaries and Limits to the Territories of Princes or Commonwealths, to ſecure them on thoſe Parts from ſudden Incurſions of Enemies. As for the Rudeneſs and Confuſion of Mountains, their cragged and broken Rocks and Cliffs, and whatever other Diſorder there may be among them, it may be accounted for, from the Manner of their firſt Generation, and thoſe other Mutations they have been ſince obnoxious to, by Earthquakes, Eruptions of
d in of their
Props and Foundations, and by Time and Weather too, by which not only the Earth
is

is washed away, or blown off from the Stones, but the very Stones and Rocks themselves corroded and diffolved, as might eafily be proved by Inftances, could I fpare time to do it.

To fum up all, relating to the Divifion and Difpofition of the Water and Earth, in brief.

1. I say, the Water being the lighter Element, doth naturally occupy the upper Place, and ftand above the Earth; and fo at firft it did. But now, we fee, it doth not fo; the Earth being, contrary to its Nature, forcibly elevated above it; being (as the *Pfalmift* phrafeth it) founded above the Seas, and eftablifhed above the Floods; and this, becaufe it was beft it fhould be fo, as I fhall clearly prove and deduce in Particulars in another Difcourfe.

2. The dry Land is not elevated only upon one Side of the Globe; for then, had it had high Mountains in the middle of it, with fuch vaft empty Cavities within, as muft be equal to the whole Bulk raifed up, the Center of Magnitude muft needs have been confiderably diftant from the Center of Gravity; which would have caufed a very great and inconvenient Inequality in the Motion of the Parts of the Earth: But the Continents and Iflands are fo equally difpers'd all the Globe over, as to counterbalance one another;

another; so that the Centers of Magnitude and Gravity concurr in one.

3. THE Continents are not of exactly equal and level *Superficies* or Convexity. For then, the Parts subject to the Course of the Sun, called the *Torrid Zone*, would have been, as the Ancients fancied them, unhabitable for Heat and Drought. But there are huge Ridges and extended Chains of lofty Mountains directed, for the most part, to run East and West; by which means, they give free Admittance and Passage to the Vapours, brought in by the Winds from the *Atlantick* and *Pacifick* Oceans; but stop and inhibit their Excursions to the North and South, either condensing them upon their Sides into Water, by a kind of external Destillation; or by streightning and constipating of them, compelling them to gather into Drops, and descend down in Rain.

THESE are great things, and worthy the Care, Direction, and Disposal of the Great and Wise Creator, and Governor of all things: And, we see, they are accordingly excellently ordered and provided by Him.

CHAP.

## Chap. IV.

*Of the Creation of Animals; some Questions resolved.*

AS to the first Creation of Animals, I have already proposed two Opinions, both consonant or reconcileable to the Scriptures.

1. THAT GOD Almighty did at first create the Seeds of all Animals, (that is, the Animals themselves in little) and dispers'd them over the superficial Part of the Land and Water, giving Power to those Elements to hatch and bring them forth; which when they had done, and all the Animals of these created Seeds were produced and perfected, there remained no more Ability in them to bring forth any more; but all the succeeding owe their Original to Generation.

2. BECAUSE some will not admit that GOD at first created any thing imperfect, we did propose that He might, by His Almighty Power, out of the Water and Earth, make the first Sett of Animals in their full State and Perfection, (as it is generally believed He did *Adam*) and give to each *Species* a Power by Generation to propagate their Like. For, His commanding the Waters and Earth to produce

duce such and such living Creatures, signifies that He did Himself efficaciously form them out of the Earth and Water; as when He saith, *Let there be Light, &c.* the Meaning is not, that He did permit or command something else besides Himself, to produce Light; but that He did, by His own Almighty Power, effectually create it. Indeed, the Scripture doth in this manner interpret itself: For, whereas it is said, *verses* 20, and 24. *Let the Waters bring forth,* &c. and, *Let the Earth bring forth the living Creature,* &c. In the next Verses it follows, *And* GOD *created great Whales, and every living Creature that moveth,* &c. *And* GOD *made the Beast of the Earth,* &c. But now there may a farther Question or two be moved, concerning the Creation of Animals.

1. WHETHER GOD created, at first, a great Number of every Kind of Animal all the Earth over, in their proper Places and Climates; or only of two of each *Species,* a Male and a Female, from which all the rest proceeded by Generation? This latter Opinion I find embraced by some modern Philosophers, and it may be made probable by several Arguments.

*First,* From the Analogy to Mankind. There being, at first, only one Man and one Woman created; it is very likely, there were no more of any other Creatures, two being

being sufficient, in a short time, to stock the World.

*Secondly*, Because, at the time of the General Deluge, there were only two of each Kind (of unclean Beasts) preserved in the Ark: And if two might thence suffice, why not as well at the first Creation? And if there were no need of creating more, what likelihood that there were more created?

BUT the first Opinion, That there were many at first created, seems more consonant to Scripture; which, in the Mention of the Creation of Aquatic Creatures, useth the Word *Abundantly*, Gen. i. 20. *And* GOD *said, Let the Waters bring forth abundantly the moving Creature that hath Life, and Fowl that may fly above the Earth, in the open Firmament of Heaven.* And, in the next Verse it is said, That *the Waters did bring them forth abundantly.* So that, at least, of Birds and Fishes, there were many Individuals at first created. As for Plants, certain it is, that they were created dispersedly all the World over; they having no locomotive Power, but being fix'd to a place, and the Seeds of many of them being ponderous, and not portable by Winds, or any other Means, and yet those of the same *Species* to be found in far distant Places, and on the Tops of high Mountains, as remote from each other, as the *Helvetick* and *Austrian Alps.*

2. CON-

2. Concerning the Creation of Animals, there may yet a farther Question be moved, *viz.* Whether all Animals that already have been, or hereafter shall be, were at first actually created by God? or, Whether hath He given to each Kind of Animal such a Power of Generation, as to prepare Matter, and produce new Individuals in their own Bodies? Some are of Opinion, that God did Himself, at first, actually create all the individual Animals that ever were, or ever shall be; and that there is no such thing as any Productions of new ones. For, say they, What were that, but a Creation of such Individuals? And, what did God at the first Creation, more than, if this be true, we see every day done, that is, produce a new Animal out of Matter, which itself prepares? All the Difference is, the doing that in an Instant which the Creature must take Time to do. For, as for the Preparation of Matter, that must be made fit, be the Agent never so Omnipotent.

Besides, the Animal-Parent cannot be the Agent or Efficient in the Generation, or Forming and Nourishing of the *Fœtus*. Because that is a Work of Art and Reason, which brute Creatures are not endued withall; nor, indeed, doth Man himself understand any thing of the Process of Generation in himself, neither is conscious of what

is

is done in the Womb; so far is he from being the Doer of it.

Again, it is most probable, if not certain, that most Animals have in them, from the Beginning, the Seeds or Eggs of all the Young they shall afterward bring forth, which when they are spent and exhaust, the Creature becomes barren, or effete. So we see all the Female *Fœtus* of viviparous Quadrupeds are brought forth with their *Testes*, or *Ovaria* in them, which are esteemed Parts of their Bodies; and all Birds have in them, from their first Formation, their Ovary or Egg-cluster, containing the Seeds of all the Eggs they shall ever lay. Now, had the Creature a Power of producing new ones, what need was there that there should be so many at first formed in them? And, why might they not breed them as well afterwards, as at the beginning?

Hereupon these Philosophers argue thus: Suppose we, that God did at first create two Animals, a Male and a Female: The Female must be created with its *Ovaries* or *Testes*, which (as we said) contained so many Seeds or Eggs as the Creature should ever bring forth Young. So it is clear, that not only the first Pair, but the first Generation of Animals, were actually created. Again, this first Generation, from their first Appearance, had each of them (the Females I mean) its *Ovaria*, or Clusters of Eggs, every one where-

E of

of had, in like manner, its Animalcule in it; so that this second Generation was also created in the first. The same may be demonstrated of the third and fourth; and so on, of all the Generations that shall be as long as the World lasts.

Against this Doctrine it may be objected, *First*, That it seems impossible that the *Ovaries* of one Female should actually include and contain the innumerable Myriads of Animals that may proceed from it in so many Generations, as have been and shall be during the Continuance of the World. Who can conceive such a small Portion of Matter to be capable of such Division, and to contain such an Infinity of Parts?

But to this it may be answered, That our Sight doth not give us the just Magnitude of Things, but only their Proportion; and what appears to the Eye as a Point, may be magnified so, even by Glasses, as to discover an incredible Multitude of Parts; nay, some Animals there are, so small, that if a Grain of Sand were broken into 8,000,000 of equal Parts, one of these would not exceed the bigness of one of those Creatures, as Mr. *Lewenhoek* affirms. And Dr. *Hook* proceeds farther, and says, that he had discovered some so exceeding small, that Millions of Millions might be contained in one Drop of Water. If these whole Creatures be so incredibly little, what shall we think of

## and Creation.

of their Parts containing and contained, their Entrails and Muscles, their Ovaries and Eggs? But for a sensible Demonstration of the Unconceivable, I had almost said Infinite, Divisibility of Matter, I might referr the Reader to the Honourable Mr. *Boyle*, of famous Memory, his Discourse concerning the strange Subtilty of *Effluviums*. I shall mention one or two Experiments. ' He dissolved one
' Grain of filed Copper in Spirit of Salt-Ar-
' *moniack*, and, upon this Solution, he poured
' so much distilled Water by degrees, as till
' the fair and deep blue Colour grew some-
' what pale, without being too dilute to be
' manifest: And then carefully weighing the
' Vessel and the Water, and subducting the
' Weight of that out of this, he found the
' Weight of the Liquor alone, when reduced
' to Grains, to amount to 28534; so that a
' Grain of Copper communicated a Tincture
' to 28534 times its Weight. Now, consider-
' ing that the Weight of Copper to the
' Weight of Water of the same Bulk, is *pro-*
' *xime* as 9 to 1, a Grain-weight of Copper
' is in bigness but the ninth part of as much
' Water as weighs a Grain; and so the for-
' merly mentioned Number of Grains of Wa-
' ter must be multiplied by 9, to give us the
' Proportion between the tinging Body and
' tinged Liquor; whence it will follow, that
' a single Grain of Copper gave a Blueness
' to above 256806 Parts of limpid Water,
' each

'each of them as big as it. And to profe-
'cute this Experiment farther, he mixt to-
'gether equal Parts of diftilled colourlefs
'Water, and of the faid tincted Liquor, and
'found, that though the Colour was very
'faint and dilute, yet an attentive Eye could
'eafily difcern it to be bluifh; whereby it
'appears, that one Grain of Copper was able
'to impart a Colour to double the Quanti-
'ty of Water above-mentioned, that is, to
'513612 Grains of Water.

OTHER Experiments there are, in the
fame Difcourfe, made in odorate Bodies:
'Having, *faith he,* for Curiofity-fake, fu-
'fpended in a Pair of exact Scales, that
'would turn with a very fmall Part
'of a Grain, a Piece of *Ambergreece* bigger
'than a Walnut, and weighing betwixt a
'hundred and fixfcore Grains, I could not
'in three days and a half, that I had Oppor-
'tunity to make the Trial, difcover, even up-
'on that Balance, any Decrement of Weight
'in the *Ambergreece,* though fo rich a Per-
'fume lying in the open Air was like, in
'that time, to have parted with good ftore of
'odoriferous Steams: And, a while after,
'fufpending a Lump of *Afafœtida* five days
'and a half, I found it not to have fuftained
'any difcernible Lofs of Weight, though, in
'fpight of the unfavourable cold Weather,
'it had about it a neighbouring Atmofphere,
'replenifhed with fœtid Exhalations, *&c.*

BUT

## and Creation.

But what can be imagined more small and subtil, than the minute Parts of the Steams of Animals? The same Author, in the same Tract, tells us, ' That a good Set-
' ting Dog, by his way of Ranging the Fields,
' and his other Motions, especially of his
' Head, would not only intimate the Kinds
' of Game, whose Scent he chanced to light
' upon, but would discover where Partridges
' had been (though, perhaps, without staying
' in that Place) several hours before." He farther tells us, ' That a very sober Gentle-
' man of his Acquaintance, who had often oc-
' casion to employ Blood-hounds, assured
' him, that if a Man had but passed over the
' Field, the Scent would lie, so as to be per-
' ceptible enough to a good Dog of that sort,
' for several hours after." And an ingenious Hunter likewise assured him, ' That he had
' observed, that the Scent of a flying and
' hunted Deer, will sometimes continue up-
' on the Ground from one Day to the next
' following." He proceeds farther; ' And
' now we may consider these three things;
' *First*, That the Substance left upon the
' Ground by the transient Tread of a Par-
' tridge, Hare, or other Animal, that doth
' but pass along his Way, does probably com-
' municate to the Grass or Ground but some
' of those Effluxions that transpire out of his
' Feet, which being small enough to escape
' the Eye, may probably not amount to one

' Grain

'Grain in Weight, or perhaps not to the
'Tenth Part of it. *Next*, That the Parts
'of fluid Bodies, as such, are perpetually in
'Motion, and so are the invisible Particles
'that swim in them, as may appear by the
'Dissolution of Salt or Sugar in Water, and
'the Wandring of aqueous Vapours through
'the Air, even when the Eye perceives them
'not. And, *Thirdly*, That though the At-
'mosphere of one of these small Parcels of
'the exhaling Matter we are speaking of,
'may oftentimes be exceeding vast in com-
'parison of the emittent Body, as may be
'guessed by the Distance, at which some Set-
'ters or Bloodhounds will find the Scent of
'a Partridge or Deer; yet, in Places exposed
'to the free Air or Wind, 'tis very likely
'that these Steams are assiduously carried a-
'way from their Fountain, to maintain the
'forementioned Atmosphere, for six, eight,
'or more hours; that is, as long as the Scent
'hath been observed to lie, there will be re-
'quisite a continual Recruit of Steams suc-
'ceeding one another. And that so very small
'a Portion of Matter, as that which, we were
'saying, the *Fomes* of these Steams may be
'judged to be, being sensibly to impregnate
'an Atmosphere incomparably greater than
'itself, and supply it with almost continual
'Recruits, we cannot but think, that the
'Steams it parts with, must be of extreme
'and scarce conceivable Minuteness." *So far*
*the*

*the Author.* To which I shall add, That by the Steams, I suppose, he means the minute Particles of which the Steams are compounded. Now these minute Particles themselves must be compound Bodies, because they affect the Sense in a particular manner, so that a sagacious Creature can distinguish by them, not only Species but Individuals; as a good Dog, by the Foot, will find out his Master, though not only several other Creatures, but several Men have passed that way: Unless we will groundlesly affirm, that those Particles are the *minima Naturalia,* and that the Creature discerns them by their Figure, or their different manner of Motion.

A second Objection of *Brunnerus* (as I find him quoted in *Peyerus* his *Merycologia*) is this: *Si cuncta Animalium membra jam formata existant in ovo, &c.* 'If all the
' Members of Animals, already formed, do
' exist in the Egg, though for their Smalness
' they escape our sight; I cannot conceive,
' how by the Force of Imagination alone, in
' a pregnant Woman, can be produced
' sometimes Calves-heads, or Feet, some-
' times a Dog's Face, or other monstrous
' Members; these Productions being a cer-
' tain and experimental Proof, that the Parts
' and Members of Animals are formed and
' delineated originally in the Womb, or
' Egg.

To this, *Peyerus* replies: 'Who then
'forms? who delineates such Monsters?
'Shall we accuse GOD the Creator? But
'He is just, and doth not make enormous
'things: Or, Will you blame Nature? that
'is, the constant Order and Will of GOD,
'which never is deficient? Will you lay
'the fault upon the plastick Vertue or
'Power residing in the Womb or Seed, and
'acting those things? But that is a *Chimæ-*
'*ra*; it is nothing, it is an Idol. There re-
'main Two Things to which the Cause
'may justly be imputed; the *Imagination of*
'*the Mother*, which may and doth often-
'times effect wonderful things in the Body
'of the tender *Embryon*; and *the Devil*. If
'you refuse to admit the former, you are
'obliged to accept the latter. And, truly,
'the Devil may, GOD so permitting, many
'ways abuse Men, and transfigure the Young
'in the Womb, to punish the wicked and
'nefarious Actions of degenerate Mankind,
'indulging themselves in obscene Imagina-
'tions, or preposterous and unnatural Im-
'purities and Pollutions. But do these Er-
'rors and Enormities take away the Order
'of Nature? By no means: For, from
'what is rare and extraordinary, and sel-
'dom happens, there is no Consequence to
'be drawn. For though Monsters are some-
'times born, nothing hinders but that we
'may still think, that the *Ideas* of the seve-
'ral

'ral *Fœtus* may be præexistent and latent
'in the Eggs; and the Event may teach us,
'that those *Ideas* or *Embryos* may, by a vio-
'lent Cause, be marred and deformed in
'the Womb; as Wax, though it be alrea-
'dy figured, while it is soft, is easily al-
'tered, and capable of receiving new Im-
'pressions.

But against this Answer we may thus plead in Defence of *Brunnerus:* As to what is said of the Devil, it seems to be but a Shift or Refuge to have recourse to, when we are at a Loss, and pinch'd with an Argument; as in the ancient Stage-plays, when they were put to a plunge, they were forced to bring in some θεὸς ἀπὸ μηχανῆς to help them out. And as for the Imagination of the Mother, strange it is, that that should have any Influence at all upon the Formation of the *Fœtus*; the Mother not knowing a-ny thing that's done in the Womb; nor being conscious to herself of any Power to form or act any thing there: The *Fœtus* being an external thing to her, and no more a Part of her, than an Egg is of the Hen that sits upon it, affording nothing to it but Warmth and Nourishment. And we see, Eggs may be hatched by the artificial Heat of an Oven, without the Incubation of a Hen. But granting, that the Imagination of the Mother may transform the *Fœtus*, why may it not as well originally form it out of prepared

pared Matter? and then, what need of an Idea or minute Animalcule in the Seed? But whatever may be said of Men, how come Monsters in Brutes, which, according to *Peyerus*, are meer Machines, and have no Imagination or Perception at all?

But not to lead the Reader into a Maze or Labyrinth, and leave him there; for my own part, I must confess, that the Argument for the Præexistence of the *Fœtus's*, or their Creation from the Beginning, taken from the due Number of Eggs that are in every Female from her first Formation, and her being effete after they are spent, weighs very much with me, as I know not how to quit myself of it. And on the other hand, if those Stories concerning Dogs and Serpents, &c. found in the Wombs of Women be true (which are well attested) I acknowledge it very difficult to give an Account, how those Animals came to be bred or formed there. But I had rather confess my Ignorance of the Manner of the Production of such præternatural and extraordinary things, than to permit it to have such Influence upon me, as to remove me from so well-grounded an Opinion concerning the ordinary Production of Animals in a natural Way.

But notwithstanding all I have said, in Defence of the Creation of the Individuals of all Animals at first, because the inconceivable

vable Smalnefs of the laſt Races of Animals make it incredible, I ſhall be content to let it paſs for a Conjecture, and not inſiſt farther upon it.

The Being of a Plaſtick Nature, ſubordinate to God, notwithſtanding *Peyerus* makes an Idol of it, and charges thoſe with Idolatry who do believe it, I am not afraid to admit: My Reaſons for which, I have given in another * Diſcourſe, and ſhall not here repeat.

* *Wiſdom of God in the Creation.*

The new Opinion of Mr. *Lewenhoek*, that all Animals proceed from an Inſect or Animalcule in the Male-ſperm, I think I have ſufficiently confuted in my Book, Entituled, *Synopſis methodica Animalium Quadrupedum*, pag. 37. & ſeqq. to which I referr the Reader: Only I ſhall repeat, that I am leſs inclinable to it, becauſe of the neceſſary Loſs of an incredible Multitude of them, which ſeems not agreeable to the Wiſdom and Providence of Nature. For, ſuppoſing every Male hath in him all the Animalcules that he ſhall or may eject; they may, for ought I know, amount to Millions of Millions, and ſo the greateſt part of them muſt needs be loſt. Nay, if we take but one *Coit*, there muſt, in uniparous Creatures at leaſt, abundance be loſt. But if we ſuppoſe the *Fœtus* to be originally in the Egg, it is not ſo. For the Eggs of all ſorts of Creatures are ſo proportioned to the Nature of the Animals, the

Time

Time that they live, the Time and Number of their Gestations, and the Number they bring forth at all times, that they will much about suffice for the Time the Creatures are fit to breed and nourish their Young: So that they may, if need be, be all brought forth, and come to Perfection.

*The End of the First Discourse.*

# DISCOURSE II.

## Of the general Deluge in the Days of NOAH, its Causes and Effects.

I Proceed now to say something concerning the General Deluge in the Days of *Noah*; which was also a Matter of ancient Tradition. I shall not enlarge much upon it, so as to take in all that might be said, but confine myself to Three Heads. 1. I shall confirm the Truth of the History of the Deluge recorded in the Scripture, by the Testimonies of some ancient Heathen Writers. 2. I shall consider the Natural Causes or Means whereby it was effected. 3. I shall enquire concerning the Consequences of it, what considerable Effects it had upon the Earth.

# Chap. I.

*Testimonies of Ancient Heathen Writers concerning the Deluge.*

FIRST then, I shall produce some Testimonies of Ancient Heathen Writers concerning the Deluge.

The first shall be those of *Berosus*, recorded by *Josephus*. The first, in his first Book against *Appion*, where he tells us, 'That '*Berosus*, following the most ancient Wri- 'tings, relates the same things with *Moses* 'concerning the great Deluge, and the De- 'struction of Men by it; and of the Ark, in 'which *Nochus*, the Author of our Stock, 'was preserved, after it rested on the Tops 'of the *Armenian* Mountains." And the se- cond, in the fifth Chapter of his first Book of *Jewish Antiquities*; Βηρωσσὸς ὁ Χαλδαῖος διηγέμενος τὰ περὶ τὸν κατακλυσμὸν, ὕτω πε διεξίεισι, &c. That is, '*Berosus* the *Chaldæan*, 'relating the Story of the Deluge, writes thus: 'It is reported, that there is some part of 'the Vessel [the Ark] still remaining at the 'Mountain of the *Gordyæans*; and that cer- 'tain Persons scraping off the *Bitumen*, or 'Pitch, carry it away; and that Men make 'use

'ufe of it for Amulets, to drive away Dif-
'eafes.

A SECOND Teftimony the fame *Jofephus* affords us in the fame Place, and that is, of *Nicolaus Damafcenus*; 'who, *faith he*, gives
' us the Hiftory [of the Ark and Deluge] in
' thefe Words: About *Minyas* in *Armenia*,
' there is a great Mountain called *Baris*, to
' which it is reported, that many flying, in
' the time of the Deluge, were faved; and
' that a certain Perfon was carried thither in
' an Ark, which refted on the Top of it; the
' Reliques of the Timber whereof were pre-
' ferved there a long time." Befides thefe, *Jofephus* tells us in the fame Place, that *Hieronymus* the *Egyptian*, who wrote the *Phœnician* Antiquities, and *Mnafeas*, and many others, whofe Words he alledges not, make mention of the Flood.

EUSEBIUS fuperadds two Teftimonies more; the one of *Melon*, to this Effect:
' There departed from *Armenia*, at the time
' of the Deluge, a certain Man, who together
' with his Sons had been faved; who being
' caft out of his Houfe and Poffeffions, was
' driven away by the Natives. This Man
' paffing over the intermediate Region, came
' into the mountainous Part of *Syria*, that
' was then defolate." This Teftimony makes the Deluge Topical, and not to have reached *Armenia*.

THE

The other is of *Abydenus* an ancient Writer, set down by *Eusebius, Præpar. Evangel. lib. 9. cap. 4.* Μεθ' ὃν ἄλλοι τε ἦρξαν, καὶ Σείσιθρος, ᾧ δὴ Κρόνος προσημαίνει μὲν ἔσεσθαι πλῆθος ὄμβρων Δεσίȣ πέμπτῃ ἐπὶ δέκα, &c. "After whom others reigned, and then *Sisithrus*, (so he calls *Noah*.) To whom *Saturn* foretold, that there should be a great Flood of Waters upon the fifteenth Day of the Month *Desius*; and commanded him to hide all Writings [or whatever was committed to writing] in *Heliopolis* of the *Syparians*: Which so soon as *Sisithrus* had performed, he presently sailed away to *Armenia*, where what God had predicted to him, immediately came to pass, [or came upon him.] The third Day after the Waters ceased, he sent forth Birds, that he might try whether they could espy any Land uncovered of Water: But they finding nothing but Sea, and not knowing whither to betake themselves, returned back to *Sisithrus*. In like manner, after some Days, he sent out others, with like Success. But being sent out the third time, they returned with their Feet fouled with Mud. Then the Gods caught up *Sisithrus* from among Men; but the Ship remained in *Armenia*, and its Wood afforded the Inhabitants Amulets to chase away many Diseases." These Histories accord with the Scripture as to the main, of the Being of a Flood, and *Noah* escaping out of it;
only

only they adulterate the Truth, by the Admixture of a deal of fabulous Stuff.

CYRIL, in his first Book against *Julian*, to prove the Deluge, alledges a Passage out of *Alexander Polyhistor*, consonant to the preceding Words of *Abydenus*. 'Plato himself '(saith he) gives us an obscure Intimation of 'the Deluge, in his *Timæus*, bringing in a 'certain *Egyptian* Priest, who related to *Solon* 'out of the Sacred Books of the *Egyptians*, 'that before the particular Deluges known 'and celebrated by the *Grecians*, there was 'of old an exceeding-great Inundation of 'Waters, and Devastation of the Earth, 'which seems to be no other than *Noah*'s 'Flood.

PLUTARCH, in his Book *De Solertia Animalium*, tells us, 'That those who have written 'of *Deucalion*'s Flood, report, that there was 'a Dove sent out of the Ark by *Deucalion*, 'which returning again into the Ark, was a 'Sign of the Continuance of the Flood, but 'flying quite away, and not returning any 'more, was a Sign of Serenity, and that the 'Earth was drained.

INDEED, *Ovid*, and other Mythologists, make *Deucalion*'s Flood to have been universal: And it's clear, by the Description *Ovid* gives of it, that he meant the general Deluge in the Days of *Noah*. And that by *Deucalion*, the Ancients, together with *Ovid*, understood *Noah*, Kircher, in his \* *Arca Noæ*, \*L.2.c.6.

F doth

doth well make out. First, For that the Poet *Apollonius* makes him the Son of *Prometheus*, in his third Book,

——————— ἔνθα Προμηθεὺς
Ἰαπετιονίδης ἀγαθὸν τέκε Δευκαλίωνα.

where *Prometheus*, the Son of *Japetus*, begat the renowned *Deucalion*. 2. *Berosus* affirms *Noah* to have been a *Scythian*: And *Lucian*, in his Book *De Dea Syria*, tells us, that many make *Deucalion* to have been so too. 3. The Scripture testifies, that Men were generally very corrupt and wicked in the Days of *Noah*. And *Andro Teius*, a very ancient Writer, testifies, that in *Deucalion*'s time there was a great abundance of wicked Men, which made it necessary for God to destroy Mankind. 4. The Scripture saith, *That Noah was a just Man, and perfect in his Generation.* And *Ovid* saith of *Deucalion*, that,

*Non illo melior quisquam, nec amantior æqui Vir fuit, aut illâ* [*Pyrrhâ* uxore ejus] *reverentior ulla Deorum.*

And a little after,

*Innocuos ambos, cultores numinis ambos.*

5. *Apollonius* saith of *Deucalion*, Πρῶτος ἀνθρώπων ἐβασίλευσε, *He first ruled over Men.* Which may very well be attributed to *Noah*, the Father and Restorer of Mankind, whose
Right

Right the Kingdom was. 6. The sending out of a Dove, to try whether the Waters were abated, and the Flood gone off, is (we have seen) by *Plutarch* attributed to *Deucalion*. 7. *Lucian,* in his *Timon*, and in his Book *De Dea Syria,* sets forth the Particulars of *Deucalion's*, after the Example of *Noah's* Flood: Δευκαλίων ᾖ μένος ἀνθρώπων ἐλίπετο εἰς γενεὴν δευτέραν εὐβελίης τε καὶ τῶ εὐσεβέος ἕνεκα, &c. *Deucalion was the only Man that was left for a second Generation, for his Prudence and Piety sake; and he was saved in this manner: He made a great Ark, and got aboard it, with his Wife and Children: And to him came Swine, and Horses, and Lions, and Serpents, and all other living Creatures, which the Earth maintains, according to their Kinds, by Pairs; and he received them all, and they hurt him not; for there was, by Divine Instinct, a great Friendship among them; and they sailed together in the Ark, so long as the Waters prevailed.* And, in his *Timon,* he saith, *That* Noah *laid up in the Ark Plenty of all Provisions for their Sustenance.*

PLINY saith of the City of *Joppa*, that it was built before the Flood.

BY all this it appears, that the Notion of a general Flood was every where current among the People, especially in those Countries where the Ark rested, and where *Noah* afterwards lived. And hence it was, that the *Apameans*, whether of *Mesopotamia*, or *Syria*, or *Bythinia*, (for there were three Cities of that Name) coined Moneys in Honour of the Emperors *Septimius Severus*, and *Philippus Arabs*, having on the Reverse the Figure of an Ark, with a Man and a Woman standing before it; and two Doves above it, one flying with a Branch of a Tree in its Mouth, another resting upon it. The Figures whereof, and a learned Discourse thereupon out of *Falconerius*, may be seen in *Kircher*'s *Arca Noæ*. Which Moneys, though they were coined long after our Saviour's Time, and the Divulgation of the Scriptures; yet being done by Ethnicks, do shew that the Story of the Deluge was known, and famous, and generally credited among them, as being near the Place where *Noah* lived and conversed after the Flood.

\* L.2.c.6.

Howbeit I do not deny, that there was such a particular Flood in *Thessaly*, as they call *Deucalion*'s, which happened seven hundred and seventy Years, or thereabouts, after the general Deluge. I acknowledge also a more ancient Flood in *Attica*, in the Time of *Ogyges*, about two hundred and thirty Years before *Deucalion*'s, by which the Country was so marred, that it lay waste and uncultivated, without Inhabitants, for almost two hundred Years.

Chap.

TAB. I.                                                    pag: 68

The two ancient Apamian Coyns taken out of
Octav. Falconieri de Nummo Apamensi Deuca-
lionæi Diluvij typum exhibente 8º Romæ.

By the Greek inscriptions they were stamp'd
under Philippus Marcus Aurelius Alexander and Septimius Severus

## Chap. II.

### Of the Causes of the Deluge.

WHAT were the instrumental Causes or Means of the Flood? Whether was it effected by natural or supernatural Means only? Whether was God no farther concerned in it, than in so ordering Second Causes at first, as of themselves necessarily to bring it in at such a time?

First, Those that hold this Deluge was altogether miraculous, and that God Almighty created Waters on purpose to serve this Occasion, and, when they had done their Work, destroy'd them again, dispatch'd the Business, and loose or cut the Knot in a few Words. And yet this *Hypothesis* is not so absurd and precarious, as at first Sight it may seem to be: For the World being already full, there needed not, nor indeed could be any Creation of Water out of nothing, but only a Transmutation of some other Body into Water. Now, if we grant all Natural Bodies, even the Elements themselves, to be mutually tra
and some think they can demonstrate; why might not the Divine Power and Providence bring

bring together at that time such natural Agents, as might change the Air, or *Æther*, or both together, into Water; and so supply what was wanting in Rains, and extraordinary Eruptions of Springs. To them that argue the Improbability of such a Change, from the great Quantity of Air requisite to the making of a little Water; it may be answered, That if Air, and all Bodies commixt with it, were together changed into Water, they must needs make a Bulk of Water of equal Quantity with themselves, unless we will grant a Peripatetical Condensation and Rarefaction; and hold that the same Matter may have sometimes a greater, sometimes a lesser Quantity or Extension.

To this may be replied; If, indeed, the whole World were full of Body or Matter, a Deluge might easily be effected this way: It were but converting the Air and other Bodies mixt with it round the Terraqueous Globe, to the Height of 15 Cubits above the highest Mountains into Water, and the Business were dispatch'd.

But there is another Being in Nature besides Matter or Body, *viz.* a *Vacuum*, or empty Space, which is intermix'd with the minute Parts of all Bodies. Those that have more of it interspers'd among their Parts, are more rare or thin; and those that have less, more dense or thick; the rarer Bodies are also lighter, the more dense heavier, according

according to the Proportion of Matter they contain. Hence perchance a cubical Foot of Air may not be equal in Weight to the hundredth Part of a cubical Foot of Water; and consequently, an hundred cubical Feet of Air will be requisite to make, by Conversion, one cubical Foot of Water. I take it for granted here, that the different Weight of Bodies depends upon the Difference of Matter they contain, so that those which have fewest empty Pores are the heaviest; those that have most, the lightest.

This Cause [the Conversion of Air into Water] the Learned Jesuite *Athanasius Kircher*, in his Book *De Arca Noæ*, alledges as the undoubted instrumental Cause or Means of the Deluge, in these Words; *Dico totum illud aëreum spatium usque ad supremam regionem aëris, præpotentis Dei virtute, in aquas, per inexplicabilem nubium coacervatarum multitudinem, quâ replebatur, conversam esse; cujus ubertas tanta fuit, ut Aer supremus cum inferiori in Oceanum commutatus videri potuerit, non naturæ viribus, sed illius cujus voluntati & imperio cuncta subsunt.* That is, *I affirm, that all that Aëreal Space that reaches up to the supreme Region of the Air, was, by the Power of the Omnipotent* GOD, *and Instrumentality of an inexplicable Multitude of Clouds amassed together, wherewith it was filled, changed into Water, so that the upper and lower Air might seem to be transmuted into*

into an Ocean, *not by the Strength of Nature, but of Him to whose Will and Power all things are subject*. And he is so confident *, that this Deluge, in which the Water was raised fifteen Cubits above the highest Mountains, was not, nor could be effected by natural Causes, but by the Right Hand of the most High GOD only; that he saith, "No Man can 'deny it, but he who doth not penetrate 'how far the Power of Nature can extend, 'and where it is limited." To conclude, this Hypothesis hath the Suffrages of most learned Men. But, because the Scripture, assigning the Causes or Means of the Inundation, makes no Mention of any Conversion of Air into Water, but only of the Breaking up the Fountains of the Great Deep, and the Opening of the Windows of Heaven, I suppose those Causes may be sufficient to work the Effect, and that we need not have recourse to such an Assistance.

* *Arca Noæ,* l. 2. c. 4.

As for those that make the Deluge Topical, and restrain it to a narrow Compass of Land, their Opinion is, I think, sufficiently confuted by a late ingenious * Author, to whom, therefore, I referr the Reader.

**Dr. Bur-net.*

I SHALL not undertake the Defence or Confutation of those, or any other *Hypothesis*; only tell you which, at present, seems to me most probable; and that is theirs, who for a Partial Cause of the Deluge, assign either a Change of the Center of the Earth, or a violent

lent Depression of the Surface of the Ocean, and a Forcing the Waters up from the subterraneous Abyss through the Channels of the Fountains that were then broken up and opened.

1. FIRST then, let us consider what Causes the Scripture assigns of the Flood; and they are two. 1. The Breaking up the Fountains of the great Deep. 2. The Opening of the Windows of Heaven. I shall first treat of this last. By the Opening of the Windows of Heaven, is (I suppose) to be understood the Causing of all the Water that was suspended in the Air to descend down in Rain upon the Earth; the Effect hereof here mentioned being a long continuing Rain of forty Natural Days; and that no ordinary one neither, but Catarracts or Spouts of Water; for so the *Septuagint* interpret the *Windows of Heaven were opened.* Καὶ αἱ καταῤῥάκται τῦ ὐρανῦ ἠνεώχθησαν. *The Catarracts or Spouts of Heaven were opened.* And that these Treasuries of the Air will afford no small Quantity of Water, may be made appear, both by Scripture and Reason. 1. By Scripture, which opposes the Waters that are above the Heavens or Firmament, to those that are under them; which if they were not ἰσόῤῥοπα, and in some Measure equal, it would never do. Gen. i. 6. GOD *is said to make a Firmament in the midst of the Waters, and to divide the Waters which were under the Firmament,*

*ment, from the Waters which were above the Firmament.* And this was the Work of a whole Day, and consequently no inconsiderable thing. 2. The same may be made appear, by Reason grounded upon Experience. I myself have observed a Thunder-Cloud in Passage, to have in less than two Hours Space poured down so much Water upon the Earth, as, besides what sunk into the parched and thirsty Ground, and filled all Ditches and Ponds, caused a considerable Flood in the Rivers, setting all the Meadows on float. [And Dr. *Wittie,* in his *Scarborough Spaw,* tells us of great Spouts of Rain that ordinarily fall every Year, some time or other, in Summer, that set the whole Country in a Flood.] Now had this Cloud, which might, for ought I know, have moved forty Miles forward, stood still and emptied all its Water upon the same Spot of Ground it first hung over, what a sudden and incredible Deluge would it have made there? and yet what Depth or Thickness of Vapours might remain uncondensed in the Air above this Cloud, who knows? That the Ocean afforded but little, appears in that the Vapours raised out of it, and brought up in Clouds, and poured down upon the Earth in Rain, are shortly carried off by the Rivers, and reassumed into the Sea: But if the Waters of the Flood encompassed the whole Terraqueous Globe, (as is most probable) then the

Ocean

Ocean contributed nothing; for the Water must be raised higher above the *Superficies* of the Ocean, than that of the dry Land; upon which yet, at the end of the forty Days Rain, the Waters were so high as to bear up the Ark, that it touched not the Ground.

MOREOVER, after this forty Days violent and impetuous Rain, it is probable, that it rained, though more gently and interruptedly, till the 150th Day, because till that time the Waters prevailed and encreased upon the Earth. All this Water that fell in Rain, must be contained in the vast Treasuries of the Middle and Superior Air, or else immediately created by GOD.

IF the whole Ocean indeed were raised up in Vapour, and that Vapour condensed into Rain, and poured forth upon the dry Land, and there suspended and miraculously stopped from going off by the Almighty Power of GOD, then might it, together with an equal Quantity of Water raised up from the great Deep, have a considerable Interest in the Deluge. But of this there cannot be any Proof gathered from the Scriptures.

I RETURN now to the first Cause or Means of the *Deluge* assigned by the Scripture, and that is, the *Breaking up of all the Fountains of the great Deep*. By the *great Deep*, in this Place, I suppose, is to be understood the subterraneous Waters, which do and must necessarily communicate with the Sea. For we see,

see, that the *Caspian*, and some other Seas, receive into themselves many great Rivers, and yet have no visible Outlets; and therefore, by subterraneous Passages, must needs discharge their Waters into the Abyss of Waters under the Earth, and by its Intervention into the Ocean again.

THAT the *Mediterranean* Sea doth not (as I sometimes thought) communicate with the Ocean by any subterraneous Passages, nor thereby impart any Water to it, or receive any from it, may be demonstrated, from that the *Superficies* of it is lower than the *Superficies* of the Ocean, as appears from the Waters running in at the Streights of *Gibraltar*; for if there were any such Communications, the Water keeping its Level, the *Mediterranean*, being the lowest, must by those Passages receive Waters from the Ocean; and not the Ocean, which is (as we have proved) the highest from the *Mediterranean*. But that it doth not receive any by subterraneous Passages, is most likely, because it receives so much above Ground. Hence it necessarily follows, that the *Mediterranean* spends more in Vapour than it receives from the Rivers, which is Mr. *Halley*'s Conclusion; though in some of his Premises, or *Hypotheses*, he is, I think, mistaken: As, 1. In that he numbers the *Tiber* amongst his nine great Rivers, each of which may yield ten times as much Water as the *Thames*, whereas

whereas I queſtion whether that yields once ſo much: And whereas he paſſes by all the reſt of the Rivers as ſmaller than it, there are two that I have ſeen in *Italy* itſelf, whereof the one, *viz.* the *Arnus*, on which *Florence* and *Piſa* ſtand, ſeemed to me not inferior in Bigneſs to the *Tiber*; and the other, *viz.* the *Atheſis*, on which *Verona* ſtands, I could not gueſs to be leſs than twice as big.  2. In that he thinks himſelf too liberal in allowing theſe nine Rivers to carry down each of them ten times ſo much Water as the *Thames* doth.  Whereas one of thoſe nine, and that none of the biggeſt neither, *viz.* the River *Po*, if *Ricciolus* his *Hypotheſes* and Calculations be good, affords more Water in an Hour, than Mr. *Halley* ſuppoſes the *Thames* to do in a Day; the hourly Effuſions of the *Po* being rated at eighteen Millions of Cubical Paces, by *Ricciolus*; whereas the daily ones of the *Thames* are computed to be no more than twenty five Millions, three hundred forty four thouſand Cubical Yards of Water, by Mr. *Halley*; but a Geometrical Pace contains five Feet, *i. e.* $1\frac{2}{3}$ of a Yard.  Now if the *Po* pours ſo much Water hourly into the Sea, what then muſt the *Danow* and the *Nile* do? each of which cannot (I gueſs) be leſs than treble of the *Po*.  *Tanais*, *Boryſthenes*, and *Rhodanus*, may equal, if not exceed it.  Howbeit, I cannot approve *Ricciolus* his *Hypotheſes*, judging

them

them to be too exceſſive, but do believe that as to the whole, Mr. *Halley* comes nearer the Truth. Sure enough it is, that in the *Mediterranean*, the Receipts from the Rivers fall ſhort of the Expence in Vapour; though in Part of it, that is, the *Euxine*, the Receipts exceed, as appears from that there is a conſtant Current ſets outward from thence through the *Thracian Boſphorus*, and *Helleſpont*.

But though the *Mediterranean* doth indeed evaporate more than it receives from the Rivers, yet, I believe, the Caſe is not the ſame with the *Caſpian* Sea; the *Superficies* whereof ſeems to me not to bear any greater Proportion to the Waters of the Rivers that run into it, than that of the *Euxine* doth to its; which we have obſerved not to ſpend the whole Receipt in Vapour.

You will ſay, Why then do not great Floods raiſe the Seas? I anſwer, as to the *Caſpian*, if it communicates with the Ocean, whether the Rivers bring down more or leſs, it's all one; if more, then the Water keeping its Level, the *Caſpian* raiſeth the Ocean; if leſs, then the Ocean communicates to the *Caſpian*, and raiſes that. But as to the *Mediterranean*, we may ſay, that when it receives more on the one Side, it receives leſs on the other, the Floods and Ebbs of the *Nilus*, and the other Rivers, counterbalancing one another: Beſides, by reaſon of the Snows lying

upon

upon the Mountains all Winter, the greatest Floods of those great Rivers in *Europe* do not happen when the *Mediterranean* evaporates least in the Winter-time, but in the Spring.

You will demand farther, if the *Mediterranean* evaporates so much, what becomes of all this Vapour? I answer, It is cast off upon the Mountains, and on their Sides and Tops is condensed into Water, and so returned again by the Rivers unto the Sea.

If you proceed to ask what becomes of the Surplusage of the Water, which the *Mediterranean* receives from the *Ocean*, and spends in Vapour; I answer, It seems to me that it must be cast farther off over the Tops of the Mountains, and supply in part Rain to these Northern Countries; for we know that the South Wind brings Rain with us, and all *Europe* over.

*Madidis Notus evolat alis.* Ovid. Metam.

As to the great Ocean, I do not believe that it evaporates so much as the *Mediterranean*: Both, 1. Because the whole *Mediterranean*, excepting the *Euxine*, lies in a hot Climate, and a great Part of it as it were in a Valley, Ridges of high Mountains, *Atlas* on one Side, and the *Alps* and *Appennine*, &c. on the other running along it. And, 2. Because the Surface of the whole *Ocean* bears a greater Proportion to the Waters it receives

from

from the Rivers of at least this Continent, than that of the *Mediterranean* doth to its. And therefore I think also that Mr. *Halley* exceeds in his Estimate of the Heat of the *Superficies* of the Sea Water. I cannot persuade myself, that were it all commixt, I mean the hotter Part with the cooler, all the Surface over to such a Thickness, it would equal the Heat of our Air in the hottest time of Summer. But I leave that to farther Tryal and Enquiry.

HERE give me leave to suggest, that we are not to think, that all the Vapours that supply our Rains and Dews proceed from the Sea; no, a great Part of them, *viz.* all that, when condensed, waters the Earth, and serves for the Nutrition of Plants and Animals; (if not the same individual Water, at least so much) was exhaled out of the Earth before; and returned again in Showers and Dews upon it: So that we receive no more from the Sea, than what the Rivers carry back, and pour into it again. But supposing Mr. *Halley*'s *Hypotheses* to be good, and that the *Ocean* doth evaporate, and cast off to the dry Land $\frac{10}{12}$ of an Inch Thickness daily, and this suffices for the Supply of all the Rivers; how intolerably extravagant must their *Hypotheses* be, who suppose the Rivers of all the World together to yield half an Ocean of Water daily? Though I must confess myself to be at a Loss, as to those vast Rivers of *America* of ninety Miles broad; for if they should run with any thing a swift Current, it is indeed ineſtimable what a Quantity of Water they may pour forth. All, therefore, that I have to ſay to them, is, That we want a true Hiſtory and Account of their *Phænomena,* from their Fountains to their Outlets.

But in contradiction to what I have ſaid, concerning the Water keeping its Level, and flowing in only at the *Straits-Mouth,* I underſtand, that it is the concurrent and unanimous Vote and Suffrage of Mariners, Voyagers, and Philoſophers, that there is an Under-Current at the Straits of *Gibraltar,* the *Thracian Boſphorus,* and the *Baltick Sound.* Particularly, *M. Marſilly* affirms, That the lower Water in the Channel of the *Thracian Boſphorus* is driven Northward into the *Euxine* Sea, whilſt the upper flows conſtantly from the *Euxine* Southward: And, That that which flows from the South is ſalter and heavier; which he found by letting down a Veſſel cloſe ſhut up, fitted with a Valve to open at pleaſure, and let in the loweſt Water, which being brought up and weighed, was obſerved to be ten Grains heavier than the upper. That the upper and lower flows contrary ways, he found by the Fiſhermens Nets, which being let down deep from Veſſels that were fixed, were always, by the Obſervation of the Fiſhermen, by the Force of the Current driven towards the *Black Sea,* and by the letting down of a Plummet; for if it were stopp'd and detain'd at about five or six Foot depth, it did always decline towards the *Marmora* or *Propontis*; but if it descended lower, it was driven to the contrary part, that is, the *Euxine*. But, I think, these Experiments are not sufficient to establish and demonstrate such an Under-Current, because, possibly there might be some Mistake in them: And Mr. *Smith* mentions no such thing as any Under-Current there. But yet the same Mr. *Smith* endeavours to prove an Under-Current, by two Experiments: The first is, the Running-Tide and Half-Tide in the *Offing*, between the *North-Foreland* and *South-Foreland*. Now where it flows Tide and Half-Tide, though the Tide of Flood runs aloft, yet the Tide of Ebb runs underfoot, that is, close by the Ground. See *Philosophical Transactions*, Numb. 158. p. 564.

The second is, an Experiment made in the *Baltick Sound:* In one of the King's Fregats they went with their Pinnace into the middle Stream, and were carried violently by the Current: Soon after, they sunk a Bucket with a large Cannon Bullet, to a certain Depth of Water, which gave check to the Boat's Motion; and sinking it still lower and lower, the Boat was driven ahead to Windward against the Upper-Current, the Current aloft being not above four

or

or five Fathom deep; and the lower the Bucket was let fall, they found the Under-Current the ſtronger.

To all this I reply; That I do not underſtand how Waters can run backward and forward in the ſame Channel, at the ſame time. For there being but one Declivity; this is as much to affirm, as that a heavy Body ſhould aſcend. It is a Croſſing of Proverbs, Ἄνω ποταμῶν, making Rivers aſcend to their Fountains, affirming that to be done, which all the World hitherto hath look'd upon as abſurd and impoſſible. And, therefore, the Matter of Fact had need be well atteſted: Which, when to me it ſhall be, I muſt then, *manus dare*, yield up the Bucklers, and ſtudy ſome Means to ſolve the *Phænomena*.

Suppose we, that the *Mediterranean* empties itſelf into the Ocean by an Under-Current; there muſt be a Declivity to carry it down, and, conſequently, the upper Superficies of this Under-Current muſt have its Declivity too, and likewiſe the contiguous Superficies of the Upper-Current; and ſo, the Upper-Current muſt needs aſcend in its Courſe inwards. If you ſay, it's forc'd in by the Motion of the Ocean, that ſeems unlikely, becauſe it runs in conſtantly, as well Ebb as Flood. And, therefore, there ſeems to be no better Account of it than the Superficies of the *Ocean* being higher than that of the *Mediterranean*.

But

But to put this Matter out of all doubt, that learned and curious Obferver of all Natural and Artificial Rarities that came in his way, Mr. *John Greaves*, in whofe time there was no talk of an Under-Current at the *Straits-Mouth*, but of contrary-fide ones, affirms of his own Knowledge and Obfervation, *That it was a great Miftake, and that there was no fuch thing as a contrary Current, but that the Water flowed equally inward, as well on the one fide of the Channel as on the other.* Pyramidograph. *p.* 101, 102.

By the Breaking up of the Fountains of the *Great Deep*, is, I conceive, meant, the making great Iffues and Apertures for thefe fubterraneous Waters to rufh out. You will fay, how could that be, fith the Water keeps its Level, and cannot afcend to a greater Height above the common Center, than the Superficies of the Sea is, much lefs force its Way, remove Obftacles, and break open Paffages?

I answer, According to them that hold that all Rivers come from the Sea by fubterraneous Paffages, it is no more than daily happens. For they muft needs grant, that the Water in fubterraneous Channels, is raifed as far above the Level of the Ocean, as are the Heads and Fountains of great Rivers. Which, confidering the Height of their firft Springs up the Mountains, the Length of their Courfes, and the Swiftnefs of their

Streams

Streams for a great part of the Way, is very confiderable, a conftant Declivity being neceffary to their Defcent. And, therefore, I can by no means affent to the Learned Doctor *Plot*, (if I underftand him aright) * *That the Valleys are as much below the Surface of the Sea, as Mountains are above it.* For, how then could Rivers defcend down to the Sea through thofe Valleys? The Sea would rather run into them, and make *Sinus's*; or elfe, if they were enclofed, the Water would ftagnate there, and make Pools.

* *Hift. Nat Stafford, p. 79.*

If this be done by way of Filtration (which feems to be the moft likely Means of raifing the Water) I do not fee, but thefe Filters may     p the whole Ocean; and if Apertures and Outlets large enough were made, pour it out upon the Earth in no long time. But I cannot be fully reconciled to this Opinion, though it hath great Advocates, efpecially the fore-mentioned very learned and ingenious Perfon, Dr. *Robert Plot*. I acknowledge fubterraneous Waters: I grant a Confluence and Communication of Seas by Under-ground Channels and Paffages: I believe, that wherever one fhall dig as deep as the Level of the Sea, he fhall feldom fail of Water; the Water making its way through Sand, and Gravel, and Stones. In like manner, as it is obferved of the River *Seine*, that in Flood-times all the neighbouring Wells and Cellars are filled with Water, and when the River decreafes decreases and sinks again, those Waters also of the Wells and Cellars diminish, and by degrees fall back into the River, so that there are scarce any Wells or Fountains in the Plains near the River, but their Waters keep the Level of the Rivers, rising and falling with it.

But this inferior constant Circulation and perpetual Motion of Water, seems to me not yet sufficiently proved and made out. I think that the Patrons and Abettors of this Opinion, have not satisfactorily demonstrated, how it is, or can be performed. To what is offered concerning the Center of Gravity being nearer to our Continent, by reason of the Preponderancy of the Earth, and the Waters lying, as it were, on an Heap in the other Hemisphere, I answer, 1. That in the present terraqueous Globe, the *New World*, which lies between the two great Seas, and almost opposite to our Continent, doth in some measure counterpoise the *Old*, and take off a great part of the Advantage, which, by reason of its Preponderancy, it might otherwise have. Moreover, I am of Mr. *Brierwood*'s Opinion, that there may be, and is a vast Continent toward the Southern Pole, opposite to *Europe* and *Asia*, to counterpoise them on that side; nay, I do verily believe, that the Continents and Islands are so proportionably scattered and disposed all the World over, as if not perfectly and exactly,
yet

yet very nearly to counter-balance one another; so that the Globe cannot walter or reel towards any Side: And that the Center of the Convex *Superficies* of the Sea, is the true Center of the whole Terrestrial Sphere, both of Motion, and of Gravity. I add also of Magnitude, which is exceedingly convenient, as well for the Facility as the Equability of the Earth's Diurnal Motion. This *Hypothesis* of the Continent's being dispers'd equally on all Sides of the Globe, makes these Centers concurr in one Point, whatever Cause we assign of the raising up the dry Land at first. Whereas if we should suppose the dry Land to have been raised up by Earthquakes only on one Side of the Globe, and to have cast off the Water to the other, and also that the Waters could find no Way into the Caverns that were left within; then the watery Side must needs preponderate the Land Side, and bring the Center of Gravity nearer to it's own *Superficies*, and so raise the Land still a great deal higher, and make a considerable Distance between the Centers of Magnitude, and of Gravity. In our *Hypothesis* of the equal Dispersion of the Continents and Islands, no such thing would happen, but each Continent, taking it with all its internal Caverns, whether lighter or heavier than its Bulk in Water, that is, whether the Water did make its way into the Caverns thereof, or did not, (for in the first Case it would be

G 4        heavier,

heavier, in the second lighter) would have its Counterpoise on the opposite Side, so that the Centers would still concurr. The Case would be the same, if the dry Land were discovered, and the Mountains raised by the immediate Application of the Divine Power. 2. The Sea being no where above a *German* Mile deep, (for which we have good Authority) in most Places not half so much, taking then, as a Middle Term, half a Mile. Suppose it every where half a Mile deep, (the Earth below the Sea, we have no reason to suppose of different Gravity) what Proportion hath this half Mile's Thickness of Water to the whole Terraqueous Globe, whose Semidiameter is, by the Account of Mathematicians, Three thousand four hundred and forty *Italian* Miles? What little Advantage then can it have of the Earth opposite to it, in Point of Preponderancy? 3. Granting the Center of Gravity should be nearer our Continent: The Center being the lowest Place, and the Water a fluid Body, unless stopped, (which it might indeed be, if it were encompassed round with high Shores, as high as the Mountains, without any Breaks or Outlets in them) where it found Declivity, it would descend as near as it could to it, without any Regard of the Earth's Preponderancy. And though we should grant, that the Dryness of the Shores might stop it, and cause it to lie on a Heap, yet would it run up

the

the Channels of Rivers, till it come as near as possible to the Center of Gravity. Indeed the Rivers themselves could not descend, but must run towards the Middle of the Continent. All this, I think, will follow from this *Hypothesis* by as good Consequence, as the Waters being forced through the subterraneous Channels out at the Springs. Dr. *Hook's* Opinion, That the Preponderancy of the salt Water above the fresh, raises up the fresh Water above the Level of the salt, as high as the Springs and Fountain-Heads, and forces it out there, would have a great Probability in it, were there continued strait Channels or Conduits from the Bottom of the Sea to the Eruption of Springs, which I believe there are not. I do not peremptorily affirm, that all Fountains do proceed from Rain; only I contend, that Rain may suffice to feed them, and that probably it doth feed ordinary Springs. This the ingenious *French* Author doth well demonstrate in the River *Seine*, and I believe it is demonstrable in most other Rivers.

The little Brook that runs near my Dwelling, and hath its Head or Source not above four or five Miles off, where there is no extraordinary Eruption of Water, all along its Course receives small Rivulets on both Sides; which though they make a considerable Stream at five Miles Distance from the Fountain-Head, yet singly are so small, that they may

may very well be conceived to drain down from the higher Grounds that lie about them. And taking the whole together, it is a very confiderable Length and Breadth of Land, that contributes to the Maintenance of this little River: So that it may eafily be believed, that all its Water owes its Original to Rain: Efpecially, if it be confidered farther, that in Winter-time, after the Rains are fallen, the Ground fated, and the Ditches full, the Stream of this River, during the whole Winter following, is for the moft part, unlefs in Frofts, double of what it was in Summer. Which Excefs can proceed from nothing but Rain and Mifts; at leaft it would be Rafhnefs to affign any other Caufe, when there is fo obvious and manifeft an one. Moreover, that Rain affords no fmall Quantity of Water, is clear alfo from great Floods, wherein it might be proved, that in few Days there defcends more Water than would fupply the ordinary Stream for a good part of Summer. Now, to compare great Things with fmall; I have feen many of the biggeft Rivers in *Europe*, the *Danow*, *Rhine*, *Rhofne*, and *Po*; and when I confider the Length of their Courfes, the Multitude of confiderable Rivers and Brooks they receive; and all thefe from their firft Rife, made up by Degrees of little Rivulets and Gills, like my neighbouring Brook; the huge Mountains and vaft Extent of higher

Grounds

Grounds they drain: To me it seems (and I have seen all their Streams near their Outlets, except the *Danow's*, and its after four hundred Miles Descent) that they do not bear any greater Proportion to the Rivers and Rivulets they receive, and the immense Tracts of Land that feed them, than my Brook doth to its small Rills and Compass of Ground.

But in this, I confess, I do not descend to the Niceness of Measuring and Calculation; but satisfy myself with rude Conjectures, taking my Measures, as the *Cestrians* say, by the Scale of the Eye.

It will here be objected, *That the Rain never sinks above ten Foot deep at most into the Earth, and therefore cannot supply the Springs.*

*Answ.* This indeed, if it were true, would much enervate, nay, quite overthrow our Opinion: And therefore we must fortify this Point, and effectually demonstrate, beyond all Possibility of Denial, or Contradiction, That Rain-water doth sink down, and make its Way into the Earth; I do not say, ten, or twenty, nor forty, but an hundred, nay, two or three hundred Foot, or more.

First, then, in *Pool-Hole*, in the *Peak* of *Derbyshire*, there are in some Places constant Droppings and Destillations of Water from the Roof: Under each of which (to note that
by

by the by) rises up a Stone Pillar, the Water precipitating some of those stony Particles, which it had washed off the Rocks in passing through their Chinks. These Droppings continue all the Summer long. Now, it seems clear to me, that the Rain-water making its Way through the Veins and Chinks of the Rocks above it, and yet but slowly, by reason of the Thickness of the Mountain, and Straitness of the Passages, supplies that Dropping all the Year round; at least, this is much more rational than any different *Hypothesis*. If the Water distills down faster in Winter-time and wet Weather, than it doth in Summer (which I forgot to ask) the Experiment would infallibly prove our Assertion. In Confirmation of this Argument, *Albertus Magnus* (as I find him quoted in Dr. *Wittie*'s *Scarborough Spaw*) tells us, *That at the Bottom of a solid Rock one hundred and thirty Fathoms deep, he saw Drops of Water distilling from it in a rainy Season.*

SECONDLY, It is well known, and attested to me by the People at *Buxton* when I was there, That out of the Mouth of the same *Pool-Hole*, after great and long continuing Rains, a great Stream of Water did usually issue forth: And I am sure it must make its Way through a good Thickness of Earth, or Rocks, before it could come in there.

THIRDLY, What becomes of all the Water that falls on *Newmarket-Heath*, and *Gogmagog Hills*,

## the Deluge.

Hills, I presume also *Salisbury-Plain*, and the like spungy Grounds all Winter long, where we see very little run off any way? It must needs sink into the Ground more than ten Foot deep.

FOURTHLY, Many Wells, whose Springs lie at least twenty Foot deep, we find by Experience, do often fail in great Droughts in Summer-time.

FIFTHLY, In Coal Delfs, and other Mines, in wet Weather the Miners are many times drown'd out, (as they phrase it) though no Water runs down into the Mouths of their Pits or Shafts. Nay, Dr. *Wittie* tells us, in his *Description of the Vertues of the Scarborow Spaw*, pag. 105. *That after great Inundations of Rain, the Miners find the Water frequently distilling through the solid Earth upon their Heads; whereas in Summer, or dry Seasons, they find no Interruption from thence at all.*

FARTHER, to confirm this Particular, I wrote to my Honoured Friend Sir *Thomas Willughby*, Bar. desiring him to examine his Colliers concerning it, and send me Word what Report they make; and from him received this Account: *If there be Springs lie before you come at the Coal, they carry the Water away; but if there be none, it falls into the Works in greater or less Quantity, according as the Rains fall.* Which Answer is so much the more considerable, in that it
gives

gives me a farther clear Proof, that Springs are fed by Rain-water, and not by any Communications from the Sea; their Original being above the Beds of Coal, they receiving the Rain-water into their Veins, and deriving it all along to their Fountains or Eruptions, above the Coals.

I MIGHT add out of him, [Dr. *Wittie*] Fifthly, *p.* 85. *That the* Scarborough *Spaw, notwithstanding it breaks out of Ground within three or four Yards off the Foot of the Cliff, which is near forty Yards high, and within a Quarter of a Mile there is another Hill, that is more than as high again as the Cliff, and a Descent all the way to the Cliff, so as the Rain-water cannot lie long upon the Ground; yet it is observable, that after a long Rain, the Water of the Spaw is altered in its Taste, and lessened in its Operation; whereas a rainy Day or two will not sensibly hurt it.* And now I am transcribing out of this Author, give me Leave to add an Observation or two in Confirmation of Rains being the Original of Springs. The first is (*pag.* 97.) this:

IN England, *in the Years* 1654, 55, *and* 56. *when our Climate was drier than ever it had been mentioned to be in any Stories, so as we had very little Rain in Summer, or Snow in Winter, most of our Springs were dried up; such as in the Memory of the eldest Men living had never wanted Water, but were of those Springs we call* Fontes Perennes, *or at*

*least*

*least were esteemed so.* He instances also a parallel Story out of *Heylin's Geography,* in the Description of *Cyprus,* where the Author relates; *That in the Days of* Constantine *the Great, there was an exceeding long Drought there, so as in thirty six Years they had no Rain, insomuch as all the Springs and Torrents, or Rivers, were dried up; so that the Inhabitants were forced to forsake the Island, and to seek for new Habitations for want of fresh Water.*

The second is, *p.* 84. *That in the* Wolds *or Downs of* Yorkshire *they have many Springs break out after great Rains, which they call* Gypsies, *which jet and spout up a great Height.*

Neither is this Eruption of Springs, after long Rains, proper and peculiar only to the *Wolds* of *Yorkshire,* but common to other Countries also, as Dr. \**Childrey* witnesseth, in these Words: *Sometimes there breaks out Water in the manner of a sudden Land Flood, out of certain Stones, that are like Rocks standing aloft in open Fields, near the Rising of the River* Kynet [*in* Kent] *which is reputed by the common People a Fore-runner of Dearth. That the sudden Eruption of Springs in Places where they use not always to run, should be a Sign of Dearth, is no Wonder. For these unusual Eruptions,* (which in Kent we call Nailbourns) *are caused by extreme Gluts of Rain, or lasting wet Weather, and never happen*

\**Britannia Baconica.*

*pen but in wet Years; witness the Year* 1648. *when there were many of them;* —— *and to our Purpose very remarkable it was, that in the Year* 1654. *several Springs and Rivulets were quite dried up, by reason of the precedent Drought, which raged most in* 1651, 1652, *and* 1653. *As the Head of the* Stour, *that rises near* Eltham *in* Kent, *and runs through* Canterbury, *was dry for some Miles Space: And the like happened to the Stream that crosseth the Road-way between* Sittingburn *and* Canterbury, *at* Ospring *near* Feversham, *which at other times ran with a plentiful Current, but then wholly failed.* So we see that it is not infrequent for new Springs to break out in wet Years; and for old ones to fail in great Droughts. And *Strabo*, in his first Book out of *Xanthus* the *Lydian*, tells us, *That in the Time of* Artaxerxes, *there was so great a Drought, that Rivers, and Lakes, and Wells of Water failed, and were dried up.*

I cannot here also forbear to add, the probable Account he [Dr. *Wittie*] gives of the Supply of the Spring-Well on the Castle-Hill at *Scarborough*; at which, I confess, I was somewhat puzzled. *This Well,* saith he, *though it be upon the Top of the Rock, not many Yards deep, and also upon the Edge of the Cliff, is, doubtless, supplied by secret Channels within the Ground, that convey the Rain and Showers into it, being placed on a dependent Part of the Rock; near unto which, there are also Cellars*

*lars under an old ruinated Chappel,* which, after a great Rain, are full of *Water,* but are dried up in a long Drought.

As for what is said concerning the River *Wogla*'s pouring out so much Water into the *Caspian Sea,* as in a Year's time would make up a Mass of Water equal to the Globe of the Earth; and of the hourly Effusions of the River *Po* in *Italy,* which *Ricciolus* hath computed to amount to 18000000 cubical Paces of Water; whence a late learned Writer hath probably inferred, that all the Rivers in the World together, do daily discharge half an Ocean of Waters into the Sea; I must confess myself to be unsatisfied therewith. I will not question their Calculations, but I suspect they are out in their *Hypotheses.*

The Opinion of Mr. *Edmund Halley,* that Springs and Rivers owe their Original to Vapours condensed on the Sides of Mountains, rather than unto Rains, I acknowledge to be very ingenious, grounded upon good Observations, and worthy of its Author; and I will not deny it to be in part true, in those hot Countreys in the Torrid Zone, and near it; where, by reason of the great Heats, the Vapours are more copiously exhaled out of the Earth, and, it's likely, carried up high in the Form of Vapours. The inferiour Air, at least, is so charged with them, and by that means so very moist, that, in some Places,

H                 their

their Knives ruft even in their Pockets; and in the Night, fo very frefh and cold, partly alfo by reafon of the Length of the Nights; that expofing the Body to it, caufes Colds and Catarrhs, and is very dangerous: Whence alfo their Dews are fo great, as in good meafure to recompenfe the Want of Rain, and ferve for the Nourifhment of Plants; as they do even in *Spain* itfelf.

I shall firft of all propofe this Opinion in the Words of the Author, and then difcourfe a little upon it. After he had enumerated many of the high Ridges and Tracts of Mountains in the four Quarters of the World, he thus proceeds: *Each of which far furpafs the ufual Height to which the aqueous Vapours of themfelves afcend, and on the Tops of which the Air is fo cold and rarified, as to retain but a fmall Part of thofe Vapours that fhall be brought thither by the Winds. Thofe Vapours, therefore, that are raifed copioufly in the Sea, and by the Winds, are carried over the low Lands to thofe Ridges of Mountains, and are there compelled, by the Stream of the Air, to mount up with it to the Tops of the Mountains, where the Water prefently precipitates gleeting down by the Crannies of the Stone; and part of the Vapour entring into the Cavities of the Hills, the Water thereof gathers, as in an Alembick, into the Bafons of Stone it finds; which being once filled, all the Overplus of Water that comes thither, runs over by the lowest Place,*

*and*

and breaking out by the Sides of the Hills, forms single Springs. Many of these running down by the Valleys, or Guts, between the Ridges of the Hills, and coming to unite, form little Rivulets or Brooks. Many of these, again, meeting in one common Valley, and gaining the plain Ground, being grown less rapid, become a River: And many of these being united in one common Channel, make such Streams, as the Rhine, and Rhosne, and the Danube; which latter one would hardly think the Collection of Water condensed out of Vapour, unless we consider how vast a Tract of Ground that River drains, and that it is the Sum of all those Springs, which break out on the South-side of the Carpathian Mountains, and on the North-side of the immense Ridge of the Alps, which is one contained Chain of Mountains from Switzerland to the Black Sea. And it may almost pass for a Rule, that the Magnitude of a River, or the Quantity of Water it evacuates, is proportionable to the Length and Height of the Ridges, from whence its Fountains arise. Now this Theory of Springs is not a bare Hypothesis, but founded on Experience, which it was my Luck to gain in my Abode at S. Helena; where, in the Night-time, on the Tops of the Hills, about Eight hundred Yards above the Sea, there was so strange a Condensation, or rather Precipitation of the Vapours, that it was a great Impediment to my Celestial Observations; for, in the clear

*Sky*, the Dew would fall so fast, as to cover each half-quarter of an Hour my Glasses with little Drops, so that I was necessitated to wipe them off so often; and my Paper, on which I wrote my Observations, would immediately be so wet with the Dew, that it would not bear Ink: By which it may be supposed, how fast the Water gathers in those mighty high Ridges I but now named. ------ At last he concludes: And I doubt not but this Hypothesis *is more reasonable, than that of those who derive all Springs from the Rain-waters, which yet are perpetual, and without Diminution, even when no Rain falls for a long space of Time.*

This may, for ought I as yet see or know, be a good Account of the Original of Springs in those fervid Regions, though even there, I doubt, but partial; but in *Europe*, and the more temperate Countries, I believe the Vapours in this manner condensed, have but little Interest in the Production of them, though I will not wholly exclude them. For,

*First*, The Tops of the *Alps* above the Fountains of four of the greatest Rivers in *Europe*, the *Rhine*, the *Rhosne*, the *Danow*, and the *Po*, are, for about six Months in the Year, constantly covered with Snow, to a great thickness; so that there are no Vapours all that while that can touch those Mountains, and be by them condensed into Water; there falls nothing there but Snow, and

and that continuing all that while on the Ground without Diſſolution, hinders all Acceſs of Vapours to the Earth; if any roſe, or were by Winds carried ſo high in that Form, as I am confident there are not. And yet, for all that, do not thoſe Springs fail, but continue to run all Winter; and it is likely too, without Diminution; which is a longer time than Droughts uſually laſt; eſpecially, if we conſider that this Want of Supply is conſtant and annual; whereas, Droughts are but rare and accidental. So that we need not wonder any more, that Springs ſhould continue to run, and without Diminution too, in times of Drought. True it is, that thoſe Rivers run low all Winter, ſo far as the Snow extends, and to a good diſtance from their Heads; but that is for want of their accidental Supplies from Showers. Nay, I believe, that even in Summer, the Vapours are but rarely raiſed ſo high in a liquid Form in the free Air, remote from the Mountains, but are frozen into Snow, before they arrive at the Height. For the *Middle Region* of the *Air*, where the Walk of the Clouds is, at leaſt the ſuperiour part of it, is ſo cold, as to freeze the Vapours that aſcend ſo high, even in Summer-time. For we ſee, that in the Height and Heat of Summer, in great Thunder-ſtorms, for the moſt part it hails: Nay, in ſuch Tempeſts I have ſeen mighty Showers of great Hail-ſtones fall, ſome as big as

Nut-

Nutmegs or Pigeons Eggs; and in some places, such Heaps of them, as would load Dung-Carts, and have not been dissolved in a day or two. At the same Seasons, I have observed, in some Showers, Hail-stones fall of irregular Figures, and throughout pellucid, like great Pieces of Ice, with several Snags or Fangs issued out of them: Which, how they could be supported in the Air till they amounted to that Bulk and Weight, is a thing worthy to be more curiously considered. For either they must fall from an incredible Height, the Vapours they encountred by the Way, condensing, and, as it were, crystallizing upon them into Ice, and in time augmenting them to that Bulk; or else, there must be some strange and unknown Faculty in the Air to sustain them. That the superiour Air doth support heavy Bodies better than the inferiour, the Flight of Birds seems to be a clear Demonstration. For, when they are mounted up on High, they fly with less Fatigue, and move forward with greater Facility, and are able to continue longer upon the Wing without Delassation, than in the lower Air they could possibly do. And, therefore, when they are to make great Flights, they soar aloft in the Air, at a great Height above the Earth. So have I often seen a a Flock of Wild-geese mounted so high, that though their Flight be swift, they seemed to make but little Way in a long time, and to pro-

proceed on their Journey with eafe, and very leifurely, by reafon of their Diftance. And yet one would think, this were contrary to Reafon, that the lighter Air, fuch as is the fuperiour, fhould better fupport a weighty Body than the heavier, that is, the inferiour. Some imagine, that this comes to pafs by reafon of the Wind, which is conftantly moving in the upper Air, which fupports any Body that moves contrary to it. So we fee that thofe Paper-kites which Boys make, are raifed in the Air, by running with them contrary to the Wind: And when they are advanced to a great Height, do but ftick down the nether End of the Line, to which they are faftned, into the Ground, they will be continued by the Wind at the fame Height they were, fo long as it lafts and abides in the fame Quarter. In like manner, the Birds flying contrary to the Wind, it fupports and keeps them up. But if this were the only Reafon, methinks it fhould not be fo eafie, but rather very laborious for Birds to fly againft the Wind, fo as to make any confiderable Progrefs in the fuperiour Air, as we fee they do. And, therefore, poffibly they may be nearer the Right, who fuppofe, that the Gravity of Bodies decreafes proportionably to their Diftance from the Earth; and that a Body may be advanced fo high, as quite to lofe its Gravity and Inclination, or Tendency to the Center: Of which I do not fee see how it is possible to make Experiment. For, to what is said by some, to have been tried, that a Bullet shot perpendicularly upward out of a great Gun, never descended again, I give no credit at all.

But to leave that, it is certain, that the Vapours, after they are mounted up to a considerable Height in the Air, are congealed and turned into the immediate component Principles of Snow, in which Form I conceive they acquire a Lightness, and are apt to ascend higher than they could do, should they retain the Form of a humid Vapour; as, we see, Ice is lighter than Water, out of which it is frozen. But whether this be the reason of their Ascent, or not, I am sure of the Matter of Fact, that these Snow-Clouds do ascend far above the highest Tops of the *Alps*; For, passing over a Mountain in the *Grisons* Country, on the very Ridge of them, in the beginning of the Spring, it snowed very fast during my whole Passage for six hours; and yet the Clouds seemed to be as far above my Head, as they do here in *England*; and a great Height they must be, for the Snow to gather into so great Flakes, and to continue so long falling; nay, it may be three times so long. Moreover, we see, that the highest Pikes and Summits of those Mountains are covered with Snow. And I am assured, that all the Winter long, at intervals, it snows upon the Tops of the *Alps*.

2. In

2. In the Spring-time, when the Snow diſſolves, ſome of theſe Rivers that flow down from the *Alpine* Mountains, run with a full Stream, and overflow their Banks, in clear Sun-ſhine Weather, though no Rain falls, as I myſelf can witneſs; and, therefore, I preſume, that all the reſt do ſo too, as the Inhabitants affirmed. But, in the Summer-time, after the Snow hath been ſome time melted, their Streams decay again, notwithſtanding any Vapours condenſed upon them, proportionable to the Droughts; neither are there any Floods, but upon Falls of Rain.

3. That the Snow diſſolved, and ſoaking into the Earth, is the Original of the *Alpine* Springs; a probable Argument may be taken from the Colour of the Water of thoſe Rivers which deſcend from the *Alps*, at leaſt on this Northern-ſide, which I obſerved to be of of a Sea-green, even to a great diſtance from their Heads; which, whence can it proceed, unleſs from the nitrous Particles of the Snow-water, of which they conſiſt? Another alſo from the *Bronchocele*, or * *gutturine Tumour*, an *Endemial* Diſeaſe of the Natives of thoſe Parts, which Phyſicians and Naturaliſts attribute to the Water they drink, not without good Reaſon; becauſe, ſay they, it conſiſts of melted Snow, which gives it that malignant Quality. † *Scaliger* ſpeaking of this Diſeaſe, ſaith, *Id ab aqua fit è nivibus liquefactis, quæ multum terreſtris & crudi continent.*

* Swoln Throats.

† *De Subtilit. Exerc.* 60. *Sect.* 2.

But

But because *Julius Palmarius* may possibly be in the right, who imputes this Disease to the Steams of the Minerals, especially Mercurial, wherewith these Mountains abound, which infect the Waters, and render them noxious to the nervous Parts; I shall not insist upon this Particular.

In confirmation of what I have said concerning the Original of the *Alpine* Springs, I shall add the Opinion of the Learned *Alphonsus Borellus*, concerning the Fountains springing up, or issuing out of the Sides of Mount *Ætna* in *Sicily*. *They are probably* (saith he) *either generated, or at least encreased, from the melting of the Snow, which doth perpetually occupy the Top of the Mountain. And this is manifest, in that they are not diminished, nor decrease in Summer, as elsewhere it happens, but often flow more plentifully.* Lib. De incendiis Ætnæ.

What Mr. *Halley* saith of Springs, That they are perpetual, and without Diminution, even when no Rain falls, for a long Space of Time. If he understands it generally of all Springs, I add, that are accounted quick ones too, I deny his Assertion: That some there may be of that Nature, I grant. A Reason whereof may be given, *viz.* that the Outlet is too small to empty the Water of all the Veins and Earth that lie above it in a long time. In our Native Country of *England*, there are living and lasting Springs rising

sing at the Feet of our small Hills and Hillocks, to which, I am sure, the Vapours contribute very little; which is so obvious to every Man, that, I think, I need not spend time to prove it.

Yet must I not dissemble or deny, that in the Summer-time the Vapours do ascend, or are carried up in that Form, by the Sides of the Mountains to their highest Tops, and above them; for there falls no Snow there, in the Heat of Summer; and that which lies there, is, for the most part, dissolved. But that Rain falls, plentifully there, I myself can witness; having been on the two highest Tops of the Mount *Jura*, (which keeps the Snow all Winter) on the one called *Thuiri* in a Thunder-shower; and on the other, called *la Dolaz*, in a smart and continuing Rain: So that I will not deny, but in Summer-time the Vapours may contribute somewhat to the Springs; as I have elsewhere intimated: Clouds almost continually hanging upon the Tops of the Mountains, and the Sun having there but little Power.

And now that I am discoursing of these things, give me leave to set down an Observation I made in the last great Frost, the sharpest that was ever known in the Memory of Man, which I had before met with in Books, but did not give firm credit to, that is, that notwithstanding the Violence of the Frost, all the Springs about us brake out, and ran

ran more plentifully than ufually they did at any other time: Which I knew not what to impute to, unlefs perchance the clofe Stopping the Pores of the Earth, and keeping in that Part, which, at other times, was wont to vapour away; which Account I neither then could, nor can yet fully acquiefce in.

To this I will here add an Abftract of a Letter, written by my honoured Friend Dr. *Tancred Robinfon.*

'YOU may, peradventure, meet with fome
' Oppofition againft your *Hypothefis* of
' Fountains, though, indeed, I am more and
' more confirm'd in your Opinion of them, and
' the Ufe of the Mountains. Father *Tachart,*
' in his fecond Voyage to *Siam,* fays, When
' he went up to the Top of the *Table Moun-*
' *tain* at the *Cape of Good Hope,* the Rocks and
' Shrubs were perpetually dropping, and feed-
' ing the Springs and Rills below, there be-
' ing generally Clouds hanging on the Sides,
' near the Top. This conftant Diftillation of
' Vapours from the Ocean, on many high
' Ridges of that great Promontory, may, per-
' adventure, be one Caufe of the wonderful
' Fertility and Luxury of the Soil, which pro-
' duces more rare Plants and Animals than any
' known Spot of Ground in the World; the
' Difcovery whereof is owing to the Curiofity
' and Wifdom of the *Dutch.* The fame Ob-
' fervation hath been frequently made by our
' *Englifh*

'*English* Merchants in the *Madera* and *Cana-*
'*ry* Iflands, (the firft of which is near in the
' fame Latitude on the North of the *Æquator*,
' that the aforementioned *Cape* is in the South)
' efpecially, in their Journeys up to the *Pike* of
' *Teneriff*, in which, at fuch and fuch Heights,
' they were always wet to the Skin, by the
' Droppings of the great Stones, yet no Rain
' over-head; the fame I have felt in paffing
' over fome of the *Alps*. The Trees, which in
' the Iflands of *Ferro*, St. *Thomas*, and in *Gui-*
' *nea*, are faid to furnifh the Inhabitants with
' moft of their Water, ftand on the Sides of
' vaft Mountains: *Voffius*, in his Notes on
' *Pomponius Mela*, affirms them to be *Arbore-*
' *fcent Ferula's*; though indeed, according to
' *Paludanus* his dry'd Sample fent to the Duke
' of *Wirtenberg*, they feem rather to be of the
' Laurel Kind; perhaps there are many dif-
' ferent Sorts of them. I believe there is fome-
' thing in the many Relations of Travellers
' and Voyagers concerning thefe Trees; but
' then I fancy they are all miftaken, when they
' fay, the Water iffues out of the Trees: The
' Vapours ftop'd by the Mountains, condenfe
' and diftill down by the Boughs. There be-
' ing no Mountains in *Egypt*, may be one Rea-
' fon why there is little or no Rain in that
' Country, and confequently no frefh Springs;
' therefore in their *Caravans* they carry all their
' Water with them in great *Borracio's*, and they
' owe the Inundation of their River *Nile* to the
' ftationary

'stationary or periodical Rains on the high
'Parts of *Æthiopia*. This may be the Cause
'that the vast Ridge and Chain of Mountains
'in *Peru* are continually water'd, when the
'great Plains in that Country are all dry'd up,
'and parch'd. This *Hypothesis* concerning the
'Original of Springs from Vapours, may hold
'better in those hot Regions, within and near
'the Tropicks (where the Exhalations from the
'Sea are most plentiful, most rarify'd, and Rain
'scarce) than in the temperate and frigid ones
'(where it rains and snows generally on the
'*Vertices* of the Mountains) yet even in our
'*European* Climates I have often observ'd the
'Firs, Pines, and other Vegetables near the
'Summits of the *Alps* and *Appennines*, to drop
'and run with Water, when it did not rain a-
'bove; some Trees more than others, accor-
'ding to the Density and Smoothness of their
'Leaves and Superficies, whereby they stop
'and condense Vapours more or less. The
'Beams of the Sun having little Force on the
'high Parts of Mountains, the interrupted Va-
'pours must continually moisten them, and (as
'in the Head of an Alembick) condense and
'trickle down; so that we owe part of our
'Rain, Springs, Rivers, and Conveniencies of
'Life, to the Operation of Distillation and Cir-
'culation by the Sun, the Sea, and the Hills,
'without even the last of which, the Earth
'would scarce be habitable. This present Year,
'in *Kent*, they have had no Rain since *March*
'last,

' laſt, therefore moſt of their Springs are dry
' at this very Day, as I am aſſured from good
' Hands. The high Spouting of Water, even
' to three Fathoms perpendicular out of innu-
' merable Holes, on the Lake *Zirknitz* in *Car-*
' *niola*, after Rains on the adjacent Hills, ex-
' ceeds the Spirting Gips, or Natural *Jet*
' *d'Eaus* we have in *England*.

Nov. 12. 1691.  *Tancred Robinſon.*

Since the Receipt of this Letter, an Experiment (give me leave ſo to call it) occur-
red to me, which much confirmed me in the
Belief and Perſuaſion of the Truth of thoſe
Hiſtories and Relations which Writers and
Travellers have delivered to us concerning
dropping Trees in *Ferro, S. Thome, Guinea*, &c.
of which before I was ſomewhat diffident;
and likewiſe in the Approbation of the *Hypotheſis* of my Learned Friend Dr. *Tancred Robinſon*, for the ſolving of that *Phænomenon.*
The ſame alſo induces me to believe, that Vapours may have a greater Intereſt in the
Production of Springs, even in temperate
and cold Regions, than I had before thought.
The Experiment or Obſervation is this:

About the Beginning of *December*, 1691,
there happened to be a Miſt, and that no
very thick one, which continued all Day;
the Vapour whereof, notwithſtanding the
Trees were wholly deveſted of Leaves, condenſed ſo faſt upon their naked Branches and
Twigs,

Twigs, that they dropped all Day at such a rate, that I believe the Water distilling from a large Tree in twenty four Hours, had it been all received and reserved in a Vessel, might have amounted to a Hogshead. What then may we rationally conjecture, would have dropped from such a Tree; had it been covered with Leaves of a dense Texture, and smooth *Superficies*, apt to collect the Particles of the Vapour, and unite them into Drops?

It is clear by this Effect, that Trees do distill Water apace, when Clouds or Mists hang about them; which they are reported by *Benzo* constantly to do about the Fountain-Tree in *Ferro*, except when the Sun shines hot upon it. And others tell us, that that Tree grows upon a Mountain too: So that it is no wonder, that it should drop abundance of Water. What do I speak of that Tree? all the Trees of that Kind grow on the Sides of vast Mountains, as Dr. *Robinson* hath noted, yet he thinks that now and then many Trees may run and distill in Plains and Valleys, when the Weather has been fair, but then this *Phænomenon* happens very rarely, whereas in the other 'tis regular and constant. Besides, that in hot Regions Trees may in the Night-time distill Water, though the Air be clear, and there be no Mist about them, seems necessarily to follow, from Mr. *Halley*'s Experiment.

Now,

·Now, if there be in Mists thus much Vapour condensed upon Trees, doubtless also there is in Proportion as much upon the Surface of the Earth and the Grass; and consequently, upon the Tops and Ridges of high Mountains, which are frequently covered with Clouds, or Mists, much more; so much as must needs have a great Interest in the Production and Supply of Springs, even in temperate Countries.

But that invisible Vapours, when the Sky is clear, do at any time condense so fast upon the Trees, as to make them drop, I never observed in *England*, or elsewhere, no not in the Night Season, though I do not deny, but upon the *Appennine* and Southern Side of the *Alps*, and elsewhere in the hotter Parts of *Europe*, in Summer Nights, they may. However, considering the Penetrancy of such Vapours, that in moist Weather they will insinuate themselves deeply into the Pores of dry Wood, so that Doors will then hardly shut, and Chinks and Crannies in Boards and Floors be closed up, I know not but that they may likewise strike deep into the Ground, and together with Mists contribute to the Feeding and Maintenance of Springs, in Winter-time, when the Sun exhales but little; it being an Observation of the learned * *Fromondus*, *Quòd hyeme nec nivali, nec imbrifera, fontes tamen aquam largiùs quàm æstate (nisi valdè pluvia sit) vomant:* That

* Meteor. lib. 5. c. 7. Artic. 3.

in *Winters* neither *snowy* nor *rainy*, yet Fountains pour forth more *Water* than in *Summer*, unless it happen to be a very wet *Season*. Yet are their Contributions inconsiderable, if compared with the Supplies that are afforded by Rains. And one Reason why in Winter Fountains flow more plentifully, may be, because then the Sun defrauds them not, nor exhales any thing out of the Earth, as in Summer-time he doth.

THEREFORE, whenever in this Work I have assigned Rain to be a sufficient or only Cause of Springs and Rivers, I would not be understood to exclude, but to comprehend therein Mists and Vapours, which I grant to have some Interest in the Production of them, even in temperate and cold Regions, and a very considerable one in hot. Though I cannot be persuaded, that even there they are the principal Cause of Springs, for that there fall such plentiful and long continuing Rains, both in the *East* and *West-Indies*, in the Summer Months: That Rains are the only Cause of the Fertility of the Earth, I am convinced by what was lately suggested to me by my honoured Friend Dr. *Tancred Robinson*, that all Dearths proceed from Droughts as well in hot Countries as in temperate and cold, be the Vapours what they will. The Scripture confirms this, by joining Rain and fruitful Seasons together.

BUT

## the Deluge.

But to return from whence we digreſſed, that is, to the Conſideration of that *Hypotheſis*, or Opinion, That all the Rivers of the Earth diſcharge into the Sea half an Ocean of Waters daily.

The Fruitfulneſs of the Earth is alſo in a great Meaſure owing to Floods, which proceed from Rain falling upon the Mountains, and waſhing down thence a great deal of Earth, and ſpreading it upon the lower Grounds and Meadows, which renders theſe ſo fruitful, that they bear plentiful Crops of Graſs yearly, without any Culture or Manuring. An eminent Inſtance of this is the Land of *Egypt*, which owes its great Luxuriancy to the annual Overflowings of the River of *Nile*.

I have read of ſome Philoſophers, who imagined the Earth to be a great Animal, and that the Ebbing and Flowing of the Sea was the Reſpiration of it. And now, methinks, if this Doctrine be true, we have a farther Argument to confirm their Opinion: For this perpetual Motion of the Water anſwers very well to the Circulation of the Blood, the Water moving faſter, in Proportion to its Bulk, through the Veins of this round Animal, than the Blood doth through thoſe of other living Creatures. To which we may add farther, that to maintain this conſtant Circulation, there is alſo, probably, about the Center of the Earth a perpetual Fire, anſwering

swering to the *Biolychnium* in the Heart; but if not about the Center, yet certainly in profound Caverns, and even under the very Bottoms of the Seas; to which some, and no mean Philosophers, have attributed the Ebbing and Flowing of its Waters.

But because (as I said before) this Opinion seems to me intolerably extravagant, I shall let it pass without any serious Consideration; and also omit the Inferences I made from it in the former Edition of this Work.

For (as I have noted before) this forty Days Rain, at the Time of the Deluge, was no ordinary one, such as those that usually distill down leisurely and gently in Wintertime, but like our Thunder-Storms and violent Showers, Catarracts, and Spouts, which pour forth more Water in an Hour than they do in four and twenty: So that in forty Natural Days the Clouds might well empty out more than eight Oceans of Water upon the Earth. And so we need not be to seek for Water for a Flood; for the Rain falling at that rate we have mentioned, would, with the Addition of as much Water from the subterraneous Abyss, or great Deep, in the Space of forty natural Days, afford Water enough to cover the Earth, so far as to set the Ark afloat, or raise it up so high, as that its Bottom should not touch the Ground.

I have but one thing more to add upon this Subject; that is, that I do not see how

their

their Opinion can be true, who hold that some Seas are lower than others, as for Example, the *Red-Sea* than the *Mediterranean*. For it being true that the Water keeps its Level, that is, holds its Superficies every where equidistant from the Center of Gravity; or if by Accident one Part be lower, the rest, by reason of their Fluidity, will speedily reduce the Superficies again to an Equality; the Waters of all Seas communicating either above, or under Ground, or both ways, one Sea cannot be higher or lower than another: But supposing any Accident should elevate or depress any, by reason of this Confluence or Communication it would soon be reduced to a Level again, as might demonstratively be proved.

But I return, to tell the Reader what I think the most probable of all the Causes I have heard assigned of the Deluge, which is, the Center of the Earth being at that time changed, and set nearer to the Center or Middle of our Continent, whereupon the *Atlantick* and *Pacifick* Oceans must needs press upon the subterraneous Abyss, and so by Mediation thereof, force the Water upward, and at last compell it to run out at those wide Mouths and Apertures made by the Divine Power breaking up the Fountains of the great Deep. And we may suppose this to have been only a gentle and gradual Emotion, no faster than that the

Waters

Waters running out at the Bottom of the Sea, might accordingly lower the Superficies thereof sufficiently, so that none needed run over the Shores. These Waters thus poured out from the Orifices of the Fountains upon the Earth, the Declivity being changed by the Removal of the Center, could not flow down to the Sea again, but must needs stagnate upon the Earth, and overflow it; and afterwards the Earth returning to its old Center, return also to their former Receptacles.

THIS *Hypothesis* gives us a fair and easy Solution of all the *Phænomena* of the Deluge, save only the Generality of it, (making it topical, and confining it to our Continent) and delivers us from that great and insuperable Difficulty of finding eight, nay, twenty two Oceans of Water to effect it : For no less is requisite to cover the whole Terraqueous Globe with Water, to the Height of fifteen Cubits above the Tops of the highest Mountains. But because the Scripture useth general Expressions concerning the Extent of the Flood, saying, *Gen.* i. 19. *And all the high Hills that were under the whole Heaven were covered*; and again, *ver.* 22. *All in whose Nostrils was the Breath of Life, of all that was in the dry Land, died.* And, because the *Americans* also are said to have some ancient Memorial Tradition of a Deluge, (as credible Authors, *Acosta, Herrera,* and others inform us) which saith, faith, *That the whole Race of Mankind was destroyed by the Deluge, except some few that escaped:* (They are the Words of *Augustine Corata,* concerning the *Peruvian* Tradition; and *Lupus Gomara* saith the same, from those of *Mexico*) And the ingenious Author of the *Theory of the Earth,* hath, by a moderate Computation, demonstrated, That there must be then more People upon the Earth than now: I will propose another way of solving this *Phænomenon,* and that is, by supposing that the Divine Power might at that time, by the Instrumentality of some natural Agent, to us at present unknown, so depress the Surface of the Ocean, as to force the Waters of the Abyss through the forementioned Channels and Apertures, and so make them a partial and concurrent Cause of the Deluge.

THAT there are, at some times, in the Course of Nature, extraordinary Pressures upon the Surface of the Sea, which force the Water outwards upon the Shores to a great Height, is evident. We had upon our Coasts, few Years ago, an extraordinary Tide, wherein the Water rose so high, as to overflow all the Sea-Banks, drown Multitudes of Cattle, and fill the lower Rooms of the Houses of many Villages that stood near the Sea, so that the Inhabitants, to save themselves, were forced to get up into the upper Rooms and Garrets of their Houses. Now, how this could

could be effected, but by an unusual Pressure upon the Superficies of the Ocean, I cannot well conceive. In like manner, That the Divine Providence might, at the time of the Deluge, so order and dispose second Causes, as to make so strong a Pressure upon the Face of the Waters, as to force them up to a Height sufficient to overflow the Earth, is no way unreasonable to believe. But because there must be another Miracle required, to suspend the Waters upon the Land, and to hinder them from running off again into the Sea; this is far more unlikely than the former Account.

THESE *Hypotheses* I propose, as seeming to me, at present, most facile and consonant to Scripture, without any Concern for either of them; and, therefore, am not solicitous to gather together, and heap up Arguments to confirm them, or to answer Objections that may be made against them, being as ready to relinquish them upon better Information, as I was to admit and entertain them.

## Chap. III.

### Of the Effects of the Deluge.

I Come now to the Third Particular proposed; that is, To Enquire concerning the Consequents of the Deluge; What considerable Effects it had upon the Earth, and its Inhabitants.

It had, doubtless, very great, in changing the *Superficies* of the dry Land. In some Places, adding to the Sea; in some, taking from it; making Islands of *Peninsulæ*, and joining others to the Continent; altering the Beds of Rivers, throwing up lesser Hills, and washing away others, &c. The most remarkable Effects, it's likely, were in the Skirts of the Continents; because the Motion of the Water was there most violent. * *Athanasius Kircher* gives us a Map and Description of the World after the Flood, shewing what Changes were made therein by it, or upon occasion of it afterward, as he fansies or conjectures. But because I do not love to trouble the Reader with uncertain Conjectures, I shall content myself to have said in general, that it may rationally be supposed, there were then great Mutations and Alterations made in the superficial Part of the Earth:

* *De Arca Noæ.* p. 192.

Earth; but what they were, though we may guess, yet can we have no certain Knowledge of: And for Particulars, referr the Curious to him.

ONE malignant Effect it had upon Mankind, and probably upon other Animals too, in shortning their Age, or the Duration of their Lives; which I have touched before, and shewn, that this Diminution of Age is to be attributed either to the Change of the Temperature of the Air, as to Salubrity, or Equality, (sudden and frequent Changes of Weather having a very bad Influence upon the Age of Man in abbreviating of it, as I could easily prove) or else to the Deteriority of the Diet; or to both these Causes. But how the Flood should induce or occasion such a Change in the Air, and Productions of the Earth, I do not comprehend.

## Chap. IV.

*Of formed Stones, Sea-shells, and other Marine-like Bodies found at great Distances from the Shores, supposed to have been brought in by the Deluge.*

ANOTHER supposed Effect of the Flood, was a bringing up out of the Sea, and scattering all the Earth over, an innumerable Multitude of Shells and Shell-fish; there being of these Shell-like Bodies, not only on lower Grounds and Hillocks, but upon the highest Mountains, the *Appennine* and *Alps* themselves. A supposed Effect, I say, because it is not yet agreed among the Learned, whether these Bodies, formerly called *petrified Shells*, but now-a-days passing by the Name of *formed Stones*, be original Productions of Nature, formed in Imitation of the Shells of Fishes; or the real Shells themselves, either remaining still entire and uncorrupt, or petrified and turned into Stone, or, at least, Stones cast in some Animal Mold. Both Parts have strong Arguments and Patrons. I shall not balance Authorities, but only consider and weigh Arguments.

THOSE for the latter Part, wherewith I shall begin, are,

*First,*

*First*, Becaufe it feems contrary to that great Wifdom of Nature, which is obfervable, in all its Works and Productions, to defign every thing to a determinate End, and, for the attaining that End, make ufe of fuch Ways, as are moft agreeable to Man's Reafon, that thefe prettily fhaped Bodies fhould have all thofe curious Figures and Contrivances (which many of them are formed and adorned with) generated or wrought by a *Plaftick Vertue*, for no higher End, than only to exhibit fuch a Form. This is Dr. *Hook*'s Argumentation. To which Dr. *Plot* anfwers, *That the End of fuch Productions is, to beautify the World with thofe Varieties; and that this is no more repugnant to the Prudence of* Nature, *than is the Production of moft* Flowers, Tulips, Anemones, *&c. of which we know as little ufe of, as of formed Stones.* But hereto we may reply, That Flowers are for the Ornament of a Body, that hath fome Degree of Life in it: A Vegetative Soul, whereby it performs the Actions of Nutrition, Auction and Generation; which it is reafonable fhould be fo beautified. And, *Secondly*, Flowers ferve to embrace and cherifh the Fruit, while it is yet tender; and to defend it from the Injuries of Sun and Weather; efpecially, for the Protection and Security of the *Apices*, which are no idle or ufelefs Part, but contain the Mafculine Sperm, and ferve to give Fecundity to the Seed.

### the Deluge.

Seed. *Thirdly*, Though formed Stones may be useful to Man in Medicine, yet Flowers afford us abundantly more Uses, both in Meat and Medicine.

YET I must not dissemble, that there is a *Phænomenon* in Nature, which doth somewhat puzzle me to reconcile with the Prudence observable in all its Works, and seems strongly to prove, that Nature doth sometimes *ludere*, and delineate Figures, for no other End, but for the Ornament of some Stones, and to entertain and gratify our Curiosity, or exercise our Wits: That is, those elegant Impressions of the Leaves of Plants upon *Cole-slate*, the Knowledge whereof, I must confess myself to owe to my learned and ingenious Friend, Mr. *Edward Lhwyd* of *Oxford*, who observed of it in some Cole-pits in the Way from *Wychester* in *Glocestershire*, to *Bristol*; and afterwards communicated to me a Sample of it. That which he found, was marked with the Leaves of two or three Kinds of *Ferns* and of *Harts-tongue*. He told me also, that Mr. *Woodward*, a *Londoner*, shewed him very good Draughts of the common *Female Fern*, naturally formed in Cole, which himself found in *Mendip* Hills; and added, That he had found in the same Pits, Draughts of the common *Cinquefoil*, *Clover-grass* and *Strawberries*. But these Figures are more diligently to be observed and considered.

DR.

Dr. *Woodward* will have these to be the Impressions of the Leaves of Plants, which were there lodged at the Time of the general Deluge.

*Secondly*, There are found in the Earth at great Distance from the Sea, real Shells unpetrified and uncorrupted, of the exact Figure and Consistency of the present natural Sea-shells, and in all their Parts like them, and that not only in the lower Grounds and Hillocks near the Sea, but in Mountains of a considerable Height, and distant from the Sea. *Christianus Mentzelius*, in his Discourse concerning the *Bononian Phosphorus*, gives us a Relation of many Beds of them found mingled with Sand in the upper Part of a high Mountain not far from *Bologna* in *Italy*. His Words are these, *Non procul monte Paterno dicto, lapidis Bononiensis patria, unico forte milliari Italico distanti (loci nomen excidit memoriâ) ingens mons imminet præruptus à violentia torrentium aquarum, quas imbres frequentes ex vicinis montibus confluentes efficiunt, atque insignes terrarum moles ab isto monte prosternunt ac dejiciunt. In hac montis ruinâ, superiore in parte visuntur multæ strages seriésve, ex testis conchyliorum omnis generis, plurimâ arenâ interjectâ, instar strati super stratum (ut chymicorum vulgus loquitur.) Et enim inter hasce testarum conchyliorum strages seriésve arena ad crassitiem ulnæ & ultra interposita. Erant autem testæ variorum conchyliorum,*

*liorum, omnes ab invicem distinctæ, nec cuiquam lapidi impactæ, adeò ut separatim omnia manibus tractari & dignosci potuerint. Effecerat hoc arena pura, nullo limo lutóve intermixta, quæ conchyliorum testas conservaverat per multa secula integras. Interea verò diuturnitate temporis omnes istæ testæ erant in albissimam calcem facilè resolubiles.* Not far from the Mountain called Paterno, where the Bononian Stone is gotten, about an Italian Mile distant, (the Name of the Place is slipt out of my Memory) is a huge hanging Mountain, broken by the Violence of the Torrents, caused by the Confluence of Waters descending from the neighbouring Mountains after frequent Showers, throwing down great Heaps of Earth from it. In this upper Part of this broken Mountain, are seen many Beds or Floors of all kind of Sea-shells, much Sand interposing between Bed and Bed, after the manner of stratum super stratum, or Layer upon Layer, as the Chymists phrase it. The Beds of Sand interceding between these Rows of Shells, were a Yard thick, or more. These Shells were all distinct or separate one from another, and not stuck in any Stone, or cemented together, so that they might be singly and separately viewed and handled with one's Hands. The Cause whereof was their being lodged in a pure Sand, not intermixt with any Mud or Clay, which kept the Shells entire for many Ages. Yet were all these Shells, by reason of the

Length

*Length of Time* they had lain there, easily refoluble into a purely white Calx or Afh. *Fabius Columna* also obferves, That in the tophaceous Hills and Cliffs about *Andria* in *Apulia*, there are found various forts of Sea-fhells, both broken and whole, uncorrupt, and that have undergone no Change. And *Ovid in Metam. lib.* 15.

*Et procul à pelago Conchæ jacuere marinæ.*

I am also informed, by my learned and worthy Friend, Dr. *Tancred Robinfon*, That Signor *Settali* fhewed him, in his *Mufeum* at *Milan*, many *Turbens*, *Echini*, *Pearl-fhells*, (one with a Pearl in it) *Pectunculi*, and feveral other perfect Shells, which he himfelf found in the Mountains near *Genoa*, and afterwards, my faid Friend took notice also of feveral Beds of them himfelf, as he paffed over Mount *Cenis*, above fifty Leagues diftant from the Sea; he affures me, That many of the great Stones about the Buildings of *London*, are full of Shells, and Pieces of them. Moreover, my forementioned Friend, Mr. *Lhwyd*, fent me perfect *Efcallop* and Sea-Urchin Shells, exactly refembling the like Sea-fhells, both for Figure, Colour, Weight, and Confiftency; which he himfelf gathered up near *Oxford:* And hath lately fent me word, That he found at a Place called *Rungewell-Hill* in *Surrey*, at a Village called *Hedley*, three Miles South of *Epfham*,

at

at least twenty Miles distant from the Sea, some Fossil Oysters, which, by the Confession of Dr. *Lister* himself, were indeed true Oyster-shells, not petrified, nor much decayed: Nay, so like they were to Oysters newly taken out of the Sea, that a certain Person seeing them, mistook them for such, and opened one of them, expecting to find a living Fish therein.

Another the like Bed of Oyster-shells found in his own Ground, my worthy and ingenious Friend Mr. *Peter Burrell*, Merchant in *London*, gave me an Account of: Which take in his own Words.

'I have a Pit, wherein is a Bed or Vein
' of Oyster-shells: About two Foot under
' the Surface of the Earth they begin; and
' are from about a Yard to one Half-yard
' deep; and then succeeds a harsh Sand, that
' goes down two or three Yards deep, or
' more. In a Rivulet that runs through my
' Garden, half a Furlong from the foresaid
' Pit, there are of the same Shells great and
' small, not lying singly, but in great Clu-
' sters of great and small together, with the
' upper and lower Valves entire. When you
' open them, those that have not been ex-
' posed to the Air, or impair'd by the Wa-
' ter, have a Concavity within, and a hard
' Mossiness sticking to the Inside of each
' Shell. Those of the Pit are amassed as
' hard as a Rock; and where there are

K    ' not

'not little Veins of Sand mixt with them,
'they break into Pieces as big as a Half-
'Peck: But, when expos'd to the Weather,
'crumble like Murle, and are good to ma-
'nure Land, especially those which have
'least Sand mixed with them. It's excel-
'lent to bind Walls; only, upon Thaws
'in the Winter-time, it relaxes a little.

'I FIND, by digging in several Places,
'that there is a Layer or Bed of these Shells,
'which runs from North-West to South-
'East, two or three Furlongs in mine and
'my Neighbour's Grounds. We are 60
'Miles distant from the Sea, though but 5
'Miles from the River of *Thames*, on the
'Edge of *Surrey*, and lie high on the same
'Level with *Croyden*." So far Mr. *Burrell*.

THE Place where this Gentleman lives, is at *Beckenham*, near *Bromley* in *Kent*, ten Miles distant from *London*. He sent me Samples of the Oyster-shells, exactly agreeing with the Account he gives of them. They seem to have been the Shells of real and living Oysters, and to have suffered no greater Change than they must needs do from the Nature of the Earth and Sand they were lodged in, and from the Water com-mixt therewith. And the Lying of them in such a Bed, is a strong Argument to prove, that this Place was some time the Bottom of the Sea, which is a thing hard to be believed.

ANOTHER

Another Instance of such a Bed of Fossil Oyster-shells, I find in the *Philosophical Transactions*, N. 261. p. 485. communicated by Mr. *James Brewer*.

'These Oyster-shells were found and
'digged up near *Reading*, in *Berkshire*.
'The Circumference of the Place where
'they have been digged up, contains (as is
'judged) between five and six Acres of
'Land. The Foundation of these Shells is
'a hard, rocky Chalk. The Shells lie in a
'Bed of green Sand, upon a Level through
'the whole Circumference, as nigh as can
'possibly be judged. This *Stratum* of green
'Sand and Oyster-shells, is (as I measured
'it) nigh a Foot deep. Now, immediately
'above this Layer or *Stratum* of green Sand
'and Shells, is a Bed of bluish sort of Clay,
'very hard, brittle and rugged; They call
'it a pinny Clay, and is of no Use: This
'Bed or Layer of Clay, I found to be nigh
'a Yard deep; and immediately above it, is
'a *Stratum* of Fullers-Earth, which is nigh
'two Foot and a half deep. This Earth is
'often made use of by our Clothiers. And
'above this Earth, is a Bed or Layer of a
'clear, fine, white Sand, without the least
'Mixture of any Earth, Clay, &c. which
'is nigh seven Foot deep. Then, im-
'mediately above this, is a stiff red Clay,
'(which is the uppermost *Stratum*) of
'which we make our Tiles. The Depth
'of

'of this cannot conveniently be taken, it be-
'ing so high a Hill; upon the Top of which,
'is, and hath been dug, a little common
'Earth, about two Foot deep; and imme-
'diately under, appears this red Clay that
'they make Tiles withal. I dug (*saith he*)
'several whole Oysters, with both their
'Valves or Shells lying together, as Oysters
'before opened; in their Cavity was got in
'some of the forementioned green Sand.
'These Shells are so very brittle, that in
'digging them up, one of the Valves will
'frequently drop from its Fellow; but 'tis
'plainly to be seen, that they were united
'together, by placing the Shell that drops
'off to his Fellow Valve, which exactly cor-
'responds; but I dug up several that were
'entire, nay, some double Oysters, with all
'their Valves united." So far Mr. *Brewer*.

For, that Nature should form real Shells, without any Design of covering an Animal, is indeed so contrary to that innate *Prolepsis* we have of the Prudence of Nature, (that is, the Author of Nature) that without doing some Violence to our Faculties, we can hardly prevail with ourselves to believe it; and gives great Countenance to the Atheists Assertion, That Things were made or did exist by Chance, without Counsel or Direction to any end.

Add hereto, *Thirdly*, That there are other Bodies besides Shells found in the Earth, resembling

sembling the Teeth and Bones of some Fishes, which are so manifestly the very Things they are thought only to resemble, that it might be esteemed Obstinacy in any Man that hath viewed and considered them, to deny it. Such are the *Glossopetræ* dug up in *Malta* in such abundance, that you may buy them by Measure, and not by Tale: And also the Vertebres of Thornbacks, and other cartilagineous Fishes there found, and sold for Stones among the *Glossopetræ*, which have no greater Dissimilitude to the Teeth of a living *Shark*, and Vertebres of a *Thornback*, than lying so long in the Earth, as they must needs have done, will necessarily induce. Mr. *Doody* has in his Custody a petrify'd Lump of Fishes, on some of which the Scales themselves still remain. And if the very Inspection of these Bodies is not enough to convince any Man that they are no Stones, but real Teeth and Bones, *Fabius Columna* proves it by several strong Arguments. 1. Those Things which have a woody, bony, or fleshy Nature, by burning are changed first into a Coal, before they go into a *Calx* or Ashes: But those which are of a tophaceous or stony Substance, go not first into a Coal, but burn immediately into a *Calx* or Lime, unless by some Vitreous or Metallick Mixture they be melted. Now these Teeth being burnt, pass presently into a Coal, but the tophous Substance adhering to them, doth not so; whence it is clear, that they are of an osseous, and no stony Nature.

Next he shews, That they do not shoot into this Form after the Manner of Salts or Crystal, which I shall have Occasion farther to treat of by and by. Then he proves it from the Axiom, *Natura nihil facit frustra;* Nature makes nothing in vain. But these Teeth, were they thus formed in the Earth, would be in vain; for they could not have any Use of Teeth; as neither the Bones of supporting any Animal. Nature never made Teeth without a Jaw, nor Shells without an Animal Inhabitant, nor single Bones, no not in their own proper Element, much less in a strange one. Farther he argues, from the Difficulty or Impossibility of the Generation of *Glossopetræ* in such Places; because, among *Tophi* and Stones in those dry Places, there could not be found Matter fit to make them of. But granting that, he queries whether they were generated at first all of a sudden, or grew by little and little from small to great, as Animals Teeth, whose Form they imitate, do. If the first be said, he demands, Whether the *Tophus*, out of which they were extracted, were generated before, or after the Teeth were perfected? If it be said before, he asks, Whether there were a Place in it of the Figure and Magnitude of the Tooth, or did the Tooth make itself a Place? If the *Tophus* were concrete before, and without

out a Cavity, the vegetative Power of the Stone now in Birth, could not by Force make itself a Place in the hard and solid *Tophus*; or if it could, and did, the *Tophus* must needs be rent. Against the Production of these Bodies in a compact Earth or Stone, *Nic. Steno* argues thus: Things that grow, expanding themselves leisurely or slowly, may indeed lift up great Weights, and dilate the Chinks and Veins of Stones, as we see the Roots of Trees sometimes do; but yet while they do thus make room for themselves, they cannot but be often hindred by the Resistance of some hard Obstacle they meet with, as it happens to the Roots of Plants, which in hard Earth, being a thousand ways writhen and compressed, recede from the Figure, which otherwise in soft Land they are wont to retain; whereas these Bodies, whereof we are now discoursing, are all like one another, whether they be dug out of soft Earth, or cut out of Stones, or pluck'd off Animals. Wherefore they seem not to be at this Day produced in those Places where they are found, because (as we have said) those things which grow in compact Places are found strangely mishapen and irregular, which these are not: Nor was the Earth compacted when they were there produced for the same reason. *Columna* proceeds, If there were a Place before ready made in the *Tophus*, then was not that Fi-

gure excavated in the *Tophus* by the vegetative Nature of the Tooth itself; but the *Tophus*, by its own Nature and precedent Cavity, gave the Form to the Tooth. If the latter Part be chosen, and it be said, that the Stone by its vegetative Power grew by Degrees; it may be answered as before, that could not be, because the Hardness of the *Tophus* could not have yielded to the vegetative Force of the Tooth, but would rather have been rent or divided by it; or rather the *Tophus* itself must have vegetated, containing a Cavity or *Uterus* of the Shape of the Tooth, into which an osseous Humour, penetrating through the Pores, and filling the Cavity of the *Uterus*, must there have coagulated, and taken the Form thereof, as is observed in Stones that have their Original from a *Fluor*. That both Tooth and Case might vegetate together, he denies, because in all the Teeth which he had seen, the *Basis* or Root was found broken, and that not with an uniform Fracture, but different in every one. Which Argument is not to be slighted, for that it shews or proves, that there was no Vegetation in the case; because in all other figured Fossils it is observed, that they are never found mutilous, broken, or imperfect. Neither can it reasonably be said or believed, that these Roots or Teeth were by some chance broken within the *Tophi*, but rather, that when they were casually overwhelmed
and

and buried in that tophous Earth, they were broken off from the Jaws of the Animal in thofe Volutations, and fo in that manner mutilated. Againſt the Generation of theſe and the like Bodies in any hard Earth or Stone, *N. Steno* argues thus, That they are not at preſent produced in hard Earth, one may thence conjecture, that in all the Parts of ſuch Earth or Stone throughout, they are all found of the ſame Conſiſtence, and encompaſſed round on all Sides with that hard Matter: For if there were ſome of them produced anew at this preſent Day, the containing or ambient Bodies ought to give way to them while they are growing, which they cannot; and the Bodies themſelves that are now produced, would, without doubt, diſcover ſomething wherein they differed from thoſe that were generated of old. Another Argument to prove them to be true Teeth, and no Stones, he brings from their various Parts and Figures, which muſt elſe have been ſo wrought and formed in vain. The Tooth being not one homogeneous Body, but compounded of Parts of a different Conſtitution, there muſt in the Formation of it be made a various Election of Humours, one for the Root, one for the inner Part, one for the Superficies of it. Then for the Figures, Magnitude, Situation or Poſture, and Fitting of them; ſome are great, and broad, and almoſt triangular; others narrower and ſmaller,

ler, others very small and narrow, of a pyramidal Figure; some streight, some crooked, bending downwards, or toward the nether Side; some inclining toward the Left, others toward the Right Side; some serrate. with small Teeth, others with great Indentures, (which is observed in the lesser triangular ones) some smooth without any Teeth, as the narrow pyramidal ones. All which Things are observed in Sharks Teeth, not only by the learned Naturalists, but also by Fishermen and Mariners. The first Row of Teeth in these Animals hanging out of the Mouth, bend forward and downward; the second Row are streight, especially toward the Sides of the Mouth, where they are triangular and broad, the other Rows bend downward toward the inner Part of the Mouth. Thus far *Columna.

*Dissert. De Glossopetra.

THIS Argument is also made use of by Agostino Scilla: 'The Apophyses also, (saith 'he) or Processes, in the Glossopetræ, de-'monstrate their Original, were there no-'thing else; since they exactly answer to 'those in Sharks Teeth, whereby every 'Tooth is inserted into its Neighbour in the 'living Animal, with those Parts porous, 'and those spongious, that are so in the Tooth 'of the Fish. Nay, whereas Sharks Teeth 'are mortissed into one another, in such a 'manner, that a Man may easily tell, which 'belongs to which Side, which lie near the
' Throat,

' Throat, which near the Snout, which lie
' to the Right, which to the Left. And
' whereas, in a Shark's Jaw, the Teeth on the
' Left Side will not fit on the Right, nor those
' above serve below; so that upon seeing a
' Tooth, one may know which Side and
' what Jaw it belongs to." He hath observed every one of these things, in his *Gloffc-
petræ*, which punctually answer in every Part
to the several Ranks of the Teeth in a living
Shark.

*Fourthly,* If these formed Stones be indeed original Productions of Nature, in Imitation of Shells and Bones, how comes it to
pass, that there should be none found that
resemble any other natural Body, but the
Shells and Bones of Fishes only? Why should
not Nature as well imitate the Horns, Hoofs,
Teeth, or Bones of Land Animals, or the
Fruits, Nuts, and Seed of Plants? Now, my
learned Friend, Mr. *Edward Lhwyd*, above
mentioned, who hath been most diligent in
collecting, and curious in observing these Bodies, of any Man I know, or ever heard of,
tells me, That he never found himself, or
had seen in any Cabinet, or Collection, any
one Stone that he could compare to any part
of a Land Animal. As for such that do not
resemble any part of a Fish, they are either
Rock Plants, as the *Aftroites, Afteriæ tro-
chites, &c.* or do shoot into that Form, after
the

the manner of Salts and *Fluors*, as the *Belemnites* and *Selenites*.

*Fifthly*, Those that deny these Bodies to have been the Shells and Bones of Fishes, have given us no satisfactory Account of the manner of their Production. For that they do not shoot into that Form after the manner of Salts, may be proved by many Arguments. *First*, All Salts that shoot, their Crystals or Concretions are of one uniform Substance; as Signor *Agostino Scilla* clearly demonstrates. ' Salt (*saith he*) is Salt as well
' within as without; A Granate and a Topaz is a Granate and a Topaz throughout;
' Diamonds and Rubies are Diamonds and
' Rubies all over; they are Agregates of si-
' milar Particles which compose the whole
' Mass, be it greater, or be it less: Where-
' as, *Glossopetræ*, for Example, like all other
' vegetating Substances, are made up of va-
' rious and dissimilar Corpuscles, put toge-
' ther in such a manner, as is peculiarly sub-
' servient to the End for which they were
' made: Accordingly, the *Cortex* is of one
' Substance, the *Medulla* of another, and
' that lodged in proper Cells, the Root di-
' stinct from them both." In other Bodies that shoot, as the *Pyrites* and *Belemnites*, one may observe streight *Radii* or Fibres proceeding from one Center. *Secondly*, Did those Bodies shoot into these Figures, after the manner of Salts, it seems strange to me,

me, that two Shells should be so adapted together at the Heel, as to shoot out to the same Extension round, and the upper and nether Valve be of different Figure, as in natural Shells. *Thirdly*, Were these Bodies produced in the manner of saline Concretions, it's strange there should be such Varieties of them, and their Shapes so regular, and exactly circumscribed: So great a Diversity of Figures, arguing a greater Variety of Salts, or of their Modifications and Mixtures, than are likely to be found in Nature; and the Concretions of Salts never, that I have yet seen, appearing in that Regularity of Figure, and due Circumscription, as in these Bodies. This Argument, *Steno*, in his Discourse concerning these Bodies, improves and urges thus; ‘ Who can deny, that the hexaedrical
‘ Figure of Crystal, the Cubes of Marcasites,
‘ and the Crystals of Salts in Chymical Operations, and infinite other Bodies coagulating and crystallizing in a Fluid, have
‘ Figures much more ordinate than are
‘ those of *Scallops*, *Cockles*, and other Bivalves,
‘ and also *Periwinckles* and *Turbens*? Yet
‘ we see, in these simple Bodies, sometimes
‘ the Top of a solid Angle cut off; sometimes many of them, without any Order,
‘ sticking one to another; sometimes their
‘ Planes differing among themselves, in Magnitude and Situation; and many other
‘ Ways receding from their usual Figure:
‘ Which

'Which being so, how much greater and
'more notable Defects must there needs
'have been in Bodies that have a far more
'compound Figure, such as are those which
'imitate the Forms of Animals, if they were
'in like manner generated? Seeing, there-
'fore, in these Bodies, which are very much
'compounded, these Defects do seldom oc-
'curr, which in those other most simple Bo-
'dies, are very frequent; seeing there are
'no Defects observed in these compound Bo-
'dies, the like whereto are not in like man-
'ner seen in the Bodies of Animals: And
'seeing that wheresoever they are found,
'they are exceeding like both among them-
'selves, and to the Parts of Animals, it is
'very unlikely they should shoot into those
'Figures after the manner of Salts; but on
'the contrary, highly probable that they
'were originally the Parts of Animals; the
'Similitude of Conformation in their Pores,
'*Striæ*, Hinges, Teeth, Prominences, Threds,
'*&c.* almost necessarily inferring a Simili-
'tude of Original; which is an Argument
'of the Government of some Principle, su-
'periour to Matter figured and moved, in
'their Formations."

*Fourthly*, Were these Bodies nothing but Concretions of Salts, or saline Mixtures, it seems no less strange, that so many Liquors impregnated with all sorts of Salts and Mineral Juices, in all Proportions, having been

at

at one time or other induſtriouſly or accidentally expoſed to cryſtallize, and let ſtand long in Veſſels, there ſhould never have been found in them any ſuch Concretions. For if any had happened, we ſhould, doubtleſs, have heard of them, and the Obſervers would have improved ſuch an Experiment to the Production of the like Bodies, at their Pleaſure.

Two farther Arguments, to prove that theſe Bodies were not primary Productions of Nature, the forementioned Signor *Scilla* affords us. ' Nature (*ſays he*) ſometimes
' produced monſtrous and defective Things.
' An Animal ſometimes wants a Limb; A
' Tree is without ſome principal Branches;
' A Fruit may want ſome of its chiefeſt
' Parts. Yet ſtill we may obſerve, that Nature covers that Defect with a Skin, or
' Bark, or Rind, ſo that it never appears
' torn off, or rent, to the naked Eye, as it
' would, if it were torn off by a Hand, or
' cut off with a Knife. This is Nature's conſtant Courſe; which evidently ſhews, that
' *luſus Naturæ* (as theſe are erroneouſly
' called) were never produced in the Earth;
' ſince all the Bruiſes and Fractures which
' they have met with, are apparent, without
' any Diſguiſe to hide them; ſuch as Nature always employs to hide the Defects of her own irregular Productions."

BUT

But this may be solved, by saying, that these Fractures and Bruises happened to them, after they were perfectly formed, and, as I may so say, out of Nature's Hands; and so, Nature not concerned to cover their Defects.

*Secondly*, All the *Echini*, or other Land-Shells, which he found upon the *Calabrian* or *Messineze* Hills, or had been brought him from *Malta*, were bruised by a perpendicular Pressure, which he explains thus: ' The
' Crust of all *Echini* has two Centers, one
' directly opposite to the other; so that if
' they happened to lie in the liquid Mud, in
' such a manner as that the lowest Center
' was perpendicular to the *Horizon*, they
' were bruised so as not to lose their circu-
' lar Figure, only they were much compres-
' sed. If they lay on one Side, they were
' squeezed out of that Shape, and the Mem-
' branes of the Ligatures parted from each
' other variously, according to the Situation
' of these Shells in the Mud, at that Time.
' All which plainly shews, that as the Mud
' dried, the superincumbent Weight pressed
' perpendicularly upon the enclosed Bodies,
' which were then compressed together in
' that Posture they happened to be in; and
' were more or less compressed, according
' as the Mud got into their Cavities, in greater
' or lesser Quantities; and, as it dried, prop-
' ped them up on the Inside, against the
' Pres-

'Preſſure of the Matter in which they lay."' So far *Scilla*. By all which it appears, That theſe Shells were not formed in the Mud where they lay; but precedently in the Sea; and were, by extraordinary Tides or Inundations of the Sea, thrown up together with the Mud; which elſe would not have had thoſe Effects upon them.

As for what may be objected out of Sir *John Narborough*'s Voyage; 'That the Hills 'round about Port S. *Julian*, are full of 'Beds of great Oyſter-ſhells, which could 'not come (*ſaith he*) from the Sea or Flood; 'becauſe there is no ſuch Shell-Fiſh in 'thoſe Seas or Shores.' I anſwer, That there might be ſuch in the Seas thereabout, although it was not Sir *John*'s Hap to meet with them, or elſe they might be brought, by tempeſtuous Wind, from a great way off, as were thoſe Shells brought into *Calabria*, which we have before mentioned out of *Agoſtino Scilla*.

So I have finiſhed what I have to alledge, in Defence of the latter Part, That theſe formed Stones were ſometimes the real Shells or Bones of Fiſhes; I mean the figured Part of them.

I PROCEED now to ſet down, what may be objected againſt this Opinion, or offered in Aſſertion of the contrary; *viz.* That theſe Bodies are Primitive Productions of Na-

L ture,

ture, in Imitation of the Shells and Bones of Fishes.

Against the former Opinion we have been pleading for, it may be objected, That there follow such strange and seemingly absurd Consequences from it, as are hardly reconcileable to Scripture, nor indeed to sober Reason. As,

*First*, That the Waters must have covered the whole Earth, even the highest Mountains, and that for a long time, there being found of these Shells, not only in the most mountainous Parts of our Country, but in the highest Mountains in *Europe*, the *Appennine* and *Alps* themselves, and that not only scattered, but amassed in great Lumps, and lying thick in Beds of Sand, as we have before shewn. Now, this could hardly be the Effect of a short Deluge, which if it had carried any Shell-Fish so high, would in all Likelihood have scattered them very thin. These Beds and Lumps of them necessarily inferring, that they must have bred there, which is a Work of Time. Whereas the general Deluge, from the Beginning to the End, lasted but ten Months and thirteen Days: That is, from the seventeenth Day of the second Month of the six hundredth Year of *Noah*'s Life, when the forty Days Rain began, till the first Day of the first Month of the six hundred and first Year thereof, when the Waters were dried up from off the Earth.

Neither

Neither is it less repugnant to Reason than Scripture; for if the Waters stood so high above the Earth, for so long a time, they must, by reason of their Confluence, be raised as high above the Sea too. But what is now become of this huge Mass of Waters, equal to six or seven Oceans; nay, to twenty or more? May not the Stoicks here set in, and help us out at a dead Lift? The Sun and Moon, say they, might possibly sup it all up. Yea, but we cannot allow Time enough for that; for according to the moderate Draughts they take now-a-days, one Ocean would suffice to water them many Ages, unless perchance, when they were young and hot, they might need more Drink. But to be serious, I have no Way to answer this Objection, but by denying that there are any Beds or great Lumps and Masses of these formed Stones to be found near the Tops of the *Alps*, or other high Mountains; but yet there might be some particular Shells scattered there by the general Deluge. Unless we should say, that those Mountains, where such Shells are found, were anciently depressed Places, and afterward raised up by Earthquakes, or subterraneous Fires. Another thing there is as difficult to give an Account of, as of the Shells getting up to the Tops of Mountains; that is, of those several Beds or Floors of Earth and Sand, &c. one above another, which are observed in broken Mountains: For one can-

cannot easily imagine, whence these Floors or Beds, in the Manner of *strata super strata* (as the Chymists speak) should come, but from the Sediments of great Floods, which how or whence they could bring so great a Quantity of Earth down, when there was but little Land above the Sea, I cannot see. And one would likewise be apt to think, that such a Bed of Sands, with plenty of Cockle-Shells intermixt, as we mentioned before in the Mountain near *Bononia* in *Italy*, must have been sometimes the Bottom of the Sea. But before one can give a right Judgment of these Things, one must view the Mountains where such Layers and Beds of Earth and Shells are found; for perchance they may not be elevated so high above the present Surface of the Sea, as one would judge by the Descriptions of them. 'Tis true (says my worthy Friend Dr. *Tancred Robinson*) *that some Shells might have been scatter'd up and down the Earth by Incampments of Armies, by the Inhabitants of Cities and Towns, whereof there are now no Remains.* Monsieur Loubere, *the late* French *Envoy to Siam, affirms, That the Monkeys and Apes, at the Cape of Good Hope, are almost continually carrying Shells and other Marine Bodies from the Sea-Side up to the Mountains; yet this will not solve the Matter, nor give any satisfactory Account, why these perfect Shells are dispers'd up and down the Earth, in all Climates and Regions,*

Regions, in the deep Bowels of vast Mountains, where they lie as regularly in Beds, as they do at the Bottom of the Sea. This to me, I confess, is at present unaccountable.

Secondly, It would hence follow, That many Species of Shell-Fish are lost out of the World; which Philosophers hitherto have been unwilling to admit, esteeming the Destruction of any one Species a dismembring of the Universe, and rendring it imperfect; whereas they think the Divine Providence is especially concerned to secure and preserve the Works of the Creation: And that it is so, appears, in that it was so careful to lodge all Land-Animals in the Ark at the Time of the general Deluge. The Consequence is proved, in that, among these petrified Shells, there are many Sorts observed, which are not at this Day, that we know of, any where to be found. Such are a whole *Genus* of *Cornua Ammonis*, which some have supposed to be *Nautili* (to which indeed they are nearly a-kin, but yet differ from them so much, that they ought to be accounted a distinct subaltern *Genus*, as I shall shew out of Dr. *Plot* by and by) which there have not any been seen either cast ashore, or raked out of the Sea, at any time, that ever I heard of. Nay, my very learned and honoured Friend Dr. *Lister* proceeds farther, and saith, That when he particularly examined some of our *English* Shores for Shells, and also the fresh

Waters and the Fields, that he did never meet with any one of those *Species* of Shells found at *Adderton* in *Yorkshire*, *Wansford-Bridge* in *Northamptonshire*, and about *Gunthorp* and *Beavoir-Castle*, &c. any where else, but in their respective Quarries. What can we say to this? Why, it is possible that many Sorts of Shell-Fish may be lodged so deep in the Seas, or on Rocks so remote from the Shores, that they may never come to our Sight.

*Thirdly*, It follows also, that there have been Shell-Fish in these cold Northern Seas, of greater Bulk and Dimensions than any now living; I do not say in these, but in the most Southernly and *Indian*, viz. *Cornua Ammonis*, of two Foot Diameter, and of Thickness answerable.

To this I answer, That there are no petrified Shells that do in Bigness much exceed those of the natural Shell-Fish found in our Seas, save the *Cornua Ammonis* only, which I suspect to have never been, nor had any Relation to any Shells of Fishes; or to imitate or resemble them, at least some of them. Against this Assertion it may be objected, That there are found in *England* many *Pectinites* bigger than any Shell-Fish of that Kind which our Seas now afford. And that there are no *Nautili*, or other testaceous Fishes with us, comparable in Bigness to that *Nautilus* Stone of twenty eight Pound found by Mr. *Waller* at *Keinsham*. To which I answer, fwer, That there may be Shell-Fish in our Seas, that do not at all, or very feldom appear, greater than we are aware of. I myfelf, in Company with Mr. *Willughby*, in the Streight between the *Isle* and *Calf* of *Man*, took up among the tall *Fuci* growing thick upon the Rocks there, two or three of thofe large *Echini Marini*, or *Sea-Urchins*, as big as a Man's two Fifts, the Shells whereof we never found caft up upon the Shores of *England*, nor ever heard that any Man elfe did. So that I queftion not, but there are lodged among the Rocks, and in the deeper Places of the Sea, remote from the Shores, many different Sorts of Shell-Fish, and excelling in Magnitude thofe that are commonly found or known. And like enough it is, that after the Flood there were many Places deferted, and thrown up by the Sea, and become dry Land, which had been Sea before; which muft needs be replete with thefe Bodies. As for the *Nautili*, they are much different from thefe *Cornua Ammonis*: For the *Nautili*, at leaft all the Species of them known to us, are (as Dr. *Plot* well obferves) extravagantly broad at the Mouth, and have not more than two other fmall Turns at the moft, whereas the Turns of the *Ophiomorphites* are proportionable one to another; and in Number many times four or five, and fometimes fix, if we may believe *Aldrovand*. And there are *Nautili Lapidei*, which do as

L 4 nearly

nearly resemble the *Nautilus* Shells, as any other *Cochlites* do their respective Prototypes, as Mr. *Lhwyd* assures me he had observed many in *Museums*. And the learned and ingenious Mr. *Richard Waller*, then Secretary to the *Royal Society*, in a Letter to me dated *Febr.* 4.---87. writes, That he had been lately at *Keinsham* in *Somersetshire*, and making a Search after the *Cornua Ammonis*, found one of the true *Nautilus* Shape, covered in some Places with a shelly Incrustation, with the Diaphragms to be seen to the Center of the *Volutæ*, and in each Diaphragm, the Hole by which they communicate one with another, by a String or Gut in the Fish. This was of a very hard Stone and large Size, weighing at least twenty eight Pound, though some part was broken off. Another Argument that they have no Relation to the common *Nautili*, is, that they break into Pieces, somewhat resembling Vertebres, as I was first advised by the fore-remembred Mr. *Lhwyd*, and have since noted myself. I also received from that very ingenious and inquisitive Gentleman, happy in making natural Discoveries, Mr. *William Cole* of *Bristol*, such an Account of a Sort or two of these *Ophiomorphous* Bodies, as is enough to stagger any Man's Belief, if not utterly to overthrow his Opinion of their owing their Original to any Sea Shell, which take in his Words: *Among others of this Kind of Bodies which I have*

have observed; I shall instance in one, which can be reduced to none but the Ophiomorphites, which I found growing between the thin Plates of a kind of brittle blue Slate in large Rocks, some a Furlong within the full Sea-Mark, and in some where the Water comes not at highest Tides, only in great Storms, when the Waves break, it is dash'd sometimes against them, being forced up by the Winds; which being broken with a convenient Tool, will shiver all into very thin Plates; between which I have found in abundance of those Stones, but as brittle as the Slate in which they grew; and of the same Consistence; but so thin, that the broadest, being about four Inches, are not so thick as a Half-Crown Piece, some not half an Inch broad, were as thin as a Groat, and so proportionably up to the largest, covered with a Superficies as thin, and exactly of the Colour of Silver-foil: And where the Sea-water washeth them, and they are exposed to the Sun and Wind when the Tide is gone, they are tarnished, and appear of a Gold, Purple, Blue and Red; as any thing on which Silver-foil is laid, being exposed a considerable time to the Sun, Wind, and Weather, will do. These have the same Spiral Figures, and as regular as the other Serpent-Stones, and being taken off with a Knife, leave the same Impressions on both Sides of the Slate.

In some such Rocks of Slate, but much harder, I found some of those Stones of another Kind,

*Kind;* thick in Proportion to their Breadth, from an Inch to twenty eight Inches broad; the broadeſt one was at the great End (on which ſome Authors have fabulouſly reported the Head to grow) ſix Inches thick; all of them covered over with a white Scale, which will be taken off, one Coat under another, as Pearls, or the Shells of ſome Fiſhes. I ſaw ſome Impreſſions as big as the Fore-Wheel of a *Chariot,* &c. What ſhall we ſay to this? Were there ever any Shell-Fiſh in ours, or other Seas, as broad as a Coach-Wheel? others as thin as a Groat? What is become of all this kind of *Ophiomorphite* Shell-Fiſh? And yet (which is ſtrange) both theſe Kinds, by Mr. *Cole*'s Deſcription, ſeem to have been covered with Shells.

By what I have ſaid concerning theſe *Ophiomorphous* Stones not to have been *Nautili,* I would not be thought to reflect upon, or detract from the Veracity or Exactneſs of the Obſervations of Dr. *Robert Hook,* whom for his Learning and deep Inſight into the Myſteries of Nature, I deſervedly honour. I queſtion not, but he found in the *Keinſham Ophiomorphites,* perfect Diaphragms of a very diſtinct Subſtance from that which filled the Cavities, and exactly of that kind which covered the Outſide, being for the moſt part whitiſh, or Mother of Pearl coloured. Mr. *Waller* fore-mentioned, atteſts the ſame, writing in his Letter to me of *Febr.* 4. 1687.

that

that in the ordinary Snake-Stones there, the shelly Diaphragms were very visible. In this respect they do resemble *Nautili*; though for their Figure they are much different, and of a distinct *Genus*. I never broke any of the *Keinsham* Stones, but of those found about *Whitby* in *Yorkshire* many; but could not observe in them any Shell-like Diaphragms, only they broke into such Pieces as I mentioned before. And my dear and much honoured Friend, Dr. *Tancred Robinson*, writes me, That he had broken several *Cornua Ammonis*, but could never find any Diaphragms or Valves in them, though he confesseth Mr. *Woodward* shew'd him one with such, in his curious Collection of Petrifactions. So that these Diaphragms are not to be found in all the Sorts of them. But if they be found in some, it is a strong Presumption, that they were at first in all, however they came to disappear.

Upon farther Consideration, I find Reason to agree with Dr. *Hook*, and other Naturalists, That these *Cornua Ammonis* are of the same *Genus* with *Nautili*, and differ only in Species. But yet these *Species* are subaltern *Genera*, each having divers Species under it.

In fine, these *Ophiomorphous* Stones do more puzzle and confound me, than any other of the formed Stones whatsoever, because, by Dr. *Hook*'s Description of those of *Keinsham*, they seem to have been, or to

owe

owe their Original to Shells; and yet there is nothing like them appears at this Day in our or any other Seas, as far as I have seen, heard, or read.

To this may be anſwered, as *Scilla* doth to the like Objection againſt the *Malteſe* Shells, &c. "And whereas it is objected, "(*ſaith he*) that great Quantities of Shells "are found in *Malta* which are foreign to "thoſe Seas, that is of no Force, ſince it is "well known, that every Eaſterly and South-"Eaſterly Wind throws whole Beds of beau-"tiful Shells upon the *Calabrian* Coaſt, none "of which Kind of Shell-Fiſh are taken by "Fiſhermen in thoſe Seas." The ſame Anſwer he returns to the Objection of the *Echini Spatagi*, being very rarely ſeen about *Malta*, and yet that great Numbers of the Shells of that *Species* of *Echinitæ* have been found there, *viz.* That he himſelf, in leſs than an Hour's time, hath taken them up by hundreds in the Port of *Meſſina*, where that ſort of Shell-Fiſh is as rarely to be found as at *Malta*.

IN like manner, theſe *Cornua Ammonis*, though altogether Strangers to our Seas, might as well be brought hither by Force of Winds or Streſs of Weather, much more than by the general Deluge, in which the Fountains of the great Deep were broken up. Eſpecially if we conſider, that ſeveral *Eaſt-India* Fruits have been brought over the
vaſt

vast Ocean, and cast upon the Western Islands of *Scotland*.

*Thirdly*, A second Argument to prove these formed Stones never to have been Shells, Dr. \* *Plot* affords us, 'Because that e-
'ven those Shells, which so exactly represent
'some sorts of Shell-Fish, that there can be no
'Exception upon the account of Figure, but
'that they might formerly have been Shells
'indeed, at some Places are found only with
'one Shell and not the other. Thus in *Cowley*
'*Common* [in *Oxfordshire*] we meet only with
'the gibbous, not the flat Shell of the petri-
'fied *Oyster*, and so of the *Escallop-Stones* in
'the Quarries near *Shotover*; which if they
'had once been the Shells of *Oysters* and *Escal-*
'*lops*, had scarce been thus parted." To this
I answer, That this Argument is not necessarily conclusive, because there may possibly be some reason of it, though we know it not, nor can easily imagine any. The like Answer may be returned to his next Argument.

\* *Hist. Nat. Oxf. p. 117.*

*Thirdly*, 'Because (saith the Doctor) I
'can by no means satisfy myself, how it
'should come to pass, that in case these Bo-
'dies had once been moulded in Shells,
'some of the same Kind should be found in
'Beds, as the *Conchites* at *Langley*, *Charl-*
'*ton*, *Adderbury*, and others scattered, as at
'*Glypton*, and *Teynton*, and so the *Ostra-*
'*cites* at *Shotover* and *Cowley*. Nor how it
'should

"should fall out, that some of these *Bi-*
"*valves* should always be found with their
"Shells separate, as the *Ostracites* and *Pe-*
"*ctines*: And others always closed toge-
"ther, as the *Conchites* in all Places I have
"yet seen.

*Fourthly,* "Because many of these formed
"Stones seem now to be *in fieri*, (which
"is the Doctor's next Argument) as the
"*Selenites* at *Shotover* and *Hampton-gay,* the
"*Conchites* of *Glympton* and *Cornwall,* ma-
"ny of which were of a perfect Clay, and
"others of Stone, &c." As for the *Sele-*
*nites,* I grant them to have been *in fieri,*
because they are formed after the manner
of Salts by Shooting or Crystallization; but
concerning the Clay Cockles, I say with
the Civilians, *ampliandum.* Since the publishing of this Treatise, happening to read
Dr. *Nicol. Steno*'s Discourse concerning these
Bodies, in his *Description* of a *Shark's Head,*
I met with a very plausible Solution of
this Argument or Objection. *First,* he gives
us the History of these Bodies, or his Observations concerning them; of which these
following are two: 1. That in *Argilla,* which
some *English,* Potters-Earth, and we may render a fat Clay, he had taken Notice that
there were Plenty of them on the *Superficies*
of the Earth, but within the Earth but a few.
2. That in the same *Argilla,* the deeper you
descend downward, the more tender those

Bodies

Bodies are, so that some of them at any the least Touch fall into Powder: And they also that were on the *Superficies*, almost all of them were without much ado reduced into a white Powder. Now (saith he) seeing in such kind of Earth, by how much deeper those Bodies lie, by so much the softer they are, and do less bear the Touch, the Earth is so far from producing them, that it doth rather destroy them. Neither is there any reason to think, that they are therefore softer, because they are not yet arrived at their Perfection, or come to Maturity: For those Things that are soft upon that account, while they are in generating, have their Parts united to one another, as it were by a kind of Glue (as is seen in the tender Shells of Pine-Nuts or Almonds) but these Bodies, being deprived and destitute of all Glue, easily moulder to Dust. Nor is it any Objection against our Opinion, that on the Surface of the Earth their Number seems to increase, for that is owing to Rains washing away the intermediate Earth; but rather their Consistence when they are on the *Superficies*, being tender and easily crumbled into Dust, doth demonstrate, that their Destruction, begun in the Earth, was interrupted by the Intervention of the Rain. But to give these Arguments their Due, tho' they be not demonstrative Proofs, yet they inferr a great Degree of Probability, and shrewdly urge and shake the contrary Opinion.

THE

The other Arguments the Doctor alledges, admit a plausible Solution, excepting such as we have already touched, and given as good an Answer to, as either the Matter will admit, or we were able to give.

To the first, 'That there are found Stones resembling Shell-Fish that stick to Rocks:' I answer, That many of them might, by Accident, be rubb'd off the Rocks they stick to, or thrust off by Birds insinuating their Bills between the Shell and Rock, to feed upon their Meat; but by what means soever it be, that they are sometimes broken off, the Matter of Fact is certain; for we find many *Patellæ* cast upon the Shores by the working of the Sea; Why then might they not be brought up by the Flood?

To the second, Why might not the Bones of Whales, Sea-Horses, all squamose Fishes, the great Shells of the *Buccina, Murices, Conchæ Veneris*, and *Solenes*, and almost all the crustaceous kind, as *Crabs* and *Lobsters*, &c. as well have been brought up and left behind by the Flood, and afterward petrified, as any of the testaceous kind? I answer, Of the great *Buccina, Murices* and *Conchæ Veneris*, there are very few or none found in our Seas: It may be there are of them in the Mountains and Quarries of the *Indies*, were any Man so curious as to search them out: Though it's likely but few, because being great Things, easy to be seen, and that Part
of

of the World having been fully peopled soon after the Flood, their Beauty might invite the Inhabitants to search them out, and gather them up. But, *Secondly*, Those other Kinds may possibly be less durable, and more apt to be wrought upon, to moulder, decay, and be dissolved in time by the Weather, Rains and Moisture of the Earth, or were not so susceptive of petrifying Juices.

The Third Argument is already answered in the precedent Discourse.

To the Fourth Argument, as to what concerns the *Selenites*, *Astroites* and *Belemnites*, we have answered already. That the Species of *Brontiæ* cannot be the petrified Shells of *Echini Spatagi*, the Arguments the Doctor alledges out of *Aristotle* and *Rondeletius* do not evince. For though in some Seas they may be πελάγοι καὶ σπάνιοι, yet in others are they plentiful enough. In our own Seas, at *Llandwyn* in the *Isle of Anglesey*, we may reasonably conjecture, they are more plentiful than the common *Echini* any where with us; because we found more of their Shells cast up there on the Shore, than of the *Echini* in any Shore about *England*: Nay, so common are they there, that even the Vulgar have taken Notice of them, and imposed a Name upon them, calling them *Mermaids Heads*. And tho' their Bristles or Prickles were but small, yet were they not few or thin set, as *Rondeletius* faith.

How the Snake-Stones about *Huntly-Nab* in *Whitby* in *Yorkshire* came to be included in Globular or Lenticular Stones, is not difficult to make out; for the Cliffs thereabout being Allom-Stone or Mine, wherein these Snake-Stones lie, the Sea in Spring-Tides and tempestuous Weather undermines and throws down Part of the Shore or Cliffs, which by the Fall break in Pieces, and the *Ophiomorphous* Stone being harder than the rest of the Cliff, is broken off from it by the Fall, or its Volutation in the Sea afterward, with some Part of the Cliff or Allom-Stone sticking to each Side of it where it is concave, and by reason of its Figure and *Striæ*, cannot easily part from it.

*Lastly*, To dissemble nothing, I have myself observed some Cockle-Stones to have seemingly different Impressions or *Striæ* upon the same *Superficies*; which *Phænomenon* it is very hard to give an Account of. I have also observed a large Stone almost as hard as Marble, that was so marked every where throughout with the Impressions of Cockles and their *Striæ*, so crossing one another in every Part of it, that if it were nothing but Shells amassed together by a stony Cement, those Shells must have, before their Concretion, been broken into infinite small Pieces or Fragments, scarce any remaining entire; which I do not see how any Floods, or Working of the Sea, could possibly effect.

So

So I have finished what I had to say concerning this supposed Effect of the *Deluge*, the Bringing in of Shells, and Scattering them all over the dry Land. But yet I must not dismiss this Particular, till I have said something to an Objection that presently occurrs to any one who considers this Matter. The Waters of the Flood having been supplied, partly by Rains, partly by the Breaking up of the Fountains of the great Deep, and not by an Irruption or Inundation of the Sea, how could any Sea-Shells at all be brought in by it?

To this I answer, That the great Deep communicates with the Sea; and the Waters rising up out of the subterraneous Abyss, the Sea must needs succeed, else would there have been an empty Space left in the Middle of the Earth, so that the Shell-Fish might as well come in this Way from the Bottom of the Sea, as by an Inundation: In like manner, as the Fish in the Lake of *Carniola*, called the *Zirchnitzer Sea*, do descend annually under Ground through many great Holes in the Bottom, and return again by the same Holes. To all this I might add, that into the Lands near the Skirts of the Sea, and lower Hills, these Shells might in part be brought by particular Floods, of which many we read of, and more possibly than are recorded in any History, may have happened since the general *Deluge*. Hence the chief Champions of the Opinion of *Mock-Shells* are not difficult to grant, that in some Countries, and particularly along the Shore of the *Mediterranean-Sea*, there may all manner of Shells be found promiscuously included in the Rocks or Earth, and at good Distances too from the Sea. Which are the Words of Dr. *Lister*, repeated and approved by Dr. *Plot*. But this will not serve their Turn; for we have before proved, that in the middle Part, and near the Center of our own Country, at a great Distance from the Sea, *viz*. in *Oxfordshire*, there are found not only Shell-like Stones, but real Shells, or Mock-Shells, (as some esteem them) for Figure, Colour, Weight, Consistency, or any other Accident, not to be distinguished from true Shells; and that not such as have been accidentally scattered there, but digg'd out of the Ground in Plenty, and of Fishes that are rarely found in our Seas: Patterns whereof were sent me by my ingenious Friend Mr. *Lhwyd*, who, I hope, will, e'er long, gratify the Curious, by publishing a general Catalogue of all the *formed Stones* found in *England*, and his Remarks upon them.

And I have likewise proved by good Authority, that beyond the Seas, in high Mountains, and many Leagues distant from the Sea too, there have been Beds of real Shells. I might have added *Sharks* Teeth, or *Glossopetræ*, as both *Goropius Becanus*, and *Georgius Agricola*, testify; if not in Beds, yet plentifully

tifully dispers'd in the Earth. There are several Medical Histories extant (as Dr. *Tancred Robinson* informs me) of perfect Shells found in Animal Bodies, in whose Glands they were originally formed, which is a considerable Objection, not easily to be removed.

Dr. *Woodward*, and others, suppose these Shells, and other Bodies, to be disposed and ranged in the Earth according to their specifick Gravity; and for the solving or giving an Account of this *Phænomenon*, hath advanced a strange and bold *Hypothesis*.

'During the Time of the Deluge,
' (*saith he*) whilst the Water was out upon,
' and covered the terrestrial Globe, all the
' Stone and Marble of the *Antediluvian*
' Earth, all the Metals of it, all Mineral Con-
' cretions, and, in a word, all Fossils what-
' soever, that had obtained any Solidity,
' were totally dissolved, and their constituent
' Corpuscles all disjoined, their Cohæsion
' perfectly ceasing. That the said Corpuscles
' of these solid Fossils, together with the Cor-
' puscles of those which were not before so-
' lid, such as Sand, Earth, and the like; as
' also Animal Bodies, and Parts of Animal
' Bones, Teeth, Shells; Vegetables, and
' Parts of Vegetables, Trees, Shrubs, Herbs;
' and to be short, all Bodies whatsoever, that
' were either upon the Earth, or that consti-
' tuted the Mass of it, if not quite down to
' the Abyss, yet, at least, to the greatest

'Depth we ever dig: I say, all these were
'assumed up promiscuously into the Water,
'and sustained in it in such manner, that the
'Water and Bodies in it together, made up
'one common confused Mass.

'That, at length, all the Mass that was,
'thus borne up in the Water, was again pre-
'cipitated, and subsided towards the Bot-
'tom: That this Subsidence happened ge-
'nerally, and as near as possibly could be
'expected in so great a Confusion, according
'to the Laws of Gravity: That Matter, Bo-
'dy, or Bodies, which had the greatest Quan-
'tity, or Degree of Gravity, subsiding first,
'in Order, and falling lowest: That which
'had the next, or a still lesser Degree of
'Gravity, subsiding next after, and settling
'upon the precedent, and so on in their se-
'veral Courses: That which had the least
'Gravity not sinking down till last of all,
'settling at the Surface of the Sediment, and
'covering all the rest: That the Matter
'subsiding thus, formed the *Strata* of Stone,
'of Marble, of Cole, and the rest; of which
'*Strata* lying one upon another, the terre-
'strial Globe, or at least as much of it as is
'ever displayed to View, doth mainly con-
'sist: The *Strata* being arranged in this
'Order, meerly by the Disparity of the Mat-
'ter of which they consisted, as to Gravity,
'..... and there being Bodies of quite dif-
'ferent Kinds, Natures and Constitutions,
'that

'that are nearly of the same specifick Gra-
'vity, it thence happened, that Bodies of
'quite different Kinds subsided at the same
'instant, and fell together into, and compo-
'sed the same *Stratum:* That, for this Rea-
'son, the Shells of Cockles, Escallops, Peri-
'winkles, and the rest, which have a greater
'Degree of Gravity, were enclosed and
'lodged in the *Strata* of Stone, Marble, and
'the heavier Kinds of terrestrial Matter; the
'lighter Shells not sinking down till after-
'wards, and so falling among the lighter
'Matter, as Chalk, and the like, *&c.*" This
being the Main of his *Hypothesis*; for the
rest I referr to the Book.

I shall not at present examine it, but re-
spite that Task till the Publication of his larger Work, wherein we expect it will be confirmed, and all Difficulties cleared up. I
shall only add, that we have sufficient Authorities to prove, That that *Phænomenon*, for
the solving whereof, I suspect he invented
this *Hypothesis*, *viz.* That these Bodies are
arranged and lodged in the Beds, according
to their specifick Gravity, is not generally
true; but that they are often mingled heavy
with Light in the same Bed or *Stratum.*

Reflecting upon the Length of this
Discourse concerning the Original of these
Bodies, I am suspicious that the vulgar and
inconsiderate Reader will be ready to demand,

mand, *What needs all this ado? To what purpose so many Words about so trivial a Subject? What Reference hath the Consideration of Shells and Bones of Fishes petrified to Divinity?* Wherefore I shall, in a few Words, shew the great Importance of this Disquisition, concerning formed Stones, and the Determination of their Original.

For, *First*, If we adhere to their Opinion, who hold them to have been original Productions of Nature, in imitation only of the Shells and Bones of Fishes; we put a Weapon into the *Atheist*'s Hands, affording him a strong Argument, to prove, that even Animals themselves are casual Productions, and not the Effects of Counsel or Design. For, to what End are these Bodies curiously figured and adorned? If for no other, but to exhibit such a Form, for the Ornament of the Universe, or to gratify the Curiosity of Man; these are but general Ends: Whereas the Parts of every Species of Body are formed and fitted to the particular Uses and Conveniences of that Body. And if Nature would delineate or imprint Figures upon Bodies, only to be Spectacles to Man, one would think it should not have made choice of those of the Shells and Bones of Fishes, but rather of such as were absolutely new and different from any frequently seen, or belonging to Animals; which serve rather to amuse than delight him. But, *Secondly*, We find in the

Earth,

Earth, not only Stones formed in Imitation of Shells, but real Shells, Teeth and Bones of Fishes, or Bodies so like them, that they are not to be distinguished by Figure, Texture, Colour, Weight, or any other Accident. Now, what greater Argument can the Atheist desire, to prove, that the Shells of Fishes were never designed by any provident Efficient for their Defence, or their Bones for the sustaining of their Bodies, but that the Fish and Shell containing it, and the Bones sustaining it, did casually concurr; than that there should be real Shells produced without any Fish in them, and that in dry Places, where no Fish ever did or could breed, or indeed live; and real Fish-Bones, where there never was nor could be any Fish?

Doth it not then concern a Divine to be acquainted with this Objection against the Bodies of Animals being the Effects of Counsel and Design, and provided with an Answer to it. For my part, I must needs confess, that this Argument weighs so with me, whether from that innate *Prolepsis* myself, and I think most other Men, have of the Prudence of Nature in all its Operations, or from mine own observing that in all other things, it acts for Ends, that it is alone sufficient to preponderate all the Arguments for the contrary Opinions, tho' I acknowledge them to be of great Force, and hard to be answered; and to incline, or rather constrain

me

me to allow, that these Bodies were either real Bones and Shells of Fishes, or owe their Figure to them. I cannot (to use the Words of *F. Columna*) prevail with myself to believe, that Nature ever made Teeth without a Jaw, or Shells without an Animal Inhabitant, or single Bones, no not in their own proper Element, much less in a strange one. Who even of the Vulgar, beholding any considerable Part of an Animal which he sees not the Use of, is not apt presently to ask what it serves for, as by that innate *Prolepsis* I mentioned before, presuming it was not made in vain, but for some End and Use. Suppose any of us should find in the Earth the complete *Skeleton* of a Man, he must be as credulous as the Atheist, if he could believe that it grew there of itself, and never had Relation to any Man's Body. Why then should we think that the entire *Skeletons* of Fishes, found sometimes in the Earth, had no other Original? nor ever were any Part of living Fishes.

*Secondly*, If we choose and embrace the contrary Opinion, *viz.* That these Bodies were the real Shells and Bones of Fishes, or owe their Figures to them, we shall find that this also is urged with many and almost insuperable Difficulties, the Principal of which I have already produced, and shall here omit, repeating only two that referr to Divinity.

1. These

1. THESE Bodies being found dispersed all over the Earth, they of the contrary Opinion demand how they come there? If it be answered, That they were brought in by the general Deluge, in Contradiction thereto they argue thus: If these Stones were found scattered singly and indifferently all the Earth over, there might be indeed some reason to imagine that they were brought in by the Flood; but being found in some particular Places only, either lying thick in great Beds of Sand and Gravel, or amassed together in huge Lumps, by a stony Cement, such Beds must in all Likelihood have been the Effect of those Animals breeding there, for a considerable time; whereas the Flood, continued upon the Earth but ten Months and thirteen Days, as I have before shewn; and, yet there are found of these Bodies upon very high Mountains, not excepting the *Appennine* and *Alps* themselves. Whence they conclude, that they were neither brought in by the Flood, nor bred during the Flood, but some other way produced. For if they were the Shells of Fishes, or their Bones, the Water must needs have covered the whole Earth, even the Mountains themselves, for a much longer Time than is consistent with the Scripture History of the Flood, and therefore we must seek some other Original of these Bodies.

If we stick to the Letter of the Scripture History of the Creation, that the Creation of Fishes succeeded the Separation of Land and Sea, and that the six Days wherein the World was created, were six Natural Days, and no more; it is very difficult to return a satisfactory Answer to this Objection: I shall therefore only add a Conjecture of my own, and that is, That possibly, at the first Creation, the whole Earth was not all at once uncovered, but only those Parts whereabout *Adam* and the other Animals were created, and the rest gradually afterwards, perchance not in many Years; during which time these Shell-Fish might breed abundantly all the Sea over, the Bottom whereof being elevated and made dry Land, the Beds of Shell-Fish must necessarily be raised together with it.

This Conjecture hath no sufficient Ground to support it, and therefore I do not insist upon it. But, truly, if it had, I see not any better Account could be given of all the *Phænomena* of them, than from thence might.

2. It will hence follow, that many Species of Animals have been lost out of the World, which Philosophers and Divines are unwilling to admit, esteeming the Destruction of any one *Species* a Dismembring of the Universe, and rendring the World imperfect; whereas they think the Divine Providence is especially concerned, and solicitous to secure and preserve the Works of
the

the Creation. And truly so it is, as appears, in that it was so careful to lodge all Land Animals in the Ark at the Time of the general Deluge; and in that, of all Animals recorded in Natural Histories, we cannot say that there hath been any one Species lost, no not of the most infirm, and most exposed to Injury and Ravine. Moreover, it is likely, that as there neither is nor can be any new Species of Animals produced, all proceeding from Seeds at first created; so Providence, without which one individual Sparrow falls not to the Ground, doth in that manner watch over all that are created, that an entire Species shall not be lost or destroyed by any Accident. Now, I say, if these Bodies were sometimes the Shells and Bones of Fish, it will thence follow, that many *Species* have been lost out of the World: As for Example, those *Ophiomorphous* ones, whose Shells are now called *Cornua Ammonis*, of which there are many Species, none whereof, at this Day, appear in our or other Seas, so far as I have hitherto seen, heard or read. To which I have nothing to reply, but that there may be some of them remaining some where or other in the Seas, though as yet they have not come to my Knowledge. For though they may have perished, or by some Accident been destroyed out of our Seas, yet the Race of them may be preserved and continued still in others. So though Wolves

and

and Bevers, which we are well assured were sometimes native of *England*, have been here utterly destroyed and extirpated out of this Island, yet there remain Plenty of them still in other Countries.

By what hath been said concerning the Nature and Original of Stones, I hope it may appear, that this is no idle and unnecessary Discourse, but very momentous and important: And this Subject, as mean as it seems, worthy the most serious Consideration of Christian Philosophers and Divines; concerning which, though I have spent many Thoughts, yet can I not fully satisfy myself, much less then am I likely to satisfy others.

But I promise myself and them more full Satisfaction shortly, from the Labours of those who are more conversant and better acquainted with these Bodies than I, who have been more industrious in searching them out, and happy in discovering them; who have been more curious and diligent in considering and comparing them, more critical and exact in observing and noting their Nature, Texture, Figure, Parts, Places, Differences, and other Accidents, than myself, and particularly that learned and ingenious Person before remembred.

According to my Hope and Expectation, since the Publishing of this Work, my learned and ingenious Friend, Mr. *Edward Lhwyd*,

hath

hath gratified the curious and inquisitive Naturalists, with the Edition of his excellent *Lithophilacium Britannicum*, or Classical Distribution of Stones and other *British* Fossils, remarkable for their singular Figure, as many as either himself hath hitherto found out, or received from Friends. To which he hath subjoined several Epistles relating to this Subject; the last of which, concerning the Original and Production of these Bodies, he hath done me the Honour to inscribe to me; which at my Request he hath translated into *English*, and enlarged with many Additions, which I shall here give the Reader.

### THE SIXTH LETTER.

*Of the Origine of Marine Fossils, Shells, and Mineral Leaves, &c.*

## To Mr. RAY.

*Honoured Sir,*

'YOU are pleased to ask, whether, af-
' ter some Years Observations, I have
' been at length able to satisfy myself, as to
' the Origine of what we call *Marine Fossils*,
' and those other Bodies no less surprizing,
' which (to distinguish them from other
' Plants) I have taken the Liberty to call
' *Mineral Leaves*, viz. Whether I conclude,
' with

'with the general Opinion, that they have
'been reposited in the Places we find them,
'at the universal Deluge, and so preserv'd to
'our Time; or that they are original Pro-
'ductions of Nature, there form'd from some
'Plastick Power of Salts, or other Minerals,
'which was the Conjecture of the late
'Dr. *Plot*[*], and other experienc'd Natura-
'lists. To this I must needs answer, That
'the frequent Observations I have made on
'such Bodies, have hitherto afforded little
'better Satisfaction, than repeated Occasions
'of Wonder and Amazement; for as much
'as I have often (I may almost say continu-
'ally) experienc'd, that what one Day's
'Observations suggested, was the next cal-
'led in Question, if not totally contradict-
'ed and overthrown. Nevertheless, so in-
'defatigable is the Curiosity, and indeed so
'successful have been the Discoveries of this
'present Age, that we are daily encouraged
'to hope, this so important a Question will
'not much longer want its final Determi-
'nation, to the great Advancement of that
'Kind of real Knowledge which relates to
'Minerals: A Part of Natural History which,
'you well know, hath been hitherto much
'more neglected, than that of Plants and
'Animals; only, as I presume, because
'these Bodies are less obvious to our View,
'and much more abstruse and unaccountable
'as to their Origine. I therefore, at spare
                                    'Hours,

[*] Pl. Nat. Hist. Oxon. p.

'Hours, continue to improve my Collection, in regard it may be hoped, that from an accurate Inspection of it, some others hereafter may frame several useful Inductions, which I myself never had the least Thoughts of. And in the mean time, because the Communicating to our Friends, what carries but some Shadow of Probability, does often contribute somewhat towards the speedier Discovery of the Truth, I shall here submit to your Examination, a Conjecture relating to the Origine of these Bodies, which I know not whether any other have as yet thought of: But in regard it is necessary, that before any new Opinion be proposed, Reasons be offer'd against those already received, give me leave here to lay before you some Objections against both the above-mentioned Accounts of the Origine of these Bodies. To begin, therefore, with that which referrs all these Marine Fossils and Mineral Leaves, Stalks, and Branches, &c. to the Deluge, I have several Reasons to offer against it, whereof (because I would not presume too much on your Time and Patience) I shall at present only propose these few:

'*First*, Therefore, as to the Marine Fossils, had these Bodies been Spoils of the Sea, brought on the dry Land by an Inundation, they would (for the Generality of them at least) either have been left on the

'Surface of the Earth, or have been lodg'd
'at no very great Depth under it; but I
'have found them buried (or inclos'd) with-
'in folid Marble on the *Face* of broken Sea
'Cliffs, of the Height of 200 Fathoms and
'more, from the Tops thereof to the Bot-
'tom, and obferv'd them to be fo continu'd
'under the Sea-Water; nor was that
'only upon the Face of thefe Rocks, but
'even, more or lefs, throughout the whole
'Mafs of them. And this is manifeft from
'divers Rocks hewn down by Workmen for
'making of Lime, and other Pieces cafually
'fallen from the Cliffs in the Ifle of *Caldey*,
'and elfewhere about *Tenby* in *Pembroke-*
'*fhire*; as alfo in feveral other Rocks and
'Mountains that confift of fuch Baftard Mar-
'ble, or Lime-ftone, throughout *Wales*, *Ire-*
'*land*, and other Countries. Now, altho'
'we fhould grant, that at the Time of the
'Deluge thefe Rocks were no other than
'Clay or Earth; and that, therefore, Sea-
'Shells, Corals, and other Marine Bodies,
'might by the Violence of the Inundation
'have been lodg'd therein; and that in Tract
'of Time, this fuppos'd Clay or Earth con-
'folidated into Lime-ftone: I fay, though
'we fhould grant all this, yet I cannot per-
'ceive by what Force fuch Bodies could be
'funk into Clay or Earth to fo great a Depth.
'If indeed thefe Bodies conftituted one con-
'tinued Mafs, fo as that one fhould bear

'hard

' hard on the other, something perhaps
' might be reply'd; but the Matter is clear-
' ly otherwise, for they are found so con-
' fusedly dispers'd throughout the Mass of
' Lime-stone, sometimes at the Distance (for
' Example) of three Foot from each others;
' sometimes two, sometimes within half an
' Inch, and not seldom two or three or more
' of them contiguous.

' *Secondly*, Such *Marine Fossils* have been
' observ'd on the Sides or Walls within our
' Lime-stone Caves, and are even sometimes
' found sticking to the Roofs of them; for I
' have gather'd *Cuthbert-Beads*, or *Entrochi*,
' which are *Vertebræ* of Sea-Stars, from the
' Roof of a Cave call'd *Lhygad Lhychwr*,
' near *Kerrig Kennen* Castle, in the County
' of *Caermarthen*; and on the Sides (as well
' as Bottom) of a noted Cave, call'd *Pòrth-
' Gogo* at *Ystrad-Velhte* in *Brecknockshire*, I
' have observ'd several Remains of Cockles,
' half worn by the Swift Current of the Ri-
' ver *Melhte* which runs through this Cave,
' and polishes its Lime-stone. Now, al-
' though I can readily grant, that the Deluge
' might have cast Marine Bodies into these
' and any other Caves, yet can I not allow
' that it could ever fasten them to their po-
' lite Roofs and Sides; and that they should
' be sunk so deep from the Top, is the Dif-
' ficulty of the former Objection. To this
' may be added, that such Lime-stone Caves

N 2 ' are

'are for the most part (as it were) wain-
'scoted with a stony Crust of *Stalagmites*,
'which is of no very old Date, but owing
'to the continu'd Dropping or Distillation of
'the Caves, in which if any Marine-like
'Bodies are found, as I can assure you the
*V. Lith. '*Entrochi* * are, I leave it to yourself, and o-
Br. p. 'ther unprejudiced Observers, to consider of
'their Origine.

'*Thirdly*, The third Reason for my que-
'stioning whether all these Things be the
'Effects of the Deluge, is, for that the Bones,
'Horns and Hoofs of Land-Animals, are
'very seldom, if at all, found inclos'd in so-
'lid Marble, or other Stone; whereas see-
'ing all perished in the Deluge, the Spoils
'of the Land might be expected (in Propor-
'tion) as well as those of the Sea.

*Fourthly*, 'Some Fossil-Shells are entirely
'compos'd of a Spar or Crystal, insomuch
'that there is no Distinction of a containing
'and contain'd Matter, but only a Crystal-
'line Body, of the Figure of a Shell, as is
'by *Steno* himself acknowledg'd; and as
'may be seen in mine, and other Cabinets
'of Form'd Stones. How so great a Change
'should happen to Sea-Shells, and yet their
'Shape or outward Form not violated, seems
'to me too difficult to explain. The like
'may be said of the Fossil Fish-Teeth, for
'these are not always of the same Matter,
'as

'as may be obferv'd from divers Specimens in my Collection.

*Fifthly,* 'Living Animals are fometimes found in thefe Foffil-Shells; for in *Miffon*'s Travels to *Italy*, we read of a Lobfter found alive in the midft of a Marble near *Tivoli* \*; and the late Defcription of *Orkney*, &c. gives us the like Account of Cockles †. Moreover, as I am credibly informed, fome Workmen very lately digging for the Foundation of a Building, near the Town of *Mold* in *Flintfhire*, met with feveral Mufcles at about three Foot Depth in the Gravel, which had living Fifh in them. Now as it would be abfurd to imagine thefe Animals could live fince the Flood, fo neither can we fuppofe that fuch Creatures being left there by the Deluge, fhould propagate their Kind ever fince; for in this cafe, there muft have been left in that Place a Heap of their Shells.

'*Sixthly,* Had thefe Marine Bodies been repofited in the Earth at the univerfal Deluge, fuch of them as adhere to each others, nay all of the fame Pits or Quarries, unlefs their Beds be of a different Matter,

---

\* Miffon's *New Voyage to* Italy, *Vol.* 2. *p.* 44. Engl. *Edit.*
† *A Gentleman in the Parifh of* Dunrefnefs *in* Zetland, *told one of the Minifters of this Country, that about five Years fince, a Plough in this Parifh did caft up frefh Cockles, though the Place where the Plough was going was three quarters of a Mile from the Sea, which Cockles the Gentleman faw made ready and eaten.* Brand's *Defcript. of* Orkney, Zetland, *&c. p.* 115.

'must necessarily have undergone the same
'Change; whereas *Steno* acknowledges, that
'he has found Testaceous Shells, adhering
'to one perfectly Crystalline †: And I have
'myself often gather'd some Crystalline Spe-
'cimens, and others Testaceous of the same
'Sort of Shell, in the same Quarry, and in
'the same *Stratum* or Layer.

† *Sten.*
*Prod. p.*

'*Seventhly*, The immense Quantity we
'have of Marine Fossils, seems no ways to
'plead for the Origine from the Deluge:
'For we may observe many thousands of
'great Stones, and even broken Pieces of
'Lime-stone Rocks throughout *Wales*, and
'the North of *England*, almost wholly com-
'pos'd of those *Vertebræ*, or broken Pieces
'of the *Radii* of Sea-Stars, which are com-
'monly call'd *Fairy-Stones*, and *Cuthbert-*
'*Beads*, whereas 'tis very rare to find on
'our Shores, three broken *Radii*, or Frag-
'ments of any Sort of Sea-Stars close toge-
'ther. Likewise one shall rarely find in the
'same Place, two single Teeth of any Fish
'on all our Coasts; whereas thousands of
'these Fossil Teeth, exactly answering those
'of divers Sorts of Sea-Fish, have been of
'late Years found in Quarries and Gravel-
'Pits about *Oxford*; nor is their Quantity at
'all diminished upon breaking new Ground.

'*Eighthly*, Some of these Marine Fossils
'are no other than as it were Shadows or
'superficial Representations of Sea Bodies:
'Nor

'Nor do they seem to have much more of
'the Matter or Consistence of those Bodies
'they mostly resemble, than a Picture hath
'of the Person or Thing it represents. And
'of this Kind is Dr. *Lister*'s *Pectinites Mem-*
'*branaceus* out of Cole-pits; * The *Mock-*
'*plaice*, or *Buglossa curta strigosa* of *Caer-*
'*marthenshire*, and † the *Islebian* Fish-Stones
'in *Germany*, of which *Olaus Wormius* gives
'us this following Account. *In the* Islebian
'*Slat* (saith he) *are seen sometimes a small*
'*Dust of the Golden* Pyrites, *which represents*
'*various Figures of Animals.  I have a large*
'*Piece of this Stone, which so lively expresses*
'*all the Lineaments of a* Barbel *in golden*
'*Colour, that the Scales, the Fins, the Tail,*
'*the Head,* &c. *could not possibly, by any Ar-*
'*tist, be ever better painted.  The Bodies of*
'*these Fish are not converted into* Pyrites; *so*
'*that we have but just the outward Linea-*
'*ments of them, and not the least Impression*
'*left of any Bones, or other Parts.*  We find
'ourselves therefore oblig'd to confess, that
'Nature reserves many things from our Know-
'ledge, the true Reasons whereof no Man will
'ever so far discover, as to be enabled to ren-
'der us a due Account of them.   Now as these
'Representations are neither Animals them-
'selves, nor the *Exuviæ* of Animals, so nei-
'ther can they be their Impressions, foras-
'much as these Lineaments are prominent,
'not impress'd: And as for the Impression

\* *Append.
ad Tract.
de Anim.
Angl. &
Conch. A-
nat. Part.
Alt.*

† *Lith.
Brit. p.
96. Tab.
22. N. 2.*

'they

'they make on one Side in the incumbent
'Stone, or other Matter, it seems not satis-
'factory, because I cannot well conceive
'how all the *Vertebræ* of a Fish, whereof
'many are frequently found in our Midland
'Quarries and Gravel-pits, should here be
'totally consum'd, and the Surface only of
'one Side be converted into this *Pyrites*, or
'*Marchasite*.

'*Ninthly*, Another Obstacle of my Assent
'to their being all of Diluvian Origine, is
'the vast Number of unknown Marine Fos-
'sils, so commonly met with throughout
'most Counties of *England*; such as we
'have nothing like, neither in our Sea
'Shores, nor rak'd by Dredges out of the
'Bottom of the Sea, by the Oyster Fishermen,
'and others who have been employed by cu-
'rious Persons on set Purpose. I have in my
'Collection above forty different Species of
'the *Fossil Nautili*, or those Shell-Stones, a
'great many Sorts whereof are commonly
'call'd *Cornua Ammonis* [*]; and have observ'd
'Plenty of most of these Species (broken or
'whole) in the Fields, Quarries, and Clay-
'Pits of the Midland Counties of *England*:
'Nor do I question, but in that excellent
'Collection of Dr. *Woodward*'s, and in those
'of some others of our curious Naturalists,
'several Species may be found that are not
'in mine: And yet I cannot understand
'that all our *British* Seas afford one Sort of
'this

[*] V. Lib. Bp. p. 15.

'this Shell. The like may be said as to se-
'veral other Kinds; particularly the *Sea-*
'*Stars*, of the broken *Radii* whereof we
'find no less a Variety: * And the *Echini*, as
'to the Prickles or *Radioli* of which, as
'well as to those of Sea-Stars, all Sorts of
'*Lapides Judaici* (as many Years since I
'hinted to you) must be referr'd; notwith-
'standing the excessive Thickness of some
'of them, and that they have that very rough
'or Graser-like Superficies†, so as to be no-
'thing like the Spines of any of the *Echini*,
'or Star-Fish of our Seas.

* *Ib. Claſ 6. p. 44.*

† *Vide Plot's Hiſt. Nat. Ox. & Lith. Br. Tab. 12. N. 1002, 1008, &c.*

'*Tenthly*, I add only one other Argument,
'which though many have already objected,
'yet hath not, that I know of, been hitherto
'answer'd to Satisfaction: And that is, that
'such Marine Substances are sometimes ge-
'nerated in Humane Bodies: For to me it
'appears a far less Wonder, that Shells and
'other Marine Bodies should be produc'd in
'the Bowels of the Earth, than their Pro-
'duction in the Bodies of Men or Animals
'at Land. And that they have been so
'found, is sufficiently attested, both by An-
'cient and Modern Authors, of a Credit
'and Character beyond all Exception. You
'know many Instances of this Kind are pro-
'duced by Dr. *Lister*, in the Second Part of
'his Anatomy of Shells; amongst which I
'remember very well to have seen that small
'*Turben*, or *Periwinkle*, discovered by

'Dr.

'Dr. *Pierce* of *Bath*, and sent to Dr. *Musgrave*, then Secretary to the *Oxford* Philosophical Society; and it was such, as I believe none could have possibly distinguish'd from a Sea-Shell. These, Sir, are the Objections I had to offer against their Opinion, who attribute the Origine of all these Marine Fossils to the universal Deluge: For whatever their true Origine is, *Marine Fossils* they ought to be term'd, in order to their better Distinction from all others. 'Tis also for the like Conveniency of Distinction, that I use the Term of *Mineral Plants* for those Fossil Leaves and Branches we find so commonly inclos'd in Stone and blue Marble at our Cole-pits, and some Iron Mines. And now to proceed to these, we shall find much the like Difficulties with what occurr'd when we consider'd the *Marine Fossils*.

'*First*, For in the first place, these subterraneous Leaves frequently (indeed most commonly) are found at the Depth of at least twenty or thirty Foot. And how they should be laid so deep by an Inundation, seems to me not so easily accountable; it being natural to suppose, that all Plants were left, by the Deluge, on the Surface of the Earth, in the manner we daily find several *America* Seeds of Leguminous Trees cast up on the Shores of *Ireland*, *Scotland*, and *Wales*; and that consequently, in a
'short

'ſhort Space, there would be no more Re-
'mains of them, than we find of thoſe Sea
'Plants we commonly dung our Land with-
'all.

'*Secondly*, Allowing they might be, by
'ſome Accident we cannot think of, buri-
'ed ſo deep, I can diſcover no Reaſon for
'their being thus lodg'd ſo plentifully in
'Cole-Slat, and Iron-Stone; and never, that
'I know of, in the Maſs of our Flint, Lime-
'ſtone, and common Rock, though there be
'infinitely the greater Quantity of theſe lat-
'ter. And this Note ſeems to deſerve our
'Conſideration, unleſs it can be made out,
'that though the Matter of Flint and Lime-
'ſtone has very entirely preſerv'd the Ante-
'diluvian Shells, yet it could not Leaves, or
'other Parts of Vegetables.

'*Thirdly*, Had they been owing to the
'Deluge, we ſhould find the Leaves and
'Branches of ſuch Plants as are Natives of
'our own Iſland, much more plentifully than
'ſuch unknown Plants as we cannot paral-
'lel: Whereas on the contrary, as far as
'Dr. *Richardſon*'s Obſervations, and my own,
'have been able to diſtinguiſh, the Genera-
'lity of theſe Mineral Leaves, are clearly
'diſtinct from thoſe of our *Britiſh* Plants.

'*Fourthly*, Had they been thus repoſited
'at the Deluge, ſome Specimens of moſt, if
'not of each Claſs of Plants, would be found
'amongſt

'amongſt them; and eſpecially of Trees,
'in regard ſuch Leaves are not only the
'moſt numerous, but alſo commonly the
'dryeſt and moſt durable. But we have not
'hitherto diſcover'd, that any of theſe Mi-
'neral Leaves anſwer to thoſe of Trees or
'Shrubs; nor are we aſſur'd that any have
'been yet found, but what may be reduced
'to three or four Claſſes.

'*Fifthly*, The ſame curious and ingenious
Gentleman hath obſerved, that theſe Mineral Leaves are, generally ſpeaking, leſs
'than thoſe they ſeem moſt to reſemble;
'which is what, in divers Specimens, I have
'ſince taken Notice of myſelf.

'*Sixthly*, Although ſometimes meer flexi-
'ble Leaves are found amongſt theſe Mine-
'ral Plants, yet the Generality of them (as
'I have before obſerved of ſome of the Ma-
'rine Foſſils) are but meer Delineations, or
'ſuperficial Reſemblances: Nor yet could
ſuch Repreſentations be owing to the Impreſſions of Plants, ſince conſum'd; becauſe, as I have ſaid before of the *Mock-
Fiſh*, they are a little raiſed above the Surface of the Stone, and not impreſs'd.

'*Seventhly*, It ſeems nothing more ſtrange
'or unaccountable, that Delineations of
'Leaves ſhould be naturally produced in
'this Coal-Slat, &c. than that Repreſenta-
'tions of Gnats ſhould be ſometimes found

'in

'in the Fossil Amber of *Prussia*\*, and of Spi-    \* *Hartm.*
'ders in the Coal-Slat in *England* †. But    *Hist. Suc-*
'if any assert, that these were once living    *cini,Pruss.* p. 85.
'Animals, they are to explain how they came    † *Lith.*
'so deep under Ground; and afterwards,    *Brit.* p.
'how they got into these entirely close Pri-    111.
'sons of Stone and Amber. I meet with
'several more Difficulties, but perhaps of
'less Moment, which I shall not therefore
'trouble you withall, till some other Occa-
'sion.

  'As to the other Opinion, which main-
'tains, that all these Bodies are form'd in the
'Earth; the greatest Difficulty it labours un-
'der, is, that we find ourselves incapable of
'giving any satisfactory Account of the Cau-
'ses and Manner of such a Production. For
'if any have Recourse, with Dr. *Plot*, to the
'Plastick Power of Salts, I see not (to go no
'farther) what they can answer to that Ob-
'jection propos'd by yourself long since, in
'your *Physico-Theological Discourses*. For
'who can reasonably imagine, that any Mi-
'neral Salts should so conspire, as that some
'of them should so exactly frame the Points
'of the *Glossopetræ*\*\*, which are Fish-Teeth,    \*\* *Lith.*
'of one Matter, and some their Roots (ad-    *Brit.*
'ding now and then a Piece of a Jaw) which    *Tab.* 13. *N.* 1270.
'are of another: That some should form
'the polite Convex Side of a *Siliquastrum*,
'and others its Appendix ††: That some    †† *Ibid.*
'should make the Socket or *Calix* of the    *Tab.* 16. *N.* 1505.
                                         'Be-

'*Belemnites*, and others its *Alveolus*, &c.
'I therefore humbly offer to your Conside-
'ration, some Conjectures I have of late Years
'entertain'd concerning the Causes, Origine,
'and Use of these surprizing *Phænomena*. I
'have, in short, imagin'd they might be part-
'ly owing to Fish-Spawn received into the
'Chinks and other *Meatus's* of the Earth in
'the Water of the Deluge, and so be deriv'd
'(as the Water could make way) amongst
'the Shelves or Layers of Stone, Earth, &c.
'and have farther thought it worth our En-
'quiry, whether the Exhalations which are
'raised out of the Sea, and falling down in
'Rains, Fogs, &c. do water the Earth to
'the Depth here required, may not from the
'*Seminium*, or Spawn of Marine Animals, be
'so far impregnated with, as to the naked
'Eye invisible, *animalcula*, (and also with
'separate or distinct Parts of them) as to
'produce these Marine Bodies, which have
'so much excited our Admiration, and in-
'deed baffled our Reasoning, throughout the
'Globe of the Earth †. I imagin'd farther,
'that the like Origine might be ascribed to
.' the

* Ibid
Tab. 21.
V. 1675,
& 1740.
& Scheuch.
Lith. Hel-
vet. Tab.
I. Fig. ii.

---

† In those accurate Microscopical Observations communicated to the Royal Society by Sir *C. H.* we find this Note:
——*Some of them also may probably be originally Water Insects, or
Fish, sui generis, and are small enough to be rais'd in Substance or
in Spawn with the Vapours, and again to fall with the Rain, and
may grow and breed again in Water when kept: And this will seem
less*

the Mineral Leaves and Branches, seeing we find that they are for the most part the Leaves of Ferns, and other *Capillaries*; and of Mosses and such like Plants, as are called less perfect; whose Seeds may be easily allow'd to be wash'd down by the Rain into the Depth here required, seeing they are so minute, as not at all to be distinguish'd by the naked Eye. And as to such of them as are not reducible to these Classes of Minute Seeds, they are such as I know not at all whither to referr.

' I am not so fond of this *Hypothesis*, as
' not to be sensible myself, that it lies open
' to a great many Objections; and, in all
' probability, you will soon discover more
' Difficulties than I shall be able to remove:
' However, those Arguments that first led
' me to it, shall be here laid before you.

' *First*, Because I observ'd, that of all
' these extraneous Figures or Representa-
' tions dug out of the Earth, there is scarce
' one in a thousand but is reducible to such
' natural Bodies as expose their Seeds either
' to the open Air or the Water: Name-
' ly, Plants, Insects, or Fish. For (as I have

---

*less strange to you, when I assure you that I have seen, and when I am so happy as to wait on you next, will shew Fishes, some as small as Cheese-Mites of different Sorts, very wonderfully made, which are of the crustaceous Kind, shell'd with many Joints, with very long Horns, fringed Tails, and have many Legs like Shrimps, &c.* Phil. Tran. for *March* and *April*, 1703. p. 1366.

' before-

' before hinted) had the Spoils of the De-
' luge been entirely (or, for the moſt part)
' preſerv'd to our Time, we might reaſon-
' ably expect Plenty of the Skeletons, and
' of the Horns and Hoofs of Quadrupeds:
' And, why ſhould not either entire or bro-
' ken Skeletons of Birds, be found preſerv'd
' likewiſe in the ſame manner and in the
' ſame places we find the Leaves of Plants?
' How happens it, at leaſt, that we find none
' at all of their Pen-feathers, which ſhould
' ſeem of a Conſtitution more durable, if
' once incloſ'd in fine Stone, than that of
' Plants? I am not ignorant, that ſome ve-
' ry learned Writers, and thoſe even emi-
' nent Naturaliſts, have inform'd us, that
' not only Bones of Land-Animals, have
' been frequently found incloſ'd on all Sides
' in ſolid Stone, but likewiſe the Repreſen-
' tations or Lineaments of Birds and Beaſts,
' and of Men and their Parts: Nay, even
' that *Monks, Hermits,* and *Saints,* have been
' exactly pourtray'd in the midſt of ſolid
' Marble. To theſe I muſt take leave to
' reply; *Firſt,* That ſome of theſe Infor-
' mations are manifeſtly erroneous; for that
' they tell us, that theſe Delineations ap-
' pear'd upon poliſhing the Marbles; where-
' as all Figures naturally delineated within
' Stones, muſt, upon poliſhing theſe Stones,
' be defac'd. *Secondly,* When we diſcover
' any unknown Foſſils, we are very ſubject
' to

## the Deluge. 193

' to make wrong Comparisons; assimila-
' ting many of them to the Parts of Land-
' Animals, which, indeed, ought to be re-
' duc'd to Sea-Shells, or other Marine Bo-
' dies; as may be observ'd in those Stones,
' call'd *Hippocepaloides, Otites, Bucardites,*
' and divers others. *Thirdly,* Although it
' be granted, that sometimes the Bones,
' Horns, and Hoofs of viviparous Animals,
' are dug out of the Earth; yet, seeing
' they are so very few, it seems much like-
' lier that they might have been bury'd by
' some other Accidents, than that they have
' been there preserv'd ever since the Deluge.
' For in the Deluge, all Land-Creatures
' whatever perish'd; nor should we so much
' expect to find their single Bones as whole
' Skeletons, thus interr'd. *Fourthly,* When-
' ever I find any Confirmation, by competent
' and credible Authors, of such Delineations
' of any sort of viviparous Animals, or
' Birds, as the *Islebian* Stones exhibit of
' Fish, I shall then readily grant, these Things
' may be also as well produc'd without
' previous Seeds; and offer no farther Ar-
' guments for this *Hypothesis.*

    Secondly, ' I am, as to my own part, a-
' bundantly satisfy'd; and others will, I
' presume, upon Sight, and accurate Obser-
' vation of some Fossils I have collected, be
' no less, that these Bodies do, in Tract of
' Time, quite lose their Forms, and become

O         ' such

'such shapeless Lumps, as, to, be distin-
'guish'd, for Marine, by none but such as
'are very conversant in Observations of this
'Kind, nor even, at last, by them neither.
'I say, I am fully satisfy'd thereof; because
'I have collected sparry or crystalline Bo-
'dies, whose Surface do only partly re-
'semble Entrochi; likewise Shells, Glosso-
'petræ and Siliquastra, consisting of a flinty
'sort of Pebble, and receding from their pro-
'per or common Figures. And, Lastly,
'Ichthyospondylli, or Fish-Vertebræ; some-
'times more, sometimes less, deform'd;
'exhibiting on their Surface, such small stel-
'lated Figures as we find on a sort of the
'* Astroites. Now seeing that, in Tract of
'Time, some of them lose their Substance
'and Form, degenerating into other Bo-
'dies, may we not suspect that others
'(considering the Intireness of many of
'them, and their vast Plenty), might be, in
'the interim, produc'd?

*V.Plot's Hist. Oxon. p. 87. & Lith.Brit. Tab. 20. Num. 1658.

*Thirdly*, 'If this *Hypothesis* may be ad-
'mitted, some Account might probably be
'given of the Fossil *Nautili*, and other
'strange Shells, by supposing, *First*, That
'many of those Clouds, which fall here, in
'Rains, &c. have been exhal'd in very re-
'mote Parts: And, *Secondly*, That such a
'Generation, as is here suppos'd, must be
'much more liable to monstrous Produ-
'ctions than the common. For, as *Agri-*
    'cola

'cola says, appositely to this Purpose, *Quan-*
'*to crassior est terra quam aqua, tanto imper-*
'*fectiores gignit formas, & quæ animalibus*
'*careant.*

*Fourthly,* ' I have often, in one and the
' same Quarry, gather'd 20 or 30 different
' Magnitudes of the same Species of Shell-
' Stones; whence I began to suspect, that
' they might have a certain vegetative
' Growth †; and that they had, therefore,
' their Generation and Corruption in the ve-
' ry Place we find them: And that hence it
' is, that we find some *Nautili, Lapides*
' *Judaici, Glossopetræ,* and *Astropodia,* of
' such monstrous Largeness, that no Seas, as
' far as our curious Naturalists have disco-
' ver'd, afford any thing comparable to
' them.

† *See the Works of the Learned for the Month of Oct.* 1703.

*Fifthly,* ' To comprize the rest in few
' Words: The burying of these Leaves of
' Plants so deep; the vast Quantity of
' these Marine Bodies; the incredible Va-
' riety of exotick or unknown Shells, Sea-
' Stars, &c. in so narrow a Compass as this
' Island; their so frequently distorted and
' uneven Surfaces; that they should be found
' at all Depths, from the Top of the highest
' Rocks to the Bottom; that they should be
' not rarely found adhering to the Roofs,
' and to the Walls, or Sides of Caves, as
' well as perpendicular Clefts of Rocks;
' and be also sometimes discover'd in Ani-
' mal

' mal Bodies at Land; and that there should
' be Sea-Shells dug at Land containing living
' Animals. I say, all these considered toge-
' ther, seem inconsistent with the Effects of
' a Deluge; and if this *Hypothesis* may be
' admitted, not very difficult.

' But before it be, I ought not to doubt,
' but that yourself and others will find many
' more Objections than I can foresee. In the
' mean time, such as occurr to my Thoughts,
' I shall here, however destructive they may
' prove to it, fairly lay down; for they who
' have no other Aim than the Search of
' Truth, are no ways concern'd for the Ho-
' nour of their Opinions: And for my part,
' I have been always, being led thereunto
' by your Example, so much the less Admi-
' rer of *Hypotheses*, as I have been a Lover of
' Natural History.

' THE main Difficulties that I can at pre-
' sent think of, are these:

*First*, ' It will be question'd, whether the
' suppos'd *Seminium* can penetrate the Pores
' of Stones.

*Secondly*, ' It will scarce seem credible,
' that such Bodies, having no Life, should
' grow, especially when confined in so seem-
' ingly unnatural a Place as the Earth, *&c.*

*Thirdly*, ' According to this *Hypothesis*,
' these Bodies should be found in much the
' same manner, lodg'd in all kind of Stone,
' *&c.* and throughout all Countries.

*Fourth-*

*Fourthly*, 'We should not find Plenty of
'Shells, &c. adhering to each others, in the
'same manner as they are found at Sea.

*Fifthly*, 'Some Fossil Shells should then be
'found so minute, as to be scarce visible, and
'others of the same Kind in their complete
'Magnitude.

*Sixthly*, 'It may be well question'd, whe-
'ther the essential Parts of this suppos'd
'Spawn of any Fish, should, being separa-
'ted, (as must be here often suppos'd) ever
'effect the End by Nature designed them, e-
'specially when brought out of their proper
'Element.

*Seventhly*, 'It will be said, that the re-
'maining Tracks of Shells that once adhe-
'red on the Surface of some of these Fossils,
'and the Pearls, which (as has been related)
'have been found sticking to others, are a
'plain Proof that they are the Spoils of once
'living Animals; also the Change of the
'Colour near the Roots of some Fossil Fish
'Teeth, as namely of some *Plectronitæ*, shew
'how far they were fasten'd in the Jaws of
'once living Fish; and that the worn Extre-
'mities of some others, do plainly discover
'that they have been once employ'd.

*Eighthly*, 'Many of these subterraneous
'Fish, as particularly several of the *Glosso-
'petræ*, are taken for the Teeth of Viviparous
'Fish; which being granted, it is impossible

O 3 they

'they should be produced in the Manner
' here proposed.

*Ninthly*, and *Lastly*, ' Such a Production
' seems clearly beside the ordinary Course
' of Nature; nor can we perceive any End
' or Use of so preternatural a Generation.

' To the First I answer, That it's mani-
' fest from Experience, upon which all solid
' Philosophy must be grounded, that the
' Spawn of Animals may insinuate itself in-
' to the Mass of Stone.

'And this plainly appears from Live
' Toads, found sometimes in the midst of
' Stones at Land, and those Shell-Fish called
' *Pholades* at Sea. If it be replied, That the
' Stones, wherein the *Pholades* are lodg'd,
' are full of large Holes, &c. I answer, That
' tho' they generally are so, yet, upon break-
' ing and examining a great many of these
' Stones, I have sometimes found of their
' Shells (though without Animals) so lodg'd,
' as that there were not any visible *Meatus's*
' from their Holes, neither directly to the
' Surface of the Stones, nor to those other
' Holes in them. *

' To the Second, That that's not so great
' a Wonder, as that Shells should be some-

---

\* *Missum est ad me alio ex litore Saxum, in quo nullæ rimæ, nullæ cavernæ, sed foramina tantùm apparebant tam exigua, ut vix aciem admitterent: Eo igitur ictibus multis confracto, cavitates internæ multæ erant, vario situ & diversæ magnitudinis in quibus conchas istas reperi.* Rondel. de Aquatilib.

' times

‘ times generated, and even grow, tho' they
‘ contain no Animals within humane Bo-
‘ dies; and within the Mass of those thick
‘ Shells of our large *Tenby* Oysters, which
‘ I formerly mentioned to you, as first shewn
‘ me by Mr. *William Cole* of *Bristol*, and have
‘ since observ'd myself. For we must grant,
‘ that the Earth, even in any Part of the In-
‘ land Country, is much fitter for their Re-
‘ ception and Augmentation than humane
‘ Bodies; especially, if we reflect, that when
‘ the *Spat* or *Seminium* here suppos'd, meets
‘ with saline Moisture in the Earth, living
‘ Animals are sometimes produc'd, as is
‘ before attested.

‘ THE Third is likewise answer'd from
‘ Experience: For we know, that Sea-Shells,
‘ and some Stones, yield to the Growth of
‘ Plants: Also, that the hardest Stones are
‘ impress'd by the *Limpets*, tho' they do but
‘ adhere to their Surface, and that our Lime-
‘ stone yields to the Growth of some *Echini*,
‘ or Sea-Urchins, as well as the *Pholades*:
‘ For, we find some of their Cells much less
‘ than others; and that 'tis certain, that all
‘ the Holes wherein they lurk, in what Stones
‘ soever they are found, are owing to their
‘ Growth.

‘ To the Fourth I answer, That this *Hy-
‘ pothesis* does not require, that these Marine
‘ Bodies should be produc'd in all Coun-
‘ tries alike. For, as in Vegetables, we find,

‘ that

‘ that *all Seeds will not be receiv'd by all Soils*;
‘ so neither can we expect, that all Earths and
‘ Minerals should be equally proper for such
‘ Productions. And, truly, I thought it well
‘ worth Observation, that, as in all these
‘ Countries, scarce any Stones at Land, ex-
‘ cepting the Lime-stone, afford Marine Fos-
‘ sils; so I never found the *Pholades* at Sea
‘ in any other, tho' in that very common;
‘ and in divers Counties of *Wales*.

‘ As to the Fifth, I pretend not to deter-
‘ mine, how long such Bodies may continue
‘ before their Dissolution; but doubt not,
‘ but that, according to the Nature of the Mi-
‘ nerals wherein they are bedded, they may
‘ last much longer in some Places than o-
‘ thers; and, therefore, we are not to won-
‘ der, if in such Places we find a far greater
‘ Plenty of them than elsewhere.

‘ To the Sixth, I answer, That at the *Ba-*
‘ *sy*'s *Leigh* Quarry, near *Oxford*, large Spe-
‘ cimens of the *Turbinites Major*, figured
‘ Table the 7th, *Numb*. 341. may be often
‘ met with; and, likewise, in the same Place,
‘ concreted Lumps of others of the same
‘ Species, very minute. I have also, in my
‘ Collection, divers other Examples of the
‘ same Kind: And *Steno* informs us, That
‘ he has discover'd amongst Fossils, some so
‘ small, as to be scarce discernible without a
‘ Microscope, and even minute Eggs of
‘ Shells.

‘ The

'The Seventh may be, in a great measure, answer'd from the numerous Histories we have of monstrous Productions: And, as to the Impropriety of the Place, the same may be answer'd here, in reference to Parts of Animals, as was to the Second Objection, in respect of Whole ones.

'Eighth, As to the Adhesion of one Shell to another, that may altogether as well happen by this Way of Generation as at Sea: And, for the Signs or Impressions made by some, that formerly adher'd to them, those might have been disjoin'd by the Workmen in digging, or by the Sinking of the Ground where they are found, or some other Accident. But, as to the Change of the Colour of the *Plectronites* towards the Root, and some of them being sharpen'd at the Point, I must confess I have little to say; but that we do not yet know, the Teeth of what Fish these *Plectronitæ* are; and, consequently, cannot tell, but they may be naturally so colour'd, and pointed: Or else, that these and many more have been thus preserv'd in the Place we find them, ever since the Deluge, which was formerly my Opinion of all these Marine* Fossils; though, for the Reason I have here given, I cannot now maintain it.

'Ninth, To the Ninth may be answer'd, That we have as yet but an imperfect Knowledge of the Generation of particular

* Phil. Transf. *for the* Month *of* May, 1693.

'Species

'Species of Fish. For whereas you have
'obſerv'd, that ſome of the Cartilagineous
'are viviparous, I have noted others to be
'oviparous; having obſerv'd Embryo's in
'the Eggs of a ſort of Dog-Fiſh, (which
'were open at the one End) caſt aſhore in
'*Angleſey, Carnarvonſhire*, and other Coun-
'tries.

'TENTH, As to the laſt, tho' we acknow-
'ledge that there is an End in all the Pro-
'ductions of Nature; yet it is no leſs cer-
'tain, that we are often but very improper
'Judges of ſuch Final Cauſes. Who, there-
'fore, can be aſſur'd, but that the Fertility of
'the Earth may, in a great meaſure, be ow-
'ing to theſe Marine Foſſils? Thus much,
'at leaſt, I have obſerv'd, that in *Wales* they
'are found, for the moſt part, in the beſt
'Countries, and that in vaſt Quantities:
'And on the other hand, in thoſe *Hun-*
'*dreds* which are moſt barren, as the moun-
'tainous Parts of *Cardigan, Montgomery,*
'*Meirionydh*, and *Caernarvon*, I could never
'find one of them. There is, at *Cleydon-*
'*Field*, near *Banbury* in *Oxfordſhire*, a Place
'call'd *Hore-Furlong*, which is noted for
'Plenty of the *Aſteriæ*, or (as there call'd)
'\* *Hore-ſtones*; and no leſs, as the Farmers
'aſſur'd me, for its Fertility. Moreover,
'we cannot be ſo poſitive, but that ſome
'Minerals may from hence derive their
'Origine, to ſay nothing of their Phyſical
'Uſe;

\* *Plot's*
Hiſt.
*Oxon.*
p. 85.
& *Lith.*
*Brit.*
p. 57,
112.

'Use; the *Lapis Judaicus* and *Lyncurius*
' having been long since well known in our
' Shops, as perhaps some others are else-
' where, and more may be hereafter. And
' these, Sir, are the Notions I had to offer to
' your Consideration, concerning the Ori-
' gine of Marine Fossils and Mineral Leaves.
' You will soon judge how frivolous they
' may be, or how probable: And as you
' find them, pass your free Censure; for
' 'tis the Truth of so important a Question
' that's the only Aim of,

SIR,

Raiadar Guy,   *Your Humble Servant*,
Mar. 10. 1698.       E. L.

FOR my part, (if my Opinion be considerable) I think that my learned Friend hath
sufficiently proved, that these Fossil-Shells
were not brought in by the universal Deluge.
He hath made it also highly probable, that
they might be originally formed in the Places
where they are now found by a spermatick
Principle, in like Manner as he supposes.
Why do I say probable? It is necessary that
at least those which are found in the *Viscera*
and Glands of Animals, be thus formed;
and if these, why not those found in the
Earth? I shall say no more, but that those
who are not satisfied with his Proofs, I wish
they would but answer them. One thing, I
confess, there is, which chiefly brought me
over

over to the contrary Opinion, *viz.* *That these Bodies owe their Original to the Sea, and were sometimes the Shells or Bones of Fishes:* That is, the Beds of Oyster-Shells found in several Parts of this Kingdom, some of which I have before-mention'd and describ'd; which Shells, all Circumstances considered, one can hardly be induced to believe to have been any other originally than the Covers of living Oysters, and the Places where they lie, than the Bottom of the Sea. But because this seems to inferr the like Original of those Beds of *Cornua Ammonis*, or *Nautili*, found at *Keinsham* in *Somersetshire*, and elsewhere, of which Sort of Shell-Fish (as I have before noted) there were never any found in our own Seas, nor indeed in any other, so far as I have heard of, I shall allow them to have been the Effects of the like Principle with their Fellows.

THE following Tables, containing some Species of the most different *Genera* of these Bodies, *viz. Shark's Teeth, Wolf-Fish's Teeth, Cockles* or *Concha, Periwinkles* or *Turbens, Cornua Ammonis* or *Serpent-Stones, Sea-Urchins* and their *Prickles, Vertebres* and other *Bones of Fishes, entire Fishes petrify'd*, and of those some singly, some represented as they lie in Beds and Quarries under Ground, for the Information of those who are less acquainted with such Bodies, were thought fit to be added to this Edition.

TAB.

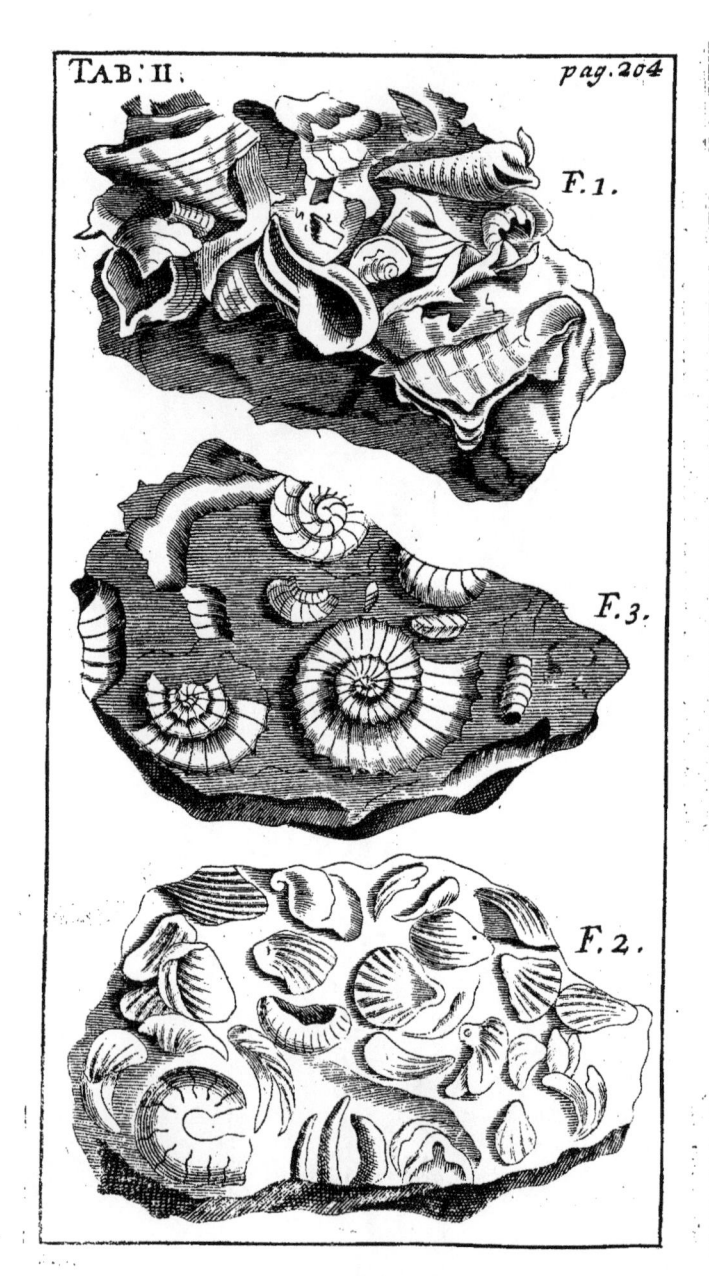

TAB. II.  pag. 204

F. 1.

F. 3.

F. 2.

TAB: III    F. 1.    pag. 204

TAB: IV                                    Pag: 204

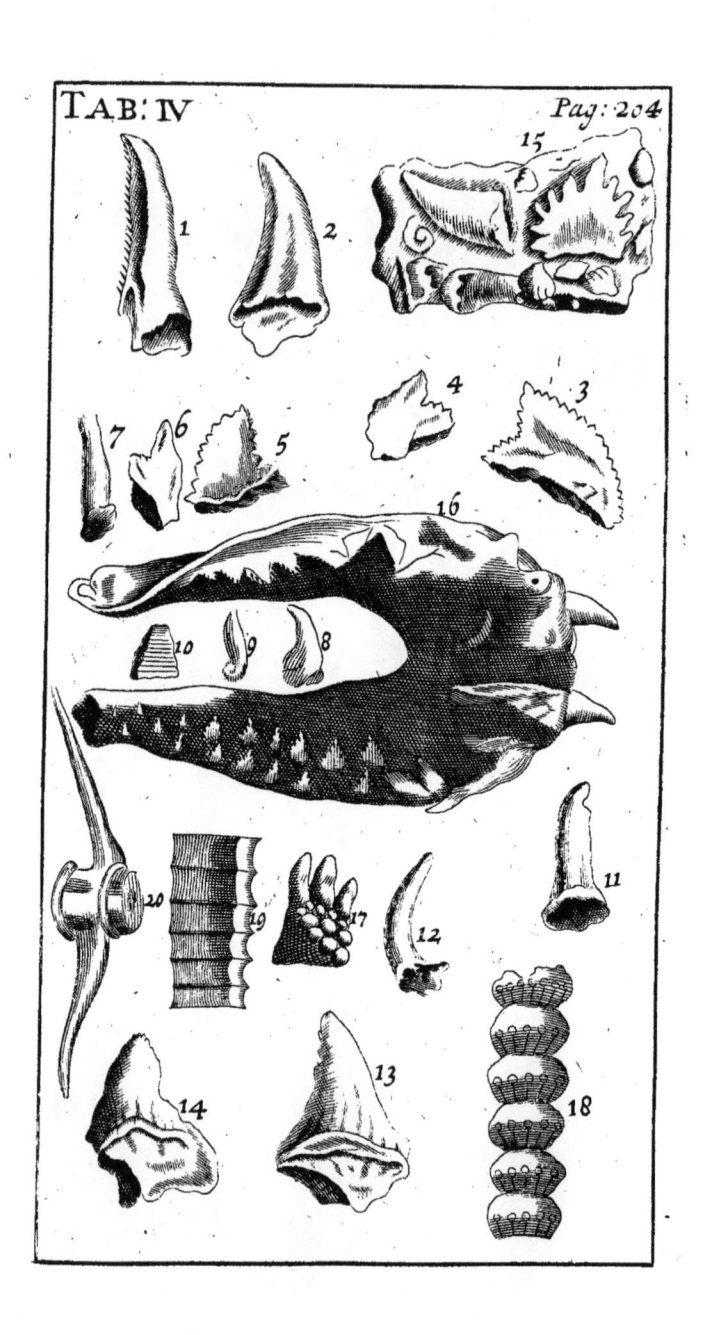

## TAB. II. Pag. 204.

FIG. 1, 2. Several Fragments and Lumps of petrify'd Shells, as they lie in Quarries and Beds under Ground; on many of these Petrifactions there still remain some *Laminæ*, or Plates of the Original Shells, which prove them not to be Stones primarily so figured.

Fig. 3. The *Cornua Ammonis* lying in Rocks with other petrify'd Bodies.

---

## TAB. III. Pag. 204.

FIG. 1, 2. Two petrify'd Fishes lying in Stone, with their Scales and Bones.

Fig. 3. A Sea-Urchin petrify'd with its Prickles broken off, which are a Sort of *Lapis Judaicus*, or *Jew-Stones*, their Insertions on the Studs or Protuberances of the Shell are here shewn. See their History and Manner of Lying in Stone and Beds, in *Agostino Scilla*, 4to. *Napoli*.

---

## TAB. IV. Pag. 204.

FIG. 1, 2, 3, 4, 5, 6, 7, 8, 9, 10, 11, 12, 13, 14. Several petrify'd Teeth of Dog-Fishes, Sharks, and other Fishes

Fig. 15, 16. The same lying in a Tophaceous Bed, and also in a Jaw-Bone.

Fig. 17. The petrify'd Teeth of a Wolf-Fish, in a Piece of the Jaw, the round ones, or Grinders, are sold in *Maltha* for petrify'd Eyes of Serpents, and by our Jewellers and Goldsmiths for Toad-stones, commonly put in Rings.

Fig. 18, 19, 20. Other petrify'd Bones of Fishes, especially Joints, or Vertebra's of Back-Bones, one with two stony Spines issuing out, f. 20. See them more at large in the Draughts of that curious *Sicilian* Painter, *Agostino Scilla*.

CHAP.

## Chap. V.

*That there have been great Changes made in the Superficial Part of the Earth since the General Deluge, and by what Means.*

I SHALL now discourse a little concerning such Changes as have been made in the Superficial Part of the Earth since the universal Deluge, and of their Causes.

THAT there have been such, I think no sober and intelligent Person can deny, there being so good Authority and Reason to prove it. *Plato*, in his *Timæus*, tells us, That the *Egyptian* Priests related to *Solon* the *Athenian* Law-giver, who lived about 600 Years before our Saviour, that there was of old Time, without the Streights of *Gibraltar*, a vast Island, bigger than *Africa* and *Asia* together, called *Atlantis*, which was afterward by a violent Earthquake and mighty Flood, and Inundation of Water, in one Day and Night wholly overwhelmed and drown'd in the Sea. Whence it may be conjectured, that the Old and New World were at first continuous, or by the Intervention of that Island, not very far remote from each other.

THAT the Island of *Sicily* was of old broken off from *Italy* by the Irruption or Insinu-
ation

ation of the Sea, is generally believed, and there is some Memorial thereof retained in the very Name of the City *Rhegium*, standing upon the *Fretum* that separates *Italy* and *Sicily*, which signifies breaking off.

> ———— * *Zancle quoque juncta fuisse*  
> *Dicitur Italiæ, donec confinia pontus*  
> *Abstulit, & mediâ tellurem reppulit undâ.*

*Ovid. Metam. lib. 15.*

In like manner, the Island call'd *Euboea*, now *Negroponte*, was of old joined to *Greece*, and broken off by the Working of the Sea.

Moreover, the Inhabitants of *Ceylon* report, that their Island was anciently joined to the Main-Land of *India*, and separated from it by the Force of the Sea.

It is also thought, and there is good Ground for it, that the Island of *Sumatra* was anciently continuous with *Malacca*, and called the *Golden Chersonese*; for being beheld from afar, it seems to be united to *Malacca*.

And to come nearer Home, *Verstegan* affirms, and not without good Reason, that our Island of *Great Britain*, was anciently Continent to *Gaule*, and so no Island but a *Peninsula*, and to have been broken off from the Continent; but by what Means, it is in his Judgment altogether uncertain: Whether by some great Earthquake, whereby the Sea first breaking through, might afterward by little and little enlarge her Passage; or whether

ther it were cut by the Labour of Man in regard of Commodity by that Paſſage; or whether the Inhabitants of one Side, or the other, by Occaſion of War, did cut it, thereby to be ſequeſtred and freed from their Enemies.

His Arguments to prove that it was formerly united to *France*, are, 1. The Cliffs on either Side the Sea, lying juſt oppoſite the one to the other; that is, thoſe of *Dover* to thoſe lying between *Callais* and *Boulogne*, (for from *Dover* to *Callais* is not the neareſt Land) being both of one Subſtance, that is, of Chalk and Flint. 2. The Sides of both towards the Sea plainly appearing to have been broken off from ſome more of the ſame Stuff or Matter, that it hath ſometime by Nature been faſtned to. 3. The Length of the ſaid Cliffs along the Sea-Shore being on one Side anſwerable in effect to the Length of the very like on the other Side, that is, about ſix Miles. And, 4. The Nearneſs of Land between *England* and *France* in that Place; the Diſtance between both, as ſome skilful Sailors report, not exceeding 24 *Engliſh* Miles. To which may be added, 5. The Shallowneſs of the Channel all along the Streight, in reſpect of the Sea at both Ends of it, which is much deeper. And, 6. The Being of Wolves and Foxes, yea, and Bears too, anciently in this Iſland; for it is not likely that they of themſelves ſhould venture to ſwim over a Channel 24 Miles broad; or if they

were

were so hardy as to venture in, should be able to hold out till they had passed it quite over: Neither is it probable that Men should transport such noisome and mischievous Creatures by Shipping. To speak in general, the Being of these wild Beasts on many Islands near the Continent, and not upon those that are far remote from it, though of sufficient Bigness to receive and maintain them, as the *Spaniards* found when they first sailed to *America*, is to me little less than a demonstrative Proof, that those Islands were anciently joined to the Continent by some Neck of Land which served as a Bridge for these Creatures to pass over, and was afterward worn through and washed away by the constant Working of the Sea.

Some of the Ancients, as *Strato*, quoted by *Strabo* in the First Book of his *Geography*, say, That the *Fretum Gaditanum*, or Streight of *Gibraltar*, was forcibly broken open by the Sea. The same they affirm of the *Thracian Bosphorus* and *Hellespont*, That the Rivers filling up the *Euxine* Sea, forced a Passage that way, where there was none before. And in Confirmation hereof, *Diodorus Siculus*, in his Fifth Book, gives us an ancient Story current among the *Samothracians*, *viz*. ‘ That before any other ‘ Floods recorded in Histories, there was a ‘ very great Deluge that overflowed a good ‘ Part of the Coast of *Asia*, and the lower ‘ Grounds

'Grounds of their Island, when the *Euxine*
'Sea first brake open the *Thracian Bospho-*
'*rus* and *Hellespont*, and drowned all the
'adjacent Countries.

This Traditional Story I look upon as very considerable for its Antiquity and Probability, it seeming to contain something of Truth: For it's not unlikely that the *Euxine* Sea, being over-charged with Waters by extraordinary Floods, or driven with violent Storms of Wind, might make its Way through the *Bosphorus* and *Hellespont*. But it will be objected, that the *Euxine* Sea doth empty itself continually by the *Bosphorus* and *Hellespont* into the *Mediterranean*, and that if it had not this Way of Discharge (the Rivers bringing in more than is spent by Vapour) it would soon overflow all its Shores, and drown the circumjacent Countries; and so it must have done soon after the Flood; and therefore it is not probable that *Samothrace* should have been inhabited before that Irruption, if any such there were.

To which I answer, 1. That Monsieur *Marsilly* thinks he hath demonstrated an Under-Current in the *Thracian Bosphorus*, by means of which the *Euxine* may receive as much Water from the *Mediterranean* as it pours forth into it. But because I have already declared myself not to be satisfied of the Being and Possibility of these Under-Currents, I answer, 2. The Annual Receipts
from

from the Rivers running into the *Euxine*, not very much exceeding what is spent in Vapour, who knows but that from the Time of the general Deluge, till the Irruption whereof we are discoursing, the *Euxine* might yearly enlarge its Bason, and encroach upon the Neighbouring Countries?

NATURAL Historians give us an Account of new Islands raised up in the Sea: *Plin. Hist. Nat. lib.* 2. *cap.* 87. enumerates *Delos* and *Rhodes*, Islands of Note; and of less Account and later Emersion, *Anaphe* beyond *Melos*, and *Nea* between *Lemnos* and the *Hellespont:* *Alone* between *Lebedos* and *Teos*, and among the *Cyclades*, *Thera* and *Therasia*, *Olymp.* 135. *An.* 4. Among the same, after 130 Years, *Hiera*, and two Furlongs distant, in his own Time, when *Junius Syllanus*, and *L. Balbus* were Consuls, *Thia*. Notwithstanding these Authorities of *Seneca*, *Pliny*, and *Strabo*, before-mentioned, Dr. *Woodward*, in his *Natural History of the Earth*, confidently affirms, ' That there is no authentick Instance of ' any considerable Tract of Land that was ' thrown up from the Bottom of the Sea by ' an Earthquake, or other subterraneous Ex-' plosion, so as to become an Island, and be ' render'd habitable. That *Rhodus*, *Thera*, ' *Therasia*, and several other Islands, which ' were supposed by the Ancients, and upon ' their Authority by later Authors, to have ' been thus raised, had really no such Ori-' ginal,

'ginal, but have ſtood out above Water as long as their Fellow-Iſlands, and ſtand now juſt as the univerſal Deluge left them.'

I CANNOT but wonder at the Confidence of this Author, in affirming this of all Iſlands, not excepting any, whenas *Seneca*, a grave and ſober Writer, and of undoubted Fidelity, tells us, *Natural. Quæſt.* lib. 6. cap. 21. *Theram & Theraſiam, & hanc noſtræ ætatis inſulam ſpectantibus nobis in Ægæo mari enatam*: And this Iſland of our own Age, which was raiſed up in the Ægæan Sea, ourſelves beholding it. But the moſt conſiderable and remarkable Mutations that have been made in the Earth have been on the Sea-Coaſts; either by carrying on the Land into the Sea, and atterrating the Bottom of the Sea; or by drowning the Lands near the Sea, by Irruptions and Inundations thereof, or undermining or waſhing away the Shores.

OF the firſt Sort of Change by Atterration, or making the Sea dry Land, we have an eminent Inſtance in the *Dutch Netherlands*, which, I eaſily conſent with *Verſtegan*, ſo far as they are eaven and plain without any Hills, have undoubtedly heretofore, in Time long paſt, been Sea; as appears, 1. From the Lowneſs of their Situation, ſome of the more Maritime Parts of them, as *Zealand* and *Holland*, and Part of *Flanders*, being ſo low, that by Breach or Cutting of the Sand Banks or Downs, which the Sea by little and little

hath

hath cast up; and the Labour of Man here and there supplied, might easily be drowned and converted into Sea again; and of the great Harms that these Parts have heretofore, by the Irruption of the Sea, sustained. But now not only those low Places that adjoin upon the Sea, as *Holland* and *Zealand*, but the greater Part of *Flanders* and *Brabant*, though they lie not so low as they, but of such Height as no Inundation of the Sea can any whit annoy them, though the Sand-Banks and Downs on the Sea-Side were never so much broken or cut through, yet are they as eaven and level as even *Holland* and *Zealand* themselves, which is a sufficient Demonstration, that they were once covered with Water: For that Water will thus level Ground it often runs over, is clear from Meadows, and from the Bottom of the Sea discovered at low Water; and we have Experience of no other Cause that doth or can effect it. And therefore *Lewis Guicciardine* erroneously argues *Hubert Thomas*, Secretary to Count *Frederick*, Palatine of the *Rhine*, of a Mistake, for saying,* in his Description of the Country of *Liege*, that the Sea hath come up even to *Tongres* Walls, now well nigh a hundred *English* Miles from the Sea: Among other good Reasons, alledging for the Proof thereof, that the great Iron Rings are there yet remaining, unto which the Ships that there sometimes arrived

ved were faſtned. I ſay erroneouſly, ſeeing all the Countries between that and the Sea are level, and of an equal *Superficies*, without any Hills or Riſings. 2. This appears, not only from the great Plainneſs and Eavenneſs of the Ground, but in that the Soil generally, both in *Flanders* and *Brabant*, is ſandy; whence it ſeems naturally to follow, that thoſe Countries were anciently the Flats, Sands, or Shores of the Sea. 3. In that digging about two Fathom more or leſs deep in the Earth, innumerable Shells of Sea-Fiſh are found, and that commonly in all Places, both of Field and Town; and in many Places the great Bones of Fiſhes.

FARTHER (ſaith *Verſtegan*) it is to be noted, that albeit digging deep in the Earth in *Brabant* and *Flanders*, great Abundance of Shells and Bones of Fiſhes are to be found; yet digging in the Earth in *Holland* and *Zealand*, none at all are perceived, howbeit on the Sands on the Sea-Shore there are very many. The Reaſon whereof may be, becauſe thoſe Parts have been in Time long paſt part of the Depth of the Sea; and the Parts aforeſaid of *Brabant* and *Flanders*, the Flats or Shore; and on the Flats, and not in the Depths, ſuch kind of Shell-Fiſh are naturally nouriſhed. This is a very plauſible Account. But yet it hath been by Experience found, that if you dig deep enough, even in *Holland* itſelf, after many Floors of ſeveral Sorts of Earth, you will at last come to Beds of Shells. For *Varenius* tells us, that Sinking a Well in *Amsterdam*, after many Beds or Layers of Earth, Sand, Turf, &c. at a hundred Foot Depth they came to a Bed of Sea-Sand mix'd with Cockle-Shells of four Foot Thickness, which doubtless was of old Time the Bottom of the Sea, and all the other Beds above it were brought down partly by Floods subsiding and settling there, partly by the Working of the Sea spreading Beds of Sand upon the Layers of the Earth, and so interchangeably. But from this Experiment it doth appear, that however deep the Sea were thereabouts, yet it was not too deep to breed or harbour Shell-Fish. Moreover, from this Instance it appears, that altho' now the Bottom of the Sea about *Holland* be not much below the Surface of the Land, yet anciently it was supposed fifty Foot; whence it will follow, that the Sea did then cover all the Land above *Holland*, which was not more than fifty Foot higher than it. This to me is a demonstrative Proof of the Atterration of the Sea thereabout.

ANOTHER great Instance of Change made in the *Superficies* of the Earth by Atterration is in our own Country, the great Level of the Fens running through *Holland* in *Lincolnshire*, the *Isle of Ely* in *Cambridgeshire*, and *Marshland* in *Norfolk*. Which that it was sometime part of the Sea, and atterrated by Land brought down by Floods from the upper Grounds, seems to me evident, in that it is near the Sea, and in that there is thereabout a Concurrence of many great Rivers, which in Flood-times, by the Abundance of Mud and Silt they bring down, there subsiding, have by Degrees raised it up. And thirdly, in that the whole Country is exactly level, like the Bottom of the Sea; it being (as I have already said) the Nature of the Water flowing over the Earth in time to level and bring to a Plain all Places that are soft and yielding, and not rocky, as is seen in Meadows, and in the Bottom of the Sea discovered at low Water.

A THIRD Instance is the *Craux* in *Provence* in *France*, anciently called *Campus Lapideus*, of which *Pliny* saith it was *Herculis præliorum memoria*; and *Strabo*, out of *Æschylus*, gives us a Poetical Fable, ' That the Stones ' were rained down by *Jupiter* in Favour of ' *Hercules* when he wanted Darts, that he ' might cast them at the *Ligurian* Army, and ' thereby break and scatter it." *Possidonius* thinks it was once a Lake, which by Fluctuation dried up, and so the Stones came to be equally dispersed over the Bottom of it. That it was a very ancient thing, is clear, having its Original in the fabulous Times before any Memoirs of true History; it continues to this Day such a kind of Place as it was in *Strabo*'s Time. It appears so evident-

ly

ly to any one who hath viewed and confidered it, to have been once Part of the Sea, from its being exactly level, and ſtrowed all over with Stones, as I have obſerved the Bottom of the Sea in many Places to be, that there is not the leaſt Reaſon to doubt of it.

The River *Arnus*, in *Tuſcany*, now falleth into the Sea, ſix Miles below *Piſa*: Whereby it appeareth, (ſaith Dr. *Hakewil*) that the Land hath gained much upon the Sea in that Coaſt; for that *Strabo*, in his Time, reporteth, it was but twenty Furlongs (that is, but two Miles and an half) diſtant from the Sea.

I might, to theſe, add many other Inſtances of Atterrations out of *Strabo*, in his firſt Book; as about the Outlets of *Iſter*, the Places called *Stethe*, and the Deſerts of *Scythia*: About thoſe of *Phaſis*, the Sea-coaſt of *Colchis*, which is ſandy, and low, and ſoft: About *Thermodon* and *Iris*, all *Themiſcyra*, the Plain of the *Amazons*, and the moſt part of *Sidene*.

To omit the whole Land of *Egypt*, which probably was covered originally with the Sea, and raiſed up by the Mud and Silt, brought down by the *Nile* in its annual Floods, ſubſiding there, as I ſhall have occaſion to ſhew afterwards.

Moreover, *Varenius* rationally conjectures, that all *China*, or a great Part of it, was originally thus raiſed up and atterrated,
having

having been anciently covered with the Sea: For that, that great and impetuous River, called the Yellow or Saffron River, coming out of *Tartary*, and very often, though not at anniverfary Seafons, overflowing the Country of *China*, is faid to contain in it fo much Earth and Sand, as make up a third Part of its Waters. The Eavenness, and Level *Superficies* of this whole Country of *China* render this Conjecture the more probable.

In fine, the like Atterrations appear to have been made about the Mouths of *Indus* and *Ganges* in the *Eaft-Indies*, and the River *de la Plata* in *America*, and the *Rhodanus* in *France*, and, doubtless, moft other great Rivers throughout the whole World.

To all which, if we add the fpacious Plains that are on each fide moft great Rivers, from their Mouths, many Miles up their Channels, as may be obferved in the *Thames* and *Trent* in *England*, which, probably, were at firft *Sinus's* of the Sea, landed up by Earth brought down from the Mountains and upper Grounds in Times of Floods; it will appear, that in this refpect there hath been a very great Change made in the terraqueous Globe, the dry Land much enlarged, and the Sea ftraitned and cut fhort.

Notwithstanding all thefe Authorities and Arguments, Dr. *Woodward*, in his *Natural Hiftory of the Earth*, confidently affirms, ‘That there were never any Iflands, or other

'considerable Parcels of Land amassed or
'heaped up, nor any Enlargement or Addi-
'tion of Earth made to the Continent, by
'the Mud that is carried down into the Sea
'by Rivers. That although the Ancients
'were almost unanimously of Opinion, that
'those Parts, where *Egypt* now is, were
'formerly Sea, and that a very considerable
'Portion of the Country was recent, and
'formed out of the Mud discharged into the
'neighbouring Sea by the *Nile*, that yet this
'Tract of Land had no such Rise, but is as
'old, and of as long standing, as any upon
'the whole Continent of *Africa*, and hath
'been much in the same natural Condition
'that it is at this day, ever since the Time of
'the Deluge: Its Shores being not advan-
'ced one jot farther into the Sea for this
'Three or Four thousand Years, nor its Sur-
'face raised by additional Mud, deposed up-
'on it by the yearly Inundations of the
'*Nile*. That neither the *Palus Mæotis*, nor
'the *Euxine*, nor any other Seas, fill up, or
'by degrees grow shallower. That *Salmy-*
'*dessus, Themiscyra, Sidene*, and the adja-
'cent Countries upon the Coasts of the *Eu-*
'*xine* Sea, were not formed out of the Mud
'brought down by the *Ister, Thermodon, Iris,*
'and the other Rivers, which discharge them-
'selves into that Sea. That *Thessaly* was
'not raised by the Mud, borne down by the
'River *Peneus*; the Islands *Echinades* or *Cur-*
'*zolari,*

' *zolari*, out of that brought by the River
' *Achelvas*; *Celicia* by the River *Pyramus*; *My-*
' *sia*, *Lydia*, *Ionia*, and other Countries of *Aná-*
' *tolia*, by the *Caycus*, *Hermes*, *Cayster*, and the
' other Rivers which pass through them. To
' be short, that no Country or Island in the
' whole World, was ever raised by this
' means." Thus far Dr. *Woodward*.

All these Particulars he ought not only to have confidently asserted, but also sufficiently proved; which till he can do, I must crave Leave to suspend my Assent.

For my part, I am of Opinion, that tho' the Ancients might be mistaken in the full Latitude of what they have delivered, concerning the Atterration of the Skirts of the Sea in the Places forementioned, about the Outlets of great Rivers; yet, that they had very good Reason for what they wrote:

*First*, The Nature of those great Levels be          a Thought to any
co           unprejudiced Person.

*Secondly*, There being undeniable Instances of such Atterrations, though in less Quantities; as, 1. That of *Ravenna* in *Italy*, which City anciently stood upon the Brink of the Sea-Shore, when it was the Head of an *Exarchate*; whereas now, by the landing up of the Shallows, it is far distant from it. 2. That at the Mouth of the River *Arnus* in *Tuscany*, just now mentioned. 3. That in the *Camarg* or Island which the River *Rhodanus* near
Arles

*Arles* in *Provence* makes, where there hath been so much lately gained from the Sea, that the Watch-Tower had been, in the Memory of some Men living, when I was there [1665] removed forward three times, as I was there credibly informed.

MOREOVER, some Confirmation it is of this Opinion, that the Earth in the Levels, about the Mouths of great Rivers, is continually raised up higher and higher, which is done by the Mud and Silt brought down by the Rivers, especially in Times of Floods, and partly also by Sand and Ouze thrown up by the Sea; which, by this means, contributes to its own straitening.

A RELATION of this Kind of Atterration, I find in the *Philosophical Transactions.* Numb. 277. pag. 1256. communicated by an innominate Person to the learned and ingenious Mr. *Ralph Thoresby,* and by him to the *Royal Society,* in these Words:

' ' Near the River *Welland,* which runs
' through the Town of *Spalding* in *Lincoln-*
' *shire,* at the depth of about 8 or 10 Foot;
' there were found Jettys (as they call them)
' to keep up the old River-Bank, and the
' Head of a Tunnel that emptied the Land-
' Water into the old River: And, at a con-
' siderable Distance from the present River,
' I guess, about 20 or 30 Yards, there were
' dug up, about the like Depth, several old
' Boats: Which things shew, that anciently
' the

' the River was much wider than now it
' is, or ran in another Place. On the o-
' ther, *viz.* the North-Weſt ſide of the River,
' and more upward, in the Town, were dig-
' ged up (at about the forementioned Depth)
' the Remains of old Tan-Vats, or Pits, a
' great Quantity of Ox-horns, Shooe-Soles,
' and, I think, the very Tanners Knebs, &c."
Which things ſhew, that the Surface of the Country lay anciently much lower than now it does.

ONE thing farther I will add, that lately, at the laying of the preſent new Sluice or Goat (as they call it) at the End of *Hamore*-Beck, as it falls into *Boſton*-Haven; taking up the Foundation of the old Goat, they met with the Roots of Trees, many of them iſſuing from their ſeveral Boles or Trunks ſpread in the Ground; which, when they had taken up, (Roots and Earth they grew in) they met with a ſolid, gravely, and ſtrong Soil, of the high Country kind, which was certainly the Surface of the old Country; the certain Depth whereof I cannot tell you, but that it was much deeper than that at *Spalding*. *What elſe could raiſe up this Ten Foot Thickneſs of Earth, but the Mud and Silt brought down by great Rivers, ſubſiding here? and partly, alſo, Sand and Ouze thrown up by the Sea, and depoſited here in Spring-Tides?*

## Of the Deluge.

A PARALLEL Instance of the raising up of the Earth, the learned Signor *Ramazzini* affords us in and about *Modena* in *Italy*.

' IN the whole City of *Modena*, and round
' about for some Miles distance, in whatever
' Place they dig, when they come to the
' Depth of about 63 Foot, they pierce the
' Ground with a *Terebra*, about 5 Foot deeper,
' and then Water springs up with so great
' Force, that, in a moment, the Well is filled
' up to the Brim. This Water is perpetual,
' doth not increase by Rain, nor decrease by
' Draught." Of this Springing up of the Water about *Modena*, we have already made mention, and given an Account out of Signor *Cassini*. ' And what is yet more remar-
' kable, from the Surface of the Ground to
' the Depth of 14 Foot, they meet with no-
' thing but Rubbish and Ruins of an ancient
' City. Being come to that Depth, they find
' paved Streets, Artificers Shops, Floors of
' Houses, and several Pieces of Inlaid-Work.
' It's very hard to conceive, how the Ground
' of this City was raised thus; we can attri-
' bute it to nothing else, but that it hath
' been ruined, and then rebuilt upon its
' Ruins, since it's not higher, but rather
' lower still than all the adjacent Country.

' AFTER these Ruins, they find a very
' solid Earth, which, one would think, had
' never been removed; but a little lower,
' they find it black, marshy, and full of Briars.

' Signor

' Signor *Ramazzini* went down one of these
' Wells, and, at the Depth of 24 Foot, he
' found a Heap of Wheat entire: In another,
' of 26 Foot, he found Filberd-Trees with
' their Nuts. They find, likewise, every six
' Foot alternatively, a Change of Earth, some-
' times white, sometimes black, with Branches
' and Leaves of Trees of different Sorts. At
' the Depth of 28 Foot, or thereabout, they
' find a Chalk that cuts very easy. It is mixt
' with Shells of several sorts, and makes a
' Bed of about 11 Foot. After this, they find
' a Bed of marshy Earth, of about two Foot,
' mixt with Rushes, Leaves and Branches.
' After this Bed, comes another Chalk-Bed,
' of near the same Thickness with the for-
' mer, which ends at the Depth of 42 Foot.
' That is followed by another Bed of marshy
' Earth like the former. After which comes
' a new Chalk-Bed, but thinner, which hath
' also another marshy Bed underneath it.
' This ends at the Place which the Workmen
' pierce with their *Terebra*. The Bottom is
' sandy, mingled with a small Gravel, in
' which they find several Shells, such as are
' on the Sea-Shores. These successive Beds
' of marshy Earth and Chalk, are to be found
' in the same Order, in whatever Part of the
' Earth you dig. The *Terebra* sometimes
' finds great Trees, which give the Work-
' men much Trouble. They see also, at
' some times, at the Bottom of the Wells,
          ' great

'great Bones, Coal, Flints, and Pieces of
'Iron.

*Ramazzini* thinks, that before the Deluge, the Gulph of *Venice* reach'd as far as *Modena*, and beyond it; but that the Waters decreasing, the Earth was raised by the Slime and Sand which they left behind them, and that the Rivers and Brooks did, in process of Time, make the abovementioned Beds. Indeed, *I cannot imagine what could make those Beds we find in Maritime Places,* ( as those we mentioned, which were found in sinking a Well at Amsterdam) *and those we see in broken Mountains; but the Sediments of the Inundations of the Sea, or of Land-Floods.*

*To say, that the Earth about* Modena *is no higher now than when the Flood left it, seems to me a very unreasonable Assertion.* For though we should grant, that the Earth was dissolved at the general Deluge, and that the different Parts thereof did subside, according to their different Gravities and Form, several Strata, or Beds; yet, how comes it to pass, that there should be so many alternate Beds of Chalk, and *moorish* Ground, one above another, in the Earth about Modena? And, how comes the Country round about to be as high as the present City, which is 14 Foot higher than the Streets of the City, upon whose Ruins it seems to have been built?

Q                N.B.

*N. B.* This Relation I transcribed out of the History of the *Works of the Learned.*

That the Rivers do bring down a great deal of Earth from the Mountains, upon Shots of Rain, is demonstratively proved by the lowering of the Mountains, because it can proceed from no other Cause imaginable. But that the Mountains are continually lowered or depressed, I shall hereafter, by two Instances, undeniably prove. And, the learned Jesuite *Josephus Blancenus* mentions the Lowering of Mountains, as a thing well known to the Mountaineers: For that, formerly, some intermediate Mountain intercepted the Sight of a Castle, or Tower, situate in a more remote Mountain, which, after many Years, the intermediate Mountain being depressed, came clearly into View.

I shall add hereto the Judgment of the most curious Observer of these things, *Nicolaus Steno,* in his *Prodromus, &c.* p. 106, 107. of the *English* Translation; *This is certain,* (saith he) *that a great Parcel of the Earth is every Year carried into the Sea,* (*as is obvious to him that shall consider the Largeness of the Rivers, and the long Passage through the Mid-land Countries, and the innumerable Number of Torrents; in a Word, all the Declivities of the Earth:*) *And, consequently, that the Earth, carried away by the Rivers, and joined to the Sea-Shores, does every day leave new Lands fit for new Inhabitants.*

But

## the Deluge.

But you will say, Hath there been no Compenſation made for all this? Hath not the Sea otherwhere gained as much as it hath loſt about the Mouths of the Rivers? If not, then the Sea will in time be ſo far landed up, or ſtraitned, till it be compelled to return again, and overflow the whole Earth.

To which I anſwer, That where the Shores are earthy, or argillaceous, or gravely, or made of any crumbling and friable Matter, the Sea doth undermine and ſubvert them, and gain upon the Land; which I could prove by many Inſtances, ſome of which I ſhall afterward touch. But whether the Sea doth, in theſe Places, gain proportionably to what it loſes in the forementioned, according to the vulgar Proverb, is to me ſomewhat queſtionable.

To proceed now to diſcourſe a little concerning the Changes that have been made by the Irruptions and Inundations of the Sea, or by its undermining and waſhing away the Shores.

That there have been of old great Floods, and much Land laid under Water by Inundations of the Sea, is clear, many ſuch being recorded in Hiſtory.

The moſt ancient of all, next to the general Deluge in the Days of *Noah*, *viz.* that of *Ogyges* King of *Bœotia*, or rather *Attica*, ſeems to have been of this Nature: So doth that of a great Part of *Achaia* in *Peloponneſus*,

Q 2  wherein

wherein the Cities of *Bura* and *Helice* were overwhelmed and laid under Water.

*Cambden* out of *Gyraldus* reports, 'That 'anciently a great Part of *Pembrokeshire* ran 'out, in the Form of a Promontory, towards '*Ireland*; as appears by that Speech of King '*William Rufus*, That he could easily, with 'his Ships, make a Bridge over the Sea, so 'that he might pass, on foot from thence to '*Ireland*." This Tract of Ground being all buried in deep Sands, during the Reign of King *Henry* the Second, was, by the violence of a mighty Storm, so far uncovered, that many Stumps of great Trees appeared fastned in the Earth : *Ictusque securium tanquam hesterni,* (saith *Gyraldus*) *and the Strokes of the Axes in them, as if they had been cut but yesterday ; ut non littus jam, sed lucus esse videretur, mirandis rerum mutationibus!* So that now it made Shew of a Wood rather than of a Strand ; such is the wonderful Change of all things!

Here I might take occasion to discourse of subterraneous Woods and Fossil Trees, and not impertinently; because some have supposed them to have been thrown down by the universal Deluge, and to have lain buried in the Earth ever since, tho' erroneously. I shall, therefore, give a twofold Account of their Original. The *First*, From Inundations of the Sea, or the Force of violent and tempestuous Winds : The *Second*, By the Labour of

Men,

Men, who felled them down in the Places where they now lie.

*First,* By Inundations of the Sea. "Near 'Bruges, in *Flanders,* (*as* Boetius de Boot, '*who was Native of that City, relates*) dig- 'ging 10 or 20 Ells deep in the Earth, they 'find whole Woods of Trees, in which the 'Trunks, Boughs, and Leaves, do so exact- 'ly appear, that one may easily distinguish 'the several Kinds of them, and very plainly 'discern the Series of Leaves which have 'fallen yearly. These subterraneous Woods 'are found in those Places, which, 500 Years 'ago, were Sea, and afterwards either left 'or thrown up by the Sea, or gained from 'it; the Tides being kept off by Walls and 'Fences. But before the forementioned 'Term of 500 Years, there is no Memory 'that these Places were Part of the Conti- 'nent. And yet, seeing the Tops of these 'Trees do, for the most part, lie Eastward, 'because, as it is probable, they were thrown 'down by the Easterly Winds, (which, on 'this Coast, are most boisterous and vio- 'lent) it will necessarily follow, that in the 'most ancient Times, and before all Memo- 'ry of Man, these Places were firm Land, 'and without the Limits of the Sea." *So far he.* Afterwards, this Land, with the Trees upon it, being undermined and over- whelmed by the Violence of the Sea, the Land and Trees continued so long under

Water, till the Sea, either by its own Working, bringing up Sand and Stones, &c., or by Earth brought down by the Land-Floods, still subsiding to the Bottom, or by the Tide's being kept off by Walls and Fences, was filled up, and the Tops of the Trees covered; and so this Space again added to the firm Land.

On the Coast of *Suffolk*, about *Dunewich*, the Sea hath, for many Years past, very much encroached upon the Land, undermining and overwhelming, by degrees, a great deal of high Ground, insomuch that ancient Writings make mention of a Wood a Mile and a half to the East of *Dunewich*; which is, at present, so far within the Sea. Now, if in succeeding Ages (as likely enough it is) the Sea shall, by degrees, be filled up by the Means beforementioned, and this Space be added again to the firm Land, these Trees will be found under Ground, in like manner as those about *Bruges* were.

I find, in a Letter from that learned and ingenious Naturalist, Dr. *Richardson*, registred in the *Philosophical Transactions*, Numb. 228. 'An Account of some subter-
'raneous Trees, dug up at *Youle* in *York-*
'*shire*, about 12 Miles below *York*, upon the
'River *Humber*: Some are so large, that
'they are used for Timber in building Hou-
'ses; which are said to be more durable
'than Oak itself: Others are cut into long
'Chips,

'Chips, and tied up in Bundles, and sent
'to the Market Towns several Miles off, to
'light Tobacco. Those that I have viewed,
'were all broken off from the Roots, I sup-
'pose, by Violence of Storm, or Water, or
'both; and, upon Enquiry, do find, that
'they are all after the same manner. They
'affirmed to me, that their Tops lay all
'one way, *viz.* with the Current of Wa-
'ter. So it seems, that these are of this first
'Kind, that were thrown down by Floods,
'and the Force of Water, and not cut down
'by the Hand of Man.

'Upon the first Sight of these (*saith the
'Doctor*) I was induced to believe, that
'they are really Fir-Trees. The Bate or
'Texture of the Wood is the same with
'Fir, easily splitting. If burnt, it sends
'out the same resinous Smell; and it af-
'fords the same Coal. The Branches gene-
'rally grow in Circles, as the Knots do yet
'testify. The Knots do easily part from
'the Wood, as is usual in Fir-Wood.
'The Straitness and Length of these
'Trees, are also a Presumption that they
'must be such."—

In the *Isle of Man* are also found of these subterraneous Trees, whereof we have an Account in a late Description of that Island. In a Bog of 6 Miles long, and 3 Miles over, called the *Curragh* in *Kirk-Christ Lezayre*, are Fir-Trees frequently found, which tho' they lie 18 or 20 Foot deep, yet their Roots are still growing upright in the Ground, and all firm and entire, but the Bodies broken off, with their Heads lying to the N. E.

These Trees (as it seems to me) were broken down, and prostrated by the Force of violent and tempestuous Winds, and the boggy Earth raised above them, in the manner we have before shewn. Hence the Head of them lie to the N. E. because the most violent Winds blow from the *Atlantick* Ocean which lies to the S. W. of this Island. The Manner of the Discovery of these Trees is very remarkable, since there are no Dews ever seen upon those Parts of the Surface of the Bog where they are found, though they lie 20 Foot interred.

Secondly, Some, and that the greatest Number of those subterraneous Trees, were burnt or cut down by the Labour of Man, in the Places where they now lie.

In *England*, there are found of them in most of the great Morasses, Mosses, Fens, and Bogs, in *Somersetshire*, *Cheshire*, *Lancashire*, *Westmorland*, *Yorkshire*, *Staffordshire*, *Lincolnshire*, and other Counties. The Wood of them is usually called Moss-Wood, and is black as Ebony.

These Trees, I say, were anciently burnt or cut down by the Labour of Man, as Mr. *De la Pryme* does clearly make out, in a
Letter

Letter to Dr. *Sloane*, regiſtred in the *Philoſophical Tranſactions*, Numb. 275. ' In that 'many of theſe Trees have been burnt, ' ſome quite through, ſome all on one ſide; ' ſome have been found chopt and ſquared, ' ſome bored through, others half riven with ' great wooden Wedges and Stones in them, and broken Ax-Heads . . . . . . And it is ' very obſervable, that upon the Confines of ' the Low Country, between *Burningham* ' and *Brumley* in *Lincolnſhire*, are ſeveral ' great Hills of looſe Sand, which, as they ' are yearly worn, and blown away with ' the Wind, there are diſcovered under them ' many Roots of great Firs, with the Im' preſſes of the Ax, as freſh upon them as if ' they had been cut down but a few Weeks; ' which I have ſeveral times, with Pleaſure, ' taken notice of, as I rode that way."

You will ask, Who felled theſe Trees? and for what Reaſon did they fell them? Mr. *De la Pryme* tells us, and proves it by ſufficient Authorities, ' That the *Romans* did ' it, to take away theſe Shelters from the ' *Britans*, and to ſecure their Conqueſts. ' For (*faith he*) the ancient *Roman* Wri' ters and Hiſtorians frequently tell us, That ' when their Armies and Generals purſued ' the wild *Britans*, they always fled into ' the Faſtneſſes of miry Woods, and low ' watry Foreſts. *Ceſar* himſelf confeſſes the ſame, and ſays, ' That *Caſſibelane* and his
'  *Britans*,

'Britans, after their Defeat, passed the
' Thames, and fled into such low Morasses
' and Woods, that there was no possibility
' of following them. We find also, that the
' stout Nation of the Silures did the same,
' when they were set upon by Ostorius and
' Agricola. The like did Venutius, King of
' the Brigantes. And Herodian plainly tells
' us, That it was the Custom of the wild
' Britans, to keep in the fenny Bogs, and
' thick marshy Woods; and when Oppor-
' tunity offered, to issue out, and fall upon
' the Romans; who were at length so
' plagued with them, that they were forced
' to issue out Orders for the destroying and
' cutting down all the Woods and Forests
' in Britain, especially all those that grew
' on low Grounds and Morasses. This
' Order was executed, and they were ac-
' cordingly cut down, as is evident in ma-
' ny Writers, who tell us, That when Sue-
' tonius Paulinus conquered Anglesey, he cut
' down all the Woods there. 'Galen the
' Physician tells us, That the Romans kept
' their Soldiers continually employed in
' cutting down of Woods, draining Mar-
' shes and Fens, and in paving of Bogs. It
' is manifest also, they did not only do this
' themselves, but imposed the same heavy
' Task upon the Captive Britans. For
' Galgacus, in his Speech to his Soldiers,
' tells them, That the Romans made Slaves
' of

'of them, and wore out their Bodies in
'cutting down of Woods, and in cleansing
'of Bogs, amidst a thousand Stripes and
'Indignities. But that which is most ob-
'servable, is, what *Dion Cassius* tells us,
'*viz.* That the Emperor *Severus* lost 50000
'of his Men, in a few Years time, in cut-
'ting down the Woods, and cleansing the
'Fens and Morasses of this Nation." Thus
far Mr. *De la Pryme*; who adds much
more of the famous Levels of *Hatfield*
Chace, and the adjoining Countries, which
may be seen in the Letter quoted before. Moreover, not only the *Romans* have
taken this Course of cutting down the Woods,
for the Reasons alledged, but other great Generals and Conquerors of Countries. So
our *Henry* II. when he conquered *Ireland*,
cut down all the Woods that grew upon the
low Countries thereof, the better to secure
his Conquest and Possession of the same, to
keep the Country in a settled Peace, and to
disarm the Enemy, who commonly trusting
to such Advantages, are apt to rebell. For,
safe Retreats are often observed not to make
more Thieves than they do Rebels; as Mr.
*De la Pryme* well writes. The like did *Edward* I. (as *Hollinshed* and other Historians
tell us) when he conquered *Wales*; for being not able to get near the *Welsh* to fight
them, by reason of their Skulking and Continuance in boggy Woods, he commanded
them

them all to be destroyed, and cut down by the Fire and Ax.

The like Original, no doubt, had those great Numbers of subterraneous Trees, which the Describer of *Amsterdam* tells us, are found and digged up in Mosses and Fenny Grounds, where they dig for Turves in *Friesland* and *Groningland*.

If it be demanded, how these Trees came to be sunk so deep in the Mosses, I answer, partly by the Rotting of their smaller Branches and Leaves, partly by the Earth and Silt brought down by Rivers, especially in Times of Floods, subsiding and spreading itself over these Trees; partly by Rain-water precipitating a copious Sediment, for the Nourishment of Moss growing abundantly, with other Plants on the Morass, and shooting down innumerable Roots, and those amassed together to a great Depth; as we see in Turf-Pits, that which is the most firm Part of the Turfs, and holds them together, being these Roots. Indeed it seems to me, that the lower Part of the *Superficies* of the Moss is changed continually into Roots, and raises up the Moor.

It may be objected, that the greatest Part of the Moss-Wood seems to have been Fir; but Fir-Trees are not Native of *England*. To which I answer, That this is a great Mistake. For that anciently there were abundance of Firs growing, even in the great
Level

Level about *Hatfield-Chace*, or in other the like Places, Mr. *De la Pryme* hath sufficiently proved, in a Letter to Dr. *Sloane*, regifter'd *Philofoph. Tranfact.* Numb. 277. And I myfelf have feen a Remnant of thefe Fir-Trees growing on a Hill near *Wareton*, a Village in *Staffordfhire*, about 2 Miles diftant from *Newport* in *Shropfhire*.

So, I think, I have given a fufficient and fatisfactory Account of all the *Phænomena* of thefe fubterraneous or Foffil Trees, or on Mofs-Wood.

Since the Writing of this, happening to read Part of the Learned Dr. *Leigh*'s Natural Hiftory of *Chefhire*, *Lancafhire*, and the *Peak* of *Derby*, I find that the Doctor adheres to the ancient Opinion concerning the Original of thefe Foffil-Trees, *viz.* That they were brought in by the general Deluge, and depofited in the Places where they now lie, and rejects that of Dr. *Plot*, which we embrace; That thefe Moraffes were the Product of the Woods that grew upon them, which by Putrefaction of the Leaves, Rains and Dews, may (as we daily fee) be converted into Bogs and Moraffes; and that the Firs found there, were not brought thither by any Deluge, but were the Products of the Soil, and in Probability ruined by the *Britans* in Revenge to the *Danes*, the Pine being their Darling Tree.

That

That these Trees grew originally in the Places where they are now found, I am of Accord with Dr. *Plot*, but cannot agree with him that they were thrown down by the *Britans* for the Reason he alledges. I rather think them to have been prostrated and overwhelmed by the Force of the Waters in some Inundation of the Sea, (not in the universal Deluge in the Days of *Noah*) and afterwards the Sea by Degrees receding, to have been covered with the Sediment of the Waters, and their own Branches and Leaves, with Moss and other Plants rotting upon them. This *Hypothesis* answers Dr. *Leigh's* second and third Arguments against Dr. *Plot's* Opinion, *viz.* 2. That he had seen seven or eight Fir-Trees of a vast Thickness contiguous to each other, so that whosoever considers the Circumference of them, must necessarily conclude, they could not grow there in that Order, it being impossible there should be a Distance between each Tree for their ascending Boughs. 3. Under these are frequently found the *Exuviæ* of Animals, as Shells and Bones of Fishes, *&c.* which could not come from any other Cause but a Deluge. If he had said, some particular Inundation of the Sea, I could easily have agreed with him. For that there have been such particular Inundations of the Sea is manifest from several Histories, and particularly that transcribed out of *Cambden* a little before, to which

which I referr the Reader. As to his Opinion, that Firs are not, nor ever were, Native of *England*, I have already said, that I think it a great Mistake; Mr. *De la Pryme* producing many Testimonies that they were, particularly in the great Levels about *Hatfield-Chace*, and in *Lincolnshire*, &c. For the Readers Satisfaction, I shall here relate his Words.

'BEING the other Day at *Hatfield*, I was
'told by several Gentlemen, that about 20
'Years ago died one *Sanderson* of that Town,
'aged near 80 Years, whose Father, much
'of the same Age, did frequently assure
'him, and other Gentlemen that were curi-
'ous in the Matter, that he could very well
'remember many hundreds of great Fir-
'Trees, standing one here and another there,
'in a languishing decaying Condition, half
'as high as Houses, and some higher, whose
'Tops were all dead, yet their Boughs and
'Branches always green and flourishing,
'growing all of them in these Levels. And
'*John Hatfield*, of *Hatfield*, Esq; Counsellor
'at Law, who is not above 40 Years of
'Age, has by him a large Twig that his Fa-
'ther plucked off from the Sprout of a green
'and flourishing Shrub of Fir, that grew
'at the Root of one of the same Kind in
'these Commons. And an old Man of *Croul*
'tells me, that he has heard his Father say,
'that he could remember Multitudes of
                                                  ' Shrubs

'Shrubs and small Fir-Trees growing here, while this Country was a Chace, and while the Vert was preserved before the Drainage. And lastly, in many old Charters that I have seen of the pious *Roger de Mowbray*, Lord of *Axholm*, who lived in the Year 1100, relating to *Hurst*, *Belwood*, *Ross*, *Santoft*, &c. that then all these Places were covered with a great old decaying Forest or Wood, and not them only, but also all that low Common between *Croul-Caussey*, and *Authrop* upon *Trent*. And tho' there be not one Stick of any such thing now to be found, yet it is not only plainly manifest, that the same was true from the Roots there found, but also from the said Roots that most of the Trees that then grew there were Firs.'' Thus far Mr. *De la Pryme*. To which, if we add what Dr. *Richardson* observed of the subterraneous Trees found at *Youle* in *Yorkshire*, together with the Remnant of these Trees at this Day growing near *Wareton*, which we before-mentioned, all together make up a demonstrative Proof that Fir-Trees were not only Native of *England*, but grew abundantly in the great Levels in many Counties thereof.

As for the Authority of *Julius Cæsar* to the contrary, I make little Account thereof.

## the Deluge. 241

For, 1. It's likely he never march'd so far up the Country, as to come to the Levels in which these Fir-Woods grew.

2. He denies the *Fagus* to this Island, whereas the Beech-Tree, which is most certainly by the Authority of all Botanists the true *Fagus* of the *Latins*, grows plentifully here in many Places; and not a distinct Sort of *Fagus*, as Dr. *Leigh* fancies, from no better Proof than the Epithet *Patula*, or Spreading, (which *Virgil* attributes to the *Fagus*) which our Beech is not. But by his Leave, I myself have seen Beech-Trees with Heads sufficiently spread, to denominate them *Patula*.

To conclude: It's a vain thing to dispute by Argument against clear Matter of Fact; or to go about to prove, that all these Fossil-Trees were brought in by the universal Deluge, when we have sufficient Testimony, that the greatest Part of them that are found with us were cut or burnt down by the Hand of Man; the very Stroaks of the Axes appearing in them, as if they had been fell'd but Yesterday. So I shall leave this Subject, and return from whence I have digressed.

In the Time of King *Henry* the first of *England*, there happen'd a mighty Inundation in *Flanders*, whereby a great Part of the Country was irrecoverably lost, and many of the poor distressed People, being bereft of

R       their

their Habitation, came into *England*, where the King, in Compassion of their Condition, and also considering that they might be beneficial to his Subjects, by instructing them in the Art of Cloathing, first placed them about *Carlisle* in the North, and after removed them into *South-Wales*, where their Posterity hath ever since remained.

In the Year 1446, there perished 10000 People by the Breaking in of the Sea at *Dordrecht* in *Holland*, and thereabouts; and about *Dullart* in *Friesland*, and in *Zealand*, above 100000 were lost, and two or three hundred Villages drowned, some of their Steeples and Towers, when the Tide is out, still appearing above Water.

Mr. *Carew* of *Antony*, in his *Survey of Cornwal*, affirmeth, That the Sea hath ravened from that Shire the whole County of *Lioness*. And that such a County there was, he very sufficiently proves by many strong Reasons. *Cambden*, in his *Britannia*, reports out of ancient Records, ‘ That upon the *Kentish* Coast, not far from *Thanet*, is a sandy ‘ dangerous Place (which the Inhabitants call ‘ *Goodwyns Sands*) where an Island (being the ‘ Patrimony of Earl *Goodwyn*) was swallow- ‘ ed up in the Year 1097.

But the greatest Change of this Kind that ever was made (if it be true) was the Submersion of the vast Island of *Atlantis*, whereof we have already spoken.

As

## the Deluge. 243

As for the Changes that have been made by undermining and washing away the Shores, they have been partly the diminishing of the Land, and partly the raising up of several Islands not far from the Shores. So the *Baltick* Sea hath invaded the Shores of *Pomerania*, and destroyed a famous Mart-Town, called *Vineta*. So the ancient Borough of *Donewich*, in *Suffolk*, is almost quite eaten away and ruined by the Encroachments of the Sea. And it is said, that the Ocean hath cut off twenty Miles from the North Part of the Island of *Ceylan* in *India*, so that it is much less at this Day than formerly it was. And many the like Examples there are. And for the Raising up of Islands near the Shore, very likely it is, that the Sea continually preying upon the Shore, and washing away abundance of Earth from thence, cannot carry it far to any great Distance from the Shores, but lets it fall by little and little in their Neighbourhood; which subsiding or settling continually for some Ages, at last the Heaps ascend up to the very *Superficies* of the Water, and become Islands. Hence, in the Middle of the Ocean, there are no Islands, or but a very few, because those Parts are too remote from the Shores for any Earth washed from thence to be carried thither; and if it were, yet the Sea thereabout is too deep to have any Heap raised in it so high: Besides, the Motions of the Water in those Depths, were there Earth enough, would overthrow any Heap before it could be advanced any thing near the Top. But all Islands in general, a very few excepted, are about the Shores, or not far from the Shores of the great Continents. Which Thing is especially to be remarked in all the great Heaps or Swarms of numerous Islands, they being all near to the Continents; those of the *Ægean* Sea to *Europe* and *Asia*; the *Hesperides* to *Africa*; and the *Maldivæ*, (which are thought to amount to eleven thousand) to *India*; only the *Flandricæ* or *Azores* seem to be situate in the Middle of the Ocean, between the *Old* and *New* World.

Besides these Changes about the Sea-Coasts, by the prevailing of the Land upon the Sea, in some Places, and the Sea upon the Land in others, the whole Continents seem to suffer a considerable Mutation by the Diminution, and Depression or Sinking of the Mountains, as I shall have Occasion to shew afterward in the Third Discourse.

*Ælian*, in his eighth Book, *cap.* 11. telleth us, That not only the Mountain *Ætna*, but *Parnassus* and *Olympus*, did appear to be less and less to such as sailed at Sea, the Height thereof sinking. Of this Lowering and Diminution of the Mountains, I shall not say much in this Place, but taking it for granted at present, only in brief intimate the Causes of it, assigned by that learned Mathematician

*Josephus*

*Josephus Blancanus*, which are partly Rain-Water, and partly Rivers, which by continual Fretting by little and little, wash away and eat out both the Tops and Sides and Feet of Mountains, and fill up the lower Places of the Valleys, making the one to encreafe, and the other to decreafe; whereby it appears (faith Dr. *Hakewil*) that what the Mountain loseth, the Valley gains; and consequently, that in the whole Globe of the Earth nothing is lost, but only removed from one Place to another; so that in Procefs of Time the highest Mountains may be humbled into Valleys: And again (which yet I will not allow him) the lowest Valleys exalted into Mountains. He proceeds, *Anaxagoras* (as *Diogenes Laertius* reports in his Life) being demanded what he thought, Whether the Mountains called *Lapsaceni* would in time be covered with Sea? answered, *Yes, unless Time itself fail;* which Answer of his seems to confirm the Opinion of *Blancanus De Mundi Fabrica*, cap. 4. where he maintains, That if the World should last long enough, by reafon of this continual Decreafe of the Mountains, and the Levelling of the Valleys, the Earth would again be overflown with Waters, as at first it was.

BESIDE these more eminent and remarkable Changes, which in Procefs of time, after a long Succession of many Ages, threaten some great Effect; indeed, no lefs than a Reduction

duction of the World to its primitive State before the Separation of the Land and Water; there have been many other lesser Mutations made either by Earthquakes and Eructations of Burning Mountains, or by great Floods and Shots of Rain, or by violent or tempestuous Winds and Hurricanes, some whereof are mentioned by Naturalists and Historians, *Strabo, Pliny, Seneca, Ovid,* and others.

For Earthquakes, *Possidonius,* quoted by *Strabo,* in his first Book, writes, 'That there 'was a City in *Phœnicia,* situate above *Sidon,* swallowed up by an Earthquake, and 'that almost two Thirds of *Sidon* itself fell 'therein, though not suddenly, and all at 'once, so that there was no great Destru-'ction or Slaughter of Men happened. The 'same extended almost over all *Syria,* tho' 'not violently, and reached as far as some 'of the *Cyclades* Islands, and *Eubœa,* where 'the Fountains of *Arethusa* in *Chalcis* were 'stopped up by it, and after many Days 'broke forth again at another Source; nei-'ther did it cease to shake the Island by Parts, 'till the Earth opening in the Field *Lelantus* 'vomited out of a River of fiery Clay.

The same *Strabo* tells us, 'That *Democles* 'mentions huge Earthquakes of old in *Lydia* and *Ionia,* extending as far as *Troas,* 'by which many Villages were swallowed
'up,

'up, and Sipylus overthrown when *Tantalus*
'reigned, and great Lakes made of Fens.

   And that *Duris* saith, 'That the *Rhagades*
'Islands by *Media*, were so called from the
'Lands about the *Caspiæ Portæ*, being torn
'and broken by Earthquakes, so that many
'Cities and Villages were overthrown, and
'several Rivers received Alterations.

   And *Demetrius Calatianus*, relating the
Earthquakes that happen'd throughout *Greece*,
writes, 'That a great Part of the *Lichades*
'Islands and *Cenæus* had been drowned
'thereby; and that the hot Baths at *Ædep-*
'*sus*, and in *Thermopylæ*, having been stopt
'for three Days, flowed again, and those of
'*Ædepsus* from new Sources. That the
'Wall of *Oreus* on the Sea-Side, and seven
'hundred Houses, were thrown down; and
'a great part of *Echinus* and *Heraclea Tra-*
'*chinia*; but the whole Building of *Phalar-*
'*nus* was overturned from the very Soil or
'Plain of it; the like happened to the *La-*
'*rians* and *Larissæans*; and that *Scarphia*
'was utterly demolished and subverted from
'the very Foundations, and not fewer than
'1700 Persons overwhelmed and buried;
'and more than half that Number of the
'*Thronii*.

   *Pliny*, in his first Book, *cap.* 84. tells us,
'That in the Reign of *Tiberius Cæsar*, there
'happened an Earthquake (the greatest that
'ever was in the Memory of Man) wherein
'twelve

'twelve Cities of *Asia* were proftrated in
one Night.

But what is that to what S. *Auguftine* writes, [*Lib.* 2. *De Miraculis SS. cap.* 3.] if that Book be his, '*In famofo quodam terræmotu centum Libyæ Urbes corruiffe*: *That in a famous Earthquake a hundred Cities of* Libya *were demolifhed.*

The City of *Antioch*, where the Difciples of Christ were firft called *Chriftians*, with a great part of *Afia* bordering upon it, was almoft wholly fubverted and fwallowed up by an Earthquake in *Trajan*'s time, as *Dion Caffius* writes; *Trajan* himfelf then wintering there.

The fame City of *Antioch*, in the Time of *Juftinian*, in the Year of our Lord 528, was again fhaken with a terrible Earthquake, wherein were overwhelmed and buried in the Ruins of the Houfes above 40000 of the Citizens.

And laftly, in the 61ft Year after the laft mentioned Earthquake, being again fhaken by a new one, it loft 60000 of its Inhabitants: *Gregory*, the then Bifhop, being by the Divine Favour, and in a manner miraculoufly preferved, the Houfe wherein he abode falling down prefently after his going out of it.

*Eufebius* and *Spartanus* make Mention of an Earthquake in the Emperor *Adrian*'s Time, wherein *Nicomedia* and *Nicæa* of *Bithynia*,

*thynia*, and *Nicopolis* and *Cæsarea*, Cities of *Palæstina*, were thrown down and ruined.

In the Year 1182, when *Saladin* set himself to overthrow the Kingdom of *Jerusalem*, there happened an Earthquake, in which *Antiochia*, *Laodicea*, *Alapia*, *Cæsarea*, *Emissa*, *Tripolis*, and other famous Cities, were almost wholly thrown down and destroyed.

To omit many that are recorded in ancient Histories, and to come near to our Times:

*Æneas Sylvius*, afterwards Pope by the Name of *Pius* the Second, in a Letter of his to the Emperor *Frederick*, thus pitifully describes an Earthquake that fell out in his time; *Audies ex latore præsentium quàm mirabilia & incredibilia damna fecerit Terræmotus in Regno* Apuliæ, *nam multa oppida funditùs corruerunt, alia magnâ ex parte collapsa sunt.* Neapoli *omnes fere Ecclesiæ & maxima Palatia ceciderunt; plusquam triginta millia corpora oppressa ruinis traduntur, populus omnis habitat in Tentoriis,* i.e. *You shall understand by the Bearer of these Presents, what wonderful and incredible Losses an Earthquake hath wrought in the Kingdom of* Apulia; *for many Towns are utterly ruined, others for the greatest part fallen. In* Naples, *almost all their Churches and fair Palaces are overthrown; more than* 30000 *Persons are said to have been slain; all the Inhabitants dwell in Tents.*

This

This Kingdom of *Naples*, especially *Apulia* and *Calabria*, hath, I think, been oftner shaken, and suffered more by Earthquakes than any other Part of *Europe*. For *Cluverius* tells us, That in the Year 1629, there were dreadful Earthquakes in *Apulia*, by which 17000 Men are said to have perished.

And *Athanasius Kircher* the Jesuite, in the Preface to his *Mundus Subterraneus*, gives us a sad Narrative of a dismal Earthquake in *Calabria*, in the Year 1638, wherein himself was, and out of which he hardly escaped with his Life: Nothing to be seen in the whole Country he passed by for two hundred Miles in Length, but the Carcasses of Cities, and the horrible Ruins of Villages, the Inhabitants wandring about in the open Fields, being half dead with Fear and Expectation of what might follow. But most remarkable was the Subversion of the noted Town of S. *Eufamia*, which was quite lost out of their Sight, and absorpt, and instead thereof, nothing left but a stinking Lake. But for a full Account thereof, I referr the Reader to the said Preface.

Not many Years ago, the famous City of *Ragusa* was almost wholly subverted and destroyed by a terrible Earthquake; and *Smyrna* has lately been demolished by one. From the *West-Indies* we hear frequently of great Damages done in our Plantations by Earthquakes. The printed Transactions and Journals

nals are full of thefe great Concuffions and Subverfions.

IN the Year 1692, on the Seventh Day of *June*, there happened a dreadful Earthquake in the Ifland of *Jamaica*, which made great Ruins and Devaftations throughout the whole Country, but efpecially in the Capital Town of *Port-Royal*, which was almoft fwallow'd up and overflow'd by the Sinking of the Earth, and Irruption of the Sea: A full Account whereof contained in two Letters fent from the Minifter of the Place, the one dated *June* the 22d, the other the 28th of the fame Month, 1692, from Aboard the *Granada* in *Port-Royal* Harbour, to a Friend of his in *England*, and publifhed by Authority, I fhall give the Reader, with fome Remarks.

1. HE tells us in general, That this Earthquake threw down almoft all the Houfes, Churches, Sugar-Works, Mills and Bridges throughout the whole Ifland: That it tore the Rocks and Mountains [others tell us, that it leveled fome Mountains, and reduced them to Plains] that it deftroy'd fome whole Plantations, and threw them into the Sea; but that *Port-Royal* had much the greateft Share in this terrible Judgment.

2. THEN he acquaints us, what for to fave the Reputation of the People, and to avoid the laying a perpetual Blot upon them, I fhould rather fupprefs and conceal, but for the

the Vindication of the Divine Providence and Juſtice, and to deterr others from the like Enormities, I think neceſſary to publiſh, That the Inhabitants of that Place were a moſt ungodly and debauched People, and ſo deſperately wicked, that he was even afraid to continue among them; for that very Day this terrible Earthquake was, as ſoon as Night came on, a Company of lewd Rogues, whom they call Privateers, fell to Breaking open Warehouſes and Houſes deſerted, to rob and rifle their Neighbours, whilſt the Earth trembled under them, and ſome of the Houſes fell upon them in the Act. [The like Robbers and Plunderers we were told wander'd up and down the Country, even in the very Smoke, during the laſt great Burning and Eruption of *Ætna* in *Sicily*.] And thoſe audacious Whores that remained ſtill upon the Place, were as impudent and drunken as ever; and that ſince the Earthquake, when he was on Shore to pray with the bruiſed and dying People, and to Chriſten Children, he met with too many Drunk and Swearing. And in his ſecond Letter, he ſaith poſitively, That there was not a more ungodly People on the Face of the Earth.

3. The Account he gives of the Motions and Effects of the Earthquake is as followeth: The Day when this Calamity befell, the Town and Iſland was very clear, affording not any Suſpicion of the leaſt Evil. [This is

is observed of most Earthquakes, and particularly of our last here in *England*, the Morning before it, being clear and calm.] But in the Space of three Minutes, about half an Hour after Eleven in the Morning, *Port-Royal*, the fairest Town in all the *English* Plantations, [and well might he call it so, if, as he writes in another Place of his Letter, most of the Houses upon the *Wharf* were built of Brick, and as fair as those in *Cheapside, London*] the best *Emporium* and Mart of this Part of the World, exceeding in Riches and abounding in all good Things, was shaken and shattered to Pieces, and covered for the greatest part by the Sea. The Wharf was entirely swallowed by the Sea, and two whole Streets beyond it. Himself, with the President of the Council, being in a House near where the Merchants meet, hearing the Church and Tower fall, ran to save themselves: He having lost the President, made toward *Morgan*'s Fort, because being a wide open Place, he thought to be there securest from the falling Houses, but as he was going he saw the Earth open, and swallow up a Multitude of People, and the Sea mounting in upon them over the Fortifications: Moreover he tells us, That their large and famous Burying-Place, called the *Palisado's*, was destroyed by the Earthquake; and that the Sea washed away the Carcasses of those that were buried out of their Graves, their

Tombs

Tombs being dashed to Pieces by the Motion and Concussion. That the whole Harbour, one of the fairest and goodliest that ever he saw, was covered with the dead Bodies of People of all Conditions floating up and down without Burial. That in the Opening of the Earth, the Houses and Inhabitants sinking down together, some of these were driven up again by the Sea which arose in those Breaches, and wonderfully escaped: Some were swallowed up to the Neck, and then the Earth shut upon them, and squeezed them to Death; and in that Manner several were left buried with their Heads above Ground, only some Heads the Dogs have eaten, others are covered with Dust and Earth by the People which yet remain in the Place, to avoid the Stench. So that they conjecture, that by the Falling of the Houses, the Opening of the Earth, and the Inundation of the Waters, there are lost Fifteen hundred Persons, and many of good Note, as Attorney General *Musgrove*, Provost Marshal *Reeves*, Lord Secretary *Reeves*, &c.

FARTHER he tells us, That after he was escaped into a Ship, he could not sleep all Night for the Returns of the Earthquake almost every Hour, which made all the Guns in the Ship to jar and rattle. And he supposes that the whole Town of *Port-Royal* will in a short time be wholly swallowed by the Sea; for few of those Houses that yet stand are left whole, and that they heard them fall every Day, and that the Sea daily encroached upon them. That they had Accounts from several Parts of those Islands of Mischiefs done by the Earthquake. From St. *Anne*'s they heard of above 1000 Acres of Wood-Land changed into Sea, carrying with it whole Plantations. And, lastly, That he was told by some, that they still heard Bellowings and Noises in the Mountains, which made them very apprehensive of an Eruption of Fire; which if so, he feared might be more destructive than the Earthquake. [But I think causlesly, for I never heard or read of any great Destruction of Men made by any Eruptions of Fire, even out of burning Mountains.]

4. The Account he gives of his own unexpected and strange Preservation, take in his own Words: *After I had been at Church reading Prayers, (which I did every day since I was Rector of the Place, to keep up some Shew of Religion) and was gone to a Place hard by the Church, where the Merchants meet, and where the President of the Council was, who came into my Company, and engaged me to take a Glass of Wormwood Wine, as a Whet before Dinner; he being my very great Friend, I staid with him: Upon which he lighted a Pipe of Tobacco, which he was pretty long in taking; and not being willing to leave him before it was out, this detain'd me*

me from going to Dinner to one Captain Ruden's, whither I was invited. Whose House, upon the first Concussion, sunk first into the Earth, and then into the Sea, with his Wife and Family, and some that were come to dine with him. Had I been there, I had been lost. But to return to the President, and his Pipe of Tobacco: Before that was out, I found the Ground rolling and moving under my Feet; upon which, I said to him, Lord! Sir, what is this? He replyed very composedly, being a very grave Man, It is an Earthquake; be not afraid, it will soon be over: *But it increased*, &c. Then he relates, how he went to his own Lodging, and found all things in Order there, nothing stirred out of its place; and, going into his Balcony to view the Street, he saw never a House down there, nor the Ground so much as crack'd: And that, after he had prayed with the People, at their earnest Request, and given them some serious Exhortations to Repentance, in which Exercises he spent near an hour and half, there came some Merchants of the Place to him, desiring him to go aboard some Ship in the Harbour, and refresh himself, telling him, that they had gotten a Boat to carry him off; whom he accompanied: And passing over the Tops of some Houses, which lay leveled with the Surface of the Water, got first into a Canoe,

and

and then into a Long-Boat, which put him on board a Ship.

5. The last thing I shall take notice of in these Letters, shall be the Influence and Effect this Judgment had upon the Remainder of the People, to bring them to a Sense of their Sins, and Repentance for them, and to resolve upon, and begin a Reformation and Amendment of their Lives. It is a true Saying, *Vexatio dat intellectum*: *In their Affliction they will seek me early*. The pious Inclination of the People appeared, in that they were so glad to see their Minister in the midst of this Disaster, and so earnest with him to come down and pray with them, when they saw him in the Balcony beforementioned; and that when he came down into the Street, every one laid hold on his Cloaths, and embraced him, so that with their Fear and Kindness he was almost stifled. And that not only at the instant of the Distress, but afterwards when he went ashore to bury the Dead, and pray with the Sick, and baptize the Children, and preach among them, the People were overjoy'd to see him, and wept bitterly when he preached to them. Fear is a more powerful Passion than Love: And whatever creates Terror, is a more effectual Curb to restrain and rule Men as well as Children, than any Favours or Benefits, the most powerful Motives of Love and Affection: For though the *Bonds*

*of Love* are called the *Cords of a Man*, and are indeed very ſtrong ones to rational and ingenuous Perſons, yet the greateſt part of Mankind are ſo far degenerated, that *they have broken theſe Bonds, and caſt theſe Cords from them;* and upon Trial, one ſhall find little of Gratitude or Ingenuity among them.

I ſhall add one or two Remarks upon the precedent Paper.

*Firſt,* It is very remarkable, that the Day, when all this befell *Port-Royal* and the whole Iſland of *Jamaica*, was very clear, not affording the leaſt Suſpicion of any Evil; ſo that the Inhabitants had no Warning at all of it, but were ſurprized of a ſudden, without time ſufficient to eſcape and ſave themſelves. For, in the ſhort Space of three Minutes, the Town was ſhaken and ſhattered to pieces, and ſunk into, and covered, for the greateſt part, by the Sea. In which reſpect, this Judgment reſembled thoſe on the Old World and on *Sodom*, which, the Scripture tells us, were, to the People involved in them, ſudden and unexpected; as alſo the Second Coming of Chriſt, and future Diſſolution of the World by Fire, is predicted to be.

That the Cauſe of Earthquakes is the ſame with that of Thunder, I doubt not, and moſt learned Men are agreed; that is, Exhalations or Steams ſet on fire, the one in the Clouds, the other in the Caverns of the Earth; which

which is sufficiently proved from the great Deflagrations and Eruptions of *Vulcano*'s or burning Mountains; they being always either preceded or attended by Earthquakes: And Earthquakes, even here in *England*, being, as far as I can understand, for the most part, accompanied with a Noise. But now of what Nature this Steam is, that is thus inflamed, and what causes the Accension, I must confess myself not to be yet fully satisfied. That it is at least partly Sulphureous is certain, and well proved by Dr. * *Lister*, from the Sulphureous Stink of Waters smelt before, and of the very Air itself after them: That it conceives Fire of itself, and is not kindled after the Manner of Gun-powder by the Touch of Fire, is as clear, there being no Fire præexisting in the Clouds; but how it should kindle, unless by a Colluctation of Parts after the manner of Fermentations, I cannot conceive. And if so, then the Steam must be a dissimilar Body composed of Parts of different Natures; else would there be no Colluctation, and consequently no Accension, the Parts friendly conspiring and agreeing in the same Motion.

* *Philos. Transact.* N. 157.

I AM not ignorant, that Water, either in the gross Body, or in Vapour, may and doth so far work upon some solid Bodies, as for Example, Quick-Lime, Hay in a Mow, the *Pyrites* or Fire-stone, &c. as to cause an Incalescency, and even an Accension; but still this

this is by the Difcord or Contrariety of the Parts of Water or Vapour, and thofe of the forementioned Bodies meeting and ftruggling together. So in Tempefts of Thunder and Lightning, the Fume contain'd in the Clouds, which my honoured Friend Dr. *Martin Lifter* fuppofes and proves to be no other than the Breath of the *Pyrites* encountring with the Vapour of Water, there may very likely, by the Concourfe and Conflict of thefe two, be produced firft a great Heat, and afterwards an actual Fire.

As for Thunder, after the Steams inclofed in the Cloud are once inflamed, I conceive the Fire goes not out till the End of the Tempeft; but when the inflamed Matter is fo much dilated, that the Cavity of the Cloud cannot contain it, it rends the Cloud, and forces its Way through, where it is moft yielding, fo much of the Fire efcaping at the Breach, till the Cloud overcomes the Refiftance of the Remainder, and clofes itfelf again; and continues fhut, till there be fo much of the fulphureous Steam anew inflamed, as to have Strength enough to tear it, and break out the fecond time, which Procefs is repeated, till the whole Steam be burnt and confumed, and the Fire go out; or till the Cloud be quite condenfed and fallen down in Rain. That this Vapour, or Steam in the Clouds, heats gradually before it comes to Accenfion, I think probable, becaufe before

any

any considerable Tempest the Air beneath is sultry, (as we call it) that is, suffocatingly hot.

So likewise in the Caverns of the Earth, it is not unlikely that the Steams or Damps that cause Earthquakes before Ignition, may be gradually heated by a Colluctation of Parts; but their Accension seems to be very sudden, and in manner of Explosion, like that of Gun-powder; the Succussion coming unexpectedly without any Notice-giving, and being also very transient, and of short Continuance. I mean Earthquakes where there are no Eructations of Fire, such as ours in *England* are.

THERE is a Sort of Damp which some call a Fire-Damp or Fulminating-Damp, of which I had the first Notice from my honoured Friend *Francis Jessop* Esq; *An.* 1668. whereof I find a Relation since communicated by him in a Letter to Dr. *Lister*, published in the *Philosophical Transactions*, Num. 117. and a farther Account from him in Answer to some Queries proposed by the Honourable Mr. *Boyle*, in the *Philosophical Transactions*, Numb. 119. wherein he writes, That this Sort of Damp presently takes Fire at the Touch of a lighted Candle, or other flaming Matter, and flies out of the Mouth of the Bink or Shaft, with a Crack like a Gun. He instances in three Persons that had been hurt by it; one in the Coal-Mines in *Hasleberg* Hills,

S 3 who

who had his Arms and Legs broken, and his Body ſtrangely diſtorted by it: A ſecond in thoſe at *Wingerſworth,* who going into a Bink, where this Kind of Damp was, to fetch ſome of his Tools, with a Candle in his Hand, found himſelf on a ſudden environ'd with Flames, ſo that his Face, Hands, Hair, and a great part of his Cloaths were very much burnt. He heard very little Noiſe, but one who was working at the ſame time in another Bink, and thoſe that were above Ground, heard a very great one, like a Clap of Thunder, wherewith the Earth ſhook; which hearing, they ran in a great Amazement to ſee what the Matter was, with their Candles in their Hands, which were twice extinguiſh'd, but held upon the third Lighting. They ſaw nothing, but met with an intolerable Stench of Brimſtone, and a Heat as ſcalding as an Oven half heated, which made them glad ſpeedily to quit the Place. A third at the ſame Place met with the ſame Accident: And the fore-mentioned Perſon happening then to ſtand at the Mouth of the fired Bink, was ſhot forth about two or three Yards, and had his Head broken and Body bruiſed againſt the farther Side; the ſame alſo a third time incurred the like Diſaſter. That it ſhot off the Turn at the Mouth of the Pit to a conſiderable Height: That they could perceive no Smell before the Fire, but afterwards a very ſtrong one of Brimſtone. That the

Damp

Damp hung about the Top of the Bink, and therefore they were forc'd to go with their Candles very low, elſe it would have taken Fire. That the Flame would continue in the Vault two or three Minutes, ſometimes more after the Crack. That he could never hear of any Damps that kindled of themſelves. That from the Breaking of theſe Fulminating-Damps proceeded a black Smoak of the Smell and Colour of that from Gun-powder fired.

This Sort of Fire-Damp, Mr. *Beaumont* tells us, they have alſo in ſome Coal-Works bordering on *Mendip* Hills. See *Philoſoph. Collect.* 1. And Mr. *George Sinclair*, in a Land called *Werdy*, Weſt of *Leith*, which even in the Day-time is ſometimes ſeen in Coal-works in little Holes, ſhining like kindled Sulphur. But the moſt ſtrange Fire-Damp was that which happen'd at *Moſtyn* in *Flintſhire*, at the ſame time with that at *Wingerſworth* [1675.] which as ſoon as the Colliers were ſcanted of Air, appeared in the Creviſſes or Slits of the Coal, where Water had been before, in a ſmall bluiſh Flame, flaſhing and darting like Sword-Blades from Side to Side of the Pit; and being kindled, had the ſame and more violent Effects than thoſe of *Haſleberg* or *Wingerſworth*, leaving a foul ill-ſcented Smoak behind it. In the laſt there mention'd (*Philoſoph. Tranſact.* Numb. 136.) firing of it by one who ran indiſcreetly with his Candle over the Eye of the damp Pit, it flew to and fro over all the Hollows of the Work with a great Wind and mighty Roaring, tore the Mens Cloaths from their Backs, findging and burning them, as also their Hair and Skins, carrying some of them 15 or 16 Yards from their first Station, beating them against the Roof of the Coal and the Posts. As it drew up to the Day-Pit, it caught one that was next the Eye along with it, and up it comes and was discharged out of the Mouth of the Shaft with a terrible Crack, not unlike, but more shrill than a Cannon, so that it was heard fifteen Miles off. The Man's Body, and other things from the Pit, were seen in the Air above the Tops of the highest Trees that grew on the Brow of the Hill (eighteen Yards above the Pit) more than 100 Yards. The Barrel of an Horse Engine for winding up the Rope of above 1000 Pound Weight, though fasten'd to the Frame with Locks and Bolts of Iron, together with the Buckets and Rope were thrown up, and carried a good way from the Pit, and Pieces torn off from it scattered about the Woods. And lastly, the whole Frame of the Engine moved out of its Place. The whole Relation deserves well to be read.

THAT which seems to me most strange and Romantick, is the Motion of the Damp, that as if it had been a living thing, it should fly up with a long sharp Flame to lighted Candles

dles set over the Eye of the Pit, and put them out. And yet Mr. *Jessop* also mentions a like Motion in that of *Wingersworth*; *For if*, says he, *in the Bink where it was, they held their Candles any higher than ordinary, they could see the Damp, which lay near the Roof, to descend like a black Mist, and catch hold of the Flame, lengthening it to two or three Handfuls.*

By these Descriptions, this Damp should seem to be but Gun-powder in a Vapour, and to partake the Sulphur, Nitre, and *Bitumen*, as the learned Dr. *Plot* well proves in his *Natural History of Staffordshire, c. 3. sect. 47.* to which I referr the Reader. But for the Accension of it, whether it ever takes Fire of itself, I am in some Doubt. Mr. *Jessop* denies it of those of *Hasleberg* and *Wingersworth*; and how far those Relators that affirm it are to be credited, I know not.

If in this Particular I were satisfied, I should readily accord with the Doctor, That our Earthquakes in *England*, and any others that have but one single Pulse, owe there Original to the Kindling and Explosion of Fire-Damps.

You will say, That Fire is the Cause of Thunder we readily grant, because we see it plentifully discharged out of the Clouds; but what Reason have we to think so of this Sort of Earthquakes, where we see no Lightning or Eruption of Fire at all? What becomes of the inclosed Flame?

IN Answer hereto, I demand, What becomes of it in the open Air? It diffuses itself through the Caverns of the Earth, till the Deflagration be made, and is there dissipated and dissolved into Fume and Ashes. It breaks not forth, I conceive, because by reason of the Depth of the Caverns wherein it is lodged, it is not able to overcome the Resistance of the incumbent Earth, but is forced *quà data porta ruere*, to make its Way where it finds easiest Passage through the strait *Cuniculi* of the Earth: As in a Gun the inflamed Powder, though if it were at Liberty, and found equal Resistance on every Side, it would spread equally every Way; yet by reason of the Strength and Firmness of the Metal, it cannot tear the Barrel in Pieces, and so break out; but is compelled to fly out at the Muzzle, where it finds an open, tho' strait Passage. For the Force of Flame, though very great, is not infinite.

IT may be farther objected, We hear not of any Eruption of Fire at *Port-Royal*, or elsewhere in this Island, and yet the Earth opened, and the Roofs of the Caverns fell in, therefore Fire could not be the Cause of this Earthquake; for if it had, at those Apertures and Rifts of the Ground, it must needs have issu'd forth and appear'd abroad.

To which I answer, that the Vaults and Cavities wherein the inflamed Matter was imprison'd, and the Explosion made, lay deep in the Earth, and were cover'd with a thick and impenetrable Coat of hard Stone, or other solid Matter which the Fire could not tear; but that above this Coat there were other superficial Hollows in a more loose and crumbling Earth, which being not able to sustain the Shock, and hold out against the impetuous Agitations of the Earthquake, the Roofs might yield, open, and subside, as we hear they did, and give Way to the Sea to rush in and surmount them.

You will reply, This may be a tolerable Account of our *English* Earthquakes, which are finished at one Explosion, but what shall we say to those of *Jamaica*, which like a Tempest of Thunder and Lightning in the Clouds, have (as we learn by this Relation) several Paroxysms or Explosions, and yet no Discharging of Fire?

To which I answer, That I conceive the Caverns of the Earth wherein the inflamed Damps are contained, are much larger there than ours in *England*; and the Force of the Fire, joined with the Elatery of the Air, being exceeding great, may of a sudden heave up the Earth, yet not so far as to rend it in sunder, and make its Way out, but is forced to seek Passage where it finds least Resistance through the lateral *Cuniculi*. So the main Cavern being in a great Measure emptied, and the Exterior Parts of the extended Matter within cooling and shrinking, the Earth

may

may subside again, and reduce the Cavern to its former Dimensions. Yet possibly there may not be a perfect Deflagration and Extinction of the Fire, and so new Damps ascending out of the Earth, and by Degrees filling the Cavern, there may succeed a second Inflamation and Explosion, and so a third and fourth till the Steams be quite burnt up and consumed. But in this, I confess, I do not satisfy myself. They who have a more comprehensive Knowledge of all the *Phænomena*, may give a better Account.

But as for those Earthquakes that are occasion'd by the Burning of *Vulcano's*, they are, I conceive, of a different Nature. For in them the Fire burns continually, and is never totally extinct, only after the great Eruptions, in which, besides Smoak and Fire, there is an Ejection of abundance of Ashes, Sand, Earth, Stones, and in some Floods of melted Materials, the Raging is for a time qualified; but the Fire still continuing, and by Degrees increasing in the combustible Matter it finds in the Hollows of the Mountains, at last swells to that Excess, that it melts down Metals and Minerals where it meets with them, causing them to boil with great Fury, and extending itself beyond the Dimensions of the Cavities wherein it is contained, causes great Succussions and Tremblings of the Earth, and huge Eruptions of Smoak, and casts out such Quantities of

Ashes,

Ashes, Sand, and Stones, as we just now mention'd; and after much Thunder and Roaring by the Allision and Repercussion of the Flame against and from the Sides of the Caverns, and the Ebullition and Volutation of the melted Materials, it forces out that boiling Matter, either at the old Mouths, or at new ones, which it opens where the incumbent Earth is more thin and yielding. And if any Water enters those Caverns, it mightily encreaseth the Raging of the Mountain. For the Fire suddenly dissolving the Water into Vapour, expands it to a vast Dimension; and by the Help thereof throws up Earth, Sand, Stones, and whatever it meets with. How great the Force of Water converted into Vapour is, I have sometimes experimented by inadvertently casting a Bullet in a wet Mold, the melted Lead being no sooner poured in, but it was cast out again with Violence by the Particles of Water adhering to the Mold, suddenly converted into Vapour by the Heat of the Metal.

*Secondly,* The People of this Plantation being generally so ungodly and debauched in their Lives, this Earthquake may well be esteemed by this Gentleman, the Minister of *Port-Royal,* a Judgment of God upon them.

For tho' it may be a senile Complaint, and popular Mistake, that the former Times were better than these, and that the World

doth

doth daily degenerate, and grow worse and worse. *Ætas parentum pejor avis tulit hos nequiores, mox daturos Progeniem vitiosiorem.* For had this been true, Vice would long before this Time have come to the Height and greatest possible Excess; and this Complaint hath been made as well in the best as worst of Times. Though, I say, this be partly an Error, yet I do verily believe, that there are certain Times when Iniquity doth abound, and Wickedness overflow in a Nation or City; and that long Peace and Prosperity, and great Riches, are apt to create Pride and Luxury, and introduce a general Corruption of Manners: And that at such Times GOD usually sends some sweeping Judgment, either utterly destroying such a People who have filled up the Measure of their Iniquity, or at least grievously afflicts and diminishes them. So when in the old World *the Wickedness of Man was great upon the Earth, and every Imagination of the Thoughts of his Heart was only Evil continually,* Gen. vi. 5. *And the Earth was corrupt before* GOD, *and filled with Violence, all Flesh having corrupted their Ways,* vers. 11, and 12. GOD brought in the Flood, and drowned them all. The like Vengeance we find executed on the Cities of *Sodom* and *Gomorrha,* after such a monstrous Height of Wickedness as the Inhabitants were generally arrived at. And we shall find it noted by Historians, That before any great

publick

publick Calamity, or utter Excision of a Nation, the People were become universally vicious and corrupt in their Manners, and without all Fear of GOD, or Sense of Goodness. For GOD doth not stand by as an idle and unconcerned Spectator, and suffer Things to run at Random, but his Providence many times interposes, and stops the usual Course and Current of Natural Causes: Nay, I believe and affirm, That in all great and notable Revolutions and Mutations, He hath the greatest Hand and Interest; Himself ordering and governing them by His special Superintendence and Influence. So, though the Instruments and Materials wherewith this Devastation in *Jamaica* was made, as a subterraneous Fire and inflamable Materials, were before in the Earth, yet that they should at this time break forth and work, when there was such an Inundation of Wickedness there, and particularly and especially at *Port-Royal*, this we may confidently say, was the Finger of GOD, and effected perchance by the Ministery of an Angel.

MOREOVER, this Relator's being called aside, and stopped from going to a Place, whither if he had then gone he had certainly perished, we have good Reason to think an Effect of Providence, designing thereby his Preservation; as *Gregory* the Bishop of *Antioch* his going out of the House wherein he abode immediately before it fell down,

was

was rationally thought to be in respect of him.

But to proceed; I should now have done concerning Earthquakes, it being my design only to take notice of such as have made confiderable Mutations in the superficial Part of the Earth, passing by those, which after a short Trembling and Succussion, have left the Earth as they found it, making no Alteration at all therein. But at the very time this Sheet of Earthquakes was Composing, there happening a notable one, though of this latter Kind, in our own Country; I was, partly by the Coincidence of it with the Composure before-mentioned, partly at the Request of the Bookseller, induced to make some Mention of it, and add what I knew or could learn of its History; which is, indeed, very little and inconfiderable, we having as yet but a very lame and imperfect Account of the Accidents of it.

As for the Time when it happened, it was the 8th of *September*, 1692, about 4 Minutes past Two of the Clock in the Afternoon, as was observed at *London*: Hereabouts I can hear of no body that was so critical in noting the Time, only they agree that it was about Two of the Clock. Had we a punctual and exact Notice of the very Minute that it happened in far distant Places, we might thence gather something concerning the Motion and Progress of it. However, it is remarkable,

markable, that it happened in the *Autumn*, one of the Seasons, in which, *Aristotle* tells us, such Effects are most frequent, the other being the Spring; and likewise in the Month of *September*; in the which, that about *Oxford* in the Year 1683. fell out; and, moreover, in a wet Season, as that also did: Though the Forenoon of the Day was clear and fair, yet, in the Afternoon, when the Earthquake was past, it rained hard till Night; the whole precedent Summer (to this I mean) having been cold and wet: Which, what Influence it can have toward the Production of an Earthquake, unless by stopping the Pores of the Earth, and hindring the Evaporation of those sulphureous Steams, which are the Efficients of it, I know not. The same Night succeeded some Strokes of Thunder and Flashes of Lightning, both here and at *London*; and since then, we have had great Storms of Wind. I might have taken Notice, that, for some Mornings before, we had smart Frosts for the time of the Year.

SINCE this was written, and sent away in order to printing, I am advis'd, by Letter from my honoured Friend Dr. *Tancred Robinson*, that this Earthquake was not confin'd to some Counties of *England*, as *Middlesex*, *Essex*, *Kent*, *Sussex*, *Hampshire*, &c. but spread far into Foreign Parts; an Account whereof I shall give you in the Doctor's own Words. *The Concussion or Vibration of our late Earth-*

T *quake*

*quake was felt in most Parts of the Dutch and Spanish Netherlands, as also in* Germany *and* France: *It affected Places most upon the Sea-Coasts, and near the great Rivers, as* Zealand, Cologn, Mentz, *and the Bridge of* London. *It went not beyond 52 Degrees and 46 Minutes of Northern Latitude; how far it reach'd to the South and East, is not yet certainly known, for Want of good Intelligence; we have already traced it beyond* Paris, *to the 48 Degree of N. Latitude, and beyond the* Rhine, *on the East to* Francfort; *so that we know, at present, of 260 Miles square shaken by it. The Motions of some Machines were very sensibly stop'd or retarded by the* Choc, *especially Pendulums: And there were some Alterations in the Air, (as to its Smell, Spring, and Gravity) both before and after. The Time of its happening here in* England, *and beyond the Seas, seems to vary some Minutes; but that may easily be accounted for by the Difference of Meridians.* Thus far the Doctor. Dat. Septemb. 22.

The Duration or Continuance of it (as I am informed by some curious and attentive Observers) about *London*, was about two Minutes; here not so long.

The Manner of the Motion, as I am assured by my learned and ingenious Friend and Neighbour Mr. *Allen*, Physician in *Braintree*, who had it from several intelligent and observant Persons hereabouts, and that lived in distant Places, was first a manifest Heaving upwards, and after that a Trembling, or Vibration, or Agitation to and fro. So that in the first respect, its Motion seemed to resemble that of the Blood in an Artery, stretching the Channel as it passed.

THE Motion of it was most considerable upon the Hills, and in Valleys.

THE Effect it had upon those who were sensible of it, was a Swimming or Dizziness in their Heads; and this was general upon all. In some it affected their Stomachs, and created a Loathing, and Inclination to Vomit: Some of the tenderer Sex found in themselves such a Disposition as they have had before a swooning Fitt. All which must be the Effects, either of the Heaving, or tremulous Motion, or both; and yet, no Motion of Boat or Coach doth so suddenly affect and disturb the Head or Stomach.

*Lastly,* It was attended with a Noise, as our Earthquakes generally in *England* are, as is observed by Mr. *Pigot* in that of *Oxford* in the Year 1683. and by myself when I lived in *Sutton-Cofield,* in one that happen'd there in the Winter-time, as I remember, in the Year 1677. and extended at least 40 Miles in Length into *Worcestershire.* The Noise I heard, seem'd to be in the Air. This Noise, hereabouts, was heard but in few Places, and by few Persons; but yet I am well assured by some, and those of the Vulgar and Ignorant sort,

sort, who reported it of themselves, having no reason to feign it, and who had never heard that any such thing accompanied Earthquakes.

From many of the afore-mentioned Particulars, it may be collected, That the Caverns, in which the inflamed Damp, causing this Earthquake, was contained, lie deep in the Earth.

For, 1. It could not else have shook such a vast Extent of Ground, both Hills and Valleys in *England*, and beyond Seas, (the Motion not being stopt by the Channels of great Rivers or even Creeks of the Sea) unless, I say, the containing *Cuniculi* or Conduits had passed under the very Bottom of the narrow Seas: Which is a great Confirmation of what we have before delivered concerning the Mountains of *Ætna*, *Stromboli*, and *Vesuvius*, communicating by submarine Vaults.

2. If the Caverns had not lain deep, the enclosed Damp would, in all likelihood, somewhere or other, have rent the superincumbent Earth, and broken forth in the Form of a Flame.

And yet, notwithstanding the Depth, it should seem, it found so much Vent as to affect the external Air, and create a Sound: For if the Caverns, wherein the Damp was, had been close shut up with such a thick Coat of Earth, I doubt whether the Trembling

## the Deluge.   277

bling and Vibration of the soft Earth alone, would have produced such a Noise abroad in the Air; and the Vapour of it also made a shift to struggle through the Pores of the Earth into the open Air, in such Quantity as to affect the Sense;
ing
and after the Concussion.

It is, moreover, very remarkable, That there were some particular Spots which were not at all stirred in those Countries where the Places, not far distant round about, were shaken; as *Sturbridge-Fair* before-remembred, and that where my Dwelling is; neither myself, nor any of my Family, though they were Above-stairs, nor any of our near Neighbours, being sensible of the least Motion or Impression of it, and yet those living within less than half a Mile, had their Houses considerably shaken by it.

It is also worth the noting, That both this, and all other Earthquakes I have heard or read of in *England*, have been very short, and finished at one Explosion; which is an Argument that the Cavities and *Cuniculi*, wherein the inflamed Matter is contained and moves, are very strait, and of small Di-
xplosion I call it, because by the Quickness of the Motion, it seems rather to resemble that of Powder in a Gun, than that of a Squib running in a Train of Powder. Though others I have read of, whose Motion

T 3                              was

was very flow; as that obferved by the Honourable Mr. *Boyle*, and defcribed in the *Philofophical Tranfactions*, Numb. 11. Had we certain Knowledge where the greateft Force of this Earthquake was, we might thence learn where its firft Accenfion was, and which way it fpread itfelf. But I have not time to enlarge farther concerning it, or to give an Account of all its *Phænomena*, left I injure the Printer by ftopping the Prefs: Neither, indeed, would it be Prudence to attempt it, till we have a more particular and perfect Hiftory of it.

SINCE this was written and fent away to the Printer, Intelligence is come from beyond the Seas, that *Flanders*, and all *Holland*, Part of *France* and *Germany*, were fhaken by this Earthquake, and, confequently, the interjacent Provinces; which is a clear Demonftration of our Opinion, That the inflamed Damp, which caufed it, was lodged deep in the Earth, the *Cuniculi* or Caverns, which contained it, paffing under the very Bottom of the Sea. It is alfo a great Confirmation of what we have delivered concerning the Mountains of *Ætna*, *Stromboli*, and *Vefuvius*, communicating by fubmarine Paffages. Add hereto, that *Gaffendus*, in the Life of *Peireskius*, reports, That at the Mountain *Semo* in *Æthiopia*, there happened a Burning at the fame time with that of *Vefuvius* in *Campania*, viz. in the Year 1633.

1633. So that not only *Vesuvius* communicates with *Ætna* by subterraneous Vaults, but also (as he rationally inferrs) *Ætna* with the Mountains of *Syria*, the Tunnels running under the Depths of the *Mediterranean* Sea, and those with the *Arabian*; and, lastly, the *Arabian* with Mount *Semo* in *Æthiopia*.

That an inflamed Damp or subterraneous Fire is the Cause of all Earthquakes in general, and not only such as precede the Eruptions of *Vulcano's*, may be proved by an eminent Instance of an Earthquake happening *May* 12. 1682. which shook the greatest Part of *France* and *Switzerland*, and reach'd as far as *Collen* in *Germany*: An Account whereof we have in the *Journal des Scavans*, set forth *June* 1. 1681. inserted in the *Weekly Memorials* printed for Mr. *Faithorne*, Numb. 23. In which they write, That it was perceived in *Lionnois*, (which was wont to pass for a Place exempt from such Accidents) in *Dauphiny* and *Beaujolois*, though very little, and without any ill Consequence. That at *Mets* in *Lorrain*, the Watch-place of a Bulwark was thrown down into the Ditch, with the Soldier that stood Centinel there.

That at *Tonnerre*, the Houses and Churches were so terribly shaken, as if several Coaches with six Horses had driven along full speed through the Streets; and that it threw

T 4          down

down several Rocks on the side of *Bourbirant*. They tell also, that it stopt a Fountain at *Raviere*, hard by, (which at fifty Paces from its Head, turns a Mill) for half an Hour.

THAT it was perceived in *Provence*, by the Shaking of Windows and Beds, and Opening of Doors; and that it had two several Motions or Pulses, as ours also was, by some, observed to have: And that the Domestick Animals, as Sheep, Cows, Horses, and Poultry, did discover their Fear by unusual Motions and Cries. And the Sheep at *Dijon* in *Burgundy*, could not be stop'd from getting into their Stalls at Four of the Clock in the Afternoon, which were not then wont to betake themselves thither till Sun-set.

THAT the Cities of *Orleans, Troyes, Sens, Chalons, Joinville, Reims, Soissons, Laon, Mascon, Dole, Strasbourg, &c.* felt the Effects of it.

BUT at *Remiremont* upon the *Moselle*, where it exerted its greatest Force; throwing down several Houses, insomuch that the Inhabitants were forced to betake themselves into the Fields for six Weeks time; there was a Noise heard like Thunder, and Flames frequently broke out of the Earth of a noisome Scent, but not sulphureous, and which burnt nothing; yet was there no Rift or Chap in the Ground, save only in one Place; the Depth whereof was in vain search'd, search'd, and which afterwards closed up. And before this Earthquake also, Flames appeared for four Days upon a Mountain near *Geneva*.

It is very strange and remarkable, that the Flames that issued out, were of the Nature of an *Ignis fatuus*, and burnt nothing; and that the Earthquake raged every Night, and never in the Day-time.

Concerning Earthquakes, I shall only add two Observations.

1. That it is not likely that they spend all their Strength upon Cities, but do indifferently shake, break in sunder, and throw down Mountains and Rocks; and seeing few Cities there are but have been shaken, and many ruined and subverted by them, and leveled with the Ground; there is good Reason to think, that few Rocks or Mountains have escaped their Fury, but have suffered the like Concussions and Alterations.

2. That the Changes that have hitherto happened in the Earth by Earthquakes, have not been so considerable as to threaten a Dissolution of the present System of the Terraqueous Globe, should there be a like Succession of them to Eternity. Unless we will except that unparallel'd universal One, which happened in the Days of *Valentinian* the First, (which we have already mentioned) by which the whole known World, both Land and Sea, and it's like the then unknown too, were

violently

violently shaken; which might seem to be a Prelude to the future Conflagration, or Destruction of the whole, by such a Confusion and Dashing in Pieces of all the Parts of it, one against another, as the *Stoicks* speak of.

Of the Effects of burning Mountains, or *Vulcano's*; I have already said something, and shall, afterwards, have occasion to say more. In brief, 1. They cast forth out of their Mouths, and scatter all over the Country, sometimes to a very great Distance, abundance of Sand and Ashes. *Dion Cassius* reports, That in the noted Deflagration of *Vesuvius*, in the Time of *Titus* the Emperor, there was so much Cinders and Ashes vomited out of its flaming Tunnel, and with that Fury and Violence, that they were transported over Sea, into *Africa*, *Syria*, and *Egypt*; and, on the other side, were carried as far as *Rome*, where they darkned the very Air, and intercepted the Sun-beams. At which time, by the Fury of this Burning and Tempest, the whole Mountain and Earth thereabouts was so shaken, that two adjoining Cities, *Herculanium* and *Pompeii*, were destroyed with the People sitting in the Theater. And the famous Natural Historian *Pliny* the Elder, then Admiral of the *Roman* Navy, out of a Curiosity of searching out the Causes and Nature of the Deflagration, approaching too near the Mountain, and staying too long there,

there, was suffocated with the sulphureous Smoke and Stench thereof.

Of another Eruption of the same *Vesuvius*, we read, in the Time of *Leo* the Emperor, wherein the Ashes thereof, transported in the Air, obscured all *Europe*, being carried as far as *Constantinople*; and that the *Constantinopolitans* being wonderfully affrighted therewith, (insomuch as the Emperor forsook the City) in memory of the same did yearly celebrate the Twelfth of *November*.

2. They also pour out huge Floods of melted Minerals, Stones, and other Materials, running down like Rivers for many Miles together; as did the Mountain *Ætna* in that last and most famous Eruction, disgorging such mighty Streams of fiery running Matter, as flowed down to *Catana*, above twenty Miles distant, and advanced a considerable way into the very Sea itself.

2. The next thing I shall mention, is the extraordinary Floods caused by long continuing Showers, or violent and tempestuous Storms and Shots of Rain.

The most ancient and memorable of this Kind is that of *Deucalion*, of which we have already discoursed sufficiently. S. *Hierome*, in the Life of *Hilarion*, (as I find him quoted by Dr. *Hakewill*) speaks of a Flood and Inundation after the Death of *Julian*, in which *Naves ad prærupta montium delatæ pependerunt*, the Ships being landed upon

the

the Tops of the Mountains, there stuck: Which, whether it proceeded from Rain, or from an Irruption of the Sea, or from both Causes together, he doth not say: But if it were literally true, and not hyperbolically exaggerated, then may some Credit be given to what *Sabin*, in his Commentaries upon *Ovid*'s *Metamorphosis*, reports, *Ex Annalium monumentis constat Anno* 1460. *in Alpibus inventam esse Navim cum anchoris in cuniculo per quem metalla effodiuntur*: *It appears by by the Monuments of History, that in the Year 1460. in a Mine of the* Alps, *was found a Ship with its Anchors*; in Confirmation of what that Poet writes:

*Et vetus inventa est in montibus anchora summis.*

In the Year of our Redemption 590. in the Month of *October*, *Gregory* being then Bishop of *Rome*, there happened a marvellous Overflowing in *Italy*, and especially in the *Venetian* Territory, and in *Liguria*, accompanied with a most fearful Storm of Thunder and Lightning; after which followed the great Plague at *Rome*, by reason of many dead Serpents cast up, and left upon the Land, after the Waters decreased and returned.

STROZIUS SIGOG, in his *Magia omnifaria*, telleth of an Inundation in *Italy*, in the Time of Pope *Damasus*, in which also many

Cities

Cities of *Sicily* were swallowed: Another in the Time of *Alexander* the Sixth. Also, in the Year 1515. *Maximilian* being Emperor, he also remembers a perilous Overflowing in *Polonia* about *Cracovia*, by which many People perished.

LIKEWISE *Vignier*, a *French* Historian, speaketh of a great Flood in the South Part of *Languedoc*, which fell in the Year of our Lord 1557. with so dreadful a Tempest, that all the People attended therein the very End of the World and Judgment-Day, saying, That by the violent Descent of the Waters about *Nismes*, there were removed divers old Heaps and Mountures of Ground, and many other Places torn up and rent; by which Accident, there was found both Coin of Silver and Gold, and divers Pieces of Plate, and Vessels of other Metal, supposed to be hidden at such time as the *Goths* invaded that Province. These Stories related in the three last Paragraphs, I have borrowed of Sir *Walter Raleigh* his *History of the World*.

To which I shall add one of late Date happening in *Sicily*, a Narrative whereof communicated in a Letter from *Palermo*, dated *June* the 25th, 1682. I met with in the *London Gazette*, Numb. 1742. in the following Words: *We have an Account from the Town of* Tortorica, *That on the Sixth Instant, about Seven a Clock in the Evening, after so great a Darkness that no Object could be* be distinguished at the Distance of four Paces, there arose such a great Storm of Rain, Lightning, and Thunder, which lasted Six and thirty Hours, that about One a Clock the next Morning, great Torrents of Water, caused by these Rains, fell down from the neighbouring Mountains with so great Rapidity, that they carried with them Trees of an extraordinary Bigness, which threw down the Walls and Houses of the Town they happened to beat against. The Waters were so violent that they overthrew the Church of S. Nicholas; and the Arch-Deacon of the Town, who retired thither, perished there with many other Persons: There remaining only one Abby, and about fifty Houses, and those so shattered, that they fell one after another. There were about Six hundred of the Inhabitants drown'd, the rest being abroad in the Field gathering their Silk, fled to the Mountains, where they suffered very much for Want of Provisions. The Goods, Trees, Stone, Sand, and other Rubbish, which the Waters carried away, were in so great Abundance, that they made a Bank above the Water, two Miles in Length, near the Mouth of the River, where, before, the Sea was very deep. This Town is situate in that Part of Sicily called the Valley of Demona, on the side of the River Tortorica, about Five and twenty Miles from the Tuscan Sea. The Towns of Randazzo and Francaville,

and

*and* several others, have likewise been destroyed by this great Flood. It is added, that Mount Ætna casts out such abundance of Water, that all the neighbouring Country is drowned. Which if it be true, (as I see no Reason to doubt it) this is a farther Proof against *Borellius*, that the Caverns of *Ætna* are more than superficial, and reach down to the very Roots and Foundations of that Mountain, communicating with the subterraneous Abyss, and the Sea itself, from whence, in all likelihood, these Waters were derived, as is evident in those poured out by *Vesuvius*.

MANY other Floods we read of in Histories, whether caused by Rains or Inundations of the Sea, is uncertain; and, therefore, I shall not spend time in setting them down. The Effect of all which, relating to the Earth in general, is, the Wasting and Washing away of Mountains and high Grounds, the Raising of the Valleys and Bottoms, and, consequently, Leveling of the Earth, and Landing up of the Sea.

3. THE last thing I shall mention, which hath effected considerable Changes in the Earth, is boisterous and outrageous Winds and Hurricanes, of which I need not give Instances, they every Year almost happening. These, I conceive, have a great Interest in the Inundations of the Sea we have before mentioned. These raise up those great Hills or

Downs

Downs of Sand we see all along the Coasts of the *Low-Countreys*, and the Western-Shores of *England*, and the like Places. These sometimes blow up so much Sand, and drive it so far as to cover the adjacent Countrys; and to mar whole Fields, yea, to bury Towns and Villages. They are also a concurrent Cause of those huge Banks and Shelves of Sand, that are so dangerous to Mariners, and bar up Havens, and ruin Port-Towns; of which many Instances might be given.

I FIND in Dr. *Hakewill's* Apology, a Story, or two, shewing the great Force and Strength of Winds; the one taken out of *Bellarmine's* Book, *De ascensu mentis in Deum per scal. creat. grad.* 2. *Vidi ego* (saith the Cardinal) *quod nisi vidissem non crederem, à vehementissimo vento effossam ingentem terræ molem, eamque delatam super pagum quendam ut fovea altissima conspiceretur, unde terra eruta fuerat; & pagus totus coopertus, & quasi sepultus manserit, ad quem terra illa devenerat:* i. e. 'I myself have seen, which if I had not seen, I should not have believed, a very great Quantity of Earth, digged out and taken up by the Force of a strong Wind, and carried up a Village thereby, so that there remained to be seen a great empty Hollowness in the Place from whence it was lifted, and the Village upon which it lighted was in a manner all covered over and buried in it.

THE

The other out of *Stow*, who reports, That in the Year 1095. during the Reign of King *William Rufus*, there happened in *London* an outrageous Wind, which bore down in that City alone Six hundred Houses, and blew off the Roof of *Bow-Church*, with which the Beams were borne into the Air a great Height, six whereof being 27 Foot long, with their Fall were driven 23 Foot deep into the Ground, the Streets of the City lying then unpaved.

Now then to sum up what we have said; The Changes and Alterations that have been made in the superficial Part of the terraqueous Globe, have been effected chiefly by *Water, Fire,* and *Wind.* Those by *Water* have been either by the Motions of the *Sea*, or by *Rains;* and both either ordinary or extraordinary: The ordinary Tides and Spring-Tides of the *Sea* do wash away the Shores, and change Sand-Banks, and the like. The extraordinary and tempestuous Motions of the Sea, raised by raging and impetuous Winds, subterraneous Fires, or some other hidden Causes, overwhelm Islands, open *Fretums,* throw up huge Beds and Banks of Sand, nay, vast Baiches of Stone, extending some Miles, and drown whole Countrys. The ordinary *Rains* contribute something to the daily Diminution of the Mountains, filling up of the Valleys, and atterrating the Skirts of the Seas. The extraordinary *Rains*

U causing

causing great Floods and Deluges, have more visible and remarkable Influences upon such Mutations, doing that in a few Days which the ordinary Weather could not effect, it may be, in a hundred Years.

In all these Changes the Winds have a great Interest; the Motion of the Clouds being wholly owing to them, and, in a great measure also, the Overflowings and Inundations of the Sea.

Whatever Changes have been wrought by Earthquakes, Thunders, and Eruptions of *Vulcano's,* are the Effects of Fire.

All these Causes co-operate toward the lowering of the Mountains, leveling of the Earth, straitning and landing up of the Sea, and, in fine, compelling the Waters to return upon the dry Land, and cover the whole Surface of it, as at the first. How to obviate this in a natural way, I know not, unless by a Transmutation of the two Elements of Water and Earth one into another, which I can by no means grant. 'Tis true indeed, the rocky Parts of the Mountains may be so hard and impenetrable, as to resist and hold out against all the Assaults of the Water, and utmost Rage of the Sea; but then all the Earth and Sand being washed from them, nothing, but as it were their *Skeletons,* will remain extant above the Waters, and the Earth be in effect drowned.

But

But tho' I cannot imagine or think upon any natural Means to prevent and put a Stop to this Effect, yet I do not deny that there may be some; and I am the rather inclinable so to think, because the World doth not in any Degree proceed so fast towards this Period, as the Force and Agency of all these Causes together seem to require. For, as I said before, the Oracle predicting the Carrying on the Shore of *Cilicia* as far as *Cyprus*, by the Earth and Mud that the turbid River *Pyramus* should bring down, and let fall in the interjacent Strait, is so far from being filled up, that there hath not any considerable Progress been made towards it, so far as I have heard or read, in these 2000 Years. And we find by Experience, that the longer the World lasts, the fewer Concussions and Mutations are made in the upper or superficial Region of the Earth; the Parts thereof seeming to tend to a greater Quiet and Settlement.

In this Conjecture I find myself mistaken. For since the Writing hereof there have happened as terrible and destructive Earthquakes as any we read of in History, particularly those of *Sicily* in the Year 1692-3. the first on *Jan.* 9. about four Hours and a half after Sun-set; the second on the 11th of the same Month, about the 21st Hour of the Day, according to the *Italian* Reckoning, that is, three Hours before Sun-set. In both which there perished 93000 Souls; were destroyed and much damnified 2 Bishopricks, 700 Churches, of which 22 Collegiate ones, 250 Monasteries, 49 Cities and Villages, whereof the most remarkable was the City of *Catania*, one of the fairest and largest in the Island, which was wholly overthrown and buried in its Ruins, scarce any Footstep of it remaining, wherein perished above 15000 Souls: Of which the learned and ingenious Signor *Paulo Bonone* gives a particular Account, in his Book entituled, *Musæum Physicum & Experimentale*; and besides affords us many curious Remarks and Observations, concerning the Signs, Concomitants and Effects of these Earthquakes, which being too long to transcribe, it not being my Design to write a complete Treatise of Earthquakes, but only to discourse a little of them occasionally, as they, or rather the Cause of them, might possibly have been the Means or Instruments the Almighty made use of at first to raise up the dry Land, and cast off the Waters; I referr the Reader to the Book itself.

2. THOSE of *Naples*, or *Terra di Lavoro*, anciently called *Campania Felix*, happening on the fifth of *June* 1688. of which Mr. *Misson* gives us an Account at the End of his *New Voyage to* Italy, *Vol.* 1. sent in a Letter from an *English* Merchant then living in

in *Naples* to his Friend, in thefe Words: *Sir, About eight Days ago we all believed the World was at an End. We felt a moft terrible Earthquake in this Town of* Naples: *It lafted but three Minutes, but in that little time fuch Things happened, as without all Doubt were done by the Hand of the Almighty. About a quarter of an Hour after four in the Afternoon, a terrible Earthquake fhook the whole City all of a fudden, and put the People into fuch a Confufion as cannot be expreffed. Mount* Vefuvius *being quiet, no Body miftrufted any fuch Thing: And though they perceived the Houfes to ftoop, and to recover again, to part from one another, to move every where, and in fome Places to fall, their Aftonifhment was fo great, and their Eyes fo dazzled, that fome cried out Fire, others fancied to themfelves fome popular Sedition, and very few gueffed what it really was. But another more violent Earthquake fucceeding the firft, a fubterraneous Noife, furpaffing that of Thunder, was heard and accompanied by a Domeftick Noife of all the Houfhold Goods, which were overturned, and a good Part of them either broken or bruifed. The Bells rang in all the Steeples, the Cifterns vomited up their Waters, feveral Houfes parted from each other, fome rejoined, others fell, and fome ftood as if they were ftooping and ready to fall. Then every one was fenfible that it was an Earthquake,*

U 3

quake, &c. To this succeeded a third Trembling, which the Writer only mentions. Not many People were lost in this Earthquake at Naples; but the Damage sustained by it was reckoned by knowing Persons to amount to Ten Millions of Crowns. At the Town of Benevento there were 1567 Persons crushed to Pieces, and buried under Ruins; so that that Town is nothing now but a Heap of Stones. We have here a List of 800 Persons more killed in twelve or thirteen Villages about the said City of Benevent. The Town of Ceretto, belonging to the Duke of Mattalone, was entirely overturned, and 4000 Persons perished therein. Five Hundred were also lost at Mirabella, 1000 at S. Lupo, 300 at S. Lawrence Major, 400 at Pierra Roya, and every Soul, without any ones escaping, at the Boroughs of Civitella, S. Lawrence Minor, and Guardia S. Framondi.

3. To these may be added the terrible Earthquake in the Island of *Jamaica*, whereof we have already discoursed at large.

BESIDES, the *Superficies* of the Sea, notwithstanding the Overwhelming and Submersion of Islands, and the Straitning of it about the Outlets of Rivers, and the Earth it washes from the Shores subsiding, and elevating the Bottom, seems not to be raised higher, nor spread farther, or bear any greater Proportion to that of
the

the Land than it did a Thousand Years ago.

So have I finished my second Discourse concerning the Deluge, and its Effects; and the Mutations that have been since made in the Earth, and their Causes.

# DISCOURSE III.

## OF THE DISSOLUTION OF THE WORLD.

## THE INTRODUCTION TO THE Third Discourse.

THERE is implanted in the Nature of Man a great Desire and Curiosity of fore-knowing future Events, and what shall befall themselves, their Relations and Dependents in time to come; the Fates of Kingdoms and Commonwealths,

especially

especially the Periodical Mutations, and final *Cataſtrophe* of the World. Hence, in ancient Times, Divination was made a Science or Myſtery, and many Nations had their Colleges or Societies of Wiſe-Men, Magicians, Aſtrologers and Sooth-ſayers; as for Example, the *Egyptians, Babylonians* and *Romans*. Hence the Vulgar are very prone to conſult Diviners and Fortune-Tellers.

To gratify in ſome Meaſure this Curioſity, and that his People might not in any Privilege be inferiour to the Nations about them, it pleaſed GOD, beſides the ſtanding Oracle of *Urim*, not only upon ſpecial Occaſions to raiſe up among the *Jews* extraordinary Prophets, by immediate Miſſion; but alſo to ſettle a conſtant Order and Succeſſion of them, for the Maintenance and Upholding whereof, there were Colleges and Seminaries inſtituted for the educating and fitting young Men for the Prophetick Function. Theſe were the Sons of the Prophets, of whom we find ſo frequent Mention in Scripture.

MOREOVER, it pleaſed GOD ſo far to condeſcend to the Weakneſs of the *Jews*, that in the Infancy of their State, He permitted them to conſult His Prophets concerning ordinary Accidents of Life, and Affairs of ſmall Moment: As we ſee *Saul* did *Samuel* about the Loſs of his Father's Aſſes, which it's not likely he would have done, had it not been u-

ſual

sual and customary so to do. In the latter Times of that State, we read of no Consulting of Prophets upon such Occasions. At last also by their own Confession, the Spirit of Prophecy was quite taken away, and nothing left them but a Vocal Oracle, which they called *Bath col*, *i. e.* the Daughter of a Voice, or the Daughter of Thunder, a Voice out of a Voice. This Dr.* *Lightfoot* thinks to have been a meer Fancy or Imposture. *Quæ de Bath Kol referunt Judæi, ignoscant illi mihi si ego partim pro Fabulis habeam Judaicis, partim pro præstigiis Diabolicis. What the Jews report concerning* Bath Kol, *I beg their Pardon, if I esteem them no other than either Jewish Fables, or Diabolical Illusions.* It is a Tradition among them, that after the Death of the last Prophets, *Haggai*, *Zachary*, and *Malachi*, the Holy Spirit departed from *Israel*. But why, I beseech you, was Prophecy withdrawn, if Celestial Oracles were to be continued? Why was *Urim* and *Thummim* taken away, or rather not restored, by their own Confession, after the Babylonish Captivity? It were strange indeed, that GOD taking away His ordinary Oracles from a People, should bestow upon them one more or equally noble; and that, after they were extremely degenerated and fallen into all manner of Impiety, Superstition and Heresy, &c. And a little after, if I may freely speak what I think, those innumerable Stories,

\* *Horæ Hebr. in Matth. cap.* 3. *v.* 17.

Stories, which every where occurr [in the Jewish Writings] concerning *Bath Kol*, are to be reduced to two Heads, *viz.* 1. The most of them are meer Fables, invented in Honour of this or that Rabbin, or to gain Credit to some History. 2. The rest meer Magical and Diabolical Illusions, *&c.*

In the Primitive Churches of Christians planted by the Apostles, there was also an Order of Prophets, 1 *Cor.* xii. 28. GOD *hath set some in the Church, first Apostles, secondarily Prophets,* &c. This Spirit of Prophecy was an extraordinary and temporary Gift, as were the Gifts of Healing and Speaking with Tongues, continuing not long after the Death of the Apostles, and Consignation of the Canon of Scripture. So that now we have no Means left us of Coming to the Knowledge of future Events, but the Prophecies contained in the Writings of the Holy Penmen of Scripture, which we must search diligently, consider attentively, and compare together, if we desire to understand any thing of what shall befall the Christian Church or State in Time to come.

THIS Text which I have made Choice of for my Subject, is Part of a Prophecy concerning the greatest of all Events, the Dissolution of the World.

2 PETER

## 2 PETER iii. 11.

*Seeing then all these Things shall be dissolved, what manner of Persons ought we to be in all holy Conversation and Godliness?*

### CHAP. I.

*The Division of the Words and Doctrine contained in them, with the Heads of the following Discourse.*

THESE Words, contain in them two Parts: 1. An Antecedent, or Doctrine, *All these things shall be dissolved.* 2. A Consequent, or Inference thereupon, *What manner of Persons ought we to be?*

THE Doctrine, here only briefly hinted, or summarily proposed, is laid down more fully in the precedent Verse; *But the Day of the* LORD *will come as a Thief in the Night, in which the Heavens shall pass away with a*

*great*

*great Noife, and the Elements fhall melt with fervent Heat, the Earth alfo, and the Works that are therein fhall be burnt up.*

These Words are, by the Generality of Interpreters, Ancient and Modern, underftood of the final Deftruction or Diffolution of Heaven and Earth; in which Senfe I fhall choofe rather to accept them at prefent, than with the Reverend and Learned Dr. *Hammond*, and fome few others, to ftem the Tide of Expofitors, and apply them to the Deftruction of *Jerufalem* and the Jewifh Polity. I fay then,

> *That this World, and all things therein contained, fhall one Day be diffolved and deftroyed by Fire.* Doctr.

By *World*, in this Propofition, *We*, and by *Heaven* and *Earth* in this Place, the moft rational Interpreters of Scripture, do underftand only the whole *Compages* of this Sublunary World, and all the Creatures that are in it; all that was deftroyed by the Flood in the Days of *Noah*, and is now fecured from perifhing fo again; that I may borrow Dr. *Hammond*'s Words, in his Annotations on this Place. "And again, the Word *Heavens* '(*faith he*) being an Equivocal Word, is ufed "either for the fuperiour Heavens, whether ' Empyreal or Ethereal, or for the fublunary ' Heavens, the Air, (as the Word *World* is ei-';ther the whole *Compages* of the fuperiour

' and

'and inferiour World, as the Author of the Book *De Mundo*, ascribed falsly to *Aristotle*, defines Κόσμος, σύςημα ἐξ οὐρανῦ καὶ γῆς καὶ τῶν ἐν τέτοις περιεχομένων φύσεων, *The System or* Compages *of Heaven and Earth, and the Beings therein contained:* Or else only of the sublunary Lower World) we may here resolve, that the Οὐρανοὶ and ςοιχεῖα, Heaven and Host, or Elements thereof, are literally the sublunary Aereal Heavens, and all that is therein, Clouds and Meteors, &c. Fowls and flying Creatures, and so, fit to join with the Earth and Works that are therein.

In Prosecution of this Proposition, and in Order to the Proof and Confirmation, and likewise the Clearing and Illustration of it, I shall, (1.) Give you what I find concerning the Dissolution of the World: 1. In the Holy Scripture. 2. In ancient Christian Writers. 3. In the Heathen Philosophers and Sages. (2.) I shall endeavour to give some Answer to these seven Questions, which are obvious and usually made concerning it.

1. WHETHER there be any thing in Nature, which might prove and demonstrate, or argue and inferr a future Dissolution of the World?

2. WHETHER shall this Dissolution be brought about and effected by Natural, or by extraordinary Means and Instruments;

and

and what those Means and Instruments shall be?

3. Whether shall the Dissolution be gradual or sudden?

4. Whether shall there be any Signs and Fore-Runners of it?

5. At what Period of Time shall the World be dissolved?

6. How far shall this Conflagration extend? Whether to the *Ethereal* Heavens, and all the Host of them, Sun, Moon, and Stars, or to the *Aereal* only.

7. Whether shall the Heavens and Earth be wholly dissipated and destroyed, or only refined and purified?

---

## Chap. II.

*The Testimonies of Scripture concerning the Dissolution of the World.*

1. THEN, let us consider what we find delivered in the Holy Scriptures, concerning the Dissolution of the World. And first of all, This Place, which I have made Choice of for my Text, is in my Opinion the most clear and full, as to this Particular, in the whole Scripture; and will give Light for the Solution of most of the proposed

posed Questions. Verf. 10. *The Day of the* LORD *shall come as a Thief*, &c. This answers the third Question, Whether the Dissolution shall be gradual or sudden? *Wherein the Heavens shall pass away with a great Noise, and the Elements shall melt with fervent Heat, the Earth also, and all the Works that are therein, shall be burnt up.* And again, Ver. 12. *Wherein the Heavens being on Fire shall be dissolved, and the Elements shall melt with fervent Heat.* This answers the second Question, What the Means and Instruments of this Dissolution shall be? Ver. 13. *Nevertheless we, according to his Promise, look for a new Heaven and a new Earth, wherein dwelleth Righteousness.* This gives some Light toward the answering of the last Question, Whether shall the Heavens and the Earth be wholly burnt up and destroyed, or only renewed and purified? These Words, as clearly as they seem to referr to the Dissolution of the World, yet Dr. *Hammond* doubts not to be understood of the remarkable Destruction of *Jerusalem*, and the Jewish State, he thus paraphrasing them.

> Verse 10. *But the Day of the* LORD *will come as a Thief in the Night, in which the Heavens shall pass away with a great Noise, and the Elements shall melt with fervent Heat, and the Earth also, and*
> *the*

*the Works that are therein shall be burnt up.*

But this Judgment of Christ, so remarkable on the *Jews*, shall now shortly come, and that very discernably; and the Temple shall suddenly be destroyed, the greater Part of it burnt, and the City and People utterly consumed.

> Verse 11. *Seeing then all these Things shall be dissolved, what Manner of Persons ought ye to be in all holy Conversation and Godliness?*

Seeing then this Destruction shall thus involve all, and now approacheth so near, what an Engagement doth this lay upon us to live the most pure strict Lives that ever Men lived?

> Verse 12. *Looking for and hastning unto the Coming of the Day of God, wherein the Heavens, being on Fire, shall be dissolved, and the Elements shall melt with fervent Heat.*

Looking for the Coming of Christ for our Deliverance, and by our Christian Lives quickning and hastning God to delay it no longer; that Coming of His, I say, which as it signifies great Mercy to us, so it signifies very sharp Destruction to the whole *Jewish* State.

Verse 13. *Nevertheless we, according to His Promise, look for new Heavens and a new Earth, wherein dwelleth Righteousness.*

Instead of which we look for a new Christian State, wherein all Provision is made by Christ for Righteousness to inhabit, according to the Promise of Christ concerning the Purity that He should plant in the Evangelical State.

How he makes out and confirms this Paraphrase, see in his *Annotations* upon this Place. So confident is he of the Truth of this his Interpretation, that he censures the usual one as a great Mistake, in his *Annotation* on *ver.* 10. where he thus writes; 'What 'is here thus expressed by S. *Peter*, is ordina-'rily conceived to belong to the End of the 'World, and by others applied to the End of 'this World, and the Beginning of the *Millen-*'*nium*, or Thousand Years. And so, as S. *Peter* 'here saith, *ver.* 16. many other Places in 'S. *Paul's* Epistles, and in the Gospel, especi-'ally *Matth.* xxiv. are mistaken and wrested. 'That it doth not belong to either of those, 'but to this fatal Day of the *Jews*, sufficiently 'appears by the Purport of this whole Epistle, 'which is, to arm them with Constancy and 'Perseverance till that Day come; and par-'ticularly in this Chapter, to confute them 'who object against the Truth of Christ's
'Pre-

' Predictions, and resolve it should not come
' at all: Against whom he here opposes the
' Certainty, the Speediness, and the Terrible-
' ness of its Coming. That which hath given
' Occasion to those other common Mistakes, is
' especially the Hideousness of those Judg-
' ments which fell upon the People of the
' *Jews*, beyond all that ever before are rela-
' ted to have fallen upon them, or indeed a-
' ny other People, which made it necessary
' for the Prophets, which were to describe it,
' (and who use Tropes and Figures, and not
' plain Expressions, to set down their Predi-
' ctions) to express it by these high Phrases, of
' the *passing away* and *dissolving* of *Heaven* and
' *Earth,* and *Elements, &c.* which sounding
' very tragically, are mistaken for the great
' and final Dissolution of the World." So far
the Doctor. Two Things there are in this
Chapter, which seem to contradict this Interpretation: First, That the Destruction
here spoken of, is compared with *Noah*'s
Flood; and the Heaven and Earth to be dissolved by this, made parallel, and of equal
Extent to the World destroyed by that. Of
this the Doctor was well aware, and therefore grants, 'that the seventh Verse, *But the
Heavens and the Earth which are now, by the
same Word are kept in Store, reserved unto Fire
against the Day of Judgment, and Perdition of
ungodly Men,* is to be understood of the general and final Destruction of the World by

X 2 Fire,

Fire; but the following Verses to be an Answer to the first Part of the Atheists Objection, viz. *Where is the Promise of His Coming?* To me it seems, that all referr to the same Matter. The second Thing which seems to contradict the *Doctor's* Interpretation, is, the Apostle's citing for the Instruction, and Confirmation of the Believers, and in Answer to the Atheists Objection, (*Where is the Promise of His Coming?*) that Place of the *Psalmist, Psal.* xc. 4. *That one Day is with the* Lord *as a thousand Years, and a thousand Years as one Day.* For the Apostle seems to suppose, that the Time of Christ's Coming might possibly be a thousand Years off; and that they were not to think much, or distrust the Promise, if it were so: For though it were predicted as a thing shortly to come, yet they were to consider, that a thousand Years in God's Sight is but a very short Time; so that it might be foretold as shortly to come, tho' it were a thousand Years off. Whereas it might seem improper to mention a thousand Years to support them in Expectation of an Event that was not twenty Years to come.

Another Place, where Mention is made of Christ's coming to Judgment, and the Dissolution of the World, is *Matth.* xxiv. to which may be added as Parallel, *Mark* xiii. and *Luke* xxi. In which Places you have considerable, 1. The Suddenness of Christ's Coming, *ver.* 27.

27. *As the Lightning comes out of the East, and shineth even unto the West, so shall the Coming of the Son of Man be.* 2. The Signs of His Coming, v. 29. *Immediately after the Tribulation of those Days shall the Sun be darkned, and the Moon shall not give her Light, and the Stars shall fall from Heaven, and the Powers of Heaven shall be shaken.* 3. The Manner of His Coming, v. 30. *And then shall appear the Sign of the Son of Man in Heaven; and then shall all the Tribes of the Earth mourn, when they shall see the Son of Man coming in the Clouds of Heaven with Power and great Glory. And He shall send His Angels with a great Sound of a Trumpet, and they shall gather together His Elect from the four Winds, from one End of Heaven to the other.* 4. The Uncertainty of the Time of His Coming, and this Dissolution as to us. *But of that Day and Hour knoweth no Man, no not the Angels in Heaven:* And *Mark* adds, *neither the Son, but the Father only.*

All this Prophecy Dr. *Hammond* understands of the Destruction of the City and Temple of *Jerusalem*, and whole Nation of the *Jews*; as may be seen in his *Paraphrase* and *Annotations* upon this Place. And indeed, our Saviour Himself seems to limit it to this, saying, verse 24. *Verily I say unto you, this Generation shall not pass away, till all these things be fulfilled.* For if these Prophecies look farther than the Destruction of

*Jerusalem*, even to Christ's coming to Judgment, how could it be true, that that Generation should not pass away till all those Things were fulfilled? Whereas we see that that Generation is long since passed away, and yet the End is not come? And indeed, Expositors that understand them of the End of the World, and Christ's second coming to Judgment, are hard put to it to answer this Objection. S. *Chrysostom* will have this Word γενεὰ to be understood not of the Generation of Men then living, but of the Generation of the Faithful, which should not fail till the End of the World. Οἶδε γὰρ (saith he) γενεὰν ἐκ ἀπὸ χρόνων χαρακτηρίζειν μόνον, ἀλλ' ἀπὸ τρόπε θρησκείας καὶ πολιτείας, ὡς ὅταν λέγῃ, Αὕτη ἡ γενεὰ ζητέντων σε, &c. *He denominates a Generation not only from living together in the same time, but from having the same Form and Manner of religious Worship and Polity; as in that Place, This is the Generation of them that seek thee, that seek thy Face, O* Jacob. *Beza* understands γενεὰ of the present Age, and will have it to be of the same Valour with דור in *Hebrew*, and πάντα ταῦτα, to referr not to all Particulars mentioned in this Chapter, but only to those which are spoken of the Destruction of the City and Nation of the *Jews*: But (saith he) if any one urgeth the universal Particle, *Vertere licebit, Fiant omnia, viz. quæ ultimam illam diem præcessura dixit. Nam ab illo*

*tempore*

*tempore cœperunt fieri, & adhuc perseverant illa signa; suo demum tempore Filio hominis venturo.*

But on the other Side, 1. Some Passages there are in this Chapter, which are hardly applicable to the Destruction of *Jerusalem*, and the Dissolution of the *Jewish* Commonwealth; as *the Appearing of the Sign of the Son of Man in Heaven, and the Tribes seeing the Son of Man coming in the Clouds of Heaven, with Power and great Glory. And His sending His Angels with a great Sound of a Trumpet.* 2. The Coming of Christ is in like manner described in Places which undoubtedly speak of His coming to Judgment at the End of the World. As in 1 *Cor.* xv. 52. Mention is made of the *Trumpets sounding* at the Time of Christ's Coming; And 1 *Thess.* iv. 16. it is said, *The* Lord *Himself shall descend from Heaven with the Voice of the Archangel, and with the Trump of* God; and. v. 17. *We that are alive shall be caught up together with them* [that are risen] *in the Clouds to meet the* Lord *in the Air.* All which Places are perfectly parallel, and seem manifestly to allude to the fore-mentioned Words, *Matth.* xxiv. 30, 31. I am apt to think that these Prophecies may have a double Respect; one to the City, Temple, and Nation of the *Jews*; another to the whole World at the great Day of Doom: And that the former is indeed typical of the latter: And so they have a double Completion; the first in the Destruction of *Jerusalem* and the *Jewish* Polity: In Reference to which it is truly said, *This Generation shall not pass away till all these things be fulfilled.* The second in the final Dissolution of the World, which is yet to come.

But to proceed; Another Place which is usually understood of the Dissolution of the World by Fire, is 2 *Thess.* i. 7, 8. *When the* LORD JESUS *shall be revealed from Heaven with His mighty Angels in flaming Fire,* &c. Other parallel Places may be seen, *Rev.* vi. 12, 13, 14. *Rev.* x. 6. *Rev.* xxi. 1. *And I saw a new Heaven and a new Earth, for the first Heaven and the first Earth were passed away, and there was no more Sea,* Hebr. xii. 26, 27. These Places speak more directly of the Dissolution of the World, and the Coming of CHRIST to Judgment. Others there are, that speak only concerning the Time of it, 1 *Pet.* iv. 7. *But the End of all Things is at hand.* James v. 9. *Behold the Judge standeth before the Door.* 1 John ii. 18. *Little Children, it is the last time;* or as some translate it, the last Hour, ἐσχάτη ὥρα. Hebr. x. 37. *Yet a little while, and He that shall come will come, and will not tarry,* μικρὸν ὅσον ὅσον. Luke xviii. 17. *I tell you he will avenge them speedily.* All these Places the forementioned Dr. *Hammond* still applies to that famous Period of the Destruction of the City, Temple and

and Polity of the *Jews*; only in his Note upon ὄλεθρος αἰώνιος, that everlasting Destruction mentioned 2 *Theff.* i. 9. he hath some Qualification, saying thus: *Mean while, not excluding the eternal Torments of Hell-fire, which expect all impenitent Sinners that thus fall, but looking particularly on the visible Destruction and Vengeance which seizeth on whole Nations or Multitudes at once in this Life.* And in Conclusion hath left us but one Place in the New Testament, to prove the general Conflagration of the World, *viz.* 2 Pet. vii. 7.

Now, because some have been offended at these Interpretations of his, others have spoken very slightingly of them: I shall briefly sum up what hath been alledged in Defence of them by this great Man.

1. THAT the Prophets use to set down their Predictions in Tropes and Figures, and not in plain Expressions, (*their Style being Poetical.*) And therefore, in describing those hideous Judgments which fell upon that People of the *Jews*, beyond all that ever before fell upon them, or indeed any other People, they found it necessary to employ those High and Tragical Phrases of the passing away and dissolving Heaven, and Earth, and Elements. And that this was the Manner of the Prophets, may be proved; because we find the Destruction of other Places described in as high Strains, as lofty and tragical Expres-

sions as this of *Jerusalem*. For Example, that of *Idumæa*, Isa. xxxiv. 9. *The Streams thereof shall be turned into Pitch, and the Dust thereof into Brimstone, and the Land thereof shall become burning Pitch. It shall not be quenched Night nor Day, the Smoke thereof shall go up for ever.* And in the 4th Verse he seems but to preface to this Destruction, in these Words; *And all the Host of Heaven shall be dissolved, and the Heavens shall be rolled together as a Scroll; and all their Hosts shall fall down as the Leaf falleth off from the Vine, and as a falling Fig from the Fig-Tree; for my Sword shall be bathed in Heaven: Behold it shall come down upon Idumæa.* And in the Burden of *Babylon*, cap. xiii. 8, 9. we have these Words, *Behold the Day of the* LORD *cometh, cruel both with Wrath and fierce Anger to lay the Land desolate: For the Stars of Heaven, and the Constellations thereof shall not give their Light: The Sun shall be darkened in his going forth, and the Moon shall not cause her Light to shine.*

2. ALL the Predictions in that famous Place, *Matth.* xxiv. to which all other Places in the New Testament relating to this Matter, are parallel, are by our Saviour Himself restrained to the Destruction of *Jerusalem*, and the full Completion of them limited to the Duration of that Age: Verse 34. *Verily I say unto you, This Generation shall not pass till all*

*all these Things be fulfilled.* What Reason then can we have to extend them farther?

3. In most of the Places where this Coming of CHRIST is mentioned, it is spoken of as near, and at hand; as in the Places last cited. Now, (saith the learned Doctor) in his Note upon *Luke* xviii. 7. *I tell you he will avenge them speedily.* 'All which, if (when
'it is said to approach and to be at the door)
'it belonged to the Day of Judgment (now
'after so many hundred Years not yet come)
'what a μακροθυμία were this? What a Delay-
'ing of His Coming? And consequently,
'What an Objection against the Truth of the
'Christian Religion? As *Mahomet*, having
'promised after his Death he would presently
'return to Life, and having not performed his
'Promise in a thousand Years, is by us justly
'condemned as an Impostor.

4. THAT this Place of S. *Peter*, out of which I have taken my Text, doth not belong to the End of the World, sufficiently appears (saith he) by the Purport of this whole Epistle, which is to arm them with Constancy and Perseverance till that Day come, and particularly in this Chapter to confute them who object against the Truth of CHRIST's Predictions, and resolve it should not come at all; against whom he here opposes the Certainty, the Speediness, and the Terribleness of its Coming. And for that other famous Place, 2 *Thess.* i. 8, 9. that it

belongs

*Of the Dissolution*

belongs to the same Period. See how he makes it out in his Annotations.

I SHALL now superadd some Places out of the Old Testament, which seem to speak of the Dissolution of the World, *Job* xiv. 12. *Man lieth down and riseth not till the Heavens be no more.* Psal: cii. 5, 6. quoted Hebr. i. 10, 11. *Of old hast thou laid the Foundations of the Earth, and the Heavens are the Works of Thy Hands. They shall perish, but Thou remainest; and they all shall wax old as doth a Garment, and as a Vesture shalt Thou change them, and they shall be changed,* Isai. xxxiv. 4. *And all the Host of Heaven shall be dissolved, and the Heavens shall be rolled together as a Scroll, and all their Host shall fall down as a Leaf falleth from the Vine,* &c. Isai. li. 6. *The Heavens shall vanish away like Smoke, and the Earth shall wax old like a Garment,* Joel ii. 31. *The Sun shall be turn'd into Darkness, and the Moon into Blood, before that great and terrible Day of the* LORD *comes.* Malachi iv. 1. *Behold the Day cometh that shall burn like an Oven,* &c. Deut. xxxii. 22. *For a Fire is kindled in my Anger, and shall burn to the lowest Hell, and shall consume the Earth with her Increase, and set on Fire the Foundations of the Mountains.* I must confess, that the Prophetick Books are full of Figurative Expressions, being written in a Poetick Style, and according to the Strain of the Oriental Rhetorick, which is much different from the

the *European*, affecting lofty and tumid Metaphors, and excessive *Hyperbola's* and Aggravations, which would either sound harsh to our Ears, or import a great deal more to us than they did to them. This is obvious to any one that reads their Books; and may clearly be demonstrated from the Titles that their Kings assumed to themselves, as well anciently as lately, *viz. Sons of the Sun, Brethren of the Sun and Moon, Partners of the Stars, Lions crowned in the Throne of the World, endued with the Strength of the whole Heaven, and Virtue of the Firmament.* Now, we cannot possibly imagine them so vain, as to think themselves literally to be such: No sure, all they meant by these Expressions, was, that they were great, and honourable, and powerful. Now, the Prophetick Books of the Old Testament being written in a Style somewhat conformable to the Oratory of those Countries, are not (I humbly conceive) in every Tittle to be so exactly scanned and literally expounded, but so to be interpreted, as a *Jew* or an *Asiatick* would then have understood them. And this I rather think, because there be divers Passages in the Prophets, which cannot be verified in a strict literal Sense; as in the Place before quoted, *Isa.* xxxiv. 9. it is said of the *Streams of* Idumæa, *that they should be turned into Pitch, and the Dust thereof into Brimstone; and the Land thereof should become burning Pitch,*

*and*

and should not be quenched Night nor Day; but the Smoke thereof should go up for ever. And of the City of *Tyre* it is said, Ezek. xxvi. 14. *It shall be built no more.* And ver. 19. *When I shall make thee a desolate City, like the Cities that are not inhabited, when I shall bring up the Deep upon thee, and great Waters shall cover thee.* And *Verse* 21. which is thrice repeated, *I will make thee a Terror, and thou shalt be no more; though thou be sought for, thou shalt never be found again, faith the* LORD GOD. And yet we see that the City of *Tyre,* tho' it was indeed wholly dispeopled at that Time, the Inhabitants transferring themselves into *Africa,* when it was besieged by *Nebuchadnezzar*; yet was it afterward peopled again, and continues a City inhabited to this Day. And of *Babylon,* it is said, that *there should none remain in it, neither Man nor Beast, but that it should be desolate for ever,* Jer. li. 62. Isai. xiii. 20. and of the Land of *Babylon,* v. 29. *that it should be a Desolation without an Inhabitant.* And though indeed this Prophecy was, I think, as to the City, at last verified in the Letter; yet did *Babylon* long continue a great City after this Prophecy: And the Land of *Babylon* is now inhabited, there being at this Day a great City not far from the Place where *Babylon* stood. So that these Places import no more, than that there should be a very great Destruction and Devastation

of

of those Cities and Countries. As for those Places in the Old and New Testament, wherein Mention is made of the last Days and the last Times, it is clear that they are to be understood of the Age of the Messiah, all the time from the Exhibition of the Messiah to the End of the World. *Isaiah* ii. 1. *And it shall come to pass in the last Days, that the Mountain of the* LORD's *House shall be established in the Top of the Mountains, and shall be exalted above the Hills, and all Nations shall flow to it;* which very Words we have repeated *Micah* iv. 1. So in that Prophecy of *Joel* ii. 28. quoted *Acts* ii. 17. *And it shall come to pass in the last Days, saith* GOD, *I will pour out of my Spirit upon all Flesh,* &c. it is clear the last Days are to be understood. The Apostle *Peter* interpreting the Prophecy, (*ver.* 16.) of the *Gift of Tongues* bestowed upon the Disciples at that time. Hence the *last Days* have among the *Jews* proverbially signified the Days of the Messiah, as Doctor *Hammond* in his Annotations upon this Place tells us; who also notes, that in that Place of *Joel*, the *last Days* do literally signify the last Days of the *Jews*, immediately preceding their Destruction, called there the *great and terrible Day of the* LORD. So *Hebr.* i. 2. by ἐπ' ἐσχάτων τῶν ἡμερῶν τέτων, *in these last Days,* is meant the Days of the Messias. So 1 *Pet.* i. 20. 2 *Pet.* iii. 3. 1 *Tim.* iv. 1. 2 *Tim.* iii. 1. Mention is made
of

of the last Days in this Sense. In like manner, the End of the World, συντελεια τȣ αιῶνος, Heb. ix. 26. *But now once in the End of the World hath He appeared to put away Sin by the Sacrifice of Himself.* And τα τελη τῶν αιώνων, *the Ends of the World,* in 1 *Cor.* x. 11. *upon whom the Ends of the World are come,* signify the Age of the Messias, though indeed the former seems more peculiarly to denote the Shutting up of the *Jewish* Age or OEconomy.

✳✳✳✳✳✳✳✳✳✳✳✳✳✳✳✳

## Chap. III.

*The Testimonies of the Ancient Fathers and Doctors of the Church, concerning the Dissolution of the World.*

2. I PROCEED now to what the Ancient Fathers of the Church and Christian Writers have delivered concerning the Dissolution of the World.

That there should be a Dissolution of this World, and that it shall be by Fire, is so certain and clear among them, that it would be superfluous to cite Particulars to prove it: Nay, so general and unanimous is the Consent of all Christians in this Point, that, as *Origen*

*gen* observes in his third περὶ Ἀρχῶν, and the learned Doctor *Hakewill* after him, whereas there can hardly be named any Article of our Faith, which some Hereticks have not presumed to impugn or call in Question, yet not any to be met with who question this; but herein all agree, being compelled (saith *Origen*) by the Authority of the Scriptures. As for the Time of this Dissolution, the ancient Christians held it to be at hand, as might easily be proved by many Testimonies, were it not granted on all Hands. And here it may be worth the observing, that the longer the World stood, the farther off generally have Christians set the Day of Judgment, and End of it. Many of the Ancients did conceive, that the Dissolution should be at the End of six thousand Years. As for Example, *Justin Martyr*, in *Quæst. & Resp. ad Orthodoxos*, if he be the Author of that Piece, where this Question (*When the End of the World should be?*) being put, the Answer is, Ἔνεςι διὰ πολλῶν γραφικῶν μαρτυριῶν, &c. *We may rationally conjecture and conclude from many Scripture Expressions, that they are in the right, who say that the World will last six thousand Years.* For in one Place it saith, In these last Days; and in another, Upon whom the Ends of the World are come; and in a third, When the Fulness of Time was come. *Now it is evident,*

dent that these things were spoken in the sixth Millenary.

IRENÆUS *adv. hæres. lib.* 5. *cap. ult.* who gathers so much from the Similitude of the six Days Creation, after which six Days was the Sabbath, that is, the Day of Rest; *Hoc autem* (saith he) *est & præteritorum narratio, & futurorum prophetia. Dies enim unus mille annos significabat, sicut Scriptura testatur;* * *Mille anni ante Dominum sicut Dies unus: ergo sicut consummatus fuit mundus in sui creatione intra sex dierum spatium, & postea quies; sic in sui fine consummabitur intra spatium sex millium annorum, deinde vera & perpetua quies subsequetur.* This is both a Narration or History of what is past, and a Prophecy of Things to come. For one Day signified a thousand Years, as the Scriptures testify, A thousand Years in the Sight of GOD are but as one Day. Therefore, as the World at the first Creation was consummated in the Space of six Days, and afterwards followed the Sabbath or Rest; so, in the end, its Duration shall be consummated within the Space of Six thousand Years; and then shall follow the true and perpetual Rest.

* 2 Pet. iii.

To these I might add *Lactantius*, in his Seventh Book of *Institut.* cap. 14. who useth the same *Argument* with *Irenæus, Ergo quoniam sex diebus cuncta Dei opera perfecta sunt: per secula sex, id est, sex annorum millia manere in hoc statu mundum necesse est.*

*Dies*

*Dies enim magnus Dei mille annorum circulo terminatur, sicut indicat Propheta, qui dicit, Ante oculos tuos, Domine, mille anni tanquam dies unus,* &c. Therefore, because all the Works of GOD were perfected (or finished) in six Days, it is necessary (or necessarily follows) that the World shall continue in this State six Ages, that is, Six thousand Years. For, the great Day of GOD is terminated in a Circle of Six thousand Years; as the Prophet intimates, who saith, A thousand Years in Thy Sight, O LORD, are but as one Day. *S. Augustin, l. 20. de Civitate Dei. S. Hieronymus Comment. in Mich. cap. 4.* Most clear and full to this purpose is *Eustath.* in his Comment. in *Hexaemeron*, Λογιζόμεθα γὰρ διαμεῖναι τὴν κτίσιν, &c. We reckon (saith he) *that the Creation shall continue till the End of the sixth Chiliad, because* GOD *also consummated the Universe in six Days; and, I suppose, that the Deity doth account Days of a thousand Years long; for that it is said,* A thousand Years are in the Sight of the LORD as one Day. Howbeit, the most of them did not propose this Opinion as an undoubted Truth, but only as a modest Conjecture. And S. *Austin* is very angry with them, who would peremptorily conclude from so slight an Argumentation.

THIS Conceit is already confuted, and the World hath long outlasted this Term, according to their Computation who followed the *Septuagint* or *Greek* Account, and reckoned that *Phaleg* lived about the Three thousandth Year of the World, and had his Name from his living in the Division of Time, there being to come after him Three thousand Years, that is, just so many as were past before him.

As concerning the future Condition of the World after the Conflagration, I find it the general and received Opinion of the ancient Christians, that this World shall not be annihilated or destroyed, but only renewed and purified. So *Eusebius*, Οὐ παντελῶς πρὸς φθορὰν ὁ κόσμος χωρήσει, ἀλλὰ πρὸς ἀνακαινισμόν. *The World shall not be wholly destroyed, but renewed.* Divers other Passages I might produce out of him to the same purpose: *Cyril of Jerusalem*, Catech. 15. Εἱλίσσει ϳ τὰς ὀρανὰς, ἐκ ἵνα ἀπολέσῃ τέτες, ἀλλ᾽ ἵνα καλλίονας ἐγείρῃ. *He folds up the Heavens, not that he might destroy them, but that he might rear them up again more beautiful.* Again, *Cyril* upon this Place, Θάνατον δὲ τῶν ςοιχείων εὐφυῶς ὀνομάζει τὴν εἰς τὰ ἀμείνω μεταβολὴν, &c. *He acutely or ingeniously calls the Death of the Elements their Change into better.* So that this Renovation in respect of the Creation, shall be such a kind of thing as the Resurrection in reference to Man's Body. *OEcumenius*, upon this Place, He saith, *new Heavens, and a new Earth,* ἐκ ἑτέραν δὲ τῇ ὕλῃ, *yet not different in Matter.* And again, ἐκ εἰς ἀφανισμὸν ἀλλ᾽ εἰς κάθαρσιν.

*They*

*They shall not be destroyed or annihilated, but only renewed and purified.* And upon *Rev.* xxi. 2. Τȣτο ȣ τὴν ἀνυπαρξίαν δηλῶν τῆς κτίσεως, ἀλλὰ τὸν ἀνακαινισμόν. This he saith, *not denoting the Non-existence of the Creation, but the Renewing.* In this manner he expounds *Psalm* cii. 5, 6. and proceeding, saith, *We may here take Notice, that the Apostle doth not use the Word* ἀπῆλθεν, *as if the Heaven and Earth were annihilated and brought to nothing; but* μετέβη, *they passed away, or removed, or changed State.* S. *Hierome* upon the Psalms, *Psalm* cii. saith, *Ex quo ostenditur perditionem cœlorum non interitum sonare, sed mutationem in melius. From which Words* [as a Vesture shalt thou change them] *may be shewn and made out, that the Dissolution of the Heavens doth not signify their utter Destruction or Annihilation, but only their Change into a better State.* I might add abundance more Testimonies, but these, I think, may suffice.

Y 3    CHAP.

## Chap. IV.

*The Opinions of the Ancient Heathen Philosophers, and other Writers concerning the Dissolution.*

3. **I**T follows now that I give you an Account what the ancient Philosophers and Sages among the *Heathens* thought and delivered concerning this Point. Two of the four principal Sects of Philosophers held a future Dissolution of the World, *viz.* The *Epicureans* and *Stoicks*.

As for the *Epicureans*, they held, that as the World was at first composed by the fortuitous Concourse of Atoms, so it should at last fall in Pieces again by their fortuitous Separation, as *Lucretius* hath it, *lib.* 5.

*Principio maria ac terras cœlúmque tuere,*
*Horum naturam triplicem, tria corpora, Memmi,*
*Tres species tam dissimiles, tria talia texta*
*Una dies dabit exitio, multósque per annos*
*Sustentata ruet moles & machina mundi.*

*But now to prove all this; first cast an Eye,*
*And look on all below, on all on high,*
*The solid Earth, the Seas, and arched Sky:*
*One fatal hour at last must ruin all,*
*This glorious Frame, that stood so long, must fall.*

This

## Of the Dissolution.

This Opinion of theirs is consonant enough to their wild Principles, save only in that Point of its Suddenness, *Una dies dabit exitio*, &c. *One day shall destroy or make an end of it.*

The *Stoicks* were also of Opinion, that the World must be dissolved, as we may learn from the Seventh Book of *Laertius*, in the Life of *Zeno*, Ἀρέσκει δ' αὐτοῖς, &c. They hold, that the World is corruptible for these Reasons; 1. Because it was generated, and had a Beginning. 2. Because That is corruptible in the whole, whose Parts are corruptible: But the Parts of the World are corruptible, being daily transmuted one into another. 3. That which is capable of Mutation, from better to worse, is corruptible. But such is the World; sometimes being afflicted with long Heats and Droughts, sometimes with continued Showers and Inundations. To these we may add, 4. according to some of their Opinions, Because the Sun and Stars being fed with Vapours exhaled from the Earth, all the Moisture will at length be drawn out, and the World fly on fire. They were afraid, * *Nè humore omni consumpto totus mundus ignesceret.* The Poet *Lucan*, who seems to be of the *Stoick* Sect, in the Beginning of his First Book, describing the Dissolution of the World, makes it to be a Falling in Pieces of the whole Frame of

* Minut. Felix.

Heaven

Heaven and Earth, and a Jumbling and Confounding of all their Parts together.

    ――― *Sic cùm compage solutâ*
*Secula tot mundi suprema coëgerit hora ;*
*Antiquum repetent iterum Chaos omnia ; miſtis*
*Sydera ſyderibus concurrent.; ignea Pontum*
*Aſtra petent, tellus extendere littora nolet,*
*Excutiétque fretum ; fratri contraria* Phœbe
*Ibit, & obliquum bigas agitare per orbem*
*Indignata diem poſcet ſibi.; totáque diſcors*
*Machina divulſi turbabit fœdera mundi.*

    ――― So when the laſt Hour ſhall
So many Ages end, and this disjointed, All
To Chaos back return ; then all the Stars ſhall be
Blended together ; then thoſe burning Lights
  on high
In Sea ſhall drench ; Earth then her Shores
  ſhall not extend,
But to the Waves give Way ; the Moon her
  Courſe ſhall bend
Croſs to her Brothers, and diſdaining ſtill to
  drive
Her Chariot Wheel athwart the heavenly Orb,
  ſhall ſtrive
To rule the Day ; this Frame to Diſcord bent,
The World's Peace ſhall diſturb, and all in
  ſunder rent.

This Diſſolution of the World, they held, ſhould be by Water and by Fire alternately at certain Periods, but eſpecially by Fire, which they call ἐκπύρωσιν. *Philo,* Οἱ δὲ Στωϊκοὶ τῆς φθορᾶς τῦ κόσμυ αἰτίαν φασὶ τὴν ὑπάρχυσαν ἐν τοῖς ὖσι πυρὸς ἀκαμάτυ, δύναμιν, χρόνων μακραῖς περιόδοις ἀναλύεσαν τὰ πάντα εἰς ἑαυτόν. *The Stoicks say, that the Cause of the Destruction of the World is the irresistible Force of Fire that is in things, which, in long Periods of Time, consumes and dissolves all things into itself.* Euseb. Præp. l. 15. Ἀρέσκει ᾗ τοῖς πρεσβυτάτοις τῶν ἀπὸ τῆς αἱρέσεως, ἐξαερῦσθαι πάντα κατὰ περιόδυς τινὰς μεγίςας, εἰς πῦρ αἰθερῶδες ἀναλυομένων πάντων. *The most ancient of that Sect held, That at certain vast Periods of Time all things were rarified into Air, being resolved into an Ethereal Fire.* This Ἐκπύρωσις of the *Stoicks* we find mentioned by many, both *Christian* and *Heathen* Writers, as besides the fore-quoted *Minutius Felix, Justin Martyr, Clemens Alexandrinus* in 5. *Strom. Plutarch, Seneca,* and others. The Time of this Conflagration *Seneca* determines not, but saith only, it shall be when GOD pleases. 3 *Quæst. Nat. cap.* 20. 8. *Cùm Deo visum, vetera finire, ordiri meliora; When it shall seem good to* GOD *to put an End to old things, and to begin better.* Some there be who tell us of the *Annus Platonicus* or *Magnus,* by which they understand such a Period of Time, as in which all the heavenly Bodies shall be restored to the same Site and Distance they were once in, in respect of one another: As supposing that all the Seven Planets

nets were at the Moment of Creation in the first Degree of *Aries*, till they come all to be in the same Degree again; all that Space of Time is called the Great Year, *Annus Magnus*. In this Year they tell us, that the Height of Summer is the Conflagration, and the Depth of Winter the Inundation; and some Astrologers have been so vain as to assign the Time both of the Inundation and Conflagration. *Seneca*, 3 *Quæst. Nat. cap.* 20. *Berosus, qui Belum interpretatus est, dicit, cursu ista syderum fieri, & adeò quidem affirmat, ut conflagrationi atque diluvio tempus assignet. Arsura enim terrena contendit, quando omnia sydera in Cancro convenerint: inundationem futuram, quando eadem syderum turba in Capricorno convenerit.* Berosus, who interpreted Belus, saith, *That those things come to pass according to the Course of the Stars: and he so confidently affirms it, that he assigns the Time both for the Conflagration and Inundation. For that all earthly Bodies will be burnt up, when all the Stars shall meet in* Cancer; *and the Inundation will fall out, when the same shall be in Conjunction in* Capricorn. Concerning the Manner of this Conflagration, they held it should be sudden. *Senec. Natura subitò ad ruinam, & toto impetu ruit; licet ad originem parcè utatur viribus, dispensétque se incrementis fallacibus. Momento fit cinis, diu sylva,* &c. Nature doth suddenly, and with all its Force, rush on to Ruin; though, to the Rise and Formation

*mation* of *Things*, it *useth its Strength sparingly, dispensing its Influence, and causing them to grow by insensible Degrees; a Wood is long in growing up, but reduced to Ashes almost in a Moment.* And some of them were so absurd as to think, that the Stars should justle and be dashed one against another. *Senec. lib. de consolatione ad Marciam: Cùm tempus advenerit, quo se mundus revocaturus extinguat, viribus ista se suis cædent; & sydera syderibus incurrent; & omni flagrante materia, uno igne, quicquid nunc ex disposito lucet, ardebit.* When the *Time* shall come, that the *World*, again to restore and renew itself, shall perish, these things shall batter and mall themselves by their own Strength, the Stars shall run or fall foul upon one another, and all the Matter flaming, whatsoever now, according to its settled Order and Disposition, shines, shall then burn in one Fire. Here, by the way, we may, with Dr. *More*, [*Soul's Immortality, lib.* 3. cap. 18.] take notice, how coarsly, not to say ridiculously, the *Stoicks* philosophize,
' when they are turned out of their Road-
' way of Moral Sentences, and pretend to
' give an Account of the Nature of Things.
' For, what Errors can be more gross than
' they entertain of GOD, of the *Soul*, and of
' the *Stars?* they making the two former
' corporeal Substances, and feeding the lat-
' ter with the Vapours of the Earth; affirm-
' ing that the Sun sups the Water of the
                                    ' great

' great Ocean to quench his Thirst, but that
' the Moon drinks off the lesser Rivers and
' Brooks; which is as true as that the *Ass*
' drank up the *Moon*. Such Conceits are
' more fit for *Anacreon* in a drunken Fitt to
' stumble upon, who, to invite his Compa-
' nions to tipple, composed that Catch,

Πίνει θάλασσα δ' αὔρας,
Ὁ δ' ἥλιος θάλασσαν.

*The Sea drinks up the Vapours,*
*And the Sun the Sea.*

' than to be either found out or owned by a
' serious Philosopher. And yet *Seneca* migh-
' tily triumphs in this Notion, of foddering
' the Stars with the thick Fogs of the Earth,
' and declares his Opinion with no mean
' Strains of Eloquence, *&c.*

As for the Extent of this Conflagration, they held, that not only the Heavens should be burnt, but that the Gods themselves should not escape Scot-free. So *Seneca*, *Resoluto mundo, & Diis in unum confusis*. *When the World shall be dissolved, and the Gods confounded and blended together into one.* And again, *Atque omnes pariter Deos perdet nox aliqua & Chaos*. *And, in like manner, a certain Night and Chaos shall destroy all the Gods.* Is not this wise Philosophy? If their Morality were no better than their Physicks, their *Wise Man* they boast of, might be so denominated, κατ' ἀντίφρασιν, as they of *Gotham*.

But

But let us look a little farther, and we shall find, that the *Stoicks* were not the first Authors of this Opinion of the Conflagration; but that it was of far greater Antiquity than that Sect. Others of the more ancient Philosophers having entertained it, *viz. Empedocles*, as *Clemens Alexandrinus* testifies in his 5 *Strom.* Ὡς ἐσομένης ποτὲ εἰς τὴν τῦ πυρὸς ἐσίαν μεταβολῆς· *That there shall some time be a Change of the World into the Nature or Substance of Fire.* 2. *Heraclitus*, as the same *Clemens* shews at large out of him in the same place, ὅπως ἢ πάλιν ἀναλαμβάνεται καὶ ἐκπυρῦται, &c. And *Laertius*, in the Life of *Heraclitus*, he taught, Ἕνα εἶναι τὸν κόσμον, γεννᾶσθαί τε αὐτὸν ἐκ πυρὸς, καὶ πάλιν ἐκπυρῦσθαι κατὰ τινὰς περιόδες ἐναλλὰξ τὸν σύμπαντα αἰῶνα· *That there is but one World, and that it was generated out of Fire, and again burnt up or turned into Fire, at certain Periods alternately throughout all Ages.* I might add to these the Ancient *Greek* Poets, *Sophocles* and *Diphilus*, as we find them quoted by *Justin Martyr*, and *Clemens Alexandrinus*. Neither yet were these the first Inventers and Broachers of this Opinion, but they received it by Tradition from their Forefathers, and look'd upon it as an Oracle and Decree of Fate. *Ovid* speaks of it as such, in the First of his *Metamorphosis*:

*Esse*

*Esse quoque in fatis reminiscitur, affore tempus,*
*Quo mare, quo tellus, correptáque regia cœli*
*Ardeat, & mundi moles operosa laboret.*

    ———— Besides by Doom
Of certain Fate, he knew the Time should
 come,
When Sea, Earth, ravish'd Heav'n, the curi-
 ous Frame
Of this World's Mass should shrink in purging
 Flame.

\* Lib. 7. And *Lucan* \*;

*Hos Cæsar, populos si nunc non usserit ignis,*
*Uret cum terris, uret cum gurgite ponti:*
*Communis mundo superest rogus ossibus Astra*
*Misturus.* ——

*If now these Bodies want their Fire and Urn,*
*At last with the whole Globe they'll surely burn;*
*The World expects one general Fire: And thou*
*Must go where these poor Souls are wandring*
 *now.*

Now, though some are of Opinion, that by *Fata* here are to be understood the *Sibylline Oracles,* and to that Purpose do alledge some Verses out of those extant under that Title, as *Lactantius,* in his Book De ira Dei, cap. 23.

Καί ποτε τὴν ὀργὴν Θεὸν ὀυκέτι πραΰνοντα,
Ἀλλ' ἐξεμβρίθοντα, καὶ ἐξολύοντά τε γένναν
Ἀνθρώπων ἅπασαν ὑπ' ἐμπρησμῦ πέρθοντα.

          And

*And it shall some time be, that* GOD *not any more mitigating His Anger, but aggravating it, shall destroy the whole Race of Mankind, consuming it by a Conflagration.*

And in another Place there is Mention made, of a River of Fire that shall descend from Heaven, and burn up both Earth and Sea.

*Tunc ardens fluvius cælo manabit ab alto
Igneus, atque locos consumet funditus omnes,
Terrámque, Oceanúmque ingentem, & cærula
 ponti,
Stagnáque, tum fluvios, fontes, Ditémque se-
 verum,
Cælestémque polum, cæli quoque lumina in u-
 num
Fluxa ruent, formâ deletâ prorsùs eorum,
Astra cadent, etenim de cælo cuncta revulsa.*

Then shall a burning Flood flow from the
 Heav'ns on high,
And with its fiery Streams all Places utterly
Destroy, Earth, Ocean, Lakes, Rivers, Foun-
 tains, Hell,
And heav'nly Poles, the Lights in Firmament
 that dwell,
Losing their beauteous Form shall be obscur'd,
 and all
Raught from their Places, down from Heav'n
 to Earth shall fall.

Now

Now because the Verses now extant under the Name of *Sibylline Oracles* are all suspected to be false and *Pseudepigrapha*; and many of them may be demonstrated to be of no greater Antiquity than the Emperor *Antoninus Pius* his Reign; and because it cannot be proved, that there was any such thing in the Ancient genuine *Sibylline Oracles*; I rather think, (as I said before) that it was a Doctrine of ancient Tradition, handed down from the first Fathers and Patriarchs of the World. *Josephus*, in his *Antiquities*, runs it up as high as *Adam*, from whom *Seth* his Son received it; his Father, saith he, foretelling him, ἀφανισμὸν τῶν ὅλων ἔσεσθαι, τὸν μὲν κατ' ἰσχὺν πυρὸς, τὸν ᾽ϳ κατὰ βίαν καὶ πλῆθος ὕδατος· *That there should be a Destruction of the Universe, once by the Violence of Fire, and again by the Force and Abundance of Water*; in Consequence whereof he erected two Pillars, one of Brick, which might endure the Fire, and another of Stone, which would resist the Water; and upon them engraved his Astronomical Observations, that so they might remain to Posterity: And one of these Pillars, he saith, continued in *Syria* until his Days. Whether this Relation be true or not, it may be thence collected, that this was an universal Opinion, received by Tradition, both among *Jews* and Gentiles, That the World should one Day be consumed by Fire. It may be proved by good Authority, that the

the ancient *Gauls*, *Chaldæans*, and *Indians*, had this Tradition among them; which they could not receive from the *Greek* Philosophers or Poets, with whom they had no Intercourse; but it must, in all Probability, be derived down to both from the same Fountain and Original; that is, from the first Restorers of Mankind, *Noah*, and his Sons.

I NOW proceed to the Third Particular proposed in the Beginning; that is, to give Answer to the several Questions concerning the Dissolution of the World.

## Chap. V.

*The first Question concerning the World's Dissolution, Whether there be any thing in Nature that may probably cause or argue a future Dissolution? Three probable Means propounded and discussed.*

### Sect. I.

*The Waters again naturally overflowing and covering the Earth.*

THE first Question is, Whether there be any thing in Nature, which may prove and demonstrate, or probably argue, and inferr a future Dissolution? To which I answer, That I think there is nothing in Nature which doth necessarily demonstrate a future Dissolution: But that Position of the *Peripatetick* Schools may, for ought I know, be true Philosophy; *Posito ordinario Dei concursu mundus posset durare in æternum.* Supposing the ordinary Concourse of GOD [with second Causes] *the World might endure for ever.* But though a future Dissolution by Natural Causes, be not demonstrable; yet some possible, if not probable, Accidents there are, which, if they should happen, might inferr such a Dissolution. Those are Four: The Possibility of

1. THE Waters again overflowing and covering the Earth.
2. THE Extinction of the Sun.
3. THE Eruption of the *Central Fire* enclosed in the Earth.
4. THE Driness and Inflammability of the Earth under the Torrid Zone, and the Eruption of all the *Vulcano's* at once.

BUT before I treat of these, it will not be amiss, a little to consider the old Argument for the World's Dissolution, and that is, its daily Consenescence and Decay; which, if it can be proved, will in Process of time necessarily inferr a Dissolution. For as the Apostle saith in another Case, *That which decayeth and waxeth old is ready to vanish away*, Heb. viii. 13. That which continually wastes, will at last be quite consumed; that which daily grows weaker and weaker, will in time lose all its Force. So the Age, and Stature, and Strength of Man, and all other Animals, every Generation decreasing, they will in the End come to nothing. And that all these and all other things do successively diminish and decay in all Natural Perfections and Qualities, as well as Moral, hath been the received Opinion, not only of the Vulgar, but even of Philosophers themselves from Antiquity down to our Times:

Times. *Plin. Nat. Hist. l. 7. c. 16. In plenum, autem cuncto mortalium generi minorem indies mensuram staturæ propemodum observatur: rarosque patribus proceriores consumente ubertatem seminum exustione; in cujus vices nunc vergat ævum.* In sum; It is observed, that the Measure of the Stature of all Mankind decreases and grows less daily: And that there are few taller than their Parents; the Burning (to which the Age inclines) consuming the Luxury of the Seeds.

*Terra malos homines nunc educat atque pusillos.*
Juvenal Sat.

The Earth now breeds Men bad and small.

And *Gellius, Noct. Att. lib. 3. c. 10. Et nunc quasi jam mundo senescente rerum atque hominum decrementa sunt.* And now, as if the World waxed old, there is a Decrement or Decay both of Things and Men. I might accumulate Places out of the Ancients and Moderns to this Purpose, but that hath been already done by others.

But this Opinion, how general soever it was formerly, was inconsiderately, and without sufficient Ground, taken up at first; and afterwards without due Examination embraced and followed, as appears by Dr. *Hakewill's Apology*, wherein it is so fundamentally confuted, that it hath since been rejected by all considerate Persons. For that Author hath
at

at large demonstrated, that neither the pretended Decay of the Heavenly Bodies in regard of Motion, Light, Heat, or Influence, or of any of the Elements; neither the pretended Decay of Animals, and particularly and especially of Mankind, in regard of Age and Duration, of Strength and Stature, of Arts and Wits, of Manners and Conversation, do necessarily inferr any Decay in the World, or any Tendency to a Dissolution. For tho' there be at Times great Changes of Weather, as long continuing Droughts, and no less lasting Rains; excessive Floods and Inundations of the Sea; prodigious Tempests and Storms of Thunder, Lightning and Hail; which seem to threaten the Ruin of the World, violent and raging Winds, Spouts and Hurricanes, which turn up the Sea to the very Bottom, and spread it over the Land; formidable and destructive Earthquakes, and furious Eruptions of *Vulcano's* or Burning Mountains, which waste the Country far and wide, overwhelming or subverting great Cities, and burying their Inhabitants in their Ruins; or as the Scripture speaks, *Making of a City a Heap, of a defenced City a Ruin.* Though these and many other Changes do frequently happen, at uncertain Seasons as to us, yet are they so ordered by the wise Providence of the Almighty Creator and Governour of the World, as nearly to balance one another, and to keep all things in an *Æquilibrium*; so that as it is said of the Sea, that *what it gains in one Place, it loses in another*, it may be said proportionably of the other Elements and Meteors; That, for Example, a long Drought in one Place is compensated probably at the same time by as long a Rain in another; and at another time, the Scene being changed, by as durable a Drought in this, as lasting a Rain in that. The same may be said of violent and continuing Heats and Colds in several Places, that they have the like Vicissitudes and Changes, whereby in the whole they so balance and counterpoise one another, that neither prevails over other, but continue and carry on the World as surely and steddily, as if there were no such Contrarieties and Fights, no such Tumults and Commotions among them. The only Objection against this Opinion, is the Longævity of the *Antediluvian* Patriarchs, and of some also (I mean the first) of the *Postdiluvian*. For immediately after the Flood, the Age of Man did gradually decrease every Generation in great Proportions; so that had it continued so to do at that Rate, the Life of Man had soon come to nothing. Why it should at last settle at Threescore and ten Years, as a mean Term; and there continue so many Ages, without any farther Change and Diminution, is, I confess, a Mystery too hard for me to reveal: However, there must be

a great

a great and extraordinary Change at the Time of the Flood, either in the Temperature of the Air, or Quality of the Flood, or in the Temper and Constitution of the Body of Man, which induced this Decrement of Age. That the Temper and Constitution of the Bodies of the *Antediluvians* was more firm and durable than that of their Posterity after the Flood: And that this Change of Term of Life was not wholly to be attributed to Miracle, may both be demonstrated from the gradual Decrease of the Age of the *Postdiluvians*. For had it been miraculous, why should not the Age of the very first Generation after the Flood have been reduced to that Term? And what Account can we give of their holding out for some Generations against the Inconveniencies of the Air, or Deteriority of Diet, but the Strength and Firmness of their Constitutions? which yet was originally owing to the Temperature of the Air, or Quality of their Diet, or both; seeing a Change in these (for there was no other visible Cause) did by Degrees prevail against, and impair it. What Influence the lying so long of the Water upon the Earth might have upon the Air and Earth, in changing them for the worse, and rendring them more unfit for the Maintenance and Continuance of Humane Life, I will not now dispute. But whatever might be the Cause of the Longævity of the

*Antediluvians*, and the Contracting of the Age of the *Postdiluvians*, it is manifest, that the Age of these did at the last settle, as I said, at or about the Term of Threescore and ten, and hath there continued for Three thousand Years without any Diminution.

I PROCEED now to the Accidents which might possibly, in Process of Time, inferr a Dissolution of the World.

1. THE Possibility of the Water, in Process of Time, again overflowing and covering of the Earth.

FOR, first of all, the Rains continually washing down and carrying away Earth from the Mountains, it is necessary, that as well the Height as the Bulk of them that are not wholly rocky, should answerably decrease; and that they do so, is evident in Experience. For, as I have elsewhere noted, I have been informed by a Gentleman of good Credit, that whereas the Steeple of *Craich*, in the *Peak* of *Derbyshire*, in the Memory of some old Men then living [1672.] could not have been seen from a certain Hill lying between *Hopton* and *Wirksworth*, now not only the Steeple, but a great Part of the Body of the Church may from thence be seen; which comes to pass by the Sinking of a Hill between the Church and the Place of View: A parallel Example whereto the learned Dr. *Plot* gives us, in a Hill between *Sibbertoft* and *Hasleby* in *Northamptonshire*, *Hist. Nat. Stafford.*

*Stafford.* p. 113. And thus will they continue to do so long as there falls any Rains, and as they retain any Declivity, that is, till they be leveled with the Plains.

In Confirmation of this Particular, I have received from my ingenious Friend Mr. *Edward Lhuyd*, some notable Observations of his own making concerning the Mountains of *Wales*; which do demonstrate that not only the looser and the lighter Parts of the Mountains, as Earth, Sand, Gravel, and small Stones, may be washed down by the Rains: But the most solid and bulky Rocks themselves, by the violent Descent of the Waters down their Chinks and Precipices, be in time undermined and subverted. Take them in his own Words:

'Upon the reading of your Discourse of
'the Rains continually washing away, and
'carrying down Earth from the Mountains,
'I was put in mind of something pertinent
'thereto, which I have observed in the Moun-
'tains of *Caernarvonshire*, viz.

1. First, 'That generally the higher the
'Hills are, the more steep are their Preci-
'pices and Declivities, (I except the Sea
'Rocks) thus *Moel y Wydhrha, y Grib gôtch,*
'and twenty others that might be named,
'reputed the highest Hills in *Wales*, have the
'steepest Rocks of any Mountains I have
'seen; and that not only in their highest
'Cliffs, but also in most of their other Crags,
'till

'till you descend to the lower Valleys: This
'I can ascribe to nothing else but the Rains
'and Snow which fall on those high Moun-
'tains, I think, in ten times the Quantity
'they do on the lower Hills and Valleys.

2. 'I HAVE observed a considerable Quan-
'tity of the Chips or Parings (if I may so
'call them) of these Cliffs to lie in vast
'Heaps at the Roots of them; and these
'are of several Sorts and Materials; being
'in some Places covered with Grass, and in
'others as bare as the Sea Shore: And those
'bare Places do consist sometimes of Gra-
'vel, and an innumerable Number of Rock
'Fragments, from a Pound Weight to twen-
'ty, &c. and are sometimes composed of
'huge Stones, from an hundred Pound
'Weight to several Tuns.

3. 'IN the Valleys of *Lhanberys* and *Nant-*
'*Phrancon*, the People find it necessary to
'rid their Grounds often of the Stones
'which the Mountain Floods bring down;
'and yet notwithstanding this Care, they of-
'ten lose considerable Parcels of Land.

4. 'I AFFIRM, That by this means not
'only such Mountains as consist of much
'Earth and small Stones, or of softer Rocks,
'and such as are more easily dissoluble, are
'thus wasted, but also the hardest Rocks in
'*Wales*; and they seem to be as weighty,
'and of as firm and close a Texture as Mar-
'ble itself. It happen'd in the Valley of
'*Nant-*

' *Nant-Phrancon, Anno* 1685. that Part of
' a Rock of one of the impendent Cliffs,
' call'd yr *Hyſvae*, became ſo undermined,
' (doubtleſs by the continual Rains and ſub-
' terraneous Veins of Water occaſioned by
' them) that loſing its Hold it fell down in
' ſeveral Pieces, and in its Paſſage down a
' ſteep and craggy Cliff, diſlodged thouſands
' of other Stones, whereof many were in-
' tercepted e'er they came down to the Val-
' ley, but as much came down as ruin'd a
' ſmall Piece of Ground; and ſeveral Stones
' were ſcatter'd at leaſt 200 Yards aſunder.
' In this Accident one great Stone, the big-
' geſt remaining Piece of the broken Rock,
' made ſuch a Trench in its Deſcent, as the
' ſmall Mountain Rills commonly run in;
' and when it came down to the plain
' Ground, it continued its Paſſage through
' a ſmall Meadow, and a conſiderable Brook,
' and lodged itſelf on the other ſide it.
' From hence I gather, that all the other vaſt
' Stones that lie in our mountanous Val-
' leys, have by ſuch Accidents as this fallen
' down. Unleſs perhaps we may do better
' to referr the greateſt Part of them to the
' univerſal Deluge. For conſidering there
' are ſome thouſands of them in theſe two
' Valleys [of *Lhanberys* and *Nant-Phran-*
' *con*] whereof (for what I can learn) there
' are but two or three that have fallen in the
' Memory of any Man now living; in the
' ordina-

'ordinary Course of Nature we shall be
'compelled to allow the rest many thou-
'sands of Years more than the Age of the
'World." So far Mr. *Lhuyd*.

To this last Particular, and for a farther Account of it, may be added, That sometimes there happen strange and violent Storms and Hurricanes, wherein the Rain is driven with that Force upon the Tops and Sides of the Mountains by furious and tempestuous Winds, as to do more Execution upon them by breaking in Pieces, tearing and throwing down Rocks and Stones, in a few Days, than in the ordinary Course of Nature, by the usual Weather is effected in many hundred Years.

2. By reason of the Abundance of Earth thus washed off the Mountains by Shots of Rain, and carried down with the Floods to the Sea; about the Out-lets of the Rivers, where the violent Motion of the Water ceases, settling to the Bottom, and raising it up by Degrees above the Surface of the Water, the Land continually gains upon, and drives back the Sea: The *Egyptian Pharos*, or Light-House, of old Time stood in an Island a good Distance from Land, which is now joined to the Continent, the interjacent *Fretum* having been filled up by the Silt brought down by the River *Nilus* in the Time of the Flood subsiding there. Indeed, the ancient Historians do truly make the whole Land of *Egypt* to have been δῶρον ποταμᾶ, the Gift of
the

the *River*, and by this means gained from the Sea. *Seneca,* in the Sixth Book of his *Nat. Quest.* chap. 26. gives this Account, *Ægyptus ex limo tota concrevit. Tantum enim (si Homero fides) aberat à continenti Pharos, quantum navis diurno cursu metiri plenis lata velis potest. Sed continenti admota est. Turbidus enim defluens Nilus, multumque secum limum trahens, & eum subinde apponens prioribus terris, Ægyptum annuo incremento semper ultra tulit. Inde pinguis & limosi soli est, nec ulla intervalla in se habet; sed crevit in solidum arescente limo, quo pressa erat & cedens structura, &c.* that is, all Egypt *is but a Concretion of Mud. For (if* Homer *may be believed) the* Pharos *was as far distant from the Continent, as a Ship with full Sail could run in a Day's time· but now it is joined to it. For* Nilus *flowing with troubled Waters brings down a great deal of Mud and Silt, and adding it to the old Land, carries on* Egypt *farther and farther still by an annual Increase. Hence it is of a fat and muddy Soil, and hath no Pores or Cavities in it. And this Reason he gives why it is not troubled with Earthquakes.* Which also may be the Reason why it hath no fresh Springs and Fountains: For though indeed Dr. *Robinson* doth very probably impute its Want of Rain and Springs to the Want of Mountains; yet because (as we shall afterwards prove) Springs may be derived from Mountains at a good
Distance,

Distance, I know not whether all Mountains are so far remote from *Egypt*, as that there may be no subterraneous Channels of that Length, as to derive the Water even thither from them; and, therefore, probably one Reason of their Wanting of Springs may be the Density and Thickness of the Soil, whereby it becomes impenetrable to the Water; and it may be, should they use the same Artifices there, which the Inhabitants of the Lower *Austria*, and of the Territory of *Modena* and *Bologna* in *Italy* do, that is, dig and bore quite through this Coat of Mud till they come to a Sand, or looser Earth; they might, in like manner, procure themselves Fountains of springing Water. Thus, by Reason of the great Rivers, *Po*, *Athesis*, *Brenta*, and others, which empty themselves into the *Lagune*, or Shallows about *Venice* in *Italy*, and in Times of Floods bring down thither great store of Earth; those *Lagune* are in danger to be in time atterrated; and with the City situate in the midst of them, added to the firm Land, they being already bare at every Ebb, only Channels maintain'd from all the neighbouring Places to the City, not without considerable Charge to the State in Engines and Labourers in some Places to clear them of the Mud, wherewith otherwise they would indanger to be obstructed and choaked up; which Engines they call *Cava-fango's*. Thus in the

*Camarg,*

*Camarg*, or Isle that the River *Rhosne* makes near *Arles* in *Provence*, there hath been so much lately gained from the Sea, that the Watch-Tower had, in the Memory of some Men living 1665, been removed forward three times, as we were there informed; which I have already entred in this Work. And it seems to me probable, that the whole *Low-Countrys* were thus gained from the Sea: For, *Varenius* in his Geography tells us, ' That sinking a Well at *Amsterdam*, at ' near a hundred Foot depth, they met with ' a Bed or Floor of Sand and Cockle-Shells; ' whence it is evident, one would think, that ' of Old Time the Bottom of the Sea lay so ' deep, and that that hundred Foot Thickness ' of Earth above the Sand arose from the Se- ' diments of the Waters of those great Rivers, ' the *Rhine, Scheld, Maes, &c.* which there- ' abouts emptied themselves into the Sea, and, ' in Times of Floods, brought down with ' them abundance of Earth from the upper ' Grounds." The same Original, doubtless, had that great Level of the Fens, running through the Isle of *Ely*, *Holland* in *Lincoln-shire*, and *Marshland* in *Norfolk*. That there hath been no small Quantity of Earth thus brought down, appears also in that along the Channels of most great Rivers; as for Example, the *Thames* and *Trent* in *England*, especially near their Mouths or Out-lets, between the Mountains and higher Grounds

on

on each Side, there are large Levels and Plains, which seem to have been originally Part of the Sea, raised up, and atterrated by Earth and Silt brought down by those Rivers in great Floods.

*Strabo*, in the First Book of his Geography, hath much to this purpose: Ἡ γὰρ πρόσχωσις περὶ αὐτὰ συνίςαται τὰ ςόματα τῶν ποταμῶν· οἷον περὶ μὲν τὰ τῦ Ἴςρυ τὰ λεγόμενα Στήθη, καὶ ἡ Σκυθίων ἐρημία· περὶ ᾳ τὰ τῦ Φάσιδος ἡ Κολχικὴ παραλία, δίαμμος, καὶ ταπεινὴ, καὶ μαλακή ὅσα· περὶ ᾳ τὸν Θερμόδοντα καὶ τὸν Ἴριν ὅλη ἡ Θεμίσκυρα, τὸ τῶν Ἀμαζόνων πεδίον, καὶ τῆς Σιδύνης τὸ πλέον. Οὕτω ᾳ καὶ ἐπὶ τῶν ἄλλων, ἅπαντες γὰρ μιμῦνται τὸν Νεῖλον, ἐξημπειρῦντες τὸν πρὸ αὐτῶν πόρον, οἱ μὲν μᾶλλον, οἱ δ᾽ ἧττον· ἧττον μὲν οἱ μὴ πολλήν τε καὶ μαλακόγειον χώραν ἐπιόντες παὶ χειμάρρυς δεχόμενοι πολλύς· ὧν ἐςι καὶ ὁ Πύραμος, ὁ τῇ Κιλικίᾳ πολὺ μέρος προσθείς· ἐφ᾽ ᾧ καὶ λόγιον ἐκπέπτωκέ τι τοιῦτον,

Ἔσσεται ἐσσομένοις ὅτε Πύραμος εὐρυοδίνης
Ἠιόνα προχέων ἱερὴν ἐς Κύπρον ἵκηται.

And after a while, he adds, Οὕτω μὲν ὂν ἐνδέχεται προσχωσθῆναι τὸ πέλαγος πᾶν ἀπὸ τῶν αἰγιαλῶν ἀρξάμενον, ἂν συνεχεῖς ἔχῃ τὰς ἐκ τῶν ποταμῶν ἐπιρρύσεις. That is, *For this Landing up and Atteration of the Skirts of the Sea, is, for the most part, about the Mouths of Rivers, as about the Out-lets of* Ister, *the Places called* Στήθη, *and the Deserts of* Scythia; *about those of* Phasis, *the Sea-coast of* Colchis, *which is sandy,*

*sandy, and low, and soft;* about Thermodon and Iris, *all* Themiscyra, *the Plain of the* Amazons, *and the most Part of* Sidene. *And the like may be said of other Rivers. For all of them imitate the* Nile, *adding to the Continent or Main Land the Part lying before their Mouths, some more, some less; those less, that bring not down much Mud; and those more, that run a great way over soft and loose Ground, and receive many Torrents: Of which Kind is the River* Pyramus, *which hath added a great Part of its Land to* Cilicia. *Concerning which there is an Oracle come abroad, importing, That there will a Time come in future Ages, when the River* Pyramus *shall carry on the Shore and Land up the Sea as far as* Cyprus. . . . . . . . *So it might in Time happen, that the whole Sea should gradually be landed up, beginning from the Shores, if the Effusions of the Rivers, that is, the Earth and Mud they bring down, did spread so wide as to be continuous.* Thus far *Strabo*. But the Oracle he mentions, predicting the Carrying on and Continuation of *Cilicia* as far as *Cyprus*, and the joining that Island to the Continent, proves false; there having not been as yet, that we hear or read of, any considerable Advance made towards it, in almost 2000 Years.

Now, the Rain thus continually washing away, and carrying down Earth from the Mountains and higher Grounds, and raising up the Valleys near the Sea, as long as there is any Descent for the Rivers, so long will they continue to run, carry forward the low Ground, and streighten the Sea; which also by its Working, by reason of the Declivity, easily carries down the Earth towards the lower and middle Part of its Channel [*Alveus,*] and by Degrees may fill it up. Monsieur *Loubere*, in his late Voyage to *Siam*, takes Notice of the Increase of the Banks and Sands in and near the Mouths of the great Rivers of the Oriental Kingdoms, occasion'd by the Sediments brought down from the Countries by the several Streams; so that, *says he,* the Navigation into and up those Rivers grows more and more difficult, and may in Process of Time be quite interrupted. The same Observation, I believe, may be made in most of our great *European* Rivers, wherein new Beds are rais'd, and old ones enlarged. Moreover, the Clouds still pouring down Rain upon the Earth, it will descend as far as there is any Declivity; and where that fails, it will stagnate, and, joining with the Sea, cover first the Skirts of the Earth, and so, by Degrees, higher and higher, till the whole be covered.

To this we may add, that some Assistance toward the leveling of the Mountains, may be contributed by the Courses and Catarracts of subterraneous Rivers washing away the Earth continually, and weakning their

Foundations, so by Degrees causing them to founder, subside, and fall in. That the Mountains do daily diminish, and many of them sink; that the Valleys are raised, that the Skirts of the Sea are atterrated, no Man can deny. That these things must needs, in Process of Time, have a very considerable and great Effect, is as evident; which what else can it be, than that we have mentioned?

MOREOVER, towards this levelling of the Mountains, and filling up of the Sea, the Fire also contributes its Mite. For the burning Mountains or *Vulcano's*, as for Example, *Ætna* and *Vesuvius*, vomit at Times out of their Bowels, such prodigious Quantities of Sand and Ashes, and with that Force, that they are by the Winds carried and dispersed all over the Country, nay, transported over Seas into foreign and remote Regions; but let fall so copiously in the circumjacent Places, as to cover the Earth to a considerable Thickness; and not only so, but they also pour forth Floods of melted Stones, Minerals, and other Materials, that run down as low as the Sea, and fill up the Heavens, as of old one near *Catana*; and make Moles, and Promontories, or Points, as in the last Eruptions both of *Ætna* and *Vesuvius*; the Tops of these Mountains falling in, and subsiding proportionably to the Quantity of the ejected Matter, as *Borellus* proves. Meeting with a Quotation in Dr. *Hakewill's* Apology out of

*Jo-*

*Josephus Blancanus* his Book *De Mundi Fabricâ*, I earneſtly deſired to get a Sight of that Book, but could not procure it till the Copy of this Diſcourſe was out of my Hands, and ſent up to *London*, in order to its Printing. But then obtaining it, I found it ſo exactly conſonant to my own Thoughts, and to what I have here written concerning that Subject; and ſome Particulars occurring therein by me omitted, that I could not forbear tranſlating the whole Diſcourſe into *Engliſh*, and annexing it to this Chapter, eſpecially becauſe the Book is not commonly to be met with. The Diſcourſe is firſt ſet down in his Book *De locis Mathematicis Ariſtotelis* more at large; and afterward repeated in his Book *De Mundi Fabricâ* more briefly.

Pergratum *Lectori fore exiſtimavi, ſi rem ſcitu digniſſimam expoſuero,* &c. I thought it might be very acceptable to the Reader, if I ſhould diſcover to him a thing moſt worthy to be known; which I have long ago, and for a long time obſerved, and am daily more confirmed in; eſpecially, ſeeing no former Writer that I know of hath publiſhed any thing concerning it. It is this, That the *Superficies* of the whole Earth, which is now rough and uneaven by reaſon of Mountains and Valleys, and ſo only rudely Spherical, is daily from the very Beginning of the World reducing to a perfect Roundneſs, inſomuch that it will neceſſarily come to paſs

pass in a Natural way, that it be one Day overflown by the Sea, and rendred unhabitable.

First then, that we may clearly apprehend the Causes of this Thing, we must lay down as a Foundation from Holy Writ, That the Terraqueous Globe was, in the Beginning, endued with a more perfect spherical Figure, that is, without any Inequalities of Mountains and Valleys; and that it was wholly covered with the Sea, and so altogether unfit for terrestrial Animals to inhabit: But it was then rendred habitable, when by the Beck or Command of its Creator, the greatest Part of the Land was translated from one Place to another; whereupon here appeared the Hollows of the Seas, there the Heights of the Mountains: And all the Waters, which before covered the Face of the whole Earth, receded, and flowing down, filled those depressed and hollow Places; and this Congregation of Waters was called the *Sea.* Hence some grave Authors doubt not to assert, That the Mountains were made up of that very Earth which before filled the Cavities of the Sea. Whence it follows, that the Earth, as now it is, is mountainous and elevated above the Waters, hath not its natural Figure, but is in a violent State: but *Nullum violentum est perpetuum.* Besides, the Earth being heavier than the Water, none of its Parts ought to be extant, and appear above its Superficies; and yet we see that the Earth is really higher than the Sea, especially the mountainous Parts of it: In which respect also, both Land and Water are in a violent State. Wherefore, it is very convenient to the Nature of both, that they should daily return towards their ancient and primigenial State and Figure; and, accordingly, we affirm that they do so.

Moreover, we say, that the Waters, both of Rains and Rivers, are the Cause of this Restitution, as will appear by the following Observations.

1. We see that Rivers do daily fret, and undermine the Roots of the Mountains; so that here and there, from most Mountains, they cause great Ruins and Precipices, whence the Mountains appear broken; and the Earth, so fallen from the Mountains, the Rivers carry down to the lower Places.

From these Corrosions of the Rivers, proceed those slow, but great Ruins, called, *Labinæ, à labendo*; in which some Streets and whole Villages are precipitated into the Rivers.

2. We daily see, that the Rain-Waters wash away the *Superficies* of the Mountains, and carry them down to the lower Places. Hence it comes to pass, that the higher Mountains are also harder and more stony than the rest, by means whereof they better resist the Water. Hence also it comes to pass, that

that ancient Buildings in Mountains, their Foundations being by Degrees discovered, prove not very durable. For which Reason, the Foundations of the *Roman Capitol* are now wholly extant above-ground; which of old, at its first Erection, were sunk very deep into it. This same thing all the Inhabitants of the Mountains do confirm; all saying, that this Lowering of Mountains was long since known to them; for that, formerly, some intermediate Mountains intercepted the Sight of a Castle, or Tower, situate in a more remote Mountain; which, after many Years, the intervenient Mountain being depressed, came clearly into View. And *George Agricola* is of Opinion (which I very much approve of) that the Rivers produced the Mountains and Hills in this manner. In the Beginning of the World, there were not so many particular divided Mountains, but only perpetual eminent Ridges of Land, not dissected into so many Valleys as we now see. So, for Example, our *Appennine* was at first one continued, eaven, eminent Ridge of Land, not divided into any particular Mountains and Hills by intervening Valleys, as now it is; but that after the Rivers began to flow down from the Top of it, by little and little fretting and corroding the Ground, they made Valleys, and daily more and more; and by this means the whole *Appennine* came to be divided into many Hills and Mountains.

A a 4      3. I N

3. In Plains we see the directly Contrary happens; for the Plains are daily more and more elevated, because the Waters do let fall, in the plain and hollow Places, the Earth they brought down with them from the Mountains. Hence we see that ancient Buildings in such Places, are almost wholly buried in the Ground. So in *Rome*, at the Foot of the *Capitoline* Mountain, we see the *Triumphal Arch of Septimius* almost wholly overwhelmed in the Earth; and every where in ancient Cities, many Gates and Doors of Houses almost landed up, little thereof being extant above Ground.

From which it appears, that this Sinking and Demersion of Buildings into the Earth is a manifest Sign of their Antiquity, which is so much the greater, by how much the deeper they are sunk. So, for Example, at *Bononia* in *Italy*, many of the ancient Gates of the City, which the *Bolognese* call *Torresotti*, are very deeply sunk, which is a certain Argument of their Antiquity; and thence it appears to be true that Histories relate, that they were built in the Time of S. *Petronius*, about 1200 Years ago. But here it is to be noted, that other things agreeing, those are deeper depressed that are built in lower Places, than those in higher, for the Reason abovesaid. So at *Bononia*, that old Port, called *Il Torresotto di S. Georgio*, is deeplier buried, or landed up, than that which is called

led *Il Torrefotto di Stra Caftilione*, becaufe that is fituated in a lower Place, and therefore the Earth is more eafily raifed up about it.

4. The fame is affirmed by Architects, who, when they dig their Foundations, do every where, in plain Places, firft of all remove the Earth, which they call *Commota*, [loofe or fhaken] which is mixt with Fragments of Wood, Iron, Rubbifh, Coins, ancient Urns, and other things; which when it is thrown out, they come to another fort of Earth that hath never been ftirred, but is folid, compact, and not mixt with any heterogeneous thing, efpecially artificial. That moved [*Commota*] and impure Earth, is it which the Waters have by little and little brought down from the higher to the more depreffed Places, which is not every where of equal Depth. But now, becaufe in the Mountains there is no where found fuch moved or new Earth, as is plain from the Experience of Architects, it is manifeft that the Mountains do by no means grow or increafe, as fome dream.

5. Our Obfervation is proved from that Art, which is now much practifed, of elevating and landing up depreffed Places by the Waters of Rivers, and depreffing the higher by running the Water over them.

The fame things happen about the Sea; for, whereas the Bottom of the Sea is more

de-

depressed than the *Superficies* of the Earth; and all the great Rivers empty themselves into the Sea, and bring in with them a great Quantity of Earth and Sand, there must needs be great Banks or Floors of Earth raised up about the Sea Shores, near the Mouths of Rivers, whereby the Shores must necessarily be much promoted and carried forward into the Sea, and so gain upon it, and compell it to recede.

This may be proved, first by the Authority of *Aristotle, lib.* 1. *Meteor. cap. De permutatione terræ ac maris*; and that of the ancient Geographers and Historians. To omit that Proof from *Egypt*; *Aristotle*'s second Example of this Landing up of the Sea, is the Region of *Ammonia*, whose Lower and Maritime Places (faith he) it's clear, were by this Landing up first made Pools and Fens, and in Process of time these Pools were dryed up, and raised to be firm Land, by Earth brought down. A third Example is that of the *Mæotis Palus*, whose Skirts are so grown up by what the Rivers bring down, that the Waters will not carry any thing so great as Ships, as they would have done sixty Years ago. A fourth is the *Thracian Bosphorus*, which for Brevity's-sake may be seen in him. Add hereto, in the fifth Place, the Testimony of *Pliny*, who tells us, that much new Land hath been added to the Earth, not only brought

brought in by the Rivers, but deserted by the Sea.

So the Sea hath receded ten Miles from the Port of *Ambracia*, and five from that of *Athens*, and in several other Places more or less. What he adds out of *Strabo*, concerning the River *Pyramus*, is already enter'd.

6. NEITHER are later and nearer Experiments wanting. Of old time *Ravenna* stood upon the Brink of the Sea Shore, which is now by reason of the Landing up the Shallows far distant from it. The Sea washed the Walls of *Padua*, which is now Twenty five Miles remote therefrom. In fine, our *Rhene* of *Bologna*, though it be but a small Torrent, yet in a few Years, since it hath been by an artificial Cut let into the *Po*, it hath so filled it up, and obstructed its Channel with Sand and Mud, that it hath much endamaged the neighbouring Fields. Seeing then by these various Aggerations of Sand and Silt, the Sea is daily cut short, and driven back, and its Basin or Receptacle straitned, and the Bottom thereof raised, it will necessarily come to pass in time, that it will begin to overflow; as now it happens in many Places, for Example, in the *Baltick*, *Danick*, and *Holland* Shores, in which Places they are forced to erect and maintain long and high Banks and Fences against the Inundations of the Sea.

THEREFORE, after this manner, that Earth which now makes up the Mountains, being
by

by the Water little by little brought down into the Cavities of the Sea, is the Cause why the Sea gradually here and there overflows the *Superficies* of the Earth; and so the Globe of the Earth, by the Affusion of the Waters, will be again render'd unhabitable, as at first it was in the Beginning of the World; and the Earth and Water will return to their primitive State and Figure, in which they ought naturally to rest.

Hence we may deduce some Consectaries worthy to be known, *viz.* That the World, or at least the Earth, was not endued with that Figure which we now see; neither can the World endure for ever. For if this mountainous Figure had been in it from Eternity, all those Protuberancies of the Mountains had been long since eaten away and wasted, or consumed by the Waters. Nor can this World be Eternal; because, as we have proved, in Process of time it will be reduced to a perfect Rotundity, and be overflown by the Sea; whereupon it will become unhabitable, and Mankind must necessarily perish. Wherefore, unless that Deluge were prevented by the Fire which the Holy Scriptures mention, the World would nevertheless be destroyed by Water. Long after I had committed these things to writing, I met with *Philo Judæus* his Book *De Mundo*, wherein he touches this Matter but obscurely, and in a very few Words.

Thus

Thus far *Blancanus*, whose Sentiments and Observations concerning this Matter thus punctually concurring, and according with mine, to my great Wonder and Satisfaction, I could not but think that the Conclusion hath a high Degree of Probability. Only he takes no Notice, that in Compensation of what the Rivers gain from the Sea about their Outlets, the Sea may gain from the Land by undermining and washing away the Shores that are not rocky, (as we see it doth in our own Country) perhaps as much as it loses, according to the vulgar Proverb before remember'd. However, all contributes towards the filling up of the Sea, and bringing on an Inundation, as I shall afterwards shew.

But it may be objected, That if the Waters will thus naturally and necessarily in Process of time again overflow and cover the Earth, how can God's Promise and Covenant be made good, *Gen.* ix. 11. That *there should not any more be a Flood to destroy the Earth.*

To which I answer, 1. That though this would follow in a natural way, yet the Power of God may interpose to prevent it, and so make good His Promise. 2. Though it might come to pass in the Course of Nature, yet would it be after so many Ages, that it is not at all likely the World should last so long; but the Conflagration or Destruction of it by Fire, predicted by the Scriptures, will certainly prevent it. 3. Possibly there may be something in Nature which may obviate this Event, though to us at present unknown, which I am the more inclinable to believe, because the Earth doth not hasten so fast towards it, as some of the Ancients imagined, and as the Activity of such Causes might seem to require, as I have already intimated.

*Varenius*, in his Geography, putting the Question, Whether the Ocean may again come to cover all the Earth, and make an universal Deluge? answers, That we may conceive a way how this may naturally come to pass. The Manner thus; Supposing that the Sea by its continual Working doth undermine and wash away the Shores and Cliffs that are not rocky, and carry the Earth thereof down towards the Middle, or deepest Parts of its Channel, and so by Degrees fill it up. By doing this perpetually, it may, in a long Succession of Time, carry all away, and itself cover the whole Earth. That it doth thus subvert and wash away the Shores in many Places, is in Experience true. About *Dort* in *Holland*, and *Dullart* in *Friesland*, and in *Zealand* many Villages, some say Three hundred, have been drown'd by the Encroachments of the Sea, as some of their Towers and Steeples still extant above the Waters do testify. On the *Tuscan* Shore,

*Kircher*

*Kircher* tells us, That not far from *Ligorn,* he himself had observed a whole City under Water, that had been in former Times drown'd by the Inundation of the Sea. And overagainst *Puteoli,* in the *Sinus* of *Baia,* he tells us, That in the Bottom of the Sea, there are not only Houses but the Traces and Footsteps of the Streets of some City manifestly discernible. And in the County of *Suffolk,* almost the whole Town of *Donewich,* with the adjacent Lands, hath been undermined and devoured by the Sea.

THIS Washing away of the Shores is, I conceive, in great Measure to be attributed to the forementioned streightning and cutting short of the Sea, by the Earth and Silt that in the Times of Floods are brought down into it by the Rivers. For the Vulgar have a Proverbial Tradition, *That what the Sea loses in one Place, it gains in another.* And both together do very handsomly make out and explain, how the Earth in a Natural way, may be reduced to its primitive State in the Creation, when the Waters covered the Land. But this, according to the leisurely Proceedings of Nature, would not come to pass in many Ages, I might say, in Ages of Ages: Nay, some think, that those vast Ridges and Chains of Mountains, which run through the Middle of the Continents, are by reason of their great Height, Weight and Solidity, too great a Morsel ever to be

de-

devoured by the Jaws of the Sea. But whether they be or not, I need not dispute, though I incline to the Negative; because this is not the Dissolution the Apostle here speaks of, which must be by Fire.

But I must not here dissemble an Objection I see may be made, and that is, That the *Superficies* of the Earth is so far from being depressed, that it is continually elevated. For in ancient Buildings, we see the Earth raised high above the Foot of them. So the *Pantheon* at *Rome*, which was at first ascended up to by many [eight] Steps, is now descended down to by as many. The Basis and whole Pedestal of *Trajan*'s Pillar there was buried in the Earth.

Dr. *Tancred Robinson*, in the Year 1683, observed in some Places the Walls of old *Rome* to lie Thirty and Forty Foot under Ground; so that he thinks the greater Part of the Remains of that famous ancient City is still buried, and undiscovered; the prodigious Heaps of Ruins and Rubbish inclosed within the Vineyards and Gardens, being not half digged up or searched, as they might be, the Tops of Pillars peeping up and down. And in our own Country we find many ancient *Roman* Pavements at some Depth under Ground. My learned and ingenious Friend Mr. *Edward Lhwyd*, not long since inform'd of one, that himself had seen buried deep in the Church-yard

yard at *Wychester* in *Glocestershire*. Nay, the Earth in time will grow over and bury the Bodies of great Timber Trees, that have been fallen, and lie long upon it; which is made one great Reason, that such great Numbers (even whole Woods) of subterraneous Trees are frequently met with, and dug up at vast Depths in the *Spanish* and *Dutch Netherlands*, as well as in many Places of this Island of *Great Britain*.

To which I answer, as to Buildings, 1. The Ruins and Rubbish of the Cities wherein they stood, might be conceived to bury them as deep as they now lie under Ground. And, by this means it's likely the *Roman* Pavements we find, might come to be covered to that Height we mentioned. For that the Places where they occurr, were anciently *Roman* Towns subverted and ruined, may easily be proved; as particularly in this we mention'd, from the Termination *Chester*; whatever Town or Village hath that Addition to its Name, having been anciently a *Roman* Town or Camp; *Chester* seeming to be nothing but *Castra*:

2. It is to be consider'd, That weighty Buildings do in time overcome the Resistance of the Foundation, unless it be a solid Rock, and sink into the Ground.

Nay, the very soft Water, lying long upon the Bottoms of the Sea or Pools, doth so compress and sadden them by its Weight, that the very Roads that are continually beaten with Horses and Carriages, are not so firm and sad: And in the Sea, the nearer you dig to the low Water-Mark, still the sadder and firmer it is: And it's probable, still the farther the sadder; which seems to be confirmed by the strong fixing of Anchors. [This Firmness of the Sand, by the Weight of the incumbent Water, the People inhabiting near the Sea are so sensible of, that I have seen them boldly ride through the Water cross a Channel three Miles broad, before the Tide was out, when in some Places it reach'd to the Horses Belly.] A Resemblance whereof we have in Ponds, which being newly digg'd, the Water that runs into them, sinks soon into the Earth, and they become dry again; till after some time, by often filling, the Earth becomes so solid, through the Weight of the Water, that they leak no more, but hold Water up to the Brink. *Wittie Scarborough Spaw*, p. 86.

WHAT Force a gentle, if continual Pressure hath, we may understand also by the Roots of Trees, which we see will sometimes pierce through the Chinks of Stone Walls, and in time make great Cracks and Rifts in them; nay, will get under their very Foundations. The tender Roots of Herbs overcome the Resistance of the Ground, and make their way through Clay or Gravel. By the

by,

by, we may here take Notice, that one reaſon why Plowing, Harrowing, Sifting, or any Comminution of the Earth, renders it more fruitful, is, becauſe the Roots of Graſs, Corn, and other Herbs can, with more Facility, creep abroad, and multiply their Fibres in the light and looſe Earth.

THAT the Rotting of the Graſs, and other Herbs upon the Ground, may in ſome Places raiſe the *Superficies* of it, I will not deny; that is, in Gardens and Encloſures, where the Ground is rank, and no Cattel are admitted to eat off the Fog or long Graſs; but elſewhere, the Raiſing of the Superficies of the Earth is very little and inconſiderable; and none at all, unleſs in level Grounds, which have but little Declivity: For otherwiſe the Soil would by this time have come to be of a very great Depth, which we find to be but ſhallow. Nor do I think, that ſo much as the Trunks of fallen Trees are by this means cover'd; but rather, that they ſink by their own Weight, in time overcoming the Reſiſtance of the Earth, which without much Difficulty yields, being ſoaked and ſoftned by the Rains inſinuating into it, and keeping it continually moiſt in Winter-time. But if theſe Buildings be ſituate in Valleys, it is clear, that the Earth brought down from the Mountains by Rain, may ſerve to land them up. Again, the Superficies of the Earth may be raiſed near the Sea Coaſt, by the

con-

continual Blowing up of Sand by the Winds. This happens often in *Norfolk*, and in *Cornwall*, where I obſerved a fair Church, *viz.* that of the Pariſh called *Lalant*, which is the Mother Church to *S. Ives*, and above two Miles diſtant from the Sea, almoſt covered with the Sand; little being extant above it, but the Steeple and Ridge of the Roof. Nay, a great Part of *S. Ives* itſelf lies buried in the Sand: And I was told there, that in one Night there had been a whole Street of Houſes ſo covered with Sand, that in the Morning they were fain to dig their way out of their Houſes through it. All along the Weſtern Shore of *Wales*, there are great Hills of Sand thus blown up by the Wind. We obſerved alſo upon the Coaſt of *Flanders* and *Holland*, the like ſandy Hills, or Downs, from which Weſterly Winds drive the Sand a great way into the Country. But there are not many Places liable to this Accident, *viz.* where the Bottom of the Sea is ſandy, and where the Wind moſt frequently blows from off the Sea; where the Wind ſets from the Land toward the Sea this happens not; where it is indifferent, it muſt in reaſon carry off as much as it brings on, unleſs other Cauſes hinder.

S E C T.

## Sect. II.

*The Second possible Cause of the World's Destruction in a Natural Way, the Extinction of the Sun.*

II. THE Possibility of the Sun's Extinction: Of which Accident I shall give an Account of Dr. *More*'s Words, in the last Chapter of his Treatise of the *Immortality of the Soul*. " This (*saith he*) though it may seem 'a *Panick Fear* at first Sight; yet if the Matter be throughly examined, there will appear no contemptible Reasons that may induce Men to suspect, that it may at last fall out, there having been at certain Times such near Offers in Nature towards this sad Accident already." *Pliny* speaks of it as a thing not unfrequent, that there should be *Prodigiosi & longiores Solis defectus, qualis occiso Dictatore* Cæsare, *& Antoniano bello, totius anni pallore continuo*, Hist. Nat. lib. 2. cap. 30. *Prodigious and lasting Defects of the Sun, such as happened when* Cæsar *the Dictator was slain, and in the War with* Anthony, *when it was continually pale and gloomy for a whole Year.* The like happened in *Justinian*'s Time, as *Cedrenus* writes; when for a whole Year together, the Sun was of a very dim and duskish Hue, as if

## Of the Dissolution

he had been in a perpetual Eclipse: And, in the Time of *Irene* the Empress, it was so dark for Seventeen Days together, that the Ships lost their Way in the Sea, and were ready to run one against another, as *Theophanes* reports. But the late accurate Discovery of the Spots of the Sun by *Scheiner*, and the Appearing and Disappearing of Fixt Stars and Comets, and the Excursions of these last, do argue it more than possible, that after some vast Periods of Time, the Sun may be so inextricably inveloped by the *Maculæ*, that he may quite lose his Light; and then you may easily guess what would become of the Inhabitants of the Earth: For without his vivifick Heat, neither could the Earth put forth any Vegetables for their Sustenance; neither if it could, would they be able to bear the Extremity of the Cold, which must needs be more rigorous, and that perpetually, than it is now under the Poles in Winter-time. But this Accident, tho' it would indeed extinguish all Life, yet being quite contrary to a Dissolution by Fire, of which the Apostle speaks, I shall pass it over without farther Consideration, and proceed to a Third.

SECT.

### Sect. III.

*The Third possible Cause of the World's Destruction, the Eruption of the Central Fire.*

III. THE Possibility of the Eruption of the Central Fire, if any such there be, inclosed in the Earth. It is the *Hypothesis* of Monsieur *des Cartes*, that the Earth was originally a Star, or Globe of Fire, like the Sun, or one of the Fixt Stars, situate in the Center of a *Vortex* continually whirling round with it. That by Degrees it was covered over, or incrustated with *Maculæ*, arising on its Surface like the Scum on a boiling Pot, which still increasing and growing thicker and thicker, the Star losing its Light and Activity, and, consequently, the Motion of the celestial Vortex about it growing more weak, languid, and unable to resist the vigorous Incroachments of the neighbouring *Vortex* of the Sun; it was at last drawn in, and wholly absorpt by it, and forced to comply with its Motion, and make one in the Quire of the Sun's *Satellites*. This whole *Hypothesis* I do utterly disallow and reject. Neither did the Author himself (if we may believe him) think it true, that the Earth was thus generated. For he saith, *Quinimo ad ad res naturales melius explicandas, earum causas altius hic repetam quam ipsas unquam extitisse existimem. Non enim dubium est, quin mundus ab initio fuerit creatus cum omni suâ perfectione, ita ut in eo & Sol, & Terra, & Luna, & Stellæ extiterint.......  Hoc fides Christiana nos docet; hocque etiam ratio naturalis planè persuadet. Attendendo enim ad immensam Dei potentiam, non possumus existimare illum unquam quidquam fecisse, quod non omnibus suis numeris fuerit absolutum:* That is, *Moreover, for the better explicating of Natural Things, I shall bring them from higher or more remote Causes than I think they ever had. For there is no doubt, but the World was originally created in its full Perfection, so that in it were contained both Sun, and Moon, and Earth, and Stars,* &c. *For this the Christian Faith teacheth us, and this also Natural Reason doth plainly persuade; for attending to the immense Power of* GOD, *we cannot think that He ever made any thing that was not complete in all Points.* But tho' he did not believe that the Earth was generated, or formed according to his *Hypothesis,* yet surely he was of Opinion, that it is at present such a Body as he represented it after its perfect Formation, *viz.* with a Fire in the middle, and so many several Crusts or Coats inclosing it; else would he have given us a meer Figment or Romance instead of a Body of Philosophy.

BUT

But tho' I do reject the *Hypothesis*; yet the Being of a Central Fire in the Earth is not, so far as I understand, any way repugnant to Reason or Scripture. For first of all, the *Scripture* represents Hell as a Lake of Fire, *Mark* ix. 43, 44, &c. *Rev.* xx. 10, 14, 15. and, likewise, as a low Place beneath the Earth. So *Psal.* lxxxvi. 13. and *Deut.* xxxii. 22. it is called the *nethermost Hell*, Prov. xv. 24. *The Way of Life is above to the Wise, that he may depart from Hell beneath.* 2. Many of the Ancients understand that Article of the Creed, *He descended into Hell*, of our Saviour's Descent into that local Hell beneath the Earth, where He triumphed over the Devil, and all the Powers of Darkness. And, particularly, *Irenæus* interprets that Saying of our Saviour, That *the Son of Man should be three Days in the Heart of the Earth*, of his being three Days in the Middle of the Earth, which could not be meant (*saith he*) of the Sepulchre, because that was hewn out of a Rock in its *Superficies*. 3. It is a received Opinion among the Divines of the Church of *Rome*, that Hell is about the Center of the Earth; insomuch as some of them have been solicitous to demonstrate, that there is room enough to receive all the Damned, by giving us the Dimensions thereof.

Neither is it repugnant to the History of the Creation in *Genesis*. For tho' indeed *Moses* doth mention only Water and Earth, as

the

the Component Parts of this Body; yet doth he not aſſert, that the Earth is a ſimple, uniform, homogeneous Body; as neither do we, when we ſay, *Upon the Face of the Earth,* or, the like. For the Earth, we ſee, is a Maſs made up of a Multitude of different *Species of* Bodies, *Metals, Minerals, Stones,* and other Foſſils, *Sand, Clay, Marl, Chalk,* &c. which do all agree, in that they are conſiſtent and ſolid more or leſs, and are in that reſpect contradiſtinguiſhed to Water; and together compound one Maſs, which we call Earth. Whether the interior Parts of the Earth be made up of ſo great a Variety of different Bodies, is to us altogether unknown. For tho' it be obſerved by Colliers, that the Beds of Coals lie one way, and do always dip towards the Eaſt, let them go never ſo deep; ſo that, would it quit Coſt, and were it not for the Water, they ſay, they might purſue the Bed of Coals to the very Center of the Earth, the Coals never failing or coming to an End that way; yet that is but a raſh and ungrounded Conjecture. For, what is the Depth of the profoundeſt Mines, were they a Mile deep, to the Semidiameter of the Earth? not as One to Four thouſand. Comparing this Obſervation of Dipping with my Notes about other Mines, I find that the Veins or Beds of all generally run Eaſt and Weſt, and dip towards the Eaſt. Of which, what Account or Reaſon can we give, but the

the Motion of the Earth from West to East? I know some say, that the Veins, for Example, of Tin and Silver, dip to the North, tho' they confess they run East and West, which is a thing I cannot understand, the Veins of those Metals being narrow things. Sir *Tho. Willoughby*, in his forementioned Letter, writes thus: ------ 'I have talked
' with some of my Colliers about the Lying
' of the Coal, and find, that generally the Bas-
' set-End (as they call it) lies West, and runs
' deeper toward the East, allowing about
' twenty Yards in Length to gain one in
' Depth; but sometimes they decline a little
' from this Posture; for mine lie almost South-
' West, and North-East. They always sink to
' the East more or less. There may, therefore,
' for ought we know, be Fire about the Cen-
' ter of the Earth, as well as any other Body,
' if it can find a *Pabulum*, or Fewel there to
' maintain it. And why may it not? since the
' Fires in those subterraneous Caverns of *Æt-*
' *na*, *Vesuvius*, *Stromboli*, *Hecla*, and other
' burning Mountains or *Vulcano's*, have found
' wherewith to feed them for Thousands of
' Years. And as there are at some, tho' un-
' certain Periods of Time, violent Eruptions
' of Fire from the *Craters* of those Mountains,
' and mighty Streams of melted Materials
' poured forth from thence: So, why may
' not this Central Fire in the Earth, (if any
' such there be) receiving accidentally extra-
' ordinary

"ordinary Supplies of convenient Fuel, either
"from some inflamable Matter within or from
"without, rend the thick exterior *Cortex*
"which imprisons it, or finding some Vents
"and Issues, break forth and overflow the
"whole *Superficies* of the Earth, and burn up
"all Things." This is not impossible; and
we have seen some *Phænomena* in Nature
which bid fair towards a Probability of it.
For, what should be the Reason of new Stars
appearing and disappearing again? as that noted one in *Cassiopeia*, which at first shone with
as great a Lustre as *Venus*, and then by Degrees diminishing, after some two Years vanish'd quite away? But that by great Supplies of combustible Matter, the internal Fire
suddenly increasing in Quantity and Force,
either found, or made its Way through the
Cracks or Vents of the *Maculæ* which inclosed it, and in an instant, as it were, overflowed the whole Surface of the Star, whence
proceeded that illustrious Light; which afterwards again gradually decayed, its Supply
failing. Whereas other newly appearing Stars,
which either have a constant Supply of Matter, or where the Fire hath quite dissolved
the *Maculæ*, and made them comply with
its Motion, have endured for a long time,
as that which now shines in the Neck of
*Cygnus*, which appears and disappears at certain Intervals.

But

BUT because it is not demonstrable that there is any such Central Fire in the Earth, I propose the Eruption thereof rather as a possible than probable Means of a Conflagration: And proceed to the last Means whereby it may naturally be effected; and that is:

### SECT. IV.

*The Fourth Natural Cause of the World's Dissolution, the Earth's Dryness and Inflammability.*

IV. THE Dryness and Inflammability of the Earth under the Torrid Zone, with the Eruption of the *Vulcano's* to set it on fire. Those that hold the Inclination of the *Equator* to the *Ecliptick* daily to diminish, so that after the Revolutions of some Ages they will jump and consent, tell us, that the Sun-Beams lying perpendicularly and constantly on the Parts under the *Equator*, the Ground thereabout must needs be extremely parch'd and rendred apt for Inflammation. But for my part, I own no such Decrement of Inclination. And the best Mathematicians of our Age deny, that there hath been any since the eldest Observations that are come down to us. For tho', indeed, *Ptolemy* and *Hipparchus* do make it more than we find it by above twenty Minutes, yet that Difference is not
so

so considerable, but that it may well be imputed to the Difference of Instruments, or Observations in Point of Exactness. So that not having decreased for Eighteen hundred Years past, there is not the least ground for Conjecture, that it will alter in Eighteen hundred Years to come, should the World last so long. And yet if there were such a Diminution, it would not conduce much (so far as I can see) to the bringing on of a Conflagration. For tho' the Earth would be extremely dried, and perchance thereby rendred more inflammable; yet the Air being by the same Heat as much rarified, would contain but few nitrous Particles, and so be inept to maintain the Fire, which, we see, cannot live without them: It being much deaded by the Sun shining upon it; and burning very remissly in Summer-time, and hot Weather. For this Reason, in Southern Countries, in extraordinary hot Seasons, the Air scarce sufficeth for Respiration. To the clearing up of this, let us a little consider what Fire is. It seems to consist of three different Sorts of Parts. 1. An extremely thin and subtil Body, whose Particles are in a very vehement and rapid Motion. 2. A (supposed) Nitrous *Pabulum*, or Fewel, which it receives from the Air. 3. A sulphureous or unctuous *Pabulum*, which it acts and preys upon, passing generally by the Name of Fewel. This forementioned subtil Body

agita-

agitating the (suppofed) Nitrous Particles it receives from the Air, doth by their Help, as by Wedges, to ufe that rude Similitude, penetrate the unctuous Bodies, upon which it acts, and divide them into their immediate component Particles, and at length, perchance into their firft Principles; which Operation is called the Chymical Anatomy of mix'd Bodies. So we fee Wood, for Example, divided by Fire into Spirit, Oil, Water, Salt, and Earth.

That Fire cannot live without thofe Particles it receives from the Air, is manifeft, in that, if you preclude the Accefs of all Air, it is extinguifhed immediately: And in that, where and when the Air is more charged with them, as in cold Countries, and cold Weather, the Fire rages moft: That likewife it cannot be continued without an unctuous *Pabulum*, or Fewel, I appeal to the Experience of all Men.

Now then, in the rarified Air in the Torrid Zone, the nitrous Particles being proportionably fcattered and thin fet, the Fire that might be kindled there would burn but very languidly and remifly, as we faid juft now: And fo the Eruptions of *Vulcano's*, if any fuch happened, would not be like to do half the Execution there that they would do in cold Countries. And yet I never read of any fpreading Conflagration caufed by the Eruptions of any *Vulcano's*, either in hot Countries,

tries, or in cold. They usually cast out abundance of thick Smoak, like Clouds darkning the Air; and likewise Ashes and Stones, sometimes of a vast Bigness; and some of them, as *Vesuvius*, Floods of Water; others, (as *Ætna*) Rivers of melted Materials, running down many Miles: As for the Flames that issue out of their Mouths at such Times, they are but transient, and mounting upwards, seldom set any thing on fire.

But not to insist upon this, I do affirm, that there hath not as yet been, nor for the future can be, any such Drying or Parching of the Earth under the *Torrid Zone*, as some may imagine. That there hath not yet been, I appeal to Experience, the Countries lying under the Course of the Sun, being at this Day as fertile as ever they were, and wanting no more Moisture now than of old they did; having as constant and plentiful Rains in their Seasons as they then had. That they shall for the future suffer any more Drought than they have heretofore done, there is no Reason to believe or imagine; the Face of the Earth being not altered, nor naturally alterable, as to the main, more at present than it was heretofore. I shall now add the Reason, why, I think, there can be no such Exsiccation of the Earth in those Parts. It's true indeed, were there nothing to hinder them, the Vapours exhaled by the Sun-Beams in those hot Regions, would be

cast

cast off to the North, and to the South, a great way, and not fall down in Rain there, but towards the Poles: But the long and continued Ridges or Chains of exceeding high Mountains are so disposed by the great and wise Creator of the World, as, at least in our Continent, to run East and West, as *Gassendus* in the Life of *Peireskius* well observes, such are *Atlas*, *Taurus*, and the *Alps*, to name no more: They are, I say, thus disposed, as if it were on purpose to obviate and stop the Evagation of the Vapours Northward, and reflect them back again, so that they must needs be condensed, and fall upon the Countries out of which they were elevated. And on the South Side, being near the Sea, it is likely that the Wind, blowing for the most part from thence, hinders their Excursion that way. This I speak by Presumption, because in our Country, for at least three Quarters of the Year, the Wind blows from the great *Atlantick* Ocean; which was taken Notice of by *Julius Cæsar* in the Fifth of his Commentaries, *De Bello Gallico*. *Corus ventus, qui magnam partem omnis temporis in his locis flare consuevit.*

As for any Desiccation of the Sea, I hold that by meer natural Causes to be impossible, unless we could suppose a Transmutation of Principles or Simple Bodies, which for Reasons alledged in a former Discourse I cannot allow. I was then, and am still of Opinion,

C c          that

that GOD Almighty did at first create a certain and determinate Number of Principles, or variously figured Corpuscles, intransmutable by the Force of any natural Agent, even Fire itself; (which can only separate the Parts of heterogeneous Bodies) yet not an equal Number of each Kind of these Principles, but of some abundantly more, as of *Water, Earth, Air, Æther*; and of others fewer, as of *Oyl, Salt, Metals, Minerals*, &c. Now, that there may be some Bodies indivisible by Fire, is, I think, demonstrable. For how doth or can Fire be conceived to divide; one can hardly imagine any other way than by its small Parts, by reason of their violent Agitation insinuating themselves into Compound Bodies, and separating their Parts; which allowing, yet still there is a Term of Magnitude, below which it cannot divide, *viz.* it cannot divide a Body into smaller Parts than those whereof itself is compounded. For taking, suppose, one least Part of Fire, 'tis clear that it cannot insinuate itself into a Body as little or less than itself; and what is true of one, is true of all: I say, we can imagine no other way than this, unless perchance, by a violent Stroke or Shock, the Parts of the Body to be divided, may be put into so impetuous a Motion, as to fall in sunder of themselves into lesser Particles than those of the impellent Body are, which I will not suppose at present. Now, it is possible,

that

that the Principles of some other Simple Bodies may be as small as the Particles of Fire. But however that be, it is enough, if the Principles of Simple Bodies be, by reason of their perfect Solidity, naturally indivisible. Such a simple Body, I suppose, Water separated from all heterogeneous Mixtures to be: And consequently the same Quantity thereof that was at first created, doth still remain, and will continue always in Despight of all natural Agents, unless it pleases the Omnipotent Creator to dissolve it. And therefore there can be no Desiccation of the Seas, unless by turning all its Water into Vapour, and suspending it in the Air, which to do, what an immense and long-continuing Fire would be requisite? to the Maintenance whereof all the inflammable Materials near the Superficies of the Earth would not afford Fewel enough. The Sun, we see, is so far from doing it, that it hath not made one Step towards it these four thousand Years, there being in all Likelihood as great a Quantity of Water in the Ocean now, as was immediately after the Flood: And consequently there would probably remain as much in it, should the World last four thousand Years longer.

THIS Fixedness and Intransmutability of Principles secures the Universe from Dissolution by the prevailing of one Element over another, and turning it into its own Nature; which otherwise it would be in continual

Danger of. It secures likewise the Perpetuity of all the *Species* in the World, many of which, if their Principles were transmutable, might by such a Change be quite lost: And lastly, bars the Production or Creation of any new Species, as in the formentioned Treatise I have shewn.

## Chap. VI.

*Containing an Answer to the Second Question, Whether shall this Dissolution be effected by natural or by extraordinary Means, and what they shall be?*

2. AS to the Second Question, Whether shall this Dissolution be brought about and effected by natural or by extraordinary Means and Instruments, and what those Means and Instruments shall be? I answer in brief, That the Instrumental Efficient of this Dissolution shall be natural. For it is clear, both by Scripture and Tradition, and agreed on all hands, that it shall be that Catholick Dissolvent, *Fire*. Now, to the Being and Maintenance of Fire, there are four Things requisite. 1. The active Principle of *Æther*. 2. *Air*,

or

or a Nitrous *Pabulum* received from it: These two being commixt together, are every where at hand. 3. *Fewel*, which, considering the Abundance of combustible Materials, which are to be found in all Places upon or under the Surface of the Earth, can no where be wanting. 4. The Accension, and the sudden and equal Diffusion of this Fire all the World over. And this must be the Work of GOD, extraordinary and miraculous.

SUCH a Dissolution of the World might indeed be effected by that natural Accident mentioned in the Answer to the precedent Question, *viz.* The Eruption of the Central Fire. But because it is doubtful, whether there be any such Fire in the Middle of the Earth or no; and if there ever were, it is hard to give an Account, how it could be maintained in that infernal Dungeon for want of Air and Fewel. And, because, if it should break forth into the Consistency of a thin Flame, it would in all Likelihood speedily like Lightning mount up to Heaven, and quite vanish away; unless we could suppose Floods, nay Seas of melted Materials, or liquid Fire, enough to overflow the whole Earth, to be poured forth of those Caverns. For these Reasons I reject that Opinion, and do rather think that the Conflagration shall be effected by a superficial Fire. Tho' I must confess we read in *Tacitus, Annal.* 13. at the

End, of a Sort of Fire that was not so apt to disperse and vanish. '—— The City of
' the *Inhonians* in *Germany* (saith he) confe-
' derate with us was afflicted with a sudden
' Disaster; for Fires issuing out of the Earth,
' burned Towns, Fields, Villages every
' where, and spread even to the Walls of a
' Colony newly built, and could not be ex-
' tinguished, neither by Rain nor River-Wa-
' ter, nor any other Liquor that could be
' employed, until for want of Remedy, or
' Anger of such a Distraction, certain Pea-
' sants cast Stones afar off into it; then the
' Flame somewhat slackning, drawing near,
' they put it out with Blows of Clubs, and
' other like, as if it had been a wild Beast:
' Last of all, they threw in Cloaths from
' their Backs, which the more worn and
' fouler they were, the better they quenched
' the Fire." I use Dr. *Hakewill*'s Translation.

CHAP.

## CHAP. VII.

*The Third Question answered, Whether shall this Dissolution be gradual and successive, or momentaneous and sudden?*

3. THE Third Question is, *Whether shall this Dissolution be gradual and successive, or momentaneous and sudden?*

I ANSWER, The Scripture resolves for the latter, *The Day of the* LORD *shall come as a Thief in the Night:* A Similitude we have often repeated in Scripture; as in the tenth Verse of this Chapter, in 1 *Thess.* xv. 2. *Rev.* iii. 3. and xvi. 15. And the Resurrection and Change of Things, it is said, shall be *in a Moment, in the Twinkling of an Eye,* 1 Cor. xv. 52. Consonant whereto both the *Epicureans* and *Stoicks* held their Dissolutions of the World should be sudden and brief, as *Lucretius* and *Seneca,* in the Place forementioned, tell us. And it is suitable to the Nature of Fire to make a quick Dispatch of Things, suddenly to consume and destroy.

AND as it shall be sudden, so also shall it be unexpected, being compared to the Coming of the Flood in the Days of *Noah,* Mat. xxiv. 37, 38, 39. *But as the Days of Noah were, so shall also the Coming of the Son of Man be. For as in the Days that were before the Flood, they were eating and drinking, marrying and giving in Marriage, until the Day that Noah entred into the Ark; And knew not until the Flood came and took them all away; so shall also the Coming of the Son of Man be.* And the raining of Fire and Brimstone upon *Sodom.* Luke xvii. Thessal. v. 3. *For when they shall say Peace and Safety, then sudden Destruction cometh upon them as Travail upon a Woman with Child.* Now, if it shall be thus sudden and unexpected, it is not likely there should be in Nature any manifest Tendency to it, or remarkable Signs and Fore-runners of it: For such must needs startle and awaken the World into an Expectation and Dread of it. That there is at present no such Tendency to Corruption, but that the World continues still in as good State and Condition as it was two thousand Years ago, without the least Impairment or Decay, hath been, as we before noted, without any Possibility of Contradiction, clearly made out and demonstrated, by Dr. *Hakewill* in his Apology: And therefore, arguing from the past to the future, it will in all Likelihood so continue two thousand Years more, if it be so long to the Day of Doom; and consequently that Day (as the Scripture predicts) will suddenly and unexpectedly come upon the World. But if all these Prophecies (as Dr. *Hammond* affirms)

affirms) be to be restrained only to the Destruction of *Jerusalem*, and the *Jewish* Polity, without any farther Respect to the End of the World, then indeed from thence we can make no Inferences or Deductions in reference to that final Period.

## Chap. VIII.

*The Fourth Question Resolved, Whether shall there be any Signs or Fore-runners of the Dissolution of the World?*

4. THE Fourth Question is, Whether shall there be any Signs or Fore-runners of the Dissolution of the World?

In order to the Answering of this Question, we shall distinguish Signs into Natural and Arbitrarious.

1. Natural *Signs*, so the *Aurora*, or Dawning of the Day, is a Sign of the Sun-Rising. Now, if the Dissolution be effected in the Course of Nature, and by Natural Means, there will be some previous natural Signs of it. An old House will threaten Ruin before it falls. The natural Death of Men, and all Animals, hath its Harbingers, and old Men before their Dissolution feel the
Impres-

Impressions of Age; and proclaim to the World their approaching Fate, by Wrinkles, Gray Hairs, and Dimness of Sight. But we have formerly shewn, That there is no Consenescency or Declension in Nature; but that the World continues still as firm and staunch as it was three thousand Years ago; and why hereafter it should founder and decay more than it hath done for so many Ages heretofore, what Reason can be given? It is not therefore likely there should be any natural Signs of the Dissolution of the World; and consequently that it shall be effected by natural Means.

2. There are *Arbitrary Signs*, as a Garland hung out is a Sign of Wine to be sold. Now, if the Dissolution of the World be effected by Supernatural and Extraordinary Means, (as is most likely) the Signs of it must be arbitrarious. For though they may be natural Effects and Productions, yet would they not signify the Destruction of the World, if they were not ordered by Providence to happen at that time, and predicted as Forerunners of it; with which otherwise they have no natural Connexion. Such Signs are *Matth*. xxiv. the Sun being darken'd, and the Moon not giving her Light, and the Stars falling from Heaven, and the Shaking of the Powers of Heaven. These, and many other Signs of His Coming, we find mentioned in Scripture; but what the Meaning of these

Expressions may be, is not so clear. For though some of them may be taken in a literal Sense, yet it is manifest that others cannot. The Sun may indeed be so covered with a *Macula*, as to be quite obscured; and thereupon the Moon necessarily lose her Light, which she borrows only from the Sun-Beams: But how the Stars should in a literal Sense fall down from Heaven, is inconceivable; it being almost demonstratively certain, that most of them are bigger than the whole Earth. We may therefore, keeping as near as we can to the Letter, thus interpret them. There shall be great Signs in Heaven, dismal Eclipses and Obscurations of the Sun and Moon; new Stars and Comets shall appear, and others disappear, and many fiery Meteors be suspended in the Air. The very Foundations of the Earth shall be shaken, and the Sea shall roar and make a Noise. But I must not here dissemble a great Difficulty: How can such illustrious Signs and Fore-runners be reconciled to the Suddenness and Unexpectedness of Christ's Coming, and the End of the World? *Luke* xxi. 25. After the Evangelist had told us, *That there shall be Signs in the Sun, and in the Moon, and in the Stars, ----- the Sea and the Waves roaring;* he adds, as a Consequent thereof, Ver. 26. *Mens Hearts failing them for Fear, and for looking after those Things that are coming on the Earth.* And, indeed,

indeed, how could any Man possibly be buried in so profound a Lethargy of Senslesness, and Security, as by such stupendous Prodigies, not to be rowzed and awakened to an Expectation of some dismal and tremendous Event? How could he sing a *Requiem* to his Soul, and say Peace and Safety, when the World so manifestly threatens Ruin about his Ears? For the reconciling of these Expressions to this sudden Coming of our Saviour to Judgment, it were most convenient to accept them in the Figurative and Metaphorical Sense. For if we understand them of the Ruin and Devastations of Cities and Countries, and Changes of Governments, the Subversions of Kingdoms and Commonwealths, the Falls and Deposings of Princes, Nobles, and great Men; these happening more or less in every Age, tho' the serious and inquisitive Christian, who searches and understands the Scriptures, may discern them to be the Signs of the World's *Catastrophe*; yet the careless and inconsiderate, the vicious and voluptuous are not like to be at all startled or moved at them, but may notwithstanding, looking upon them as ordinary and insignificant Accidents, *dormire in utramque aurem*, sleep securely till the last Trump awaken them. Or it may be answered, That these Prophecies do belong to the Destruction of *Jerusalem* only, and

so

so we are not concerned to answer that Objection.

## Chap. IX.

*The Fifth Question answered; At what Period of Time shall the World be dissolved?*

5. THE Fifth Question is, At what Period of Time shall the World be dissolved? I answer, This is absolutely uncertain and undeterminable. For, since this Dissolution shall be effected by the extraordinary Interposition of Providence, it cannot be to any Man known, unless extraordinarily revealed. And our Saviour tells us, That *of that Day and Hour knoweth no Man, no not the Angels of Heaven*, &c. Matth. xxiv. 36. And again, *Acts* i. 17. *It is not for us to know the Times and the Seasons, which the Father hath placed in his own Power.* And this Dr. *Hakewill* brings as an Argument, that the World decays not, neither tends to Corruption; because, if it did, the Time of its actual Dissolution might be collected and foretold; which, *saith he,* the Scripture denies. We may invert this

Argu-

Argumentation, and inferr, Becaufe the World doth not decay, therefore the Time of its Diffolution cannot be known.

But yet, notwithftanding this, many have ventured to foretell the Time of the End of the World, of whom fome are already confuted, the Term prefixt being paft, and the World ftill ftanding. *Lactantius*, in his Time, faid, *Inftit. lib.* 7. *cap.* 25. *Omnis expectatio non amplius quàm ducentorum videtur annorum*; *The longeft Expectation extends not farther than Two hundred Years*. The Continuance of the World more than a Thoufand Years fince, convinces him of a grofs Miftake. *Paulus Grebnerus*, a high Pretender to a Spirit of Prophecy, fets it in the Year 1613, induced thereto by a fond Conceit of the Numeral Letters in the *Latin* Word *Judicium*. Other Enthufiaftical Perfons of our own Country have placed it in the Years 1646, and 1656. The Event fhews how ungroundedly and erroneoufly. Others there are, whofe Term is not yet expired, and fo they remain ftill to be confuted. As thofe who conceit, that the End of the World fhall be when the Pole-Star fhall come to touch the Pole of the *Equator*, which (*fay they*) ever fince the Time of *Hipparchus*, hath approached nearer and nearer to it. That it doth fo, I am not fatisfied; but if it doth, it is meerly Accidental, and hath no Connexion with the End of the World. But the

*Du Moulin.*

the most famous Opinion, and which hath found most Patrons and Followers, even amongst the Learned and Pious, is that of the World's Duration for Six thousand Years. For the strengthening of which Conceit, they tell us, That as the World was created in six Days, and then followed the Sabbath, so shall it remain Six thousand Years, and then shall succeed the Eternal Sabbath. *Heb.* iv. 9. Ἄρα ἀπολείπεται Σαββατισμὸς, &c. *There remains, therefore, a Rest or Sabbath to the People of* God. Here we see, that the Apostle institutes a Comparison between the heavenly Rest and the Sabbath. Therefore, as God rested upon the Seventh Day, so shall all the World of the Godly rest after the Six Thousandth Year. *For he that hath entred into his Rest, ceaseth from all his Works, as* God *did from His.* Of this Opinion were many of the Ancient Fathers, as I shewed before, grounding themselves upon this Analogy between the Six Days of the Creation and the Sabbath; and the Six Thousand Years of the World's Duration, and the Eternal Rest: For, saith *Irenæus* in the Place before quoted, *Hoc autem,* (that is, the History of the Six Days Creation, and succeeding Sabbath) *est, & præteritorum narratio, & futurorum prophetia. Dies enim unus mille annos significat, sicut Scriptura testatur* 2 *Pet.* iii. 8. *Psal.* xc. 4. The Scriptures reckoning Days of One thousand Years long, as in *Verse* 8. of this

this Chapter, and in *Psal.* xc. 4. This is likewise a received Tradition of the *Jewish Rabbins*, regiſtred in the *Talmud*, in the Treatiſe *Sanhedrim*, delivered (as they pretend) by the Prophet *Elias* the *Tiſhbite* to the Son of the Woman of *Sarepta*, whom he raiſed from the Dead, and by him handed down to Poſterity. I rather think with *Reuterus*, that the Author of it was ſome *Rabbi* of that Name. The Tradition is, *Sex millia annorum erit mundus : & uno millenario vaſtatio,* i. e. *Sabbathum Dei : Duo millia inane : Duo millia Lex : Duo millia dies Meſſiæ.* Two thouſand Years Vacuity : Two thouſand Years of the Law : Two thouſand Years the Days of the *Meſſiah*. But they ſhoot far wide : For, according to the leaſt Account, there paſſed a far greater Number of Years before the Law was given, 2513, ſaith *Reuterus*; and, on the contrary, leſs Time from the Law to the Exhibition of the *Meſſiah*. All theſe Proofs laid together, do ſcarce ſuffice to make up a Probability. Neither do thoſe Rabbinical Collections from the ſix Letters in בראשית the firſt Word of *Geneſis*, or from the ſix *Alephs* in the firſt Verſe of that Book, each ſignifying a Thouſand Years; or from the Six firſt Patriarchs in the Order of the Genealogy to *Enoch*, who was caught up to Heaven, and found no more, add much Weight to this Opinion. S. *Auſtin* very modeſtly concludes, after a Diſcuſſion of this

Point concerning the World's Duration; *Ego tempora dinumerare non audeo: Nec aliquem Prophetam de hac re numerum annorum existimo præfinivisse. Nos ergo, quod scire nos Dominus noluit, libenter nesciamus.* *I dare not calculate and determine Times: Neither do I think, that concerning this Matter, any Prophet hath predicted and defined the Number of Years. What therefore the* LORD *would not have us to know, let us willingly be ignorant of.*

But though none but presumptuous Persons have undertaken peremptorily to determine that Time, yet was it the common and received Opinion and Persuasion of the Ancient Christians, that that Day was not far off: And had they been to limit it, they would hardly have been induced to set the Term so forward and remote from their own Age, as by Experience we find it proves to be, but in their own Times, or shortly after: And many Places of Scripture seem to favour that Opinion; so that some have presumed to say, That the Apostles themselves were at first mistaken in this Particular, till after farther Illumination they were better informed. But though this be too bold a Conceit, yet that the Churches, at least some of them, did at first mistake the Apostles Meaning, in their Sermons and Epistles concerning this Point, and so understand them, as to think that the End of the World and

Final Judgment was at hand, appears from 2 Theff. ii. 2. *I beseech you, Brethren, that ye be not soon shaken in Mind, or be troubled, neither by Spirit, nor by Word, nor by Letter, as from us, as that the Day of* CHRIST *is at hand.* We see the Apostle labours to rectify, and for the future to prevent this Mistake: So, likewise, the Apostle *Peter*, in the 8th and 9th Verses of this Chapter. And yet this Opinion had taken such deep Root in them, that it was not easy to be extirpated; but continued for some Ages in the Church. Indeed, there are so many Places in the New Testament which speak of the Coming of CHRIST as very near, that if we should have lived in their Time, and understood them all as they did, of His Coming to judge the World, we could hardly have avoided being of the same Opinion. But if we apply them (as Dr. *Hammond* doth) to His Coming to take Vengeance on His Enemies, then they do not hinder, but that the Day of Judgment, I mean the General Judgment, may be far enough off. So I leave this Question unresolved, concluding, that when that Day will come GOD only knows.

## Chap. X.

*How far this Conflagration shall extend.*

6. **A** SIXTH Question is, How far shall this Conflagration extend? Whether to the Ethereal Heavens, and all the Host of them, Sun, Moon, and Stars, or to the Aereal only?

I ANSWER, If we follow ancient Tradition, not only the Earth, but also the Heavens and heavenly Bodies will be involved in one common Fate, as appears by those Verses quoted out of *Lucretius*, *Ovid*, *Lucan*, &c.

OF Christians some exempt the Ethereal Region from this Destruction; for the two following Reasons, which I shall set down in *Reuterus*'s Words: 1. 'Because in this Chap-
' ter the Conflagration is compared to the
' Deluge in the Time of *Noah*. But the De-
' luge extended not to the upper Regions of
' the Air, much less to the Heavens, the Wa-
' ters arising only fifteen Cubits above the
' Tops of the Mountains, if so much. There-
' fore neither shall the Conflagration tran-
' scend that Term." So *Beza*, upon 2 *Pet.*
iii. 6. *Tantum ascendet ille ignis quantum aqua altior supra omnes montes.* That Fire shall ascend as high as the Waters stood above the

*Moun-*

*Mountains.* This Passage I do not find in the last Edition of his Notes. The ordinary Gloss also upon these Words, 2 Thess. i. 2. *In flaming Fire rendring Vengeance,* saith, *Christum venturum præcedet ignis in mundo, qui tantum ascendet quantum aqua in diluvio.* There shall a Fire go before CHRIST when He comes, which shall reach as high as did the Water in the Deluge. And S. *Augustin De Civit. Dei lib.* 20. *cap.* 18. *Petrus etiam commemorans factum ante diluvium, videtur admonuisse quodammodo, quatenus in fine hujus seculi istum mundum periturum esse credamus.* Peter also mentioning the ancient Deluge, seems in a manner to have advised us how far, at the Consummation of Time, we are to believe this World shall perish.

But this Argument is of no Force, because it is not the Apostle's Design in that Place to describe the Limits of the Conflagration, but only against Scoffers, to shew, that the World should one Day perish by Fire, as it had of old been destroyed by Water.

2. The second Reason is, 'Because the 'heavenly Bodies are not subject to Passion, 'Alteration, or Corruption. They can con- 'tract no Filth, and so need no Expurgation 'by Fire.

To this we answer, not in the Words of *Reuter,* but our own; That it is an idle and ill-grounded Conceit of the *Peripateticks,* That the Heavenly Bodies are of their own Nature

Nature incorruptible and unalterable: For on the contrary it is demonstrable, that many of them are of the same Nature with the Earth we live upon, and the most pure, as the Sun, and probably too the fix'd Stars, suffer Alterations; *maculæ*, or opaque Concretions being commonly generated and dissolved in them. And *Comets* frequently, and sometimes *New Stars*, appear in the Ethereal Regions. So that these Arguments are insufficient to exempt the Heavens from Dissolution; and on the other side, many Places there are in Scripture which seem to subject them thereto: As *Psal.* cii. 25, 26. recited *Hebr.* i. 10. which hath already often been quoted, *The Heavens are the Works of Thy Hands; They shall perish.* Matth. xxiv. 35. *Heaven and Earth shall pass away.* Isa. lxv. 17. and li. 6. *The Heavens shall vanish away like Smoke.* Yet am I not of Opinion, that the last Fire shall reach the Heavens; they are too far distant from us to suffer by it: Nor indeed doth the Scripture affirm it; but where it mentions the Dissolution of the Heavens, it expresseth it by such Phrases as seem rather to intimate, that it shall come to pass by a Consenescency and Decay, than be effected by any sudden and violent Means. *Psal.* cii. 25, 26. *They all shall wax old as doth a Garment*, &c. Though I confess nothing of Certainty can be gathered from such Expressions: For we find the same used concerning the Earth, *Isa.* li. 6. *The Heavens shall vanish away like Smoke, and the Earth shall wax old as doth a Garment.* The Heavenly Bodies are none of them uncorruptible and eternal; but may in like manner as the Earth be consumed and destroyed, at what Times, and by what Means, whether Fire, or some other Element, the Almighty hath decreed and ordered.

### C H A P. XI.

*Whether shall the whole World be consumed and annihilated, or only refined and purified?*

THERE remains now only the Seventh Question to be resolved, Whether shall the World be wholly consumed, burnt up and destroyed, or annihilated; or only refined, purified, or renewed? To this I answer, That the latter Part seems to me more probable, *viz.* That it shall not be destroyed and annihilated, but only refined and purified. I know what potent Adversaries I have in this Case. I need name no more than *Gerard* in his Common Places, and Dr. *Hakewill* in his Apology, and the Defence of it,

who

who contend earnestly for the Abolition or Annihilation. But yet upon the whole Matter, the Renovation or Restitution seems to me most probable, as being most consonant to *Scripture, Reason,* and *Antiquity.* The Scripture speaks of an ἀποκατάςασις, or Restitution, *Acts* iii. 21. *Whom the Heavens must contain until the Time of the Restitution of all Things;* speaking of our Saviour: and παλιγγενεσία, or Regeneration of the World, the very Word the *Stoicks* and *Pythagoreans* use in this Case, *Matt.* xix. 28, 29. *Verily, I say unto you, That ye which have followed me, in the Regeneration, when the Son of Man shall sit on the Throne of His Glory, ye also shall sit upon twelve Thrones,* &c. Psal. cii. 26. *As a Vesture shalt thou change them, and they shall be changed.* Which Words are again taken up and repeated, *Heb.* i. 12. Now it is one thing to be changed, another to be annihilated and destroyed. 1 *Cor.* vii. 31. παράγει τὸ σχῆμα τῦ κόσμυ τύτυ, *The Fashion of this World passeth away.* As if he had said, It shall be transfigured, or its outward Form changed, not its Matter or Substance destroyed. Isa. lxv. 17. *Behold I create new Heavens and a new Earth, and the former shall not be remembred, nor come into Mind.* Isa. lxvi. 22. *As the new Heavens and new Earth, which I shall make, shall remain before me.* To which Places the Apostle *Peter* seems to referr in those Words, 2. *Pet.* iii. 13.

*Nevertheless we, according to His Promise, look for new Heavens, and a new Earth, wherein dwelleth Righteousness.* This new Heaven and new Earth we have also mentioned, *Rev.* xii. 1. *And I saw a new Heaven and a new Earth; for the first Heaven and the first Earth were passed away, and there was no more Sea.* These Places, I confess, may admit of an Answer or Solution by those who are of a contrary Opinion, and are answered by Doctor *Hakewill:* yet all together, especially being back'd by ancient Tradition, amount to a high Degree of Probability. I omit that Place, *Rom.* viii. 21, 22. *The Creature itself also shall be delivered from the Bondage of Corruption, into the glorious Liberty of the Sons of* God: Tho' it be accounted the strongest Proof of our Opinion, because of the Obscurity and Ambiguity thereof.

2. For Antiquity, I have already given many Testimonies of the ancient Fathers and Doctors of the Church, and could, if Need were, produce many more, the whole Stream of them running this way. And tho' Dr. *Hakewill* saith, That if we look back to higher Times before S. *Hierom*, we shall not easily find any one who maintained the World's Renovation; yet he hath but two Testimonies to alledge for its Abolition; the one out of *Hilary* upon the Psalms, and the other out of *Clemens* his *Recognitions*. To this Restitution of the World, after the Conflagration,

flagration, many also of the Heathen Philosophers bear Witness, whose Testimonies Mr. *Burnet* hath exhibited in his *Theory of the Earth*, lib. 4. cap. 5. Of the Stoicks, *Chrysippus de Providentiâ*, speaking of the Renovation of the World, saith, Ἡμᾶς, μετὰ τὸ τελευτῆσαι, πάλιν περιόδων τινῶν εἰλημμένων χρόνου, εἰς ὃ νῦν ἐσμὲν ἀποκαταςήσεςθαι σχῆμα· *We, after Death, certain Periods of Time being come about, shall be restored to the Form we now have.* To *Chrysippus Stobæus* adds *Zeno* and *Cleanthes*, and comprehends together with Men all natural Things, Ζήνωνι, καὶ Κλεάνθει, καὶ Χρυσίππῳ ἀρέσκει τὴν ὐσίαν μεταβάλλειν, οἷον εἰς σπέρμα, τὸ πῦρ καὶ πάλιν ἐκ τέτε τοιαύτην ἀποτελεῖσθαι τὴν διακόσμησιν οἵα πρότερον ἦν. *Zeno, and* Cleanthes, *and* Chrysippus, *were of Opinion, That the Nature or Substance of Things changes into Fire, as it were into a Seed; and out of this again, such a World or Frame of Things is effected as was before.* This Revolution of Nature, *Antoninus*, in his Meditations, often calls τὴν περιοδικὴν παλιγγεννεσίαν τῶν ὅλων, *The Periodical Regeneration of all Things.* And * *Origen*, against *Celsus*, saith of the *Stoicks* in general, Φασὶ ᾖ οἱ ἀπὸ τῆς Στοᾶς κατὰ περίοδον ἐκπύρωσιν τῷ παντὸς γίνεσθαι, καὶ ἑξῆς αὐτῇ διακόσμησιν πάντ᾽ ἀπαράλλακτα ἔχεσαν ὡς πρὸς τὴν ἑτέραν διακόσμησιν. *The* Stoicks *say, That at certain Periods of Time there is a Conflagration of the Universe; and after that a Restitution thereof*

*Apud Lactant. l.7. c.23.*

* *Lib.* 5.

having

having exactly the same Disposition and Furniture the former World had. More to the like Purpose concerning the *Stoicks*, we have in * *Eusebius* out of *Numenius*. *Nature*, saith he, *returns* εἰς τὴν ἀνάςασιν ἐκείνην τὴν ποιῦσαν ἐνιαυτὸν τὸν μέγιςον, καθ' ὃν ἀπ' αὐτῆς μόνης εἰς αὐτὴν πάλιν γίνεται ἡ ἀποκατάςασις· ἐπανελθῦσα δ κατὰ τάξιν ἀφ' οἴας διακοσμεῖν ὡσαύτως ἤρξατο, κατὰ λόγον πάλιν τὴν αὐτὴν διεξαγωγὴν ποιεῖται, τῶν τοιῦτων περιόδων ἐξ ἀιδίυ γενομένων ἀκαταπαύςως, *to the Resurrection which makes the great Year, wherein there is again a Restitution made from itself alone to itself. For returning according to the Order wherein it began first to frame and dispose Things, (as Reason would) it again observes the same OEconomy or Administration; the like Periods returning eternally without ceasing.* He that desires more Authorities of the Heathen Philosophers and Poets, in Confirmation of the World's Restitution after the Conflagration, may consult the same Mr. *Burnet* in the Place forequoted; where he also shews, that this Doctrine of the Mundane Periods was received by the *Grecians* from the Nations they call Barbarous. *Pythagoras*, saith *Porphyry*, brought it first into *Greece*: And *Origen* witnesseth of the *Egyptian* Wise Men, that it was delivered by them. *Laertius* out of *Theopompus* relates, That the *Persian Magi* had the same Tradition; and *Berosus* saith, that the *Chaldeans* also. In fine, among all the barbarous

* *Præp. Evang. l. 15.*

Nations, who had among them any Person or Sect, and Order of Men, noted for Wisdom or Philosophy, this Tradition was current. The Reader may consult the Book we referr to, where is a notable Passage taken out of *Plutarch*'s Tractate, *De Iside & Osiride*, concerning a War between *Oromazes* and *Arimanius*, somewhat parallel to that mentioned in the Revelation between *Michael* and the *Dragon*.

3. THE Restitution of the World seems more consonant to Reason than its Abolition. For if the World were to be annihilated, what needed a Conflagration? Fire doth not destroy or bring things to nothing, but only separate their Parts. The World cannot be abolished by it, and therefore had better been annihilated without it. Wherefore the Scripture mentioning no other Dissolution than is to be effected by the Instrumentality of Fire, it's clear, we are not to understand any utter Abolition or Annihilation of the World, but only a Mutation and Renovation, by those Phrases of *perishing, passing away, dissolving, being no more*, &c. They are to be no more in that State and Condition they are now in.

2. THERE must be a material Heaven, and a material Hell left. A Place for the glorified Bodies of the Blessed to inhabit and converse in; and a Place for the Bodies of the Damned, a Κολαςήριον, or Prison for them to be shut up in. Now, if the Place of the Blessed

Blessed be an Empyreal Heaven far above these visible Heavens, as Divines generally hold; and the Place of the Damned be beneath, about the Middle of the Earth; as is the Opinion of the School-Men, and the Church of *Rome*, and as the Name *Inferi* imports, and as the ancient Heathen described their *Tartarus*,

Hom. II.
———— εἰς τάρταρον ἠερόεντα
Τῆλε μάλ᾽ ἧχι βάθιςον ὑπὸ χθονός ἐςι βέρεθρον,
Τόσσον ἔνερθ᾽ Ἀΐδεω ὅσον οὐρανός ἐς᾽ ἀπὸ γαίης.

Then when all the intermediate Bodies shall be annihilated, what a strange Universe shall we have? consisting of an immense Ring of Matter, having in the Middle a vast Vacuity, or Space void of all Body, save only one small Point for an infernal Dungeon. Those that are of this Opinion have too narrow and mean Thoughts of the Greatness, I had almost said Immensity of the Universe, the glorious and magnifick Products of the Creator's Almighty Power; and are too partial to themselves, to think the whole World was created for no other End but to be serviceable to Mankind: But of this I have said somewhat in a former Discourse, and therefore shall not at present enlarge upon it.

But let us hear what they have to say for the *Abolition*.

*Hakewill's Apol. l. 4. c. 13. f. 5.* Their first and most weighty Argument is taken from the *End of the World's Creation*, which

which was partly and chiefly the Glory of the *Creator*, and partly the Use of Man, the Lord Deputy, as it were, or *Viceroy* thereof. Now for the *Glory* of the *Creator*, it being by the admirable Frame of the World manifested unto Man, Man being removed out of the World, and no Creature being capable of such a Manifestation besides him, we cannot imagine to what Purpose the Frame itself should be left, and restored to a more perfect Estate. The other *End*, being for *Man's Use*, either to supply his Necessity in Matter of Diet, of Physick, of Building, of Apparel; or for his Instruction, Direction, Recreation, Comfort and Delight; or lastly, that therein, as in a Looking-glass, he might contemplate the Wisdom, the Goodness and Power of GOD; when he shall attain that blessed Estate, as he shall have no farther Use of any of these, enjoying perfect Happiness, and seeing GOD as He is, Face to Face, the second or subordinate End of the World's Being must needs be likewise frustrate. And what other End can be given or conceived for the remaining or restoring thereof? *&c.*

To this I answer, there may be an End of the restoring of the World, tho' we are not able to find out or determine what. We are too short-sighted to penetrate the Ends of GOD. There may be a new Race of rational Animals brought forth to act their Parts upon this Stage, which may give the Creator

tor as much Glory as Man ever did or could. And yet if there should be no material and visible rational Creature made to inhabit the Earth, there are spiritual and intellectual Beings, which may be as busy, and as much delighted in searching out, and contemplating the Works of God in this new Earth, and rendring Him the Praise of His Wisdom and Power as Man could be. These Things we may conjecture; but we must leave it to the only wise God to determine what Use shall be made of it. It seems to me to be too great Presumption, and over-valuing ourselves, to think that all this World was so made for us, as to have no other End of its Creation, or that God could not be glorified but by us.

This first and principal Argument being answered, the second admits of an easy Solution. They enquire whether the Vegetables, and Creatures endued with Sense, shall all be restored, or some only? namely such as shall be found in Being at the Day of Judgment. If all, where shall we find Stowage for them? Surely we may in this case properly apply that which the Evangelist in another useth figuratively, if they should all be restored, even the World itself could not contain the Things which should be restored. If some only, then would I gladly know, why those some should be vouchsafed this great Honour, and not all; or how those

Creatures

Creatures without a Miracle shall be restrain'd from propagating and multiplying, and that infinitely in their Kinds by a perpetual Generation. Or lastly, How the several Individuals of these Kinds, shall, contrary to their Primitive Natures, live and dure immortally?

To all this I answer, That not only all Animals, but all Vegetables too, yea, and their Seeds also, will doubtless be mortified and destroyed by the Violence of the Conflagration; but that the same should be restored, and endued with eternal Life, I know no Reason we have to believe; but rather that there should be new ones produced, either of the same with the former, or of different Kinds, at the Will, and by the Power of the Almighty Creator, and for those Ends and Uses for which He shall design them. This Question being answered in this Manner, all that follows concerning the Earth remaining without any Furniture or Inhabitants, &c. falls to the Ground. So I have dispatch'd these Seven Questions concerning the Dissolution of the World, there remains now only the Inference or Use of the precedent Doctrine.

## Chap. XII.

*The Apostle's Inference from the precedent Doctrine.*

I COME now to the *Inference* the Apostle makes from the precedent Doctrine, *What manner of Persons ought we to be in all holy Conversation and Godliness?* One Word here needs a little Explication, and that is *Holy*. What is meant by a *holy* Conversation?

HOLINESS is an Equivocal Term. It is attributed either to GOD, or to the Creature. When it is attributed to GOD, it signifies either,

1. THE unspotted Purity of His Nature, and the constant and immutable Rectitude of His Will. So it is taken, 1 *John* iii. 3. *And every Man that hath this Hope in him, purifieth himself as He is pure:* And, 1 *Pet.* i. 15. *As He, which called you, is Holy, so be ye Holy in all manner of Conversation; because it is written, Be ye Holy, for I am Holy.* Psal. cxlv. 17. *The* LORD *is Righteous in all His Ways, and Holy in all His Works.*

2. HIS Sovereign Majesty and Greatness appearing in His transcendent Wisdom and Power, in His Supreme and Absolute Dominion

nion over all things: In respect whereof, He is called the *Holy One of Israel*, and His *Name* is said to be *Holy*: That is, to be invoked with the greatest Reverence. *Holy and Reverend is His Name*. Because of this His Greatness and Excellency, He is to be worshipped, and adored with the most submissive Humility and Veneration, with a transcendent and incommunicable Worship and Devotion.

When Holiness is attributed to Creatures, it signifies either an Inherent and Inward, or a Relative or Outward, Holiness.

1. Inherent or Inward Holiness is a Conformity of Heart and Life to the Will of God: Or, as * others define it, An habitual Frame of Mind: Whereby we are fitted for Vertuous Actions, but more especially for the Duties of Religion. Indeed, Holiness doth always include a Reference to God.

\* *Bishop Wilkins's Univers. Charact.*

2. Relative or Outward Holiness results from a Separation and Setting apart any thing from a prophane and common, and applying it to a sacred or religious Use. For, the Majesty of God, who at first created, and continually sustains and governs all things, being so great and inviolable, all Persons, Things, and Times, and Places, and Ceremonies, separated and appropriated to His Service and Worship, are by all Nations esteemed Sacred, and to have a Character of Holiness imprinted on them.

By Holiness, in this Place, is to be understood an *inherent* Holiness, which is well defined by Dr. Outram, *A Conformity of Heart, and Life to the Will of* God. I shall not discourse at large concerning a holy Conversation, nor instance Particulars wherein it consists. That would be to write a Body of Practical Divinity. I shall, therefore, at present, suppose the Reader sufficiently instructed in that. My Business shall be to shew, the Strength of the Apostle's Inference.

*De Sacrif.* l. 1. c. 1.

It may be said, How doth this Dissolution concern us, who may, perchance, be dead and rotten a Thousand Years before it comes? What have we to do with it?

I answer, It concerns us, 1. Because, it's possible, it may happen in our Times; it may surprize us before we are aware. The precise Time thereof is uncertain. And it shall be sudden and unexpected, *coming as a Thief in the Night,* as we have before shewn: Therefore, we ought always to be upon our Guard, *to have our Loins girt about, and our Lights burning.* This Use the Scripture, in many Places, makes of the Uncertainty of the Time of Christ's Coming, *Luke* xii. 40. *Be ye therefore ready: For the Son of Man cometh at an Hour when ye think not.* Luke xxi. 34, 35. *And take heed to yourselves, lest at any time your Hearts be overcharged with Surfeiting and Drunkenness, and Cares of this Life, and so that Day come upon you*

*you unawares. For as a Snare shall it come on all them that dwell on the whole Earth.* Parallel whereto are *Matth.* xxiv. 42. and *Mark* xiii. 33, 35. That it shall come is certain, when it shall come is uncertain, and it every day draws nearer and nearer; therefore, it is not Wisdom to remove the *Evil Day* far from us: And as in reference to the Day of Death, it is an usual and prudent Advice, so to live every Day, as if it were our last Day; or at least, as we would not be afraid to do should it be so: Because, we are sure, that one Day will be our last, and, for ought we know, the present may be it. So, likewise, it is rational Counsel, in respect of the End of the World, so to prepare ourselves for it by a holy Conversation, that we may get above the Terror and Dread, which will otherwise attend the Apprehension of the Approach of it; and that we may be provided against the worst that may follow, and be secure come what can come.

Secondly, It concerns us, should it be a Thousand Years to come. Because then is the general Resurrection both of the Just and Unjust, *Acts* xxiv. 15. and the general Judgment, *When we must all appear before the dreadful Tribunal of* CHRIST, *that every one may receive the Things done in his Body, according to that he hath done, whether it be good or bad,* 2 Cor. v. 10. which, *Rom.* ii. 5. is called *the Revelation of the righteous Judg-*

ment of GOD. *Who will render to every Man according to his Deeds*, &c. Upon this Account, I say, it concerns us much how we have our Conversation here.

I. *First.* As we hope to be acquitted at that Day, and to enter into those new Heavens, in which dwells Righteousness. Holiness is a necessary Condition, and antecedent to Happiness. Necessary, I say,

1. By GOD's Appointment, *Heb.* xii. 14. *Follow Peace with all Men, and Holiness, without which no Man shall see the* LORD. *Rom.* vi. 22. *Have your Fruit unto Holiness, and the End Eternal Life.* Psal. 50. ult. *To him, that ordereth his Conversation aright, will I shew the Salvation of* GOD. Eternal Life is the Gift of GOD. He is not obliged to bestow it upon any Man. He may make what Condition he pleases for the obtaining of it. No Man hath any Right to it: No Man can lay any Claim to it, but from this Donation, and from the Performance of these Conditions. *Rev.* xxii. 14. *Blessed are they that do His Commandments, that they may have Right to the Tree of Life, and may enter in through the Gates into the City. For without are Dogs, and Whoremongers, and Sorcerers,* &c. All the Right they have depends upon GOD's Promise, which is Conditionate, and accrues to them by the Performance of

the

the Condition, which is the Doing of His Commandments.

2. NECESSARY, not only by GOD's Appointment, but in the very Nature of the Thing. Holiness is the very Quality and Complexion of Heaven. No Man without it is qualified to be a Subject of that Kingdom: For, thereinto nothing that is impure or unclean can enter. Rev. xxi. 27. *And there shall in no wise enter into it* [the New *Jerusalem*] *any thing that defileth, neither whatsoever worketh Abomination.* In this *new Heaven dwelleth Righteousness,* 2 Pet. iii. 15. Therefore, 1 *John* iii. 3. *Every Man that hath this Hope in Him, purifieth himself as He is pure.* Heaven would naturally spue out and eject a wicked Person, as one heterogeneous to it. Heaven and Hell are not more distant in Place, than they are in Nature. There is not more Antipathy between Fire and Water, between Light and Darkness, between Streight and Crooked, neither are they more incompatible, or do more naturally resist and expell one another, than Holiness, which is the Quality of Heaven, or Wickedness, which is the Disposition and Temper of Hell. Some do think Heaven to be rather a State than a Place; and that he that is Partaker of the Divine Nature hath Heaven within him. This is true, but this is not all. The whole Notion of Heaven comprehends both a State and a Place.

Place. A Man must be in a heavenly State, before the local Heaven can receive him, or he brook it. Heaven without him would be no Heaven, to the Man who hath not Heaven within him. A wicked Person could find no Business or Employment in Heaven; nothing to satisfy his corrupt and depraved Affections, Inclinations, and Appetites. He would there meet with no suitable Company; no Persons, whose Conversation he could take any Delight and Complacency in, but rather hate and abhor. *For, what Fellowship hath Righteousness with Unrighteousness? Or, what Communion hath Light with Darkness?* 2 Cor. vi. 14. Like naturally loves Like, and unites with it, and doth refuse, resist, and hate that which is Unlike it. For every thing is made to love itself, and, consequently, whatsoever resembles and comes near it, and is as it were a Replication of it; and to hate the contrary. As, therefore, we would be glad to be Partakers of the Blessedness of the local Heaven, so let us endeavour to get into our Minds and Spirits the Qualities and Conditions of Heaven; that so we may be fit Subjects for that Kingdom, fit Companions for that Society. *This is the Time allotted us to purify ourselves from all Filthiness both of Flesh and Spirit, and to perfect Holiness in the Fear of* GOD. There is no Invention in the Grave, whither we are going, Eccl. ix. 10. Upon this Moment depends Eternity. As the

Tree falls, so it lies, Eccles. And as Death leaves, so will Judgment find us. *Quando isthinc excessum fuerit, nullus jam locus pœnitentiæ est. Hic vita aut amittitur, aut tenetur: Hic saluti æternæ cultu Dei, & fructu fidei providetur.* Cyprian. Serm. de Immortal. After we shall depart hence, there remains no more Place for Repentance. Eternal Life is here either lost or won. Here Provision is made for everlasting Salvation, by the Worship of GOD, and Fruit of Faith. We must work while it is Day, the Night [of Death] cometh wherein no Man can work, John. ix. 4. And, therefore, the Time our Bodies shall rest in the Grave, should it be a Thousand Years, will little avail us: For, if the Soul be mean while awake, the certain and dreadful Expectation of the Sentence of Condemnation to an eternal Hell at the Day of Judgment, will be little less afflictive than the Torments thereof themselves. I might add, by way of Digression, that Sin and Wickedness is naturally productive of Hell in the Soul. A wicked Man carries Hell in his Breast. Sin necessarily inferrs Misery; It is contrary to the Nature of the Soul; and whatsoever is so, must needs be grievous. Diversion and Non-Attention to his Condition, is the wicked Man's only Security: I have heard it often from a * great Divine in his Sermons, *That there is but a Thought's Distance between a wicked Man and Hell.* For, do but fix and

* Doctor Whichcot.

bind

bind his Thoughts to the Confideration of his Life and Actions, and he will anticipate Hell himfelf, he fhall need no infernal Furies to lafh him, he will be his own Tormentor: Such a Man's Preffures will be heavy enough, fhould the Divine *Nemefis* fuperadd no more. The Reafon of this I have given in a former Difcourfe, and therefore fhall now omit what elfe might have been added on this Particular.

II. *Secondly*, It much concerns us, upon account of the future Judgment which fhall be at the Diffolution of the World, to have our Converfation in all Holinefs, as we defire to avoid that Shame and Mifery which will then otherwife certainly befall us.

1. As we defire to avoid that Shame which will cover our Faces at that Day. If here Shame and Difgrace be more grievous and infupportable than Death itfelf, what will it be then, when the Soul fhall be rendred more quick, and apprehenfive, and fenfible of fuch Impreffions? There is nothing fhameful but Sin, nothing elfe hath any natural Turpitude in it. Shame follows Sin as the Shadow doth the Body. He that will commit the one, cannot avoid the other. Therefore, fuch wicked Perfons as have not quite renounced Modefty, and loft all Senfe of Shame, efpecially, if guilty of fecret Crimes, the Confideration of a future Judgment would be a powerful Curb to reftrain them

them from Sin for the future: Because then GOD *will* produce and *bring to light the hidden Things of Darkness, and disclose and make manifest the Counsels of all Hearts*, 1 Cor. iv. 5. Then *He will judge the Secrets of Men by* JESUS CHRIST, Rom. ii. 16. *Then will He bring every Work into Judgment, with every secret thing*, Ecclef. xii. 14. For, would they but consider and ponder, what Confusion will overwhelm them when this shall be done in the Face of the whole World, and before all that knew them, and they not able to make any Denial, or Excuse: This, I say, if any thing, would be a powerful Curb to withhold them from those Enormities to which this Shame is appendent. It may be thou madest a great Figure in the World for Piety and Religion, wouldst seem to be Some-body in the Eyes of Men, when thou wert false and unsound, didst harbour and nourish some Viper in thy Bosom;

*Introrsum turpis, speciosâ pelle decorus:*

When thy secret Faults shall be exposed before thy Neighbours, and Friends, and Children; *And the Shame of thy Nakedness shall be made appear*, Rev. iii. 18. How wilt thou then be confounded and astonished, and unable to lift up thy Head? What Horror will then seize thee, *when thy Confusion shall be continually before thee, and the Shame of thy Face shall cover thee?* Psal. xliv. 15. It concerns

cerns thee, therefore, to look about thee in time, and search thy Conscience to the Bottom, to remove whatever grates, to cast out whatever offends, though never so customary, never so pleasing to Flesh and Blood: To apply thyself to the Merits and Satisfaction of CHRIST JESU'S, for the Expiation of what is past; and, for the future, to resolve and endeavour the Amendment of whatsoever hath heretofore been amiss in thee; and to beg the Assistance of the Divine Grace to strengthen in thee every good Purpose and Resolution of Heart, and to enable thee to bring it to Issue and Effect. And for thy Security, I think it good Advice, to resolve so to behave thyself in thy Retirements, so to live in the Secret of thy Chamber and Closet, as though the Doors were thrown open upon thee, and all the Eyes of the World beheld thee; as though thou were't in the *Arena* of a Publick Theatre, exposed to the View of Men and Angels. I remember the ingenious Writer of Politick Discourses, *Boccalini*, doth often divert himself and his Reader, with facetious Reflections upon the Contrivance of a Window into the Breast; which, if I mistake not, he fathers upon *Lipsius*. However he may deride it, I think it would be prudent Counsel to give and take, for every Christian, so to live and carry it in the Secret of his Heart, as if there were a Window into his Breast, that

every

every one that paffed by, might look in thereat, and fee all the Thoughts and Imaginations that paffed there, that found any Entertainment or Acceptance with him. For though, indeed, G o d *fearches the Hearts, and Reins, and underftandeth our Thoughts afar off*, Pfal. cxxxix. 2. Yet fuch is the Hypocrify of Mankind, that they do, for the moft part, more reverence the Eyes of Men than of God; and will venture to do that in His Prefence, which they would be afhamed the Eyes of Man fhould fee them doing. You will fay, Is it not better to be modeft, than to be impudent? Is it not better to conceal, than to publifh one's Shame? Is it not better to reverence Man, than neither God nor Man? Doth not the Scripture condemn a Whore's Fore-head? Is it not a true Proverb, *Paft Shame, paft Grace*? Was it not good Advice of a Cardinal (as I remember) *Si non caftè, tamen cautè?* He that hath devoured Shame, what Bridle is there left to reftrain him from the worft of Evils? I anfwer, That it feems indeed to me, that publick Sins of the fame Nature, are more heinous than fecret; and that Impudence in finning, is an Aggravation of Sin. For open Sins dare God, and bid Defiance to Heaven, and leave the Sinner unreclaimable; and are of more pernicious Influence. I do not now fpeak of the Hypocrify of feigning Holinefs to ferve our own Ends, which is rightly efteemed *duplex iniquitas*;

but

but that of concealing and hiding vicious Actions, to avoid the Shame of Men. And yet, there is a great Obliquity in this too. Because, even this is a slighting and undervaluing of God, a preferring of Man before Him, setting a greater Price and Esteem upon the Praise and Commendation of Men, than the Praise and Approbation of God, *John* xii. 43. God sees the secretest Actions, yea, the most retired Thoughts. They that believe this, and yet make bold to do in His Presence, what the Fear of Man's Eye would restrain them from, it is clear that they reverence Man more than God; a poor, frail, impotent Creature like themselves, more than the most Pure and ever Blessed Creator. Nay, let the Temptation to any Sin be never so strong, and the natural Inclination never so vehement, if the Knowledge and Conscience of Men be a Motive and Consideration powerful enough to enable us to resist and repell them, had we but as firm a Belief of the Presence and Inspection of God, and as great a Reverence and Dread of Him, why should not these have the same Influence and Effect upon us? Let us then avoid the Hypocrisy of desiring to be thought better than we are, by endeavouring, to our utmost, to be as good as we would be thought to be, and, if possible, better. So shall we satisfy ourselves that we seek the Praise of GOD, more than the Praise of Men.

HERE,

HERE, before I proceed, I cannot but admire the Wisdom and Goodness of Almighty GOD, in implanting such a Passion in the Nature of Man, as Shame, to no other Use or Purpose, that I can imagine, than to restrain him from vicious and shameful Actions. A Passion I call it, because the Body, as in other Passions, suffers from it, and that in a peculiar manner; it causing a sudden Motion of the Blood to the outward Parts, especially to the Face, which is called Blushing, and a Dejection of the Eyes. If you ask me what Shame is, I answer, It is an ungrateful and afflictive Sense of Soul, proceeding from Dishonour. Now Dishonour is nothing else but Mens ill Opinion of me, or Dislike and Condemnation of my Actions, some way declared and manifested to me; which, why I should have such an Abhorrence of, and why it should be so grievous and tormenting to me, there seems not to be a sufficient Ground and Foundation in the Nature of the Thing, supposing such as have this Opinion have neither Power nor Will to hurt my Body, but only in the Ordination of GOD, who hath so made our Natures, to secure our Innocency, and withhold us from the Commission of what is disgraceful and ignominious, as all sinful Actions, and none else, are.

AND as for secret Sins, I think Shame may take Place there too. It was a Precept of the *Pythagoreans*, Πάντων ᾖ μάλις᾽ αἰσχύνεο σαυτόν·

Of all Men reverence yourself most: Be ashamed to do that before yourself, which before others you would abhorr or blush to do; otherwise you must suffer Dishonour from yourself, and condemn your own Actions, which will, in all reason, be more grievous and afflictive than the ill Opinion and Word of other Men. Hence, Conscience of Sin is esteemed a most painful and tormenting thing, by the generality of all Mankind, tho' no other Man be privy to it.

But to return from whence we digressed, though * *Shame and everlasting Contempt* shall, at the general Resurrection, be the Portion of them who persist and die in their Sins; yet a serious and unfeigned Repentance, attested by a holy Conversation for the future, is an effectual Means to deliver us from this Shame, whatever our forepast Sins have been. For, they shall not be produced against us, they shall not be objected to us at that Day; they shall be buried in eternal Silence and Oblivion; and be as tho' they had not been. And this Opinion I hold, 1. More agreeable to the Scripture, which in this Matter makes use of the Terms of hiding, and covering, and blotting out, and forgetting. *Psal.* xxxii. 1. *Blessed is the Man whose Transgression is forgiven, and whose Sin is covered.* Isa. xliii. 25. *I, even I am He, that blotteth out thy Transgressions, and will not remember thy Sins.* So *Psal.* li. 9. *Hide Thy Face from my Sins, and*

* Daniel xii. 2.

*blot*

*blot out all mine Iniquities.* Jerem. xlviii. 34. *I will forgive their Iniquity, and remember their Sin no more.* Ezek. xxviii. 22. *All his Transgressions that he hath committed, they shall not be mentioned unto him.* Mic. vii. 19. *Thou wilt cast all their Sins into the Depths of the Sea.* And as it is more consonant to the Scripture, so is it, 2. More grateful and consolatory to the Penitents. For, the meer Mentioning and Reciting of their Sins before such an Assembly, must needs refresh their Shame and Sorrow, and so diminish their Happiness and Joy. To which I might add, that it is written, our Saviour at the last Judgment, in pronouncing the Sentence, shall enumerate the Good Works of the Godly to their Praise; but not a Word said of producing their Sins. I say, I hold this Opinion more probable upon these Accounts, than theirs, who affirm they shall then be published; for the magnifying and and advancing, the declaring and illustrating the Mercy and Grace of GOD, in pardoning so great and heinous Offences.

AND truly, I do not know, but that the Sins of the Blessed may be blotted out, even of their own Memories. Some Philosophers, who were of Opinion, that Souls præ-exist before their Bodies, thought they were dipt in *Lethe,* which is a Fountain causing Oblivion, by means whereof they forgot whatever they had done before. This I look upon as a Dream, or Fancy: But, truly, I am inclinable sometimes to imagine, that the Soul of Man can hardly be entirely happy, unless it be as it were thus dipt in *Lethe*: For every sinful Action having a natural Turpitude in it, and being dishonourable, how can the Memory and Thought of it but beget such an ungrateful Passion as Shame, even to Eternity? And, what do Divines mean by saying, That the Action [of sinning] suddenly passes away, but the Stain and Blot of it remains; but that a vicious Action, even by them to whom it is pardoned, can never be thought of without Grief and Disturbance; it leaves an indelible Scar in the Soul, which can never be perfectly healed, and obliterated.

2. It concerns us much to live in all holy Conversation in this World, as we desire to avoid that Pain and Misery, which we shall otherwise most certainly be adjudged to at that Day: That *Indignation and Wrath, Tribulation and Anguish*, which God shall render to them *that do not obey the Truth, but obey Unrighteousness*, Rom. ii. 8. That *Worm that dieth not*, and that *Fire that is not quenched*, Mark ix. 44. and 46, and 48. That *outer Darkness, where is Weeping and Wailing, and Gnashing of Teeth*, Matt. viii. 12. and xxii. 13. and xxv. 30. That *Furnace of Fire*, Matt. xiii. 42, 50. That *Lake of Fire and Brimstone*, Rev. xx. 10. or of *Fire burning with Brimstone*, Rev. xix. 20. Which Places, tho' they be

not

not literally to be expounded, yet do they import at least a very sad and deplorable Estate, a high Degree of Torment and Anguish: And all this Eternal, and without Intermission, Night and Day. *These shall go into everlasting Punishment*, Matth. xxv. 46. The State of the Damned is supposed to be a State of absolute and complete Misery, made up of the Loss of the greatest Good, and a constant, fresh, and lively Apprehension of it, which Divines call *Pæna Damni*. And, 2. Excess of bodily Pain and Sufferings, and sad Distress and Trouble of Mind, occasioned by all manner of frightful Apprehensions, and vexatious Perturbations and Reflections, which they call *Pæna Sensûs*; and this without any Intermission or Hope of Deliverance eternally. *Jude* vii. it is called the *Vengeance of eternal Fire*. Rev. xiv. 11. *The Smoke of their Torment* is said *to ascend up for ever and ever.* And *Rev.* xx. 10. it is said of the Beast and false Prophet, that *they shall be tormented Night and Day for ever and ever.* If this be so, is it not our greatest Wisdom to use our utmost Diligence and Endeavour to avoid so deplorable a Condition, and to secure to ourselves an Interest in a future Estate of everlasting Bliss and Happiness, when this Life shall be ended?

But here the *Epicureans* and sensual Persons will be ready to object and argue, Here are Pleasures and Delights in this World, which

which are very inviting and taking, and do highly gratify my Senses and Appetites. I hear likewise of future Rewards and Punishments for those that deny or fulfill their Carnal Lusts and Desires. These sensual Pleasures I see and taste, and feel, and am sure of, the other I do but only hear of, and therefore they do not, they cannot so strongly affect me: Were Heaven, and the Happiness thereof, set before my Eyes, and did I see it as plainly and clearly as I do these Things below, then indeed I should not need many Motives to provoke me to endeavour the Obtaining of it. But, alas! that is far above out of our Sight, the Joys of Heaven are by the Apostle termed Things not seen. Again, these outward and temporal Enjoyments are present and easily obtainable; the other at a great Distance, future, and besides, very hard to come by; and I love my Ease, *Ut est ingenium hominum à labore proclive ad libidinem.* Should I deny myself Good in this Life, and then perchance cease to be, and so have no Reward for my Pains; nay, on the contrary, expose myself to the Hazard of many Afflictions and Sufferings, which are the Portion of the Godly in this Life, how unnecessarily shall I make myself miserable? Miserable I say, because by the Apostle's own Confession, Christians, *if in this Life only they had Hope, would be of all Men the most miserable,* 1 Cor. xv. 19. Had I not

not better make sure of what is before me? Why have I these Appetites within me, and such Objects about me, the one being so suitable to the other, is it not more natural and reasonable to fulfill, than deny them? Surely it cannot be Wisdom to lose a certain Good, for an uncertain Hope; and for an ungrounded Fear of Hell hereafter, to undergo a Purgatory here.

To this Argumentation upon the false Foundation of the Uncertainty of a future Estate of endless Happiness or Misery, accordingly as we have behaved ourselves in this Life, I answer,

That for the Futurity of such an Estate, we have the best Authority in the World, to wit, the Holy Scriptures, and universal Tradition.

1. The Holy Scriptures, whose Authority to be more than humane, hath been by many so clearly and convincingly demonstrated, that I shall take it for granted, and not waste Time to prove it. The Testimonies herein contained, concerning eternal Happiness and Misery, are so clear and full, that it seems to me impossible, without manifest Distortion, to elude or evade the Force of them. Some we have already recited, and might produce many more, Isa. xxxiii. 14. *Who among us shall dwell with the devouring Fire? Who among us shall dwell with everlasting Burnings?* Dan. xii. 2. *And many of them that sleep in*

the *Duſt of the Earth ſhall awake, ſome to everlaſting Life, and ſome to Shame and everlaſting Contempt.* 2 Theſſ. i. 9. *Who ſhall be puniſhed with everlaſting Deſtruction from the Preſence of the* Lord, *&c.* ſpeaking of them who know not God, and obey not the Goſpel of our Lord Jesus Christ. Iſai. lxvi. 24. *For their Worm ſhall not die, neither ſhall their Fire be quenched.*

The *Origeniſts*, and others, that cannot be reconciled to the Catholick Doctrine of the Eternity of the Puniſhments of the Damned, make the Word αἰὼν, from which the *Latin ævum* is derived, to ſignify ſometimes a determinate Time, as might (ſay they) eaſily be proved by many Examples, and ſo εἰς αἰῶνα, or αἰῶνας, which we tranſlate *for ever*, ſignifies, when applied to this Matter, a long indeed, but yet a finite Time; and εἰς τὰς αἰῶνας τῶν αἰώνων, which we render *for ever and ever*, may likewiſe ſignify not an eternal Duration, but a Time to which ſome Term may be ſet by God, though to us unknown. In the ſame Senſe they accept the Adjective αἰώνιος for a long, but finite Time. But I am of S. *Auguſtin*'s Opinion, that αἰώνιος doth in the New Teſtament ſignify the ſame with *æternus* in *Latin*, and is appropriated to Things that have no End; and that εἰς τὰς αἰῶνας τῶν αἰώνων, *for ever and ever*, doth in like manner always denote eternal or endleſs Duration. That the Word αἰώνιος,
when

when applied to the State of the Damned, doth signify *eternal*, S. *Augustin* well demonstrates from the *Antithesis* in that Place of *Matth.* xxv. 46. *And these shall go away into everlasting Punishment, but the Righteous into Life eternal.* Where it is in the same Sense attributed to that Life which is the Reward of the Righteous, and that Fire which is the Punishment of the Damned; there being no Reason to believe that the same Word in the same Verse, when applied to Opposites, should be taken in a different Sense. But by the Consent of all Christians it is granted, that the Life of the Blessed shall be eternal, therefore so must the Punishment of the Damned be too.

This Acception of the Word αἰώνιος for *eternal* or *endless*, when it refers to the State of those miserable Persons, receives a farther and strong Confirmation from the

Second Particular we proposed, that is, *Universal Tradition:* It being a received Opinion among the Heathen, which must needs descend down to them by Tradition from the Ancients, that Eternal Punishments awaited the Wicked after Death.

What more common Notion among the *Grecians* and *Romans*, than of an *Elysium*, and *Tartarus*? the former to reward good Men, the latter to punish wicked. And those too esteemed to be Eternal States. Of this the *Epicurean* Poet *Lucretius* is a sufficient and unexceptionable Witness: For he makes the Fear of these Punishments to be the Cause of all the Miseries of Humane Life, and the Foundation of all Religion.

*Æternas quoniam pœnas in morte timendum.*

Now, that he could derive this from no other Source but Tradition, is clear; because he lived a good while before our Saviour's Time, and the Divulgation of the Scripture among the Heathen. And because it may be objected, that *Æternas* may signify only of long Continuance, to put the Matter out of all Doubt, in another Place he saith,

*———— Nam si nullum finem esse putarent Ærumnarum homines, nulla ratione valerent Relligionibus atque minis obsistere vatum.*

And that this Opinion and Belief generally prevailed among the People before *Epicurus* his Time, the same *Lucretius* testifies in the Beginning of his first Book,

*Humana ante oculos fœdè cum vita jaceret  
In terris oppressa gravi sub Relligione,* &c.  
*Primùm Graius homo,* &c.

Long time Men lay oppress'd with slavish Fear,  
Religion's Tyranny did domineer,  
Which being plac'd in Heav'n, look'd proudly down,  
And frighted abject Spirits at her Frown.

*At laſt a mighty One of Greece began
T'aſſert the Natural Liberty of Man,
By ſenſleſs Terrors, and vain Fancy led
To Slavery; ſtreight the conquer'd Fantoms fled:*

for he makes (as we ſaw before) the Fear of eternal Pain and Miſery, to be the Foundation of all Religion.

1. Now, becauſe theſe Objectors do repreſent Religion to themſelves and others as a melancholick and diſconſolate Thing; and think and ſay, that thoſe that enter into this State, muſt bid adieu to all the Pleaſures of Senſe, and taſte no Sweetneſs in any worldly Object; I ſhall endeavour to remove this Prejudice. I ſay therefore, That our gracious GOD doth not envy us any real Good that the Creatures can afford us, and therefore hath not denied us a moderate Uſe and Fruition of any of them. And ſeeing He hath annexed Pleaſure to thoſe Actions that are neceſſary for the Support of Life, and Continuation of Kind, as a Bait to invite us to the Performance of them, it ſeems to me highly abſurd and contradictious to affirm, that He hath forbidden us to partake or taſte thoſe Enjoyments which Himſelf has appointed as effectual Means for the Security of thoſe great Ends; and which are ſo neceſſary Conſequents of thoſe Actions, that we cannot but partake them. Where the Appetite is eager, GOD hath indulged, I might ſay, commanded

a moa moderate and regular Satisfaction. And we know, nay, the Blindness of Atheism cannot deny, that the greatest Pleasure results from a moderate and well circumstantiated Use of Pleasures. *Voluptates commendat rarior usus.* Now a religious Man enjoys all the Pleasures of these worldly and sensible Goods, without any of the Pain which is annexed to the excessive and irregular Use, or indeed Abuse of them: And besides, his Pleasure is enhanced, in that he beholds and receives them as Blessings of GOD, and Tokens of His Favour and Affection, and is without all Fear of a future sad Reckoning for his Participation of them. Howbeit a Denial of ourselves for GOD's Sake and Cause, in any thing which we might otherwise lawfully enjoy, though it be not commanded, yet is accepted, and shall be rewarded by Him.

OTHERS there are who grant, That these Words grammatically signify as we contend, and that eternal Punishments are indeed threatned to the Wicked; but say they, these Threatnings are intended only as *Terriculamenta*, or Bug-bears to Children, to terrify and keep People in Awe, and to preserve the World in some tolerable Condition of Quietness. And *Origen* himself, tho' he be of Opinion, that these Threatnings signify only temporary Pains; yet he saith, that such Mysteries are to be sealed up and concealed from the Vulgar, lest wicked Men should

rush

rush into Sin with all Fury and Licentiousness, if this Bridle were taken off, who by the Opinion and Fear of eternal and endless Punishments can scarce be deterred and restrained from it.

To this I answer, 1. That it seems to me indecorous and unsuitable to the Person and Majesty of GOD, to make use of such sorry and weak Means to bring about his Ends, as grave Men can hardly condescend to. 2. I do not see how it can consist with his Veracity, in plain Terms absolutely to threaten and affirm what he never intends to do.

Indeed it is questionable, Whether it be allowable in Man; it being at best but an officious Lye; for it is a speaking what we do not think, and that with an Intention to deceive.

Secondly, I proceed now to a second Objection against the Eternity of the Pains and Sufferings of the Damned, and that is, its Inconsistency with the Justice of GOD. What Proportion can there be between a transient and temporary Act, and an eternal Punishment? The most rigid Justice can exact no more than a *Talio*, to suffer as I have done.

'Εικε πάθοι τὰ κ' ἔρεξε δίκη δ' ἰθεῖα γένοιτο.

If I have hurt, or grieved, or injured any Man, to be punished with the same, or an equivalent Suffering: If I have taken any unrea-

unreasonable Pleasure, to compensate it with an answerable Pain. Indeed, the Enormities of my Life cannot well deserve so much, if it be considered, that I have been strongly instigated and inclined, and as it were fatally driven upon all the Evils which I have committed, by those Affections and Appetites, which I made not for myself, but found in myself; and have been exposed to strong and almost inexpugnable Temptations from without; beset with Snares, encompassed about with innumerable Evils.

To this I answer, First, that every Sin, Injury, or Offence, is aggravated and enhanced by the Dignity or Merit of the Person against whom it is committed. So Parricide is esteemed a greater Crime than ordinary Murder, and by the Laws of all Nations avenged with a sorer Punishment. The like may be said of *Læsa Majestas*, or Treason. Now GOD is an infinite Person, and Sin being an Injury and Affront to Him, as being a Violation of His Law, an infinite Punishment must be due to it.

This Answer Dr. *Hammond* in his *Practical Catechism*, lib. 5. sect. 4. accounts a Nicety, and Unsatisfactory, as also that other common Answer, That if we should live infinitely, we would sin infinitely; and therefore gives us another, which in his Discourse of the Reasonableness of Christian Religion, he thus briefly sums up.

2. *That*

2. That the Choice being referred to us to take of the two which we best like, eternal Death set before us on the one hand, to make eternal *Life* the more infinitely reasonable for us to choose on the other hand, and the eternal Hell (whensoever we fall into it) being perfectly our own *Act*, neither forced on us by any absolute Decree of GOD, nor irresistible Temptation of the Devil or our own Flesh; but as truly our *Wish* and Choice, and mad *Purchase*, nay, much more truly and properly, than eternal Heaven *is*, (when our Obedience is first wrought by GOD's Grace, and yet after that so abundantly rewarded by the Doner) it is certain, if there be any thing irrational, it is *in us* unkind and perverse Creatures (so obstinate to choose what GOD so passionately warns us to take heed of; so wilfully to die, when GOD swears He wills not our Death) and not in *Him*, who hath done all that is imaginable to be done to reasonable Creatures (here in their Way or Course) to the Rescuing or Saving of us.

But to this may be replied, If the Thing itself be unjust, how can our Choosing of it make it just? Now, that it is unjust, appears, in that there is no Proportion between the Offence and the Penalty, that is, between a short and transient Act, and an eternal Punishment.

To which I answer, That GOD deals with us as with intelligent Creatures, and
that

that have Liberty of Will; and so are to be led by Motives to choose that which is good, and refuse that which is evil: And therefore, though there should be no Proportion between them, (as in the first Answer we have shewn there is) yet the Annexing such a Punishment to the Violation of His Laws may be just, because a lesser would not be a sufficient Motive to determine our Choice, and secure Obedience to them. As we see Lawgivers, in the Sanction of their Laws, are not so solicitous to make the Penalty commensurate to the Offence in Point of Duration, as that it be sufficient to enforce Obedience to the Law; not thinking it unjust to annex a Punishment much longer than the Offence, if a lesser will not serve to secure Obedience. So several other Crimes besides Murder are punished with Death, which is a kind of eternal Punishment, there being no Return to Life again: And those Laws only are unjust upon account of disproportionate Punishments, where lesser would serve the Turn.

Now, that lesser than eternal Punishments would not suffice to enforce Obedience to GOD's Commandments, is clear in Experience: And *Origen* himself, the first Broacher of the Opinion, of the Determination of the Damneds Punishments, could not but confess it, in that he saith, It is to be held as a great Secret, and carefully concealed from

the

the Knowledge of the Common People, who, if you take off this Bridle, would be apt to rush into Sin, as a Horse rusheth into the Battle. Indeed Eternity is the very Sting of Hell. Bate him but that, and the Sinner will not think it very terrible or insupportable. But the Thought of an eternal Hell intervening, (and it will often intrude itself) strikes a cold Damp to his very Heart, in the midst of all his Jollities, and will much qualify and allay all his Pleasures and Enjoyments. Rid him of this Fear, and he will be apt to despise Hell and all his Torments, be they never so grievous or lasting. He will be ready thereupon thus to argue with himself: What need I take so much Pains to strive against Sin? What need I swim against the Stream, stem the Tide of my Passions, my natural Appetites and Inclinations, and resist the Importunities of Company? What need I keep such a constant Watch and Ward against my spiritual Enemies the Devil, the World, and the Flesh? If I fall into Hell at last, that's no eternal State, it lasteth but for a time, and will come to an End. I'll venture it, I hope I shall make a Shift to rub through as well as others.

This, therefore, I think is the most solid and satisfactory Answer to that grand Objection against the Justice of God in punishing a short and temporary Offence with eternal Pains and Sufferings, becauſe leſſer are not ſufficient to enforce Obedience to His Laws.

IF any Man be diſſatisfied with the precedent Anſwers, all that I have to add farther, is, that before this Sentence adjudging to eternal Death be pronounced againſt him, and executed upon him, there ſhall be ſuch a Revelation made, as ſhall convince and ſatisfy him of the Righteouſneſs thereof. And this the Apoſtle ſeems to intimate, *Rom.* ii. 5. when he calls the Great Day of Doom, the Day of the Revelation of the righteous Judgment of GOD. Then ſhall be made appear what now to our dim-ſighted Reaſon is not penetrable; how the Juſtice of GOD can conſiſt with the eternal Damnation of the Wicked.

As for Man's being as it were fatally determined to Evil by the Strength of Temptation, and the Violence of unruly and headſtrong Paſſions and Appetites: I anſwer, That there are Motives and Conſiderations ſufficient to enable a Man to reſiſt and repell, to conquer and overcome the moſt alluring and faſcinating Temptations, the moſt urging and importunate Appetites or Affections; ſuch are, certain Shame and Diſgrace, and that not long to come, eternal Infamy and Diſhonour, preſent Death, ſtrong Fear and Dread of approaching Death; or ſad and intolerable Pains or Calamities. Now the

the Divine Threatnings are of the greatest and most formidable Evils and Miseries that humane Nature is capable of suffering; and therefore were they but firmly believed and apprehended, they would be of Force sufficient to stir up in us such strong Passions of Fear and Terror, as would easily chase away all Temptations, and embitter all the Baits of sensual Pleasure.

3. There remains yet a third Objection against an eternal Hell, and that is, that it is inconsistent with the Divine Goodness. For the Unbeliever will say, It's contrary to all the Notions and *Ideas* I have of God, to conceive Him to be so angry and furious a Being. How can it stand with Infinite Goodness, to make a Creature that he fore-knew would be eternally miserable? We Men account it a Piece of Goodness to pardon Offences: And all Punishments are intended either for the Reformation and Amendment of the Offender, or, if he be unreclaimable, to prevent the Mischief which he might otherwise do, or for an Example to others to deterr them from the like Enormities; but I do not see for what such End any Man can be eternally tormented. So that of such Inflictions one may rationally demand, *Cui bono?* What Good comes of them? How then can they come from God, who by all Mens Confession is infinitely Good?

To which I answer: *First*, That God is just as well as good. You will say, What is Justice? It is an equal Weighing of Actions, and Rendring to every one his Right or Due: A Setting streight again what was perverted by the Sins and Extravagancies of Men. Now, that the Breaking of Order and Equality in the World, this Usurping and Encroaching upon others Rights, is a great Evil, and ought to be rectified, some may take an Argument from the strong Inclination and Desire to revenge Injuries, that is implanted in the Nature of Man, and of all Creatures. You'll say, all Desire of Revenge is absolutely sinful and unlawful. I answer, I am no Patron of Revenge. I know, the very *Heathen*, by the Light of Nature, condemned it.

----- *Infirmi est animi exiguique voluptas, Ultio* -----

*Revenge is the Pleasure of a poor and weak Spirit.* Yet, let us hear what they have to say. 1. It is hard to affirm, that any innate Appetite or Desire is in itself simply and absolutely, and in all Circumstances whatsoever, unlawful; for this seems to reflect upon the Author of Nature.

To which may be answered, that a well circumstantiated Desire of Revenge may not be in itself unlawful, yet for the evil Consequents of it, it may be, and is prohibited by a positive Law. 2. Divine Persons have
prayed

prayed to God to avenge them, as *David* and the Prophets. And S. *Paul* himself, 2 *Tim.* iv. 14. prays God to *reward Alexander the Coppersmith according to his Works.* To which may be answered, That those Expressions are rather Predictions of what should befall their Enemies, than Desires that they might. Again, whereas it is said, *Rev.* vi. 9, 10. *That the Souls of them, under the Altar, that were slain for the Word of* God, *and the Testimony which they held, cried with a loud Voice, saying, How long, O* Lord, *Holy and True, dost Thou not judge and avenge our Blood on them that dwell on the Earth?* Dr. *Hammond* saith, It signifies no more, than that their Blood cries to God for Vengeance, as *Abel*'s is said to do. 3. The Nature of Forgiveness seems to imply the Lawfulness of some Desire of Revenge. For what is Forgiveness, but a Parting with, and a Renouncing the Right I have to be Avenged; and, therefore, before I Forgive, I do retain at least some Will to be Revenged. And, I am not obliged by our Saviour, to Forgive absolutely, but upon Condition of Repentance. *Luke* xvii. 3, 4. *If thy Brother sin against thee, rebuke him; and if he repent, forgive him,* &c. And in the Lord's Prayer, one Petition is, *Forgive us our Trespasses, as we forgive them that trespass against us.* But God forgives not without Repentance. To which may be answered, That

G g before

before his Repentance, I may retain a Will of having an Offender punished by the Magistrate, or by GOD, for his own Good and Reformation, but with no respect of avengeing what is past. And if his Repentance prevents his Punishment, then I am to forgive him, that is, cease to desire his Punishment. But all allow Vengeance to be just in GOD, whose Actions are not to be scanned by our Measures. He hath not permitted Vengeance to us, but hath reserved it to Himself. *Vengeance is Mine,* (saith the LORD) *and I will repay.*

 2. IF it be just with GOD to propose to us such a Choice as Heaven, upon Condition of our Obedience to His Law, or Hell, in case of Disobedience, as we see, some wise Men make no Scruple to grant; then it cannot be Injustice in Him to inflict the Punishments of Hell upon them that make it their Choice. Nay, I cannot see how it can consist with His Veracity not to do it: Why then should any Argument from His Goodness move us to distrust His Veracity? as I have before intimated. It may also be answered to the Demand, *Cui bono?* That these eternal Punishments were threatned for a very great Good, *viz.* to secure Obedience to the Divine Laws, and to restrain Men from sinning.

IT may be objected against the Goodness of GOD, and His *Philanthropy,* or Love to Man-

Mankind, How can it consist therewith, to permit Sin to enter into the World? Why did He not prevent it, and make it impossible it should enter, since He hath Wisdom enough, and Power enough, to prevent it? that I may use Dr. *Whichcot's* Words, [*Sermons, Vol.* II. *Serm.* V.]

To which I answer; Why might not God make a Creature, endued with a Faculty of Understanding, to discern that which is Good, and Freedom of Will to make Choice of it, and under no Necessity of Sinning? If He may, and hath made such an one, it doth necessarily follow, unless He frustrates His own Workmanship, that He must suffer it to act according to its own Will. Indeed, without this Freedom of Choice, there can be no such thing as Vertue or Vice. For, how can that be a vertuous Action to which the Agent is as necessarily determined, as a Stone to fall downward.

But farther to vindicate the Honour of our Maker, (*saith the forementioned Dr. Whichcot*) and to put all out of Doubt, all those things considered which are the Provision of God, Man is more sufficient to His Effect, and the Purposes of His Creation, than any other Creature whatsoever. For as that to which a Man is called and required, is of a higher Nature than that of any other Creature below him; so also are his Principles higher and nobler; and there is over and above these, the Assistance of Grace, which is supernatural, and more than is due to him. This is such an Assistance as is able to raise a Man to that which is supernatural, and to fit him for the State of Glory. You see, inferiour Nature is sufficient to its End, and hath not failed, and we are confident that it will not fail. Now, why a Man that is invested with nobler Principles should not act at a higher rate, according to those Principles and Endowments, is a thing not to be answered. But to return from whence I have digressed.

I am as unwilling as any Man to limit the Mercies of God, because I have as much need of them as any Man: Yet I must referr it to Him, whether He will be more favourable than He hath threatned, or no, whether He will remit something of the Severity of His Comminations. I am also willing to restrain and confine the Sense of these Words, αἰῶνες, and αἰῶνες αἰώνων, as far as the Context will permit. But let our Opinions and Hopes of the Mercies of God, and temporary Hell, be what they will; a temporary Hell, I say, or rather a *Purgatory*, instead of Hell: For the Word *Hell*, according to the usual Acception of it, includes Eternity.

I shall add farther, That since God hath threatned eternal Punishments, and it is no Injustice in Him to inflict them upon the

the Breakers of His Laws; and, since we can scarce reconcile it with His Veracity not to do so, it is our wisest and safest Course to believe them. For, though He should not intend to execute the Severity of them upon us, as we may groundlesly imagine; yet it is clear, that He would have them be believed by us, else they cannot have that End and Effect He designed them to: And, therefore, it must be Unbelief and Presumption in us to deny or distrust them, tho' upon Supposition, that they are irreconcilable with His Goodness; with which, yet, perhaps, they may accord well enough, tho' we cannot at present discern it. All Divine Revelations are to be believed and accepted by us, as well Threatnings as Promises; and, if we may distrust the Veracity of God in Them, I know not but we may as well do it in These: If we deny the Eternity of the Torments of Hell, I do not see but that we may, upon as good grounds, with *Origen*, deny the Eternity of the Joys of Heaven.

Let not then the Presumption of a temporary Hell encourage thee to go on in Sin: For, how if thou shouldst find thyself mistaken? If the Event frustrate thy Hopes, and fall out contrary to thy Expectation, as it is most likely it will, What a sad Case wilt thou be in then? How will the Unexpectedness thereof double thy Misery? *Im-*

† *provisa*

*provisa gravius feriunt.* How wilt thou be stricken, as it were, with a Thunderbolt, when the Almighty Judge shall fulminate against thee a dreadful indeed, but by thee formerly undreaded, Sentence, adjudging thee to endless Punishments? How wilt thou damn thine own Credulity, who by a groundless Belief of a temporary Hell, hast precipitated thyself into an eternal, which otherwise thou mightest possibly have avoided?

Well, but suppose there be some Shadow of Hope of the Determination of the Punishments of the Damned; it is by all acknowledged to be a great Piece of Folly, to leave Matters of the highest Moment, and which most nearly concern us, at Uncertainties; and a Point of Wisdom, to secure the Main Chance, and to be provided against the worst that can come. An eternal Heaven, or State of complete Happiness, is the Main Chance, and is not to come into any Competition, or so much as to be put into the Balance against a few short, transient, sordid, loathed, and, for the most part, upon their own account, repented Pleasures: To secure to ourselves an Interest in such a State, is our greatest Wisdom. And as for being provided against the worst that may or can come; What can be worse than an eternal Hell? Which there is, I do not say

say a Possibility, but the greatest Probability imaginable, that it will be our Portion, if we persist in Impenitency, and die in our Sins. But suppose the best should happen that we can hope or conceive, that Hell should last only εἰς αἰῶνας αἰώνων, *for Ages of Ages*, and at last determine: Do we think this a small Matter? If we do, it is for Want of Consideration and Experience of Acute Pains. Should any of us be under the Sense and Suffering of a raging Paroxysm of the Stone, or Gout, or Colick, I doubt not but rather than endure it for Ten thousand Years, he would willingly part with all his Expectation of a Blessed Estate after that Term were expired, yea, and his Being to boot. But, what are any of these Pains to the Torments and Perpessions of Hell? or, the Duration of Ten thousand Years to those Ages of Ages? If thou makest light of all this, and nothing can restrain thee from Sin, but the Eternity of Punishment, thou art bound to thank GOD, who hath used this only effectual Means, threatning an eternal Hell. And it ill becomes thee to complain of His Rigour and Severity, who wouldst have made so pernicious an Use of His Lenity and Goodness. But thou who hast entertained such an Opinion, and abused it, to encourage thyself to go on in thy Sins, though

others

others should escape with a temporary Punishment, surely thou hast no Reason to expect any milder Doom than to be sentenced to an eternal.

## FINIS.

### ADVERTISEMENT.

*Physico-Theology*: Or, a Demonstration of the Being and Attributes of God, from His Works of Creation. Being the Substance of Sixteen Sermons, preached in S. *Mary le Bow, London*, at the Honourable Mr. *Boyle*'s Lectures, in the Year 1711 and 1712. With large Notes; and many curious Observations. Never before Published. By *W. Derham*, Rector of *Upminster* in *Essex*, and F. R. S. Printed for *W. Innys*, at the *Princes Arms* in S. *Paul*'s Church-yard.

CPSIA information can be obtained
at www.ICGtesting.com
Printed in the USA
BVHW08*1341170918
527708BV00012B/731/P